D1484102

Love Stories

Jonathan Ned Katz

Love Stories

Sex between Men before Homosexuality

The University of Chicago Press

Chicago and London ❧

Jonathan Ned Katz is an independent scholar and historian of sexuality. He has written three books, *Gay American History: Lesbians and Gay Men in the U.S.A.* (1976), the *Gay/Lesbian Almanac* (1983), and *The Invention of Heterosexuality* (1995), and two theater pieces based on historical research, *Coming Out!* (1972) and *Comrades and Lovers.* He has received a number of awards, including the Whitehead Award for Lifetime Achievement in Lesbian and Gay Literature from the Publishing Triangle (1995), the Community Service Award from the National Lesbian and Gay Task Force (1996), and the Magnus Hirschfeld Medal for Outstanding Contributions to Sex Research from the German Association for Social Scientific Sex Research (1997).

Jonathan Ned Katz's research is ongoing, and he would like to hear of additional sources. His email address is < jnkatz1@aol.com >.

The University of Chicago Press, Chicago 60637
The University of Chicago Press, Ltd., London
© 2001 by Jonathan Ned Katz
All rights reserved. Published 2001
Printed in the United States of America

10 09 08 07 06 05 04 03 02   2 3 4 5

ISBN: 0-226-42615-7 (cloth)

Library of Congress Cataloging-in-Publication Data

Katz, Jonathan, 1938–
    Love stories : sex between men before homosexuality / Jonathan Ned Katz.
        p. cm.
    Includes bibliographical references and index.
    ISBN 0-226-42615-7 (cloth : alk. paper)
    1. Homosexuality, Male — United States — History. 2. Male friendship — United States — History. 3. Gay men — United States — Sexual behavior. 4. Gay male couples — United States — History. I. Title.

HQ76.3.U5 K375 2001
306.76'62'0973 — dc21

                                                    2001027753

For David B. Gibson and Allan Bérubé,
for friendship, love, and laughs,

and in memory of Michael Lynch,
scholar and AIDS activist,
one of many
fallen on the field of battle.

Contents

Love Stories *in Brief*

Love Stories tells of men's lust and love for men in the nineteenth-century United States, with a side glance across the Atlantic. In these tales, Walt Whitman, John Addington Symonds, and other, lesser-known men struggle to create new and affirmative ways of naming their erotic relationships with men. Inventing a new language of love, they struggle to rethink, reevaluate, and rearrange those intimacies.

Nineteenth-century society limited sex to the reproductive acts of men and women within marriage, condemning eros between men as "mutual masturbation," "sodomy," "buggery," and the "crime against nature." Renaming and remaking the attraction of men for men, Whitman and others transformed an illicit sex story into a romantic sex-love tale. Struggling against their societies' sentimental, asexual love, they pioneered the construction of modern sexual love. Their histories disclose the modernization of eros as it occurs.

Intense "love" relations between men were approved of in the nineteenth century. But these resistors wrestled mightily with the morality of men's sexual desire for men and sexual acts with them. They affirmed the sexual love of men for men by putting that emotion into words. Their "coming to terms," this book demonstrates, was a major project of these trailblazers.

This history of sexuality is a story of contests—of wars over sexual words, battles over sexual ideas, bouts over sexual values, and, finally, struggles over the institutional shaping and reshaping of sexual desires and practices. Eros, here, is always under siege, always under production. These stories dramatize and detail the historical making and remaking of sexuality.

In particular, these stories reveal gender nonconformity being newly linked with erotic deviance. These anecdotes document the decline of "sodomites," the anxiety-producing rise of "fairies," "inverts," and "homosexuals." These tales show how the early nineteenth century's narrow construction of "sodomy" was challenged at century's end by a broad, new sexual crime, sometimes called "gross indecency." That law, and others like it, first made oral-genital contacts a crime, marking a major, historic change in what Americans considered sex. The furor in 1999 over President Bill Clinton's relations with Monica Lewinsky was not the first time that Americans debated the definition of the sexual.

I hope that readers of this book will become time travelers, projecting themselves out of the sexual present into a different sexual past. This was the world before the homosexual-heterosexual hypothesis, the universe before that great sexual divide. Pondering these nineteenth-century tales, I hope that readers will question the assumptions of that time and ask of these stories' characters: What were their past words for men's sexual and affectionate intimacies with men? What were their ideas, their judgments, their native forms of eros?

At the opening of the twenty-first century I and many other historians of sexuality reject the old twentieth-century idea of homosexual desires and deeds as unchanging, ahistorical, and essential. Words, ideas, values, and institutions, I contend, are sexuality's means of production, human beings its producers. In this book, the language of lust, concepts of eros, and judgments about sexuality take on new importance. For they are the tools that humans use within society to structure their pleasures.

Other researchers have studied the histories of sexual identities. I focus here on the social history of sexual desires and acts, and their hotly disputed interpretations. I stress the importance of locating sexual lusts, behaviors, and understandings precisely in time, and I begin that historical specifying.

I hope that readers will find these stories' characters engaging, their conflicts moving, their intimacies poignant, and their histories surprising and revealing.

PART I
Searching for Words

1 *No Two Men Were Ever More Intimate*

Abraham Lincoln and Joshua Fry Speed first met on April 15, 1837, the day Lincoln rode into Springfield, Illinois, on a borrowed horse, carrying a pair of saddlebags, two or three law books, and some clothing. Lincoln had first been elected to the Illinois legislature three years earlier, and Speed had heard him speak publicly, but probably had not met him.[1]

Lincoln "came into my store . . . , set his saddle-bags on the counter," and asked about the price of bedding for "a single bedstead," Speed recalled many years later.[2]

Hearing the cost, Lincoln said: "Cheap as it is I have not the money to pay. But if you will credit me until Christmas . . . I will pay you then." If he failed as a lawyer, said Lincoln, "I will probably never be able to pay you at all."

"The tone of his voice," Speed remembered, "was so melancholy that I felt for him." Looking up at the tall Lincoln, Speed "thought then, as I think now, that I never saw so gloomy and melancholy a face in my life."

Speed then spontaneously proposed a no-cost arrangement: "I have a very large room, and a very large double-bed in it; which you are perfectly welcome to share with me if you choose."

"Where is your room?" Lincoln responded. Speed pointed to the stairs, and "without saying a word [Lincoln] took his saddle-bags on his arm, went upstairs, set them down on the floor, came down again, and with a face beaming with pleasure and smiles, exclaimed, 'Well, Speed, I'm moved.'"[3]

The swift transformation in Lincoln from melancholy to pleasure and smiles expressed his own spontaneous response to Speed. This was one of Lincoln's cross-class relationships: although both men were from Kentucky, the upward-aspiring lawyer hailed from a poor, backwoods farm family, Speed from a wealthy family whose plantation was tilled by seventy slaves.[4]

In Springfield, Lincoln chose to sleep at Speed's, though he was also immediately welcomed into the home of William Butler and his wife, who also offered him a bed. Mrs. Butler saw to Lincoln's laundry and tended his wardrobe.[5]

In the frontier town of Springfield (population 1,500), Lincoln's search for a single bed led the twenty-eight-year-old bachelor into the double bed of the twenty-four-year-old bachelor Speed. As Speed himself described

Abraham Lincoln, 1846 (the earliest known photograph). Courtesy Library of Congress.

Joshua Fry Speed, 1837 (the year he met Lincoln). Gift of Joshua F. Speed by his daughter, Miss Susan S. Speed, 1938.48. Collection of The Speed Art Museum, Louisville, Kentucky. ❧

his and Lincoln's friendship at its height, "no two men were ever more intimate."[6] Lincoln "disclosed his whole heart to me," Speed told William Herndon, Lincoln's onetime law partner and chronicler.[7] Lincoln "loved this man more than anyone dead or living," said Herndon, not excepting Mary Todd.[8] A recent biographer called Speed "the only intimate friend that Lincoln ever had," a judgment seconded by others.[9]

Intense, even romantic man-to-man friendships—an institution in nineteenth-century America—were a world apart in that era's consciousness from the sensual universe of mutual masturbation and the legal universe of "sodomy," "buggery," and the "crime against nature" (legally, men's anal intercourse with men, boys, women, and girls, and humans' intercourse with beasts). The universe of mutual onanism and sodomy was a world of carnal acts. The universe of intimate friendship was, ostensibly, a world of spiritual feeling. The radical Christian distinction between mind and body located the spiritual and carnal in different spheres. So hardly anyone then asked, Where does friendship end and sodomy begin?

And yet, from our present standpoint, we can see that these intimate friendships often left evidence of extremely intense, complex desires, including, sometimes, what we today recognize as erotic feelings and acts. Evidence survives of a surprising variety of physical and sometimes sensual modes of relating among male friends in the nineteenth century.[10]

The common custom of men casually bedding down together, for example, became uncommon, even suspect, in the consciously eroticized twentieth century after the construction, naming, publicizing, and stringent tabooing of "sexual perversion," "inversion," and "homosexuality." At the start of the twenty-first century it may even be difficult to imagine a man, especially a bachelor, offering another a place in his bed without some conscious fear or desire that the proposition will be understood as a come-on.

In the nineteenth century, Speed was probably not conscious of any such erotic possibility. His immediate, casual offer, and his later report of it, suggests that men's bed sharing was not then often explicitly understood as conducive to forbidden sexual experiments. Nevertheless, the century's custom of bed sharing did provide an important site (probably, the major site) of erotic opportunity, as we will see.

In the century's most famous *fictional* bed sharing, in *Moby-Dick,* Herman Melville describes Ishmael and Queequeg's initial night together as consecrating a symbolic marriage, a till-death-do-us-part relation. Like Melville's "cosy, loving pair," launched on their "hearts' honeymoon," Lincoln and Speed's bed sharing also initiated a marriage-like intimacy.[11]

In 1838, at least *eight months* after Lincoln and his new friend first bedded down together, Speed hired the young William Herndon to clerk in his general store.[12] Herndon later recalled that he, Speed, Lincoln, and Charles R. Hurst (another clerk), "slept in the room upstairs over the store."[13]

After Lincoln's arrival, Speed's Springfield store became a popular gathering place. "The young men who congregated about the store," explained Herndon, "formed a society for the encouragement of debate and literary efforts." "Unfortunately," he added, "we ruled out the ladies."[14]

Without girls present, the boys felt free to air their views on female foibles. "Lincoln himself entertained us," Herndon recalls, "with a few lines of rhyme intended to illustrate some weakness in women—her frailty, perhaps."[15]

Two lines of one Lincoln ditty proclaimed: "No woman ever *played* the *whore* / Unless she had a man to help her."[16] Lincoln's poem criticized women who strayed from chastity (and the era's genteel ideal of true womanhood) and defended women's purity by suggesting that men were responsible for their straying. The ditty also took a jaundiced view of relationships between men and women, affirming the day's stereotypes of seductive men and seduced women.

Lincoln never spoke of "any *particular woman* with disrespect," Abner Ellis assured posterity, "though he had many opportunities for doing so." Was Lincoln's talk of women *in general* not so polite? Lincoln's associates did tell numerous risque stories about women, Ellis added, calling Joshua Speed and another Lincoln friend "two old rats in that way."[17] Women served, in these stories, to link men with men, sparking an erotic current between them.

Led by Lincoln, these men told each other numerous sex stories. Lincoln's "great passion for dirty stories" was not strange, Ellis explained, given the early influence of his cousins, John and Dennis Hanks—a putdown of their backwoods morals.[18] Lincoln told "the boys . . . stories which drew them after him," recalled Ellis, "but modesty and my veneration for his memory forbids me to relate." Lincoln's sex stories drew *men* to him, Ellis makes clear.

Asked once why he did not collect his dirty stories in a book, Lincoln made a face, H. E. Dummer recalled, as if he smelled "a thousand dead carcases," and declared, "Such a book would stink like a thousand privies." Lincoln had two characters, Dummer thought, "one of *purity*," and the other with "an insane love in telling . . . smutty stories."[19] Lincoln's two sides mirrored his era's strict distinction between the pure (asexual) and the "smutty."

The "great majority" of Lincoln's stories were "very nasty indeed," Henry Whitney agreed, though Lincoln never "gloated over filth," having "a great ideality and also a view of grossness which displaced the ideality."[20] Lincoln's mind (like the minds of many Americans) was a house divided, split into distinct domains: whorehouse and pure hearth, lust house and love house.

Lincoln talked dirty with men, genteelly when he met with good women. The divide between the sexes was mirrored in language. The smutty and filthy were linked then with manhood, the pure and asexual with womanhood, the carnal was to men as purity was to women.

The sort of stuff Lincoln recited for his Springfield men friends is suggested by a ditty he had composed eight years earlier at the expense of his neighbors, the four Grigsby brothers (Reuben, Charles, Billy, and Nat).

As recalled imperfectly years later, Lincoln's poem began: "Reuben and Charles have married two girls / But Billy has married a boy / The girls he had tried on every side / But none could he get to agree / All was in vain he went home again / And since he is married to Natty" (his brother, Nat). The poem added that the married brothers, "Billy and Natty agreed very well / And mama's well pleased at the match / The egg it is laid but Natty's afraid / The Shell is so Soft that it never will hatch."

Among the girls Billy had pursued was Betsy (wife of his brother Reuben): "But Betsy she said 'You cursed bald head / My suitor you never can be / Besides your low crotch proclaims you a botch / And that never can answer for me.' "[21] The poem hints at rivalry or attraction between Lincoln and Billy Grigsby (the main object of derision), and the two reportedly came to blows, with the competitive Lincoln asserting: "He was the big buck at the lick" (the biggest, manliest man).[22]

Marriage and coitus between men were on Lincoln's mind, evidently, but imagined only as a poor substitute for the failed pursuit of women. The ditty's vision of sexual rivalry between brothers over women, and marriage and intercourse between brothers, curiously foreshadowed Lincoln's own marriage-like attachment to Speed, Lincoln and Speed's conflict about their intimacy, and their anxiety about marriage and sexual relations with good women.

ॐ

The intimacy of Lincoln and Speed carries us back to a foreign land of love and lust, a universe differing substantially from today's. This book explores a vast, largely uncharted territory, attempting the first nineteenth-century-long mapping of sex and affection between men in the United States. By this book's end, the evidence we find will, I hope, provide a new, impressionistic sense of that Other America.

After Sigmund Freud and Calvin Klein most of us no longer imagine a sphere of spiritual feeling separated completely from the universe of sensual desire. Our world has shifted eros from the distant margins to our culture's center. Today's readers are deeply enmeshed in a sex-conscious, sex-irradiated society, a land of well-publicized homosexualities, hetero-sexualities, and bisexualities. But Lincoln and Speed's relationship did not, in its own time, fall within that homo-hetero-bi division.

To understand Lincoln and Speed, and others of their century, we must try to comprehend their world's structuring of eros and love, their ideas, and their language. Their society had its own ways of ordering, conceiving, and naming men's affection and lust for men, and the erotic acts between them. Walt Whitman spoke in 1856 of men "saying their ardor in native forms," and that is what Lincoln, Speed, and others were attempting.[23] Creatures of a particular historical time and place, men generated their own native forms of intimacy, of sex-love and sex-acts, sex-talk and sex-silence.

As Speed said of himself and Lincoln, "no two men were ever more intimate." He suggested a degree of intimacy surpassed by the word *ever*. Lincoln called Speed his "friend," a word that, I think, inadequately expressed his depth of feeling. Lincoln and Speed had no word like "gay" to affirm their intimacy. They were at a loss for words—at least for adequate, affirmative terms—by which to name, characterize, and judge their relationship.

We may refer to early-nineteenth-century men's acts or desires as gay or straight, homosexual, heterosexual, or bisexual, but that places their behaviors and lusts within our sexual system, not the system of their time. Projected on the past, homo, hetero, and bi distort our present understanding of Lincoln's and Speed's experiences. We may find it useful sometimes to pluck men or women out of their own sexual and affectional worlds into our present kingdom of the gay, straight, and bi. But my project is, on the contrary, to rediscover men's native forms of ardor; I wish to locate the intimacies of Lincoln, Speed, and other men within the erotic and emotional institutions of their own time.

The terms *erotic* and *emotional institutions* may sound strange. Nineteenth-century acts of sodomy and buggery were, for example, formed, named, understood, and judged primarily within that age's judicial system, an institution that was completely separate from the era's particular historical structuring of romance, in which love relationships and special friendships were constituted. The age's sensual desires were produced within its own world of senses, bodies, and meanings—a sphere separate and distinct from its love world. I am arguing not just about words and ideas. I refer to the fundamental social positioning of eros, the shaping of acts and desires within a specific historical organization of sexuality and affection.

In the genteel society of Lincoln and Speed's time, character was not thought to center upon sexuality—good women and men did not have erotic orientations or sexual identities. Neither Lincoln nor Speed thought that his love for a man or for a woman made him into a certain kind of person—a man-loving man or woman-loving man, or a combination type. The *identities* homosexual, heterosexual, and bisexual had not yet been invented—neither had those terms and concepts.[24] Historians of sexuality now generally agree that sexual *categories, ideas, attitudes,* and *identities* are changing, time-specific constructions.

But many historians, it seems to me, still assume, in practice, the existence of unchanging, ahistorical homosexual, heterosexual, and bisexual *desires* and *acts*—whatever those lusts and behaviors were called in their own time.[25] In this book, I challenge that assumption and try to deepen our understanding of sexuality as a historical construct. In every society, no doubt, some men have always sexually desired and erotically interacted with men. But those desires and acts were not always structured as specifically "same-sex" phenomena, or understood as "sexual." If, in the nineteenth century, the sexual was, properly, the potentially reproductive intercourse of penis and vagina, there existed many erotic desires and acts that were not recognized as such. In this book I ask that we consider sexual desires and sexual acts, along with sexual identities, as fundamentally changing and fully historical, a still-controversial, counterintuitive idea.

But how does my historical view of eros and affection drive this book's big story, its tale of men *searching for words, coming together, coming to terms,* and *going public*? If we suspend our assumption of an unchanging essence of homosexuality and heterosexuality, these stories reveal a new past. They show us men struggling, alone and together, to construct affectionate and sexual relationships. They show us men struggling for affirmative words to name and characterize those intimacies.

If we suspend our ahistorical homo/hetero hypothesis—our notion of an essential homo- and heterosexuality—this raises four extremely useful historical questions about life before the homo/hetero divide: First, what did people then *call* sexual or affectionate relationships between men? Second, how did they *conceive* of such relationships? Third, how did they *judge* such relationships? And, fourth, how did they socially *organize* such relationships? If we view these tales with eyes not blinded by today's homo/hetero arrangement, they begin to provide some answers.

As we read these stories we can actually see their characters using language to construct their own erotic experience and the experiences of their era. Their past words, in their past context, are central to our present attempt to understand these long-gone love lives. So, in this book, I offer many quotations and pay close attention to the particular terms used, at a particular time, by particular people.

According to the old (that is, twentieth-century) view, an essential homosexuality and heterosexuality flowed through time, fundamentally unchanged. People of different eras responded differently to those same old homo/hetero things. At different times in history they called those same old things by a variety of names. Homosexuality, for example, was called "sodomy," "unnatural filthiness, "degeneracy," and "inversion." In that twentieth-century view, words went only skin deep—they were the filmy, fashionable dress covering the real, unchanging homo or hetero body. Those old words for homosexuality sounded quaint, but they certainly were not foundational. So we did not have to take them too seriously.

In contrast, according to recent historical understandings of sexuality—my own and others'—there is no such thing as an unchanging essence of homosexuality and heterosexuality. Instead, over time, human beings continually reconfigure their affectionate and erotic feelings and acts. People use words, and the ideas those words convey, as tools to reshape eros. The names people call particular erotic desires and acts play a big role in the shaping of sexualities in an era. In this historical view, even the basic idea of what is "erotic" or "sexual" changes fundamentally over time. Its character cannot be assumed; it must be investigated, with evidence sought in old diaries, letters, trial records, and newspapers.

Historians of sexuality—accountants of eros over time—now often pay lip service to the importance of understanding sexualities of the past in their past contexts. But, in practice, it seems to me, many still fall prey to an old, time-stopping, residual essentialism. They fail, therefore, to understand, as fully as they might, how those lusts and loves were structured in their own time.[26] Intelligent, thoughtful readers are also still struggling, I think, to comprehend past sexualities as fully historical. From our vantage point in the early twenty-first century, a fully historical sexuality seems only partly comprehended.

If the idea of a time-limited homosexuality and heterosexuality still disturbs—if a fully historical sexuality still seems counterintuitive—to that extent the old essence of homosexuality and heterosexuality still holds us in its time-stopping grip. This book attempts to counter that stubborn, lingering antihistorical view of sexuality and affection. It encourages us to open our eyes to pleasures fully and surprisingly timely.

As we at the beginning of the twenty-first century read these stories, we may identify sometimes with their characters' emotions and struggles. But our empathy can lead us to confuse the past with the present. The identifying reader may fail to note the surprising ways that Lincoln and Speed's universe, and other men's past sexual and affectional worlds, dif-

fered in basic ways from our present world, which is sundered by homosexuality and heterosexuality.

If we open our minds to these tales, we may find ourselves uncomprehending, sometimes, within a strange sexual landscape, a mysterious
world of affection. We will find mysteries here. So, like detectives, we
must look for clues, interpret the rediscovered evidence, and fit together
the first, tentative fragments of the puzzle. We must become tracers of
missing intimacies, sleuths of sexualities and affections past. We must
travel back in time, on the lookout for unfamiliar configurations of lust
and love.

But why should we in the present care about men's past intimacies
with men, their old ways of making love, their different ways of doing it?
For us today, these stories briefly bring the dead to life again, momentarily recapturing desires and affections, conflicts and struggles that resonate
with our own. Readers will, first of all, I hope, relish the pleasures of these
tales.

In addition, these stories can help us explore basic shifts in the social
ordering of sexuality and affection, noting the fundamentally different
settings of these past lives and our own. The vision of a changing, fully
historical sexuality is inspiring. For, if the historical ordering of eros and
amour was different in the past, it can be different in the future. We can
radically remake love and lust in ways more satisfying to our souls and to
our flesh. We can, as Walt Whitman suggested, make sexual democracy in
America.

༄

Back in Illinois, in the summer of 1837, after bedding down with Joshua
Speed, Abraham Lincoln was trying to extricate himself from an uncom-
fortable relationship with Mary Owens, a woman he had met and discussed marriage with in New Salem, Illinois. Again, Lincoln's romance
crossed classes: the educated, cultured Owens came from a wealthy family.[27] During Lincoln's first months with Speed he was trying, frantically,
to break this almost-engagement without seeming ungentlemanly. He
wrote three letters to Owens in which he provoked her to refuse him.[28]

"I can not see you, or think of you, with entire indifference," Lincoln
wrote to Owens, as if he aspired to "entire indifference" but had not yet
achieved it.

"I want in all cases to do right," Lincoln added, "and most particularly
so, in all cases with women." Doing right by women *was* a serious obli-
gation to this ambitious, aspiring professional from a poor Kentucky
family—though Owens may have noted that Lincoln expressed no spe-

cial, personal interest in her. He added: "If I *knew* it would be doing right, as I rather suspect it would, to let you alone, I would do it." He had stressed his inability to support Owens adequately in an earlier letter, and he wielded poverty as excuse in several later incidents with women.

Owens was free to "dismiss your thoughts (if you ever had any) from me forever," Lincoln told her. But she should not by any means "understand by this, that I wish to cut your acquaintance." He only desired their future to depend on her: "If you feel yourself in any degree bound to me, I am now willing to release you, provided you wish it; while on the other hand, I am willing, and even anxious to bind you faster, if I can be convinced that it will, in any considerable degree, add to your happiness."

Lincoln's tortured phrasing reveals his frantic maneuvering to extract himself from this entanglement without directly requesting it. This is a lawyer's letter, not a love letter. Not surprisingly, Mary Owens did not reply, leaving Lincoln a free man with a clear conscience.

In a supposedly humorous account of this engagement, Lincoln wrote on April Fools' Day, 1838, to a married woman friend, reporting that he had found his unnamed former sweetheart grossly "over-size."[29] Owens may have been a large woman, but other men recall her as notably attractive, as well as intelligent.[30]

He knew his fiancée "was called an 'old maid,'" Lincoln wrote, "and felt no doubt of the truth of at least half of the appellation." Suggesting that Owens was not a "maid," Lincoln insinuated unchastity, a charge that, directed at a genteel woman like Owens, was extremely serious, and revealed his own puritanical anxieties about good women's sexual conduct.

When beholding his possible future wife, Lincoln said, "I could not avoid thinking of my mother"—he mentioned a "want of teeth" and "weather-beaten appearance," suggesting his own strong, physical disgust. Lincoln's supposed humor hints at sexual loathing.

Only after this marriage proposal was safely rejected had Lincoln, "for the first time," begun "to suspect that I was really a little in love with her." But after this fiasco of a relationship, he concluded, he would "never again . . . think of marrying"—an exaggeration that may well reveal his feelings.

Years later, Owens got her own back, commenting for posterity on her lackluster suitor: "Mr. Lincoln was deficient in those little links which make up the great chain of woman's happiness, at least it was so in my case."[31]

When a woman was safely married or engaged Lincoln might take an interest in her and enjoy her friendship. Ann Rutledge, whose death Lincoln deeply grieved, had been engaged when he seems to have fallen in love with her—another man's desire helped, perhaps, to arouse his own.[32] But many who knew Lincoln agreed that he had no pressing romantic interest in women.[33]

"He didn't go to see the girls much," recalled N. W. Branson: "He didn't appear bashful, but it seemed as if he cared but little for them. Wasn't apt to take liberties with them, but would sometimes." Lincoln would just as well have the company of "all men as to have it a mixture of the sexes."[34]

"Didn't love the company of girls," and was retiring, recalled cousin Dennis Hanks.[35] Cousin John Hanks added: "I never could get him in company with women: he was not a timid man in this particular, but did not seek such company."[36]

"He was not very fond of girls," remembered Sarah Bush Lincoln, Abraham's beloved stepmother.[37] "Abe did not go much with the girls," recalled Anna Gentry.[38]

Lincoln was "shy of ladies," Abner Ellis remembered. When working as a clerk he "always disliked to wait on the ladies," and "preferred trading with the men and boys he used to say."[39] Lincoln "did not seem to seek the company of the girls," and when about them "was rather backward," said David Turnham.[40]

A dissenter, Jason Duncan recalled Lincoln's "innocent mischief," especially "among his lady acquaintances," though only with those with whom "he was well acquainted."[41]

Another dissenter, David Davis, called Lincoln "a man of strong passion for woman," though "his conscience kept him from seduction," and this "saved many a woman."[42]

William Herndon claimed that "Lincoln had a strong if not a terrible passion for women; he could hardly keep his hands off from women," adding that Lincoln "and Speed were quite familiar with the women."[43] But Lincoln and Speed's universe was inhabited by good women and bad.

Long after Lincoln's death, Joshua Speed recalled to William Herndon that, about 1839–40, he (Speed) was (in Herndon's words) "keeping a pretty woman" in Springfield, "and Lincoln, desirous to have *a little*," asked, " 'Speed, do you know where I can get *some*?' " Speed replied " 'Yes, I do, . . . I'll send you to the place with a note. You can't get *it* without a note or by my appearance.' "

In this story, Speed offered to share his mistress or a prostitute acquaintance with his most intimate man friend, perhaps the closest Lincoln and Speed ever got to genital contact with each other. A woman again facilitated an intimacy of men.

Speed wrote the note, the story continued, and Lincoln went to see the girl, handed it to her, and "after a short 'how do you do, etc.,' Lincoln told his business and the girl, after some protestations, agreed to satisfy him."

Lincoln and the girl "stript off and went to bed." But before anything happened, Lincoln asked the girl: "How much do you charge?" She answered: "Five dollars, Mr. Lincoln." To which he replied: "I've only got three dollars." The girl said "I'll trust you, Mr. Lincoln, for $2." Lincoln thought a moment and said: "I do not wish to go on credit—I'm poor & don't know where my next dollar will come from and I cannot afford to cheat you"—the same plea of poverty he had used to exit his relationship with Owens. Despite some further words of encouragement from the girl, Lincoln "got up out of bed,—buttoned up his pants and offered the girl the $3.00, which she would not take." She told Lincoln, " 'You are the most Conscientious man I ever saw.' Lincoln went out of the house bidding the girl good evening."

He returned to Speed's, "saying nothing," and "Speed asked no questions." So the matter rested until Speed saw the girl and "she told him just what was said and done." Herndon did not doubt Speed's recollection.[44]

Lincoln's unconsummated sex with Speed's mistress (or prostitute friend) reproduced his lack of success with Mary Owens, and his later, difficult, diffident courtship of Mary Todd.

Lincoln first met Todd in the Springfield home of her sister, Elizabeth Edwards, who had married into one of the richest families in Illinois. By the fall of 1840 Todd and Lincoln were edging toward engagement, and sometime around Christmas 1840 they may have become engaged.

Years later, Mary Todd's sister recalled the courtship, which she eventually adamantly opposed because Lincoln's humble origins and future prospects appeared not good enough for her sister. "I have happened in the room where they were sitting . . . and Mary led the conversation—Lincoln would listen & gaze on her as if drawn by some superior power." He "never scarcely said a word."[45]

Remarkably talkative around men, the famously eloquent political speaker was tongue-tied with this woman. Was he intimidated by her sex, breeding, family wealth, love, or all of these?

The quiet Lincoln "could not maintain himself in a continued conversation with a lady reared as Mary was," added Edwards, stressing the difference in class and gender between the two. Lincoln "could not hold a lengthy conversation with a lady—was not sufficiently educated & intelligent in the female line to do so—He was charmed with Mary's wit and fascinated with her quick sagacity—her will—her nature—and culture." Mary, reported her sister, was "quick, lively, gay," a woman who "loved glitter show & pomp & power." She was an "extremely ambitious woman" who early "contended that she was destined to be the wife of some future president."[46]

Mary Todd was "the most ambitious woman I ever saw," stressed her sister, recalling that Mary "spurred up Mr. Lincoln, pushed him along and upward—made him struggle and seize his opportunities."[47]

Todd's ambition, and her prescient choice of Lincoln, then only a struggling, small-town lawyer and legislator, demonstrated her astute sense of political possibilities as well as her own desire for power. Born into a rich banking family, Mary Todd's privileged position and unusually good education contributed, no doubt, to the humbly born Lincoln's anxieties about her and interest in her. On both their parts, this was a cross-class attraction.

Women of Todd's class and men of the professional class Lincoln was struggling to attain then inhabited separate spheres, often approaching each other warily, as strangers, across a great divide.[48] In contrast, the separate, segregated men's and women's worlds often fostered intense, eros-irradiated friendships of men with men and women with women. Lincoln's nervous courtship of Mary Todd contrasted strikingly, for example, with the easy intimacy he established with Joshua Speed. Likewise, Mary Todd's intimacy with Mercy Levering, a young friend from a well-off Baltimore family, contrasted strikingly with her troubled, on-again, off-again relationship with Lincoln.

Throughout the winter of 1839, while Levering was visiting Springfield, she and Todd became inseparable friends, and they corresponded when Levering returned to Maryland in the summer of 1840. While visiting relatives in Missouri, the twenty-one-year-old Todd wrote to Levering, sorry to be denied "the happiness of seeing" her friend, "one I love so well," and planned to return early to Springfield, especially to see her. "How much I wish you were near," said Todd, for Levering was "a congenial heart, in your presence I have almost *thought aloud*."[49]

She easily brought Levering to mind, Todd wrote, "for the brightest associations of the year are connected with thee."[50] This is the year that Todd and Lincoln were probably moving toward an engagement. If Levering decided "to settle in Missouri, *I will do so too*," said Todd, not waiting to hear any suitor's plans.[51]

Todd referred sarcastically to the attention of a young Missouri man of good family: "Shall never survive it." She added: "My beaux have *always* been *hard bargains* at any rate," a comment perhaps including Lincoln. Though her uncle thought the Missouri man talented, Mary wrote, "yet

Merce I love him not, & my hand will never be given, where my heart is not."[52] Holding out for "love" was a powerful tactic, justifying Mary Todd's rejection of an uncle-approved beau who was also talented and rich.

Back in Springfield, in December 1840, Todd wrote to Levering again, mentioning a female relative who had been visiting, "a most interesting young lady," whose "fascinations" have "drawn a concourse of beaux & company round us." Referring to the beaux, Todd said, "we have too much of such useless commodities," adding: "it takes some time for habit to render us familiar with what we are not greatly accustomed to."[53] Whether the unusual quantity of beaux or their quality was her subject, Todd's response was not enthusiastic.

Bemoaning Levering's "loss," Todd was glad to report a new female "companion," a "congenial spirit," Matilda Edwards, "a lovelier girl I never saw."[54] Todd suspected that Joshua Speed's "ever changing heart . . . is about offering *its young* affections" at Matilda Edwards's "shrine."

Speed and Lincoln *both* fell in love with and courted Matilda Edwards several well-informed sources testify—if so, one more example of a woman mediating, complicating, and stimulating the intimacy between these men.[55] As the prostitute story suggests, Edwards was not the only woman on whom Lincoln's and Speed's desires converged. Falling for the same woman might well have manifested Lincoln and Speed's love for each other.

Mary Todd added that society offered up numbers "of *marriageable gentlemen,* unfortunately only 'birds of passage' "—flighty, fly-by-night men. Among these bachelor-birds, Joshua Speed and Abraham Lincoln had new suits of clothes. Some of the "new recruits" were "gifted," Todd admitted, and "all in our humble estimation interesting"—her first positive comment about men.[56]

One female friend "appears to be enjoying all the sweets of married life," reported Todd, but she wondered of another: "Why is it that married folks always become so serious?" Marriage was on the mind of the fun-loving Todd—and it clearly implied a worrisome curtailment of freedom. Their friend Mary Lamb "is about perpetuating the *crime* of *matrimony,*" Todd joked revealingly. Todd thought the married Lamb would be "much happier"—"happier," though, perhaps, not happy.[57]

In December 1840, Todd told Levering: "We cannot do much longer without you, *your mate* misses you too much from her nest, not to marvel at the delay" in meeting. "Write very, very soon if you love me," Todd urged.[58] "Mate" was a common nineteenth-century name for same-sex intimates, suggesting an intimacy less than marriage and more than ordinary friendship.[59]

By December 1840, Mary Todd and Abraham Lincoln may have understood their relationship as an engagement. But on New Year's Day 1841, Joshua Speed sold his interest in the Springfield general store in preparation for a return to his old Kentucky home.[60] (Speed's sale of his store is the *only* event of that January first that is actually documented.) Though Speed was reportedly "about to leave" Springfield on January 24, 1841, he delayed his trip home until the spring of that year.[61] "There is nothing here" in Springfield, Speed wrote to his sister with a touch of wistful irony, "but some of the very cleverest fellows that God ever made — the truest friends and warmest hearts — that is worth living in this country for."[62]

The same January that Speed sold his store, Lincoln or Mary Todd may have suddenly decided to break their engagement — if they were engaged (the evidence is unclear about who did what, and when).[63] The evidence does show that after that January first, Lincoln was deeply distraught and depressed, perhaps at another failure as a suitor, perhaps at losing the vivacious Mary Todd, *certainly* at losing his closest male intimate, Joshua Speed.[64]

"Within the last few days," Lincoln wrote to his law partner and friend John Todd Stuart on January 20, he had "been making a most discreditable exhibition of myself in the way of hypochondriasm," and had been tended by a doctor.[65]

"I am now the most miserable man living," Lincoln confessed to Todd three days later: "If what I feel were equally distributed to the whole human family, there would not be one cheerful face on earth. Whether I shall ever be better, I cannot tell; I awfully forbode I shall not. To remain as I am is impossible. I must die or be better." A "change of scene might help," Lincoln thought, but instead he busied himself with his law practice and state politics — his manly solution to emotional distress.[66]

In June 1841, perhaps six months after Mary Todd and Lincoln's broken engagement, she wrote to Mercy Levering, reiterating "the love which I feel has ever been ours towards each other." Telling Levering that "time and absence only serve to deepen the interest with which I have always regarded you," she recalled the days they "strolled together & derived so much of happiness from each other's society."[67]

Two months later, Lincoln visited Speed in Kentucky, where Lincoln's spirits greatly improved. But that summer Speed became engaged to Fanny Henning, setting off a new emotional crisis. Lincoln was actually in Kentucky when Speed courted Henning, Speed remembered, "and strange to say something of the same feeling which I regarded as so fool-ish in him . . . took possession of me . . . and kept me very unhappy from the time of my engagement until I was married."[68] From early September 1841 to mid-February 1842, Speed shared his "immense suffering" with Lincoln, and Lincoln responded in several remarkably revealing letters. (Only Lincoln's correspondence survives.)

On January 1, 1842, Speed ended a Springfield visit with Lincoln and started back to Kentucky to marry his fiancée. Lincoln gave him an os-tensibly encouraging letter to read on the trip. It was intended, he said, "to aid you, in case (which God forbid) you shall need any aid"—Lin-coln's first foreboding.[69]

It was "reasonable," Lincoln added, "that you will feel very badly some time between this and the final consummation of your purpose"—Lin-coln's second foreboding. Lincoln's repeated references to Speed's misery were supposed to be empathetic. But can Speed have found them sup-portive?

Lincoln's reference to the "final consummation" strongly suggests that the object of Speed's and his anxiety was not marriage in general, but the marriage act in particular: the capacity sexually to consummate matri-mony with a pure, true woman. Though Lincoln and Speed may have had sexual relations with female prostitutes, probably neither had experi-enced intercourse with a woman he considered "good," and both seem to have dreaded the opportunity.

Lincoln's response to Mary Owens had focused critically on her body, admitting that it reminded him, unflatteringly, of mom, the first good woman in his life. Far from yearning for sexual intercourse with a good woman, both men seemed deeply anxious about their ability to complete such copulation—no instinctual heterosexual desire here.

For the *third* time in this letter Lincoln reiterated: "It is reasonable that you will feel very badly yet"—fear or wish? Lincoln then reminded Speed of his *"nervous temperament,"* "defective nerves," and his "intensity of thought" that sometimes turned the "sweetest idea" to "the bitterness of death." Speed's feelings were intense and convoluted, Lincoln pointedly reminded him.

Speed's anxiety, said Lincoln, was also due to "the rapid and near ap-proach of that crisis on which all your thoughts and feelings concen-trate"—the crisis of wedlock, or the crisis of its consummation, or both? Lincoln repeated for a *fourth* time that, if Speed escaped "without another 'twinge of the soul' I shall be most happily, but most egregiously de-ceived." He seemed almost peeved at the idea of Speed escaping soul twinges.

Anticipating Speed's inescapable torment, Lincoln, for the *fifth* time, wrote: "You shall, as I expect you will at some time be agonized and distressed." If so, Speed should not attribute his suffering to the "suggestion of the Devil" but to his "nervous debility," which caused the "painful difference between you and the mass of the world." Reminding Speed of his debility and difference from most other men, was Lincoln really encouraging his friend's pursuit of a wife?

Speed feared that he did "not love" Fanny Henning as he "should," said Lincoln, quoting Speed's words. Speed believed he "*reasoned*" himself into his engagement. But were not Henning's "heavenly *black eyes*" the "whole basis of all your early *reasoning* on the subject?" Lincoln asked, reminding Speed of the bodily aspect of his attraction, discussed privately by the men.

Referring *once again* to his own fears for Speed, Lincoln said that he would "be so anxious about you, that I want you to write me every mail," and signed himself "Your friend." That particular identity tag only inadequately expressed the depth and complexity of Lincoln's feeling for Speed.

A month later, on February 3, Lincoln wrote again to Speed, who was now fearing for Fanny Henning's life (though it is not at all clear how sick Henning may actually have been).[70] Was Speed's unconscious working overtime to consign his fiancée to heaven?

Lincoln, himself, seemed eager to dispatch Henning to the nether world: "Should she, as you fear, be destined to an early grave, it is indeed, a great consolation to know that she"—a religious woman—"is so well prepared to meet it." Speed had "*once* disliked" Henning's religion "so much," Lincoln reminded him. But Speed should now prize the religion that had prepared Henning to meet her maker.

Lincoln hoped that Speed's "melancholy bodings" as to Henning's death were "not well founded" (they were not, it turned out). But Speed's fear that Henning might die was actually cause for rejoicing, Lincoln now claimed. For Speed's fear was "indubitable evidence of your undying affection for her." Lincoln reasoned: if Speed "did not love her, although you might not wish her death, you would most calmly be resigned to it." Speed "might not wish her death" if he did not love Henning? Murderous rivalries and killing fantasies were playing out here behind the love talk. Lincoln then one-upped hypochondriacal Speed: he had been "quite clear of hypo since you left."

On February 15, twelve days later, far from dying, Fanny Henning was actually quite healthy enough to marry Speed. So, when Lincoln wrote to him on February 13, he knew his friend would receive his letter *after* the much anticipated consummation.[71]

Lincoln assured Speed, "My desire to befriend you is everlasting." "Befriend" is one of the few names that Lincoln gave to his desire for lifelong intimacy with Speed. "But," Lincoln added, Speed "will always, hereafter, be on ground that I have never occupied"—the ground of marriage or married copulation, or both? So, out of inexperience, Lincoln worried, "I might advise wrong." But, then, Speed "will never again need any comfort from abroad," added Lincoln, playing for sympathy, but probably expressing a real fear. Speed's marriage, Lincoln anticipated, would curtail Speed's need for and access to his old friend, as it did.

Lincoln then warned Speed once again that he might not yet be free of his old anxiety: "excessive pleasure" might "still be accompanied with a painful counterpart at times." But even in "the agony of despondency," Speed should recall that "very shortly you are to feel well again." For Lincoln was convinced, he said, that Speed did love Henning "as ardently as you are capable of loving." Support or subtle dig?

Though Lincoln thought that Speed's "nerves will fail you occasionally for a while"—yet another prognosis negative—such failures must almost be over, Lincoln surmised. But if Speed's mind was "not exactly right," he should keep busy—Lincoln's own cure for nerves.

If Speed had passed "calmly" through "the ceremony" (the marriage ceremony, explicitly, the coitus ceremony, implicitly) or "with sufficient composure not to excite alarm in any present, you are safe," concluded Lincoln. The marriage night was a dangerous occasion in Lincoln's eyes.

Then, not above a little competition in the masculinity department, Lincoln boasted in a startling postscript, "I have been quite a man ever since you left." With Speed absent, Lincoln reclaimed his manhood. Speed's presence implicitly unmanned him.

On February 16, the day after Speed's wedding—and its sexual consummation—Speed wrote to Lincoln, and Lincoln responded on February 25.[72] He had opened Speed's letter, said Lincoln, "with intense anxiety and trepidation—so much that although it turned out better than I expected, I have hardly yet, at the distance of ten hours, become calm." Lincoln was heavily invested emotionally in Speed's consummation, almost as if he was in bed again with his friend.

"I tell you, Speed," said Lincoln, "our *forebodings* for which you and I are rather peculiar, are all the worst sort of nonsense." They were both odd, Lincoln and Speed imagined, to feel so much fear of first coitus with a new wife. But a historian who has considered the matter, Charles

Rosenberg, believes that such fear possessed many nineteenth-century men. Many, perhaps most, were inexperienced, and extremely nervous about living up to the true man ideal and acting the bold, confident sexual initiator with a pure true woman. The "marriage night was an institutionalized trauma for the pure of both sexes."[73]

From the "*tone*" and handwriting of Speed's current letter Lincoln saw that his friend was now "much *happier,* or, if you think the term preferable, *less miserable.*" (After the sexual consummation? After marriage?) Speed "had so obviously improved, at the very time I so much feared, you would have grown worse." Was Lincoln glad or miffed? Lincoln typically expressed a mixture of chagrin and relief at the success of Speed's first marriage night.[74]

Lincoln quoted Speed: "Something indescribably horrible and alarming still haunts" him, a reference, it seems, to Speed's intense, lingering sexual fears. His terrors would vanish, Lincoln assured him.[75]

Despite Speed's unexpected happiness, he had complained to Lincoln that the "Elysium" of which he (Speed) had "dreamed so much, is never to be realized" (Lincoln again quoted his friend). After all the buildup, the first consummation may well have disappointed. It was "the peculiar misfortune of both you and me," Lincoln agreed, "to dream dreams of Elysium far exceeding all that any thing earthly can realize." Their romantic dreams of love and marriage, and their idealized vision of good women, were not of this world, Lincoln understood. But no real, imperfect, earthly woman, Lincoln assured Speed, could do more than Henning to realize Speed's unearthly dreams—another ambivalent reassurance. These men's perfectionist fantasy of ideal love with a good wife conflicted with the difficult, mundane reality of married life—another root of the "crisis" experienced by Lincoln, Speed, and other nineteenth-century romantics.

Lincoln then quoted his own father's maxim about men, women, and marriage, phrased in terms of economic exchange and eros: "If you make a bad bargain, *hug* it the tighter." A man made the best of a wife, the maxim suggested, by hugging his woman "the tighter." Coitus, in other words, was compensation for the bad exchange bachelors made in giving up their freedom to marry. That bit of male folklore revealed the misogynistic underside of men's idealizing of women, love, and marriage.

If Speed had indeed made a bad bargain, Lincoln concluded, "it is certainly the most *pleasant one*" Lincoln could imagine—in this imperfect world. Lincoln's implicit qualifications are telling.

With this letter to Speed, Lincoln enclosed another bland enough to show Speed's new wife, a subterfuge that separated Speed from his bride.

The second letter recreated a secret intimacy between the two men from which the wife was excluded.[76]

In the second letter, Lincoln wrote of receiving Speed's announcement that he and Henning "are no more twain, but one flesh"—another confirmation that the meshing of male and female bodies was the specific "crisis" preoccupying these nerve-wracked men. Cocksure these guys were not.

With Speed safely married, Lincoln was able to be a bit more open about his feelings for him. Lincoln felt "somewhat jealous of both of you now," he admitted. He appealed again for sympathy: "You will be so exclusively concerned for one another, that I shall be forgotten entirely." Playing the martyr, Lincoln again expressed a real fear. He regretted, Lincoln confessed, Speed's decision not to return to Illinois: "I shall be very lonesome without you." But Speed's duty to his wife's wish to stay near her family was "ten thousand times more sacred than any you can owe to others"—the pious words again positioned Lincoln as martyr, even as his trite overstatement worked with the irony of satire.[77]

"How miserably things seem to be arranged in this world," complained Lincoln. "If we have no friends, we have no pleasure; and if we have them, we are sure to lose them, and be doubly pained by the loss." Lincoln's specific loss was Speed.

A month later, on March 27, 1842, Lincoln asked Speed about a subject "of the most intense interest"—his love life.[78] It "thrills me with joy," Lincoln said, "to hear you say you are *far happier than you ever expected to be.*" **With** so bleak an anticipation of marriage, Speed was evidently surprised to find it not so bad. On one side, bleak expectation, on the other, the impossible dream.

Speed's report gave Lincoln "more pleasure" than he had "enjoyed since that fatal first of Jany. '41"—the day of Speed's decision to leave for Kentucky, and, perhaps, of Lincoln's breakup with Mary Todd. It "kills my soul," said Lincoln, that Todd might still be unhappy on his account (he was then, in March 1842, evidently toying with making up). Again offering Speed his old-style ambivalent advice, Lincoln assured him: "It is even yet possible for your spirits to flag down and leave you miserable."

The violet that Speed had enclosed in his letter, sent by his wife, had arrived "so dry, and mashed," Lincoln reported, "that it crumbled to dust at the first attempt to handle it"—an apt symbolizing, it seems, of Lincoln's feelings about Fanny Henning's fatal impact on his and Speed's intimacy.

Writing to Speed on Independence Day, four months later, Lincoln was thinking about resigning his own independence, and attempting a renewed courtship of Mary Todd.[79] Lincoln now criticized Speed for the bad advice he had offered during Lincoln's earlier failed courtship: "Had you understood my case at the time, as well as I understood yours afterwards," said Lincoln, "I should have sailed through clear." Lincoln almost blamed Speed for his own broken engagement—another reason Lincoln may have felt ambivalent about encouraging Speed's engagement.

"You have now been the husband of a lovely woman nearly eight months," Lincoln wrote on October 5, 1842, boldly inquiring: "Are you now, in *feeling* as well as judgement, glad you are married as you are?"[80] He admitted: "From any body but me, this would be an impudent question not to be tolerated." Their special intimacy permitted this personal inquiry, Lincoln asserted. Asking that personal question, in fact, recreated their old intimacy. Answer "quickly," begged Lincoln, "as I feel impatient to know." Speed must have answered quickly that he was still glad to be wed, for the following month, on November 4, 1842, Mary Todd and Abraham Lincoln suddenly married.

Lincoln and Speed's friendship continued, intermittently, into the 1860s, but without its old intensity. Marriage to women led to these men's divorce.

෧෨

Until—and, possibly, after—Lincoln and Speed each married, they were closer to one another than to their women partners, those culturally alien, female creatures with whom they had to lie for the first time, in their new beds, on their wedding nights.

So what was the character of these men's intimacy with each other? Speed experienced an immediate, profound feeling for the woebegone stranger, a falling at first sad sight. Lincoln's response to Speed was, likewise, instantaneous, and several times explicitly linked with "pleasure." The reiterated pleasures of Lincoln and Speed's friendship contrasts with Lincoln's tortured relationships with the Marys, Owens and Todd, and with the anxieties both men experienced at the prospect of Speed's intimacy with his wife. Both men's response to good women, and to intimacy and sex with them, often seems ambivalent, sometimes downright hostile. Likewise, Mary Todd was consistently more rhapsodic about women, more critical of men. Within their separate spheres, men and women sometimes formed opposed, warring armies.

Lincoln's deep depression after Speed's sale of his store registers Lincoln's strong feelings about his beloved friend's desertion. The depth and strength of Lincoln's feelings for Speed can also be inferred from what seems to me his hostile undermining of Speed's engagement. Despite his conscious desire to bolster Speed's resolve to marry, Lincoln's *repeated* references to Speed's anxieties can only have increased them. Evident in Lincoln's response to Speed's engagement are his deep love for Speed and his anger at losing his most intimate male friend to a wife—a common experience of the era's romantic men friends, as other stories show.

Lincoln and Speed's hostility to the fiancée who threatened to separate them is also evident in their response to Fanny Henning's perceived illness. Love for each other and murderous feelings toward Henning mingled here promiscuously. So Lincoln did not see that Speed's fear of Henning's death was odd evidence of his deathless devotion.

The close bond between Lincoln and Speed permitted each man to confess his fears about copulating with a good woman. The approaching "crisis" about which both men fretted was the sexual consummation of Speed's marriage. But, did not their shared, anxious concern about sexual intercourse with women electrify the men's own intimacy? Their anxious sex-talk certainly bound them closer than ever, even as each moved away from the other, traveling toward the only approved, institutionalized, legal mode of sexual relations.

The poet Carl Sandburg sniffed sexual deviance in Lincoln and Speed's intimacy, in the first edition of his popular biography of the president, published in 1926. "A streak of lavender ran through him," Sandburg said of Speed, "he had spots soft as May violets." Speed and Lincoln "told each other their secrets about women," said Sandburg, and "Lincoln too had . . . a streak of lavender, and spots soft as May violets." Lincoln believed that he and Speed "had exceptional and sensitive personalities," continued Sandburg, stressing (for a third time) that biological inheritance and fate had "given these two men streaks of lavender, spots soft as May violets." Sandburg's obsessive repetitions revealed a desire to speak the unspeakable about the iconic president.[81]

Constructing an alternative model of legitimate, erotic intimacy between men was the project that a young, Connecticut man struggled with in his diary, the same year that Lincoln and Speed first met in Illinois.

On February 2, 1837, Albert Dodd, then nineteen or twenty years old, contemplated in his diary the emotional ups and downs of his past year at Washington College (now Trinity), in Hartford, Connecticut: "First, the friend I loved," a classmate, John Heath, "the first one whom I had ever truly loved in this wide world, became estranged from me, as I indeed did from him."[1] Dodd now "thought I had been a fool for wasting my affections" on this inadequately responsive friend. For a long time he "neglected" Heath. But then, "prompted by feelings which cannot well be here expressed, I wrote to him to renew our friendship, and he was glad so to do, and now I again have my friend."

Words for his feelings did not come easily to Dodd, though his emotions were hardly unique. The sex-segregated schools and colleges of the nineteenth century inspired intense, sometimes eros-filled friendships between young, upper-class white men, as research has begun to show.

Dodd's emotional survey continued: "Then came another affliction in my list of woes." This "was to discover that *she* whom I loved," Julia Beers, "had proved fickle and deceitful." Dodd did not accuse Beers "too heartily," for "it may be that I am . . . mistaken in supposing that she ever had any peculiar regard for me." She had "never in so many words said 'I love you,'" Dodd conceded. However, her "treatment of me for a long time led me to the conclusion that the affection which she well knew I had for her was on her part returned. But from that fond dream I have awoke, and now I have ceased to think much of the affair."[2]

Two days later, Dodd was asking himself why he was "so sensitive" to John Heath's "coldness." He answered: "Because, I regard, I esteem, I *love* him more than all the rest." "Regard," "esteem," "love"—Dodd searched for the word that best fit his feeling. He addressed the absent Heath: "John, dear John I love you, indeed I love you. But you are not here, you cannot hear me confess this to you, a confession which perhaps you would care not for."

Dodd wondered what to name his feeling for Heath: "It is not friendship merely which I feel for him, or it is friendship of the strongest kind. It is a heart-felt, a manly, a pure, deep, and fervent love." This is literally a defining moment in his diary. Dodd toyed with the word "friendship," but then rejected it for "love," qualified as especially intense. Adding qualifiers to the terms "love" and "friendship" was one of the main ways that men of this time affirmed their special feeling for men.

Dodd's defensive affirmation—that his love for Heath was "pure" and "manly"—suggests the opposite: he betrays a vague perception that his "love" for Heath included a touch of feeling he considered "unmanly," a hint of emotion he considered "impure." But Dodd's perception of the carnal seems, then, to have been unconscious. In his conscious world a man's love for a man was spiritual; only man's love for woman might include, perhaps, a touch of fleshly yearning.

In Dodd's day, a sensual possibility was realized only in strongly condemned acts of man-to-man "sodomy" or "mutual masturbation." Separate and distinct from those carnalities, "love" and "friendship" inhabited another, lust-free world. Thus freed of lust, love and friendship were the two most common terms men employed to name and understand their intimacies with other men. It sometimes took a bit of mental maneuvering, however, to keep these intense attractions free of any conscious taint of fleshly desire.

Why, Dodd added, had he not told Heath "of the fire that was burning at my heart?" His emotions were strong, and he had feared that his declaration "would not meet with an equally warm welcome." Inequality of affection was the problem Dodd perceived in his relationship with Heath, *not* the fact that the object of his desire was male. Dodd repeatedly sought a democratic reciprocity of the heart. Just fifty years after the U.S. Constitution declared equality for all (except slaves, free blacks, and women), Dodd yearned for an equal exchange of affection.

The unsure, adolescent Dodd also feared, more generally, that he was "destitute of those qualities which are calculated to win the friendship, the loving friendship, of any." But then recalling the depth of his feeling restored his self-confidence: "I can love, God knows that I can love." He hoped that this "ever burning flame" would one day "kindle a like affection in the breasts of others"—sex unspecified.

Focusing again on Heath, Dodd also hoped that their recent correspondence would, as he wrote in his diary on February 4, 1837, "renew that intercourse which has been so inconspicuously broken off."

But intercourse interrupted caused anxiety. The next day, Dodd referred to "things that trouble me particularly," first among them "that —— which has long troubled me; and also ——" (two sins unwritable among that day's college students, most probably sexual sins, which Dodd represented by long dashes). "Besides there is M.O. [mutual onanism? masturbation? onanism?] —— I dare not write even here these things —— which it is my prayer may soon be settled."

Was Dodd again fending off awareness of carnal desire in his fervent love for Heath? He was plagued, it seems, by powerful, internal, moral strictures that made his troubles literally and metaphorically unspeakable. His moral antagonist lived within him, internalized from without.

Two days later, still trying to understand his worries, Dodd thought that it may be "my ——— I dare not write it in full; or it may be that my thoughts run upon ——— as much as any other thing." He prayed: "O that I could for a time forget all these sources of care, both great and small." He even half wished for death before melodramatically banishing the thought: "Away fiend, tempt me not; Avaunt, ye blue devils . . ."

Then he unabashedly wrote: "The person of whom I think most is John Heath. That is undisputed in my mind, and therefore do I conclude that he is the one most dear to my memory." Heath and Dodd's blue devils may seem associated to us, but not, apparently, to Dodd.

Reaffirming his love for Heath, Dodd wondered if he had "really loved Julia." He had once loved her, he thought, "though the passion is now nearly forgotten. Yet it seems that the nature of my affection for A. H. [Anthony Halsey, another friend] and J. F. H. [John Heath] was really the same as that which I had for Julia. Yet one was for a female, the other for . . ." Obviously, "a male" completed the thought.[3]

Here, someone, probably Dodd or a protective friend or relative, has torn away the diary page, destroying a precious document of love's history.[4] But clearly, Dodd was struck by the *similarity* of his "affection" for men and for women. That similarity of feeling contradicted his society's idea that man's love for men was free of lust, man's love for women potentially lustful. No homo/heterosexual distinction told Dodd that he was experiencing two essentially different kinds of erotic feelings.

A week later, memories of John Heath's "beloved form" had not faded, and Dodd reproached himself again for not telling Heath of "my deep and burning affection." Why, he asked, when they were together, did he not declare: "John I love you much, do you love me?" But whatever had Heath replied, "Would this satisfy *my* ardent feeling?" Dodd doubted it.

Dodd did not expect Heath to love him as much as he loved Heath: "I possess not the requisite qualifications to obtain the deep love which John, or anyone else, might possess." Reveling in self-pity, Dodd moaned: "O God, to have one's love *slighted*, neglected, treated with coldness, when it might rightly claim at least a little regard in return. It is hard, hard." Only in his "private volume, whose pages shall be surveyed by no eyes," did Dodd freely repeat his "secret avowal" of love for his "friend" and "companion" Heath, the "sole inhabitant of my heart."[5] Again, he hid his love for Heath, not because its object was male, but because he feared Heath did not reciprocate his feeling.

A month later, however, on March 21, 1837, Dodd's roving heart was heading again for Anthony Halsey, who had not answered his letter: "I do long to hear from him again. How I love him! He lately seems to have occupied my thoughts more than J. H. and I feel as if I loved him more ardently and intensely than John. I do perhaps; but both are very dear to me, and Anthony loves me in return I am sure"—a big plus given Dodd's desire for reciprocated feeling. "Dear Anthony," he added, "how I long to see you, to be with you again, to embrace you. O God, when shall we meet again?"

A few days later, Dodd received a letter from his "dear Tony" that mentioned Julia, whom Dodd called "a lovely, sweet, noble, enchanting girl." Dodd then pondered his love's character, asking: "L-o-v-e, love; what is love?" He answered: "I can't describe it. All I know is that there are three persons in this world whom I have loved, and those are, Julia, John, & Anthony. Dear beloved trio."

Then his thoughts focused again on Anthony Halsey: "What a sweet, lovely fellow he is! I do love him!" In a diary entry of March 24, 1837, he addressed Halsey directly as, a month earlier, he had addressed Heath: "Tony, how I long to see you, to embrace you, to press you to my bosom, my own dear Tony!" He wondered if his "affection would not diminish" if he should be with Halsey again, "as we were wont to be together in days of yore. I think not. *Dearest Anthony.*"

Three days later Dodd recalled his earliest, excited sightings of Anthony Halsey "as he came along down from College . . . his appearance was very interesting, he was *so handsome.*" He did not think Halsey as handsome now, "but still he is beautiful in person, in mind, and in heart."

"Well, I became acquainted with him when I entered College," Dodd recalled, and he and Halsey "became intimate, and soon too, I loved him with my whole heart. Yes, very intimate we became, and though we did not room together, yet we were with each other much of the time. How completely I loved him, how I doted on him! We often walked out into the fields together arm in arm," talking about mutual friends.

"Often, too he shared my pillow or I his," remembered Dodd. Though not roommates the two had "often" found a way to share a bed, apparently without comment or self-consciousness. Bed sharing was an emotionally loaded practice for him, though not one acknowledged to include eros.

Then, "how sweet to sleep with him," Dodd recalled of his nights with Halsey, "to hold his beloved form in my embrace, to have his arms about my neck, to imprint upon his face sweet kisses! It was happiness complete. O if those times would only return! If I could only know him again as I did then, behold his youth, beauty, and innocence of aught of evil, how sweet it would be! Dear, dearest Anthony! Thou are mine own friend. My most beloved of all! To see thee again! What rapture it would be, thou sweet, lovely, dear, beloved, beautiful, adored Anthony!"[6] Recognizing the intensity of his love for Halsey, Dodd still did not apparently see sensuality in it—even in sweet kisses and embraces shared in bed.

In a reported dream, Dodd's interest shifted again to Julia Beers, whom he imagined "attacking" another girl, "tooth and nail, real vixen like." And then Beers, "the dear, beloved girl was in my arms, crying away with very rage, her little heart beating violently against mine; and her whole frame trembling and convulsed." Dodd recalled: "O, what a sweet and thrilling embrace it was!" He then remembered a kissing game he had played with Beers a year earlier in which he gave her a kiss, "sweet and delicious," a kiss that she had returned. "Heavens!" he scolded himself, "I did not take half the advantage that I might have done, for I was so astonished, and fluttered, and confused."[7]

A double standard was operating: Dodd could sleep repeatedly with his beloved "Tony," and kiss and hug him, acts not perceived as sensual. But, with Julia, Dodd was permitted only a kissing game and a dream convulsion, acts perceived as verging dangerously toward the lubricious.

By early June, Dodd was dreaming of yet another girl: "I held you in my arms and you smiled upon me. . . . Dearest *best* Elizabeth." He thought of Elizabeth all the time, he said in a poem addressed to her. Again, no homo/heterosexual division told Dodd he was supposed to love women *or* men.

About the same time, Dodd admired "Old Webb's daughter," a "lovely, perfectly beautiful girl, of handsome form," with "the most rosy, luscious lips I ever beheld," and eyes that are "large and dark . . . and melting."

By October 10, 1837, Dodd had transferred to Yale College, where he also transferred his affection yet again, this time to Jabez Sidney Smith, a freshman, whom he saw "much less than I wish I might. It is strange how I 'fell in love with him' (if I must use the expression, and I can think of no other to express my meaning so well)."[8] A man's "falling in love" with a woman might include carnal desire, so Dodd's "falling" for Jabez made him uneasy. Finding the right word for his feelings was still a struggle.

Whether Dodd's feeling for Jabez "will ever become on my part a lasting affection I know not," he explained, for Smith "is a freshman and I am a senior, and it is somewhat unbecoming to associate with a fresh, but that makes no difference with me I am sure."

Their age disparity did clearly matter—again Dodd's affirmation suggests its contrary. This freshman-senior romance broke the rules of propriety taught informally at Yale. Of Jabez, Dodd added: "I am conscious that I love him very much and more perhaps than I do any other one." Dodd constantly readjusted his hierarchy of affections.

In December 1837 at Yale, Dodd composed or transcribed a revealing, rhymed ditty, "The Disgrace of Hebe & Preferment of Ganymede," about a dinner for the gods given by Jove, at which the beautiful serving girl, Hebe, tripped over "Mercury's wand," exhibiting, as she fell, that part "which by modesty's laws is prohibited." Men's and women's privates were on Dodd's mind—eros was now closer to consciousness. Angry at Hebe's "breach of decorum," Jove sent her away, and called Ganymede "to serve in her place. / Which station forever he afterward had, / Though to cut Hebe out . . . was too bad."

Considering Dodd's cutting out Julia Beers for John Heath, Anthony Halsey, and Jabez Smith, his poem shows him employing ancient Greek myth, and the iconic, man-loving Ganymede to help him comprehend his own shifting, ambivalent attractions.[9] At Yale, Dodd read the *Greek Anthology* and other classic texts and began to use his knowledge of ancient affectionate and sexual life to come to terms with his own—a common strategy of this age's upper-class, college-educated white men.[10]

That Dodd perhaps found the reciprocal love he sought is hinted at in his later history. After graduating from Yale in 1838, he studied law and opened an office in St. Louis, Missouri. He then moved to Bloomington, Illinois, where, about 1840–41, in his early twenties, he became a law partner of the bachelor Jesse W. Fell, then in his early thirties.[11]

Raised in Pennsylvania in a liberal Quaker family, Fell was a founder of Normal, Illinois, and, later, a founder of the state normal university, as well as McLean County's first lawyer with diploma. Fell was also a tree and flower enthusiast, a temperance advocate, and a civic leader. In 1834, Fell had begun a friendship and a long political association with Abraham Lincoln. Later, in 1860, he worked hard to win Lincoln the Republican nomination for president.

With Fell, Dodd entered Illinois political life. In June 1844, Dodd was about twenty-six and still a bachelor, when, returning from a meeting, his horse lost its footing in the swollen Mackinaw River; Dodd was drowned.[12] Later that year Jesse Fell personally carried Dodd's private papers (including, apparently, his diary) to Dodd's father in the East. Dodd's sudden, unexpected death may well have saved his diary from destruction—the fate, no doubt, of many other revealing private papers. Six months after Dodd's death, Jesse Fell married for the first time, at the advanced age of thirty-seven, and began to raise a family that eventually included eight children.[13]

The intensity of Dodd's feelings exceeded romantic friendship by including an erotic element, as Dodd himself apparently began to see. Like many men of his century, he was perplexed about what to call and how to understand his strong attraction to men as well as to women. Like Lincoln, Dodd floundered in a world with few affirmative words for his fervent response to other men. In the diary of Albert Dodd we see how men contended against the verbal void that had also left Lincoln and Speed at a loss for words to name their mutual feelings. Against such condemnatory terms as "mutual masturbation," "onanism," and "sodomy," men in the nineteenth century struggled for a new, affirmative language of sexual love. They began to develop a counterpractice, attempting to rename, rethink, and publicly affirm men's erotic desires for men, and, sometimes, their sexual acts with them. Through their oppositional search for words, they began, tentatively, to come to terms, literally and metaphorically.

Just a few years after Dodd struggled in his diary to come to terms, another young man, in New York City, was grappling for words to affirm publicly a young man's love for a still younger boy.

Walter Whitman, early 1840s. Courtesy Ed Folsom. ❧

A pioneering, resistant man struggled for an appropriate language of love in a short story published November 20, 1841, in the *New World*, a widely distributed literary weekly.[1] Recent advances in the printing press, and the subsequent economic success of mass-produced publications, provided new forums in which American writers strove to find their own voices, and their own takes on love, friendship, and, sometimes, surreptitiously, even eros.

This tale's author, a twenty-two-year-old typesetter and journalist who also wrote conventional news stories, short fiction, features, editorials, and poems for the city's press, adopted a popular form—the sentimental romance—to portray the deep, spontaneous love that a young man felt for a younger, needy youth.

The unremarkable author of this fiction was Walter Whitman. None of his literary efforts yet hinted that fourteen years later, self-transmuted into "Walt Whitman," he would publish a book of poetry that spoke publicly, eloquently, and lyrically, in an utterly unique voice, for unorthodox sex-pleasures and for all the world's downtrodden.

Whitman's tale of 1841, "The Child's Champion," begins one summer evening, in a village fifty miles from New York City, where Charles, a poor, overworked farmhand of twelve is passing a tavern. One of the era's most prominent places for men to casually meet men, taverns play a repeated role in stories of the period. Inside this eros-filled locale, the youth, "large for his age" (like Whitman as a boy), sees five or six drunken sailors dancing together and others carousing. No women are mentioned, so the sailors must be engaged in a "bull-dance," one of the "he-festivals" mentioned years later by Whitman.[2] Men publicly dancing together, for pleasure, was a common feature of sexually segregated American life until the twentieth century. Then, the passing of separate male and female spheres and anxieties about "sexual perversion" put an end to the dance of men with men, at least as mainstream entertainment.

At the tavern's open window, Charles is accosted by a one-eyed sailor with a bushy beard and "brutal appearance" who lifts him into the room. Here, bodily impairment—a missing eye—signaled sexual irregularity. "One-eyed" was also English slang for penis, a clue, possibly, to this figure's phallic character.[3] Sailors already had a reputation as violators of sexual propriety, and this sailor's untamed beard mirrors his unrestrained masculine eroticism. Whitman, who at this time sported a carefully trimmed beard, later, several times, linked hairiness and sensuality.[4]

"There's a new recruit for you," says the sailor, rather suggestively, to his mates. "Not so coarse a one, either," he adds, surveying the comely youth. The "brawny" sailor's gaze threatens to feminize young Charles,

A "bull-dance" in California, about 1849. *The Miners' Pioneer* . . . , Kurz and Allison Art Studio, Chicago, 1887. Courtesy Library of Congress.

so Whitman immediately assures his readers that the boy, "though not what is called pretty," is "fresh and manly looking." That "manly" look defends the youth against any imputation of seducing the sailor with feminine charms.

When the sailor tries to force a glass of strong brandy down Charles's throat the teetotaling lad actively rejects this coerced ingestion, knocking the glass aside. Did the forced drink hint at involuntary oral intercourse? Literary critic Michael Moon points to the fluids circulating suggestively in this text.[5]

The aggressive sailor then "bent Charles half way over, and with the side of his heavy foot" gave him "a sharp and solid kick." The bent boy and the kick suggest anal rape. "Bent," meaning "perverse; sexually deviant or unconventional," is twentieth-century slang, but Whitman could be anticipating that later usage.[6]

While the youth still hung "like a rag" from the sailor's arm, the bully is about to repeat the kick when he is stopped by a punch thrown by a new character, the outraged John Lankton.

Lankton's face, readers are told, has "the air of city life"—not a good sign—he is a dissipated twenty-one or twenty-two, just about Whitman's age at the time of publication. Lankton dresses "fashionably," in the finest black broadcloth, like those who "may be nightly seen in the dress circles of our most respectable theatres"—and like Whitman in his dandyish 1840s photos, before his self-executed makeover as working-class rough.[7]

Why was it, asked the narrator, that from the first moment John Lankton had seen Charles his "heart had moved with a strange feeling of kindness toward the boy?" The question, it seems, was too touchy to be answered. Whatever motivated Lankton's heart movements, he was "anxious to know more" of Charles, feeling "that he should love him."

"Love" is an important word in this tale, as it was in Dodd's diary. Here, it is Whitman's basic way of naming Lankton's and Charles's feelings for each other. Love is one of the key terms by which men of this era affirmatively named and characterized their erotic and affectionate feelings for other males. As such, it was *not* necessarily a code word for "sodomitical" desire nor, of course, for "sexual inversion" or "homosexuality"—terms and concepts not yet in use. Nor was the word "love" necessarily a euphemism for some other word that could not be spoken. It was one common historical way of conceptualizing a man's deep feelings for a man or youth. Naming Lankton and Charles's love, Whitman asserted this feeling's fundamental character.

As the name for this age's dominant romantic ideal, love was also sometimes appropriated from mainstream rhetoric to define and defend men's sexual and affectionate desire for men and youths. Several historical visions of such love appear in nineteenth-century texts, as we have begun to see.

Whitman's narrator comments on such outbreaks of love as Lankton is experiencing: "O, it is passing wondrous, how in the hurried walks of life and business, we meet with young beings, strangers, who seem to touch the fountains of our love, and draw forth their swelling waters." Those young, male beings who touch older men's fountains, swelling their waters, point to the age difference that often stimulated erotic-affectional exchanges between nineteenth-century American males. Love and sexual relationships between men and male youths certainly had a long history, going back in the Western tradition to ancient Greece. But different societies constructed and integrated such age-distinguished relationships in substantially different ways.

"The wish to love and to be loved," Whitman's narrator continues, "that the forms of custom, and the engrossing anxiety for gain, so generally smother, will sometimes burst forth in spite of all obstacles; and, kindled by one, who, till the hour was unknown to us, will burn with a lovely and pure brightness."

Through the lens of this age's official, romantic worldview, the pure love of Whitman's John Lankton is perceived as lust free, however burning. But in 1841, in New York City, the narrator of Whitman's story is already a bit defensive about that common genteel notion: "No scrap is this of sentimental fiction; ask your own heart, reader, and your own memory, for endorsement to its truth."[8]

"No scrap" of this "love" is "sentimental fiction"—to be sure, Walter Whitman was making fiction of feelings he had experienced. But his love feelings, purified of eros, found only sentimental and inadequate expression in his story—they were smothered within the genteel genre in which he was writing. Whitman's reference to love smothered by "the forms of custom, and the engrossing anxiety for gain" not only formulated an embryonic economic theory of sexual and affectional repression. It also described exactly what happens within this piece of commercial, popular fiction. Whitman struggles mightily here against the constrictions of the sentimental romance, trying to say more about eros between men than the form allowed.

John Lankton, Whitman went on, was "parentless—a dissipated young man—a brawler—one whose too frequent companions were rowdies, blacklegs [dishonest gamblers], and swindlers." The New York City police "were not strangers to his countenance," and "certain reporters who note the transactions there, had more than once received gratuities for leaving out his name from the disgraceful notoriety of their columns."[9] Whitman, the New York journalist, knew of men who, in trouble with the law, paid reporters to keep their names out of print. Had Whitman himself paid other journalists to keep his more notorious exploits out of the papers? Whitman's comment suggests the possibility.

John Lankton is single and wealthy, he has trained as a doctor and has mixed in "all kinds of parties where the object was pleasure."[10] Those pleasure parties were bad, it then went without saying. The era's respectable morality looked suspiciously on enjoyments, especially sensual joys. The nineteenth-century work ethic was not yet countered by a pleasure-in-consumption ethic.

Freeing Charles from the one-eyed sailor and feeling love for the boy, Lankton tells him that the next day he will also free him from his apprenticeship to a "hard-hearted," "avaricious" master.[11] Having saved Charles from sexual and economic exploitation, Lankton then suggests a plan for the night: "It would perhaps be best for the boy to stay and share his bed at the inn." And "little persuading did the child need."

As Lankton and Charles shared that bed, and Lankton embraced comely young Charles, Whitman felt it necessary to assure readers that the man's "affection" was free of lust: "As they retired to sleep," Lankton's mind filled with thoughts "of unsullied affection," and "of walking in a steadier and wiser path." Despite the physical contact, no hint of sensuality supposedly compromised Lankton's feelings: "All his imaginings seemed to be interwoven with the youth who lay by his side; he folded his arms around him, and, while he slept, the boy's cheek rested on his bosom."

But Lankton's earlier acts and desires had *not* been lust free: "Fair were these two creatures in their unconscious beauty— glorious, but yet how differently glorious! One of them [Charles] was innocent and sinless of all wrong: the other [Lankton]—O to that other, what evil had not been present, either in action or to his desires!"[12]

Despite Lankton's wayward past, the next morning, with the "earliest rays of the warm sun," a "gentle angel entered," and, "hovering over the sleepers on invisible wings, looked down with a pleasant smile and blessed them." Paying special attention to comely young Charles, Whitman's cupid then bent "over the boy's face, and whispered strange words into his ear: thus it came that he had beautiful visions." This angelic whisperer of "strange words" is an early stand-in for Whitman, the future utterer of strange, poetic words.

Whitman physicalized the image of Charles and Lankton in bed: "No sound was heard but the slight breathing of those who slumbered there in each other's arms." Cupid then bends over the boy's lips and touches them "with a kiss." The angel hesitates, however, to kiss the corrupted Lankton, for "a spirit from the Pure Country, who touches anything tainted by evil thoughts, does it at the risk of having his breast pierced with pain." Whitman's "Pure Country" posited its contrary, an impure Lust World—two worlds at war. Lankton's "evil thoughts" and past activities in Lust World threaten to pollute the Pure Country, the kingdom of spiritual love. Lust World and the Pure Country could not coexist, an allegory for the era's mind/body split, the division we found clearly reflected in Lincoln's character.

But then, suddenly, a ray of sun hit Lankton's face, and the angel knew that he had permission from on high to bestow a kiss: "So he softly touched the young man's face with his, and silently and swiftly wafted himself away."[13] With God's approval, this absolving angel blessed Lankton and young Charles's loving union.

The day after their night together, soft-hearted Lankton freed Charles from his servitude to the hard-hearted master and started on his own path to "reformation." The "close-knit love" of Charles and Lankton, the far-seeing narrator informs us, "grew not slack with time," and when Charles (or, less likely, Lankton) finally "became head of a family of his own, he would shudder when he thought of his early danger and escape." (Whitman's last, vague "he" leaves it unclear which of the two became a family man, which remained a bachelor.)[14]

In this tale, the assaultive, subliminally erotic attack inflicted by the one-eyed sailor was bested by the loving, subliminally erotic intimacy offered by John Lankton to young Charles. Though the ending explicitly suggested the triumph of "family," marriage, and procreative intercourse, it also suggested the simultaneous triumph of Lankton's and Charles's love as it was transformed, in time, into man-man love. Family values, man-woman love, man-man love, and man-boy love were not viewed as opposed or exclusive in Whitman's story—as long as the eros in this love remained unspoken, as "unconscious" as the beauty of the bedmates, Charles and Lankton. Whitman had not yet invented a literary form adequate to convey the unspeakable lusts and affections playing intensely just below his story's conventional surface.

Starting at the age of seventeen, in 1836, the young Walter Whitman had made a living by teaching briefly at one-room schools on rural Long Island, boarding with local farm families. Whitman later told a woman friend that "the grown up son of the farmer with whom he was boarding . . . became very fond of him, and Walt of the boy, and he said the father quite reproved him for making such a pet of the boy."[15] Early in the twentieth century a rumor circulated in Southold, Long Island, that Whitman had been a teacher there and had been violently run out of town after a sexual encounter with a student.[16] The eros of pedagogy may well have paid a call on Walter Whitman and his pupil, like the angel who called on and blessed John Lankton and young Charles.

But how could Whitman, in mid-nineteenth-century America, publish without scandal this affirmative, eros-tinged story of love between a young man and a still-younger boy? At this time in the Pure Country, love was *not* yet "sex-love"—that term was not invented until century's end.[17] At this moment in the Pure Country "to make love to" meant to court, not to copulate. A "lover" was the object of romantic pursuit, not a partner in sex.[18] "To sleep with" referred usually to a sleeping arrangement, not a carnal consummation.[19] Bodily love and spiritual love were thought of then as inhabiting distinct realms—the sensual and the spiritual never met and mated.

In this era, the act of sodomy, named occasionally in legal documents and newspaper reports, and persons identified occasionally as sodomites, had no association with the feelings of pure, true love that named the emotional link between Lankton and Charles. Their love inhabited a

Walter Whitman, 1848. Courtesy Library of Congress. ❧

world innocent of conscious erotic desire. Conversely, sodomy and sodomites inhabited an erotic universe devoid of love. Love and sodomy lived in separate spheres.

In Whitman's tale, spiritual love was a disembodied emotion, not linked consciously with sexuality. As such, this love could flower, officially, legitimately, and openly, between man and man, woman and woman, older and younger. Spiritual love was not exclusive, not properly limited to one sex, or one age, as love would be so clearly linked after the invention of homosexuality and heterosexuality. In contrast to the intimacies of males, the intimacies of nineteenth-century men and women might sometimes be perceived as more dangerously fraught with carnal possibilities. The age's sexual system ironically decreed more restrictions on the intimacies of men and women than on those of men with men and women with women. Whitman counted on the dominance of the asexual love ideal to keep readers from noticing the strong hints of eros in his text. He may not have been aware of them himself.

But within two months, in New York City, the ideology of spiritual love that protected Lankton and young Charles's intimacy from any imputation of eros, was called dramatically into question. Relationships between older and younger males were subjected to a new suspiciousness. The Pure Country threatened to become a sinkhole of "sodomy," New York, a city of "Sodomites."

PART II

Making Monsters

4 *Already Do the Beastly Sodomites of Gotham Quake*

Not two months after the publication of Whitman's paean to man-boy love, two of New York City's scandal-mongering newspapers began a crusade against sodomites, pictured as older men who preyed on younger men. Whitman's "The Child's Champion" had implicitly countered that particular folktale, and these newspapers' attack on sodomites implicitly countered Whitman's counternarrative. During this antisodomite crusade, Walter Whitman continued to work in sin city as editor, reporter, fiction writer, and fledgling poet.[1]

On January 29, 1842, the gossip-peddling paper, *The Whip*, published the first of a series of attacks on a "set" of men condemned collectively as "sodomites."[2] That plural is important: sodomy had earlier been organized and perceived as the temporary aberrant act of an isolated individual. Now sodomites were presented as soldiers in an army of seducers. *The Whip* knew "numerous names" of those "who follow that unhallowed practice of Sodomy."[3] Sodomy here identified a sinister band—sodomites named a class of men defined by their acts, an assigned, spoiled, group identity.

Though sodomites had been attacked earlier in London, Paris, and Amsterdam, *The Whip*'s attacks constitute the earliest-known American crusade against sodomites.[4] These attacks helped produce a new public awareness of sodomites as denizens of the New York underworld, an emerging urban type, suggesting the increasing visibility of sodomites in America's larger cities. These attacks also provide a rare, early, jaundiced peek at the emerging U.S. sodomite subculture.

The Whip singled out more than a half-dozen men by name—the earliest-known outing of sodomites in the United States.[5] Naming sodomites was a powerful regulatory tool, belying the paper's protest that it lacked a "language . . . severe enough" for condemning and exposing these alleged sinners and criminals.[6] The language it did deploy, the naming it did undertake, was powerful indeed.

"Johnson," the first sodomite named, was said to perform nightly in one of the city's "Concert Rooms"—an early American reference to the sodomite as entertainer. New York's saloons and music halls then presented a varied menu of songs and drinks, and, probably, already, a place to meet sexual partners.[7] America's new, urban pleasure palaces provided a variety of consumer satisfactions for a price. Here, as in Whitman's story, a tavern appeared as a site of erotic opportunity.

The Whip "will drive his filthy carcass from the place," it proclaimed of Johnson, even if this erotic cleansing was left to it alone. "We intend to single you out one by one—and you are the first," Johnson and his fellow sodomites were warned.

This singer was told not to open his mouth in public again, for his breath was "death to inhale"—he was contagious.[8] Another account entreated "every honest man to point the finger of scorn" at the sodomites' "polluted persons and shun them" as he would "a pestilence."[9] The popular association of sodomites with metaphorical disease long preceded psychiatrists' late-nineteenth-century medical model of "sexual inversion" as actual disease. The doctors' model adapted old folklore to a new, late-nineteenth-century sexual "science."

Ferdinand Palmo, a New York entertainment impresario, was warned that among his performers was one who "carries the soul" of a "hell-engendered Sodomite" (probably the same Johnson). The sodomite's "soul," it seems, differed substantially from the soul of ordinary men—an early version of the idea that sodomites possessed a distinct sort of psyche. But usually at this time, no basic distinction was made between the souls of sodomites and the psyches of their alleged nonsodomite victims.

The paper asked Palmo "to discharge" this sodomite, and his fellow entertainers were asked not to perform unless he was fired. Employment discrimination—or, at least, its advocacy—was an early form of sodomite persecution. *The Whip* writer appropriated moral reform rhetoric, claiming to write in order to expose the "inhuman enormities" of the sodomites—to expel them from their jobs and "to rout from our city these monsters."[10]

Palmo's customers were also asked "to aid us in driving this monster . . . from the city," ridding it of an unhuman, alien element.[11] *The Whip* also warned this sodomite "to quit the life you are leading, or shortly you will receive a thunder-bolt from us that will make you curse the hour you were born."[12]

The paper promised to call in the law and enlist the state in its antisodomite crusade: "We intend, shortly, to have one of these monsters arrested."[13] The "Law" should take action against sodomites, the paper several times suggested.

Johnson was evidently performing at the Oriental Saloon, which Ferdinand Palmo had opened at 41 Chambers Street the year of *The Whip*'s antisodomite crusade. The *New York Herald* described it as "unsurpassed" for "splendor and magnificence" by "anything of the kind in this or any other country. It is decorated in the most gorgeous style of Eastern grandeur. Mirrors and paintings adorn its walls and ceilings; a neat little stage and orchestra is erected at one end of the room, from which concerts will be nightly given free; sofas and lounges are there for the weary."[14] The exotic, erotic "Orient" was already a decorating theme and merchandising ploy. The free concerts were already in swing, apparently, when *The Whip* began its attack in 1842.

A few years later, another of Ferdinand Palmo's New York establishments was also associated with sodomy. *The Whip*'s placing a sodomite at Palmo's saloon in 1842 tallies with a scene in Herman Melville's satirical novel *Redburn*, published in 1849. In this story, outside a fashionable hotel in Liverpool, young Redburn and his effeminate friend Harry Bolton suddenly come upon a Lord Lovely, whom Bolton calls his "old chum." ("Chum," a common nineteenth-century term for a close friend, was sometimes applied to sexual intimacies. Bolton's work as a male prostitute had earlier been hinted at, and Bolton intimated that he was once Lord Lovely's kept man.)[15]

The innocent young Redburn describes Lord Lovely: "Not much of a Lord to behold; very thin and limber about the legs, with small feet like a doll's, and a small glossy head like a seal's. I had seen just such looking lords standing in sentimental attitudes in front of Palmo's on Broadway."

Outside Palmo's Broadway opera house, another of the entrepreneur's New York establishments, in the 1840s, Melville had evidently observed doll-like men with aristocratic airs lounging and posing, their "sentimental attitudes" and small feet suggesting effeminacy. (Small feet were also mentioned as an identifying sign of the effeminate male prostitutes who gathered at the Slide, in New York, in 1892.) Melville pointed here to the existence in 1840s America of effeminate men-loving men, a group documented by historians in eighteenth-century London.[16] Melville's small-footed men may also be the first report of American opera queens.

The sodomites named by *The Whip* included three "old and lechrous villains," identified specifically by their age, wealth, and alleged seduction and ruin of younger men. They were not identified, significantly, by any remarked-upon femininity. Male effeminacy was not yet routinely linked with sexual impropriety.[17]

But an urban legend, the myth of the upper-class, predatory boy molester, was already in public circulation. Lower-class and middle-class hostility against the wealthy was mobilized here against sodomites. (A quarter of a century later, after the Reverend Horatio Alger was accused of sexual indiscretions with boys in his Massachusetts church, he escaped to New York City, and there created a literary counterimage of older men as poor boys' saviors—the same theme as Whitman's "The Child's Champion.")[18]

One of these men, "an old sodomite," *The Whip* charged, had actually "murdered" a "youth of our acquaintance," who was so unfortunate as to fall within his "snare," an entanglement that had "emaciated" the youth's "form."[19]

Later, *The Whip* explicitly named and called "the attention of the police" to the youth's alleged killer, "an Englishman," Captain Collins (the second sodomite named), who, until about a year earlier, had "kept the Star House in Reade street."

Robert A. Collins, of 34 Reade Street, a block east of Broadway, was listed in the 1840 census of New York, and in New York City directories for 1840 and 1841. Residing at the same address, the census listed five persons: one free white male between fifteen and twenty years old, three between thirty and forty, and one between forty and fifty (probably Collins). The absence of female residents is striking, though the Star House probably welcomed both sexes and a variety of underworld types, not just sodomites and their customers.[20]

Referring to Collins, *The Whip* stressed: "There is no language . . . severe enough . . . to expose the fiendish enormity of this *brute,* who has been the instrumental cause of the death of a young man, who was employed by the monster as barkeeper; who was forced to nightly lie with beasts in the shape of men, by the order of his employer. Though horrid as this may seem, we can prove it by a number of young men who are now in the city, and who have also felt the inhuman embrace of this monster."[21] *The Whip* called Captain Collins "king of the Sodomites," suggesting that he had led a large entourage.

A "beastly crew," closer to the animal than the human, sodomites were also referred to repeatedly in these reports as "fiends" and "monsters," the evil opposites of men and humans.[22]

Among those who pursued the "unhallowed practice" of sodomy, *The Whip* found "no Americans, as yet—they are all Englishmen or French."[23] Johnson and Collins were both identified as English immigrants. Another was identified as a "Frenchman." Though he had "lived in this city from an early age," he remained the eternal resident alien. In the 1840s, the true American was a born American. "Among the worst of these miscreants," declared *The Whip*, "is Johnny L'Epine, of No. —— Cedar street, a man whose hair has the impress of seventy winters' snow" (the third sodomite outed, identified as "a wholesale importer").[24] This man was called "a walking libel on his country [France] and his kind" (humankind, probably, not men, since L'Epine was not described as unmanly).

The acts of sodomites, the paper emphasized, were not native to America or natural to Americans: These "horrible offences" are "foreign to our shores—to our nature they certainly are—yet they are growing apace in New York."[25] Attributing the supposedly increasing peril of sodomy to foreigners simultaneously affirmed the purity of Americans and the young American nation's need to guard against foreign corruptions. Just sixty-eight years after England's rebellious colonists declared their independence, *The Whip*'s antisodomite crusade supported the nationalistic rhetoric of young, postcolonial America. American nationalism was constructed at the expense of foreigners, including foreign sodomites. Acts of sodomy, *The Whip* suggested, were alien to Americans' "nature," another early version of the idea that sodomites' psyches differed substantially from those of ordinary men. Later, Walt Whitman would counter the idea of men's sexual relations with men as foreign affairs, celebrating the "native forms" of American men's ardor for men.

L'Epine's offense was "to perambulate the west side of Broadway and, whenever he can meet a youth of prepossessing appearance to accost and entice him with proffers of employment."[26] In 1842, the west side of Broadway was evidently known as the place to go if you were a fair-faced young man looking for paid work and open to older men's solicitations.

Numbers of unemployed young men may have been especially tempted to sell their bodies to interested men with money. A major depression, which first hit the United States in 1836, reached its nadir in New York in 1842, the year of *The Whip*'s antisodomite crusade.[27] If this depression caused a perceptible increase in the number of young men selling their favors in the streets, this visible rise in sexual trafficking may well have helped initiate *The Whip*'s sodomite hunt.

The "victims" of sodomites "are generally young men of most prepossessing looks," stressed the paper, and such handsome youths "swarm" about New York, and were "daily allured" into L'Epine's office. "Allured" suggests, more than "lured," that these youths had an active interest in men rich enough to purchase the sex they were selling.

A youth's fate at L'Epine's hands, said *The Whip* ominously, "is best known to the parties concerned. After Johnny has kept a boy a week he may be known in the street by his pallid countenance, his effeminate lip and his mincing gait."[28] The charge of "mincing" (walking in a dainty, elegant, affected manner) has long been leveled against effeminate men, especially effeminate participants in sodomy.[29] L'Epine's effeminizing of young men—his corruption of their masculinity—was almost as bad a crime, in *The Whip*'s estimate, as his alleged debauching of the youths.

Fourth on *The Whip*'s list of "nondescript victims of a morbid appetite" was a person who called himself (or herself) Sally Binns. Taking the identity of a woman, or posing as a woman, was one way some nineteenth-century men negotiated sex with men, as other stories indicate.[30] *The Whip*'s reference to Binns's "morbid appetite" again linked sodomy and sodomites with moral corruption and physical disease. "Morbid" was a common derogatory term in the arsenal of that century's pleasure police.[31]

Sally Binns was "usually to be seen on the 'four shilling side' of Broadway"—each side apparently accommodated prostitutes of specific prices. By the 1840s, in America's urban centers, the commercialization of pleasure-sex was proceeding apace, and occasionally women-like men minced among the sellers.

Binns's hair "is curled down his neck," *The Whip* reported, "he straddles [wiggles] as he walks and if anyone speaks to him, he drops a curtsy." He also "puts on female attire and enacts feminine parts in the Thespian Association over St. John's Hall, in Frankfort Street." The linking of sodomites with cross-dressing and theatrical role-playing already had a long history.[32]

"Binns wears a snuff colored frock, and fashionable pantaloons, with watch, rings and *bijouterie* [jewelry]," said *The Whip*, stressing his effeminate garb. "He has lost all sense and feeling of manhood, and is described by the poet as 'Not quite a woman; by no means a man.'"[33] Gender deviance was linked, in the case of Binns, with the sexual deviance represented by male prostitution. But *gender* bending was not yet automatically linked with sodomites' violation of *sexual* norms.

A fifth sexual nonconformist named by *The Whip* was John Emmanuel, "a Portuguese Jew, who came to this city from Lisbon about ten years ago." This alien was accused by the paper of "unnatural intercourse with a journeyman printer" in Boston, and with taking in a boy "picked up in the street." "Picked up" already referred to a sexual encounter—street pickups were an urban institution, as Walt Whitman's later diaries also suggest.

Emmanuel was also accused of "intemperate habits." As a liquor merchant on Washington Street, his sexual excess was allegedly matched by excessive drinking. Emmanuel's "intemperate habits" were still considered moral infractions, not a sickness. Drinking to "excess" would first be labeled a medically defined "disease" late in the nineteenth century, during the same period as the invention of "sexual inversion."[34]

The boys or youths "ruined" by sodomites occupied in these reports a distinct, intermediate position—not quite sodomite, not robust male. One boy in particular, "an emaciated lad," was said to have been seen leaving Emmanuel's store in the morning, "with tottering limbs and pallid countenance." A Jem Barnes (the sixth sexual nonconformist outed) was said to be one of the boys "foully ruined" by Emmanuel.[35]

Barnes's poor appearance was compared to that of "Andrews, the barber and *valet-de-chambre* of the Park Theatre" (the seventh man named).[36] Andrews's walk was said to resemble that of an actress, Mrs. Lewis, in the trouser role of Richard III—that is, Andrews was a man who walked like a woman attempting to walk like a man. His gait and occupation were offered as evidence of his sodomitical character. An effeminate walk and employment as a theatrical dresser were sometimes beginning to be seen as a sign of erotic as well as gender nonconformity. Certain kinds of work were already linked with sodomitical inclinations.

"Andrews" was the alias of Andrew Isaacs, said *The Whip*, outing him a second time, as a Jew. Sodomites "are mostly of the Hebrew race," the paper alleged, "at least, we find no laws, save in Leviticus, to punish them."[37] Though obsessed with the city's sodomites, *The Whip* reporter does not demonstrate any knowledge of New York state's sodomy statute, suggesting that such laws may not have been well known.[38]

The Whip's linking the "Hebrew race" with sodomites simultaneously denigrated both groups—both were perpetual outsiders. Its Jew/sodomite baiting was akin, via its "race" reference, to its later attack on the sexual coupling of black men with white women.

Several stories stressed how quickly the sodomites' influence worked its destructive way on the manhood of impressionable youths. The boys associated with John Emmanuel lost their manly vigor after one night; the "pallid" look of Johnny L'Epine's victim was observed after one week.[39] In these accounts, manhood was easily deflated, highly unstable, and susceptible to ruin. The age's rigid ideal of "true manhood" left little room for deviation, so when the true man fell, he broke.

The young man forced into sodomy by Captain Collins was so drained of vital energy that he had supposedly died.[40] The sodomite-as-vampire story was already being told. The "pallid" look of the sodomites' victims also closely resembled the drained appearance of the wayward youths portrayed in the abundant, perversely popular nineteenth-century literature denouncing "self-abuse," "self-pollution," "onanism," and "masturbation." Self-abuse, sodomy, and even "excessive" procreative intercourse, were said then to dangerously deplete a man's energy and his strictly limited semen supply.[41]

The sodomy/masturbation connection was made explicit in 1842, in *The Rake,* another New York paper, a competitor of *The Whip.* This paper printed a letter claiming that a "vile wretch in this city," initials "J. F. D." (another outing?), makes it "his daily practice to entice boys and young men to his hotel and office and tries all means to perform Sodomy and Masturbation. [The "masturbation" referred to here was not a solitary act.] In some cases he has succeeded; but through the medium of your columns this wretch will be compelled to cease his horrid crimes." The writer ended with a warning to this man: "Repent!"[42] Masturbation and sex between men were often identified in this era; both were derelictions of procreative duty—sins of emission.

Though sodomy was the sodomite's defining act, it remained in these reports the quintessential crime that could not be described. Was it mysterious and unknown, or was it, as several judges in sodomy trials suggested, universally understood like "murder"? Described as inde-scribable, known as unknown, sodomy was particularly strange and, therefore, an especially horrifying sexual possibility. Because of its un-spoken link with anal intercourse, sodomy was an especially frightening term, redolent of excrement, dirt, corruption, crime, and death. And be-cause sodomy was an act that men might commit with men or women, boys or girls, it was *not* an act limited to same-sex partners, as "homosex-ual" acts were later understood.

The Whip criticized New York City's leaders for their reluctance to in-vestigate and publicize sodomy "lest their children should know that such crimes can be committed."[43] The unspoken logic of this fear? If children heard of sodomy, they would be inclined to try it, and like it. Neverthe-less, for the public good, supposedly, *The Whip* risked leading the inno-cents into sin.

The Whip claimed to "have the names of men who have been acted upon by these fiends."[44] That "acted upon" made "men" the passive, powerless victims of energetic, powerful, irresistible sodomites. The sodomites of these accounts were the active initiators, the ones "to per-form Sodomy and Masturbation" upon youths and men who were pre-sented as passive, compliant, and victimized, however alluring they might find their seducers.

The Whip, in one report, characterized sodomites as "nearly all young men of rather genteel address, and of feminine appearance and man-ners."[45] But signs of effeminacy were *not,* I stress, noted in the older sodomites, Johnson, Collins, L'Epine, and Emmanuel. *The Whip's* link-ing of sodomy with effeminacy was just then starting to make the un-manly a sign of an even worse sexual irregularity. In the 1840s, the association of sodomy and effeminacy was still being constructed. Earlier, in the American colonies from 1607 to about 1750, the sodomy of men with men was *not* condemned as deviation from masculinity, but as refusal to multiply.[46] As a reproductive disorder, it was a major, capital crime against the challenged labor force and precarious state. Not until the late nineteenth century did sodomy start to be linked regularly with gender transgression, a process I will chart. And only at the nineteenth century's end did that association become common.

The "sodomites" of these reports were emphatically distinguished from the "men" and "youths" whom they corrupted, but all of those identities were fluid. Men and youths, it was suggested, joined the sodomite crew by yielding to their seductive allure. By indulging in sodomy, "sodomite" was an identity that any man could take on: it was not congenitally given, and it was not limited to certain types of men. Sodomitical desire was considered a potential of all men, not a discrete minority or a separate sexual species. So it would have made no sense to look for the origin of sodomitical desire in a deviant brain or body.

"Fear seizes the mind of the moral man" when he is "accosted" by a sodomite, said *The Whip,* and the moral man's "first impulse is to escape."[47] But his second impulse apparently made escape difficult. The pleasure lure offered by sodomites was difficult for nonsodomite men to turn down. Only with great effort did the moral man refuse the sodomite's solicitation. Again, no essential, organic difference separated moral men from sodomites, like that which later supposedly separated heterosexuals from homosexuals.

The "diabolic enticements" of sodomites exert a powerful "allure," the paper stressed.[48] It was not unusual, then, for a "man" to feel attracted to a "sodomite." Sodomitical desire was not thought of as restricted to a particular group exclusively attracted to a same sex. Andrews of the Park Theater was named, casually, as both sodomitical *and* as the "paramour" of a female brothel keeper, Celeste Thebault.[49] No basic distinction was made here between a same-sex erotic and a different-sex sexuality. Nor was Andrews considered bisexual—a third category between homosexual and heterosexual.

Sodomites were reputed to blackmail men completely innocent of sodomy. "Men of respectability are frequently made the victims of extortion" by sodomites, said *The Whip,* "for even death is preferable to the remotest connection with such a charge."[50]

The blackmailing male prostitute also figured briefly in Herman Melville's *Redburn*. There, the worldly Harry Bolton asked Carlo, a beautiful Italian youth, who played a "hand-organ" for a living, whether he did not sometimes meet "crabbed old men" who "would much rather have your room than your music?" Carlo admitted he did meet such men. Bolton then surmised, "knowing the value of quiet to unquiet men, I suppose you never leave them under a shilling."[51] The men who come to Carlo's room, Bolton suggested, were induced to leave a payment to keep their visit quiet.

Because the line between moral men and sodomites was fluid, it was rather easily breached by any association of moral men with sodomites. No respectable man, said *The Whip,* was willing to "appear at the police office . . . to prefer a charge against one of these abominable sinners."[52]

Though the talk here was of "police" and legal charges, "abominable sinners" was traditional Christian rhetoric. In these stories, sodomites were both Christian sinners and secular offenders—no separation of church and state for *The Whip.*

In 1842, *The Whip* suggested that New York City was becoming a Sodom and that sodomites were claiming their own urban space: "We know where these felons resort for the purpose of meeting and making appointments with their victims." The paper located sodomites on Broadway and in the vicinity of City Hall Park, as did some other early reports.[53]

City Hall Park was becoming "a second Palais Royal" [*sic*], said the paper, alluding to the notorious Parisian hangout of sodomites, prostitutes, pimps, and thieves.[54] Gossip about sodomite meeting places was already circulating internationally.

The existence of certain established New York City meeting places is evidence of an emerging, urban, American sodomite subculture. Discussing sodomites' behavior, *The Whip* said that "abominable and horrid stews [brothels] are kept, in which these enormities are committed."[55] The existence of whorehouses devoted, at least in part, to sodomitical activities was alluded to in this and a few other known documents.

In 1846, for example, an editorial in a New York City working-class newspaper, *The Subterranean,* called on the police of the Sixth Precinct to close a "male brothel." This was "a den of infamy kept in the Bowery not far from Pell street, which is a notorious resort for the vilest characters of men, and courtezan lovers, who deserve not the name of men."[56] This sounds like a place where effeminate men ("courtezan lovers") were paid to have sex with manly men unconcerned about morality ("the vilest . . . men").

But in the 1840s, men selling themselves to men was still too uncommon for the sellers to have their own distinct name, "male prostitutes." Only at the end of the century, when their numbers visibility increased, did the phrase "male prostitutes" come to refer, unambiguously and specifically, to men who serviced men sexually for money. For much of the nineteenth century, "male prostitutes" apparently referred to men who had sex with, or pimped for, female prostitutes.[57] The language of sexuality shifted with major changes in the social ordering of sexuality.

After its first exposé, *The Whip* reported that its sodomite hunting was having an effect: "Already do the beastly Sodomites of Gotham quake; they feel their brute souls quiver with fear."[58] (Again, the sodomite's animalistic soul was distinguished from the souls of ordinary men.) By its third exposé, however, the paper had "received a number of letters from the friends of these brutes threatening us with violence, if we persisted in our strictures upon these *harmless* young men."[59] *The Whip*'s report of those angry, threatening letters is the earliest American evidence of resistance to the persecution of sodomites. If those letters were real, sodomite sympathizers, or perhaps sodomites themselves, were already taking action against their attackers.

Did some men call themselves "sodomites," perceiving themselves as such? *The Whip*'s reports do not indicate if those denounced as "sodomites" employed that term as an identity tag of their own. It was likely, however, that the strong negative connotations of "sodomite" kept it from becoming a self-chosen label.

The attributed group identity, "sodomites," and the act, "sodomy," were major categories *against* which men engaging in sex with men in nineteenth-century America had to define themselves and their behavior. That they did actively resist the derogatory folklore of sodomy was suggested by those letters to *The Whip* defending sodomites as harmless.

These accounts also provide clues to the ideas of *The Whip* writer who so vociferously condemned sodomites, as well as to his assumptions about his readers. Little information is available about the man responsible for *The Whip*'s sodomite hunt, but whatever his personal motives, his paper spoke to the values of New York City's "sporting men."[60]

As "sporting papers," *The Whip* and *The Rake* were directed at the male participants in an antigenteel culture which, after 1820 in New York City, openly encouraged men's intercourse with female prostitutes. *The Whip* argued: "Man is endowed by nature with passions that must be gratified." The theory of imperative male passions meant that "no blame can be attached to him, who for that purpose occasionally seeks the woman of pleasure."[61] (The theory of naturally or biologically endowed desires would later be used to defend the invert and homosexual against the charge of being sinners.)

But men's imperative desires were not thought to have any built-in, necessary object—there existed no clear idea of an exclusive, inborn "sexual orientation" focused on one sex rather than another. So men had to be strongly encouraged to direct their desire for nonprocreative pleasures exclusively toward females. By passionately attacking sodomites, proponents of the sporting culture distinguished, within the terms of their own pleasure ethic, between good men and bad, permissible and taboo, erotic behaviors.

The sporting press's defense of men's pleasure-sex with female prostitutes, says historian Timothy Gilfoyle, challenged "the emerging 'respectable,' bourgeois, Christian morality" upheld "by Protestant and Catholic clergy, male and female moral reformers," entrepreneurs, and small merchants.[62] Those respectables denounced sex for pleasure, restricting authorized sex to reproductive intercourse within the institutions of true love and legal marriage. By its sexual virtue, the middle class distinguished itself from the allegedly libidinous upper orders, and supposedly lubricious lower orders. Sexual morality played a major role in the middle class's developing, collective self-consciousness.[63]

Men of the sporting culture rejected the middle-class sexual ethic, and that rejection left sporting men wide open to sodomitical temptation. For if men's nonreproductive pleasure-sex with female prostitutes was permissible (even encouraged), why was men's pleasure-sex with men not also approved? The intensity of *The Whip* writer's attack on sodomites can be understood, then, as a way to distinguish, within the terms of a pleasure ethic, between permissible and impermissible enjoyments. This distinguishing of good and bad pleasures anticipated a major project of twentieth-century sex modernists. For, if men's pleasure-sex with women was permitted, men's sodomy with men must be condemned on grounds other than the pleasure it offered, its lack of marital context, and its nonprocreative purpose. And so *The Whip* conjured up sodomy as monstrous, sodomites as vampires.

In an age dominated by the genteel ideal of spiritual love, sporting men's sexual ethic represented a minority view, but one increasingly vocal, acceptable, and mainstream as the century progressed. Walt Whitman's first three pioneering editions of *Leaves of Grass* grew, in part, out of this libertine sexual culture. But Whitman expanded the sporting culture's sex ethic to include and to celebrate the sexual intimacies of men with men.

Among the *other* sexual pleasures denounced in *The Whip* was the erotic "intercourse" of white female prostitutes and black men, "a practice worse, by far, than sodomy!"[64] The paper explicitly constructed a hierarchy of sexual infractions, a hierarchy informed by a double standard.

The sexual acts of white women with black men were extremely bad. In contrast, the intercourse of white men and black women was not mentioned, reflecting the low status of African-American women. Sex between white men and black women was apparently considered so ordinary as to be inconsequential.[65]

In judging the "intercourse" of white women and black men "worse . . . than sodomy," *The Whip* considered the copulation of different races (and different sexes) far worse than sodomy between men. Presumably, *The Whip* referred to sodomy between men of the same race— interracial sodomy may have been so uncommon it was invisible.

The Whip's pleasure norm did not view different-sex erotic acts as good, same-sex erotic acts as bad (again, no heterosexual/homosexual opposition was at work). Forced by its pleasure principle to distinguish between licit and illicit satisfactions, it condemned mixed-race intercourse between white women and black men and sodomy between males (especially sodomy between older men and youths). It thereby honored white men's pleasure-sex with female prostitutes.

In 1849, a few years after the attack on sodomites in the sporting press, a sensationalistic novel, *City Crimes,* was published in Boston by George Thompson (under the pseudonym "Greenhorn"). It promised *A Startling Revelation* of urban secrets and included two scenes in which predatory older men pursued male youths—scenes echoing the earlier attack on sodomites.[66] Nineteenth-century city lore was starting to include sodomites among it stock characters. Sodomites were joining the titillating figures that sold urban exposés.

In one episode a young woman, Josephine, attends a masquerade ball dressed as and pretending to be a boy. She finds that her ambiguous sex and pretty face attracts the interest of a foreigner. He turns out to be a nobleman and the Spanish ambassador—again, the villain is upper class and alien.

Assured by the playful, unknowing Josephine that she was indeed a male, the Spaniard responds: "You please me . . . ten thousand times more [as a boy] than as a woman. By heaven, I must kiss those ripe lips!" While he prefers young men, his erotic interest is not limited to that sex and age group.

When the still uncomprehending Josephine protests, the ambassador explains: "You may pronounce my passion strange, unaccountable, and absurd, if you will—but 'tis none the less violent or sincere. I am a native of Spain; a country whose ardent sons confine not their affections to the fairest portion of the human race alone, but—" He whispers some unquoted lurid details in Josephine's ear, and she draws back "in horror and disgust." Once more, the sodomite's act is all the more disturbing because it cannot be named. Its unspeakableness constructs it as the fascinating forbidden.

Josephine's masquerade has revealed, she tells the ambassador, "an enormity in the human character, the existence of which I have heard before, but never fully believed till now." News of men-lusting and youth-lusting men has been getting around. She then tells the Spanish ambassador: "Your unnatural iniquity inspires me with abhorrence," and he leaves her with threats of vengeance.[67] He is not easily intimidated, and he is *not,* certainly, wracked by guilt or shame.

In a second scene, on a steamboat, "a gentleman" with a "very dark" complexion (another alien, this one not quite white) pursues a "very handsome" youth between twelve and fourteen, by offering him the proverbial cake and candy; finally he produces a gold ring. "The man was a foreigner," the narrator stresses, "one of those beasts in human shape whose perverted appetite prompts them to the commission of a crime against nature." That legal phrase identifies a predatory individual representing a class of like-lusting men.

Shortly after the boy accepts the gentleman's invitation to share his stateroom and bed, the youth rushes out "with every appearance of indignation and affright," and reports the foreigner's intentions to the boat's officer. The nameless "foreign gentleman" is punished for his proposition by being set ashore in a spot far from any house, with a storm threatening. But the narrator concludes: "The miserable sodomite should have been more rashly dealt with."[68]

In an aside, the author justifies his discussion of such a topic: "It is an extremely delicate task for a writer to touch on a subject so revolting, yet the crime actually exists, beyond the shadow of a doubt, and therefore we are reluctantly compelled to give it place in our list."[69] That this sex scene helped to sell his urban exposé, this pious author was not free to admit.

He adds: "We are now about to record a startling fact: — in New York, there are boys who *prostitute* themselves thus, from motives of gain; and they are liberally patronized by the tribe of genteel foreign vagabonds who infest the city." The "principal promenade for such cattle," he says, is City Hall Park, where these prostitutes and their customers are seen nightly, and have been mentioned, more than once, in the newspapers. "Any person who has resided in New York for two or three years" (since 1846–47), he claims, "knows that we are speaking the truth."

There was formerly "a house of prostitution for that very purpose," he also claims, "kept by a foreigner, and splendidly furnished; here lads were taken as apprentices, and regularly trained for the business." These were mostly boys "taken from the lowest classes of society, and were invariably of comely appearance. They were expensively dressed in a peculiar kind of costume, half masculine and half feminine; and were taught a certain style of speech and behavior calculated to attract the beastly wretches who patronize them. For a long time the existence of this infernal den was a secret; but it eventually leaked out, and the proprietor and his gang were obliged to beat a hasty retreat from the city to save themselves from the summary justice of Lynch law."[70] Thompson's novel echoes the sporting press's description of Captain Collins.

ॐ

Reporting A SODOMITE NABBED in 1842, *The Rake* said that a man accused in New York City Police Court of sodomy had been "let off." Invoking the Biblical Sodom story, the paper warned against such lenience—even though based, in this case, on an admitted lack of evidence. "Are we to wait," the paper asked, "until the Ruler of the Universe . . . blasts us with his destroying wrath . . . ?" Pressing for stringent punishment of accused sodomites, *The Rake* warned that for the "crime against nature . . . God visited his vengeance upon the heads of the perpetrators, destroying them by the thousands."[71]

The reference was mixed, as was the animus—"crime against nature" was a secular, legal term; God's vengeance, a theological conceit. The sodomites named in *The Whip* and *The Rake,* and those portrayed in Thompson's novel, were the offspring of a mixed parentage, the creatures of a changing, biblically inspired Sodom story with a long history of varied interpretations, the subjects of an extralegal extension of sodomy law and prosecutions.[72] For the term "sodomite," and the idea of a person defined by the act of sodomy, had no standing in this nation's laws or legal decisions. Within the legal arena there was only sodomy, one of that era's quintessential forms of illicit sexual relations. A look at cases referring to sodomy that were brought for appeal to state tribunals in nineteenth-century America shows that legal system in action.

5   *Abominable and Detestable Crimes*

In September 1810, a man named William S. Davis was indicted in Baltimore County, Maryland, "for assaulting, and attempting to commit *Sodomy*" on the body of William Carpenter, a "youth" of nineteen.[1] The indictment charged that Davis, "not having the fear of God before his eyes, but being moved and seduced by the instigation of the Devil," with "force and arms," did "beat, wound, and ill-treat" Carpenter. Davis had intended, "feloniously, wickedly and devilishly," that "most horrid and detestable crime, (among christians not to be named,) called *Sodomy* . . . against the order of nature," to the "great displeasure of Almighty God." His act was also contrary to state law and "against the peace, government, and dignity of the state."

The indictment also charged that Davis had attempted "a venereal affair" with Carpenter, "that sodomitical, detestable, and abominable sin . . . called *Buggery,*" to "the disgrace of all human kind."

Claiming that he could not have "a fair and impartial trial" in Baltimore County, Davis asked the court to transfer his case to an adjoining county. He was refused.

Pleading "not guilty," Davis was tried for attempted sodomy and convicted. He then moved for a reconsideration of that judgment. He was denied.

A judge then sentenced Davis to be imprisoned in the Baltimore county "gaol" for three months, from January 9 until April 9, 1811, and to "stand in the pillory on the third Saturday of January . . . for the space of fifteen minutes, between the hours of 12 and 1 o'clock." Davis was also required to pay the state $500, and he was sent to prison until he paid his fine.

Davis appealed this verdict to the court that had tried him on the grounds, among others, that *attempted* sodomy was "no offence" in Maryland, and that the indictment was in error, technically, in failing to charge him with "an intent to have carnal knowledge of the body" of Carpenter. His motion was rejected.

Davis next petitioned the Maryland court of appeals. He argued, in part, that the alleged offense had not been clearly enough stated in the indictment for him to defend himself.

In December 1810, the appeals court affirmed the lower court's original sentence of jail, pillory, and fine. In a statement to the court one of the appeals judges compared sodomy to other "higher offences, such as murder, robbery, rape, burglary, . . . arson." He declared: "The crime of sodomy is too well known to be misunderstood, and too disgusting to be defined farther than by merely naming it."

Whatever Davis's actual behavior in this case, the words used in his prosecution conjure up a most menacing offense: Sodomy. Buggery. Seduced by the instigation of the Devil. Assaulting a youth. Beat, wound, and ill-treat. Most horrid and detestable crime. Among christians not to be named. Against the order of nature. Displeasure of Almighty God. Contrary to the act of assembly. Against the peace, government, and dignity of the state. Venereal affair. Sodomitical, detestable, and abominable sin. Disgrace of all human kind. Too well known. Disgusting.

Such accusing litanies, later secularized a bit and joined with or displaced by the "crime against nature," were repeated in various combinations in nineteenth-century America's sodomy indictments and buggery trials. That damning diction constituted nineteenth-century America's best-known way of naming, thinking about, condemning, and constructing sex between men.

The indictment of Davis mobilized the agents of a powerful judicial system—the accuser, sheriff, local magistrates, lawyers, appeals judges, jurors, and jailors. It also employed most of the major terms, concepts, and judgments used to attack carnal connections between men in this age and nation. The prosecution of Davis presented this carnality in the worst possible light, as assaultive, ungodly, and monstrous. In response, the accused Davis publicly proclaimed himself "not guilty," rejecting the prosecutor's story of his alleged "crime." He employed every legal means to invalidate that tale and extricate himself from his entanglement with the judicial system. Whatever Davis did or did not do, his repeated legal appeals show him struggling vigorously against the system that condemned him, making him one of this nation's earliest, documented sexual resistors.

᷒

Davis v. Maryland is the earliest of the 105 legal cases mentioning the words "sodomy," "buggery," or the "crime against nature" appealed to and decided during the nineteenth century by the high courts of twenty-five American states (or districts or territories), or by federal courts, and summarized in brief, published reports.[2]

These reports include cases in which men were charged with attempted or completed acts of anal (or, later, oral) intercourse with men, women, boys, or a child of unspecified sex. They also include cases in which men or women were charged with intercourse with animals. But not all these cases charged sodomy or an attempt at sodomy. They include, as well, cases in which men or women were accused of slander or libel for publicly accusing others of intercourse with animals. Some of these reports simply refer in passing to earlier sodomy, buggery, or crime-against-nature cases, or they mention state statutes or refer to sodomy, buggery, or the crime against nature. The U.S. Supreme Court referred in two cases to a New Jersey sodomy statute.[3] For the purpose of historical analysis, the language of all these reports is revealing. However, a large number of these published reports—about a third of the 105—do not specify the exact character of the act, that is, whether with human or animal, anal or oral, or the sex of the partner.

Among these appeals, Texas is represented by twenty-four cases—Texans were either especially prone to sodomy, buggery, or the crime against nature, to slandering their neighbors with accusations of such a crime, to talking about it or making a legal case of it, or to all of these. California is represented by ten cases. Was the fabled American West particularly encouraging to sodomy, accusations of sodomy, or talk of sodomy? Ohio produced seven cases; Hawaii, six; Michigan, five; Louisiana, New York, and Washington, four each; Indiana, Iowa, Montana, Pennsylvania, and Virginia, three. Two cases each occurred in Alabama, Georgia, Massachusetts, and Maryland. Colorado, Connecticut, Illinois, North Carolina, and Vermont each produced one case. This sample of cases is valuable because it covers many states, a wide geographic area, and a century-long period that permits us to assess substantial changes over time. These published cases mentioning sodomy, buggery, and the crime against nature demonstrate that nineteenth-century Americans were joined, in imagination or in the flesh, in more ways than are usually imagined.

Americans' quest for union via sodomy, buggery, and the crime against nature—or the allegation of such a quest—followed the westward movement of the frontier, roughly mirroring the nation's expansion from sea to shining sea.[4] The earliest cases occurred in Maryland in 1810, in Virginia in 1812, Alabama in 1822, and New York in 1824. They then move on to Missouri in 1846, Ohio in 1847, Indiana in 1851, Iowa in 1860, and Texas in 1867, culminating in California in 1869, the Montana Territory in 1878, and Washington in 1893. The nation's overseas expansion was reflected in the first two Hawaiian sodomy appeals cases, dating to 1860.

America's Manifest Destiny included men lying with men, women, and children, and men and women lying with animals, along with the laying of transcontinental railroads. That transportation revolution was represented in reports of two crimes against nature committed on trains—in 1893, in California, and in 1894, while chugging from Oregon to Washington toward oceans white with foam.

The century's many immigrants to the land of the free are represented in this sample by the confrontation of two Italian boys' fathers in a civil case requiring an interpreter, tried in New Haven, Connecticut, in 1890.[5] The conflict concerned the buggery of twelve-year-old Angelo Mascolo by fifteen-year-old Achillo Montesanto, who took "an early departure from the jurisdiction," probably vanishing forever from the home of the brave.

Citizens of the United States in the late eighteenth and early nineteenth centuries witnessed the abolition of Colonial America's death penalty for sodomy and buggery. They also saw the introduction of the new "crime against nature," an epochal law reform and name change realized after the American Revolution.[6] The armed uprising of England's colonial subjects caused a substantial shift in the legal organization of anal intercourse and human-beast connections.

Pennsylvania executed a man for bestiality in 1785, then abolished death for sodomy or buggery the following year (the first state to do so). Instead, the convicted one forfeited all lands and goods and served the state for a term not to exceed ten years.[7] The death penalty for sodomy and buggery was next abolished in New Jersey, New York, Rhode Island, Virginia, Massachusetts, Maryland, New Hampshire, Georgia, and Delaware, all of which declared new penalties ranging from one year, to ten years, to twenty-one years, to life.[8]

But execution for sodomy, buggery, and other crimes remained on the books in North Carolina until 1869, when the penalty became five to sixty years in prison. The death penalty remained in South Carolina as late as 1873, after which the punishment then became up to five years in prison.

Executions for sodomy had halted in eighteenth-century America even while the capital punishment laws were still on the books. But the colonial practice of capital punishment of sodomy certainly imbued that crime with associations of death for some years after the last execution.

The abolition of the death penalty no doubt pleased those accused under the new statutes. But they cannot have been happy that the new, more lenient sodomy laws caused a large increase in prosecutions, sending committers of sodomy to prison for a good many years—sometimes for what liberal-minded people now consider acts between consenting adults.[9]

The seriousness of sodomy, buggery, and the crime against nature was

reflected in punishments mentioned in the appeals reports: not less than
two years for a man's *attempted* sodomy with a dog; five years for a male
prisoner's *failed attempt* at a crime against nature with another male prisoner; ten years for two men's sodomy with another man; fifteen years for
a man's sodomy with a woman; and "hard labor for life" for a man's crime
against nature with a man.[10]

❧

The 105 appeals cases document a century-long, nationwide, and surprisingly explicit discussion focusing on two specific sexual acts, then
conceived of, legally, as related. The appeals mentioning sodomy, buggery, and crime against nature include rulings about (1) the penis-in-
vagina intercourse of men with female animals and women with male
animals. They also include decisions about (2) the penis-in-anus intercourse of human males with men, women, and boys (only one of these
published appeals cases involved human males with girls).[11] Those
linked, criminalized acts were, I stress, limited to two—until the extremely busy last decades of the nineteenth century.

Judicial practice and tradition constituted a bestiality/sodomy connection, a historically specific association of human-beast mating and
men's anal intercourse with other humans. That linking seems strange
only to readers who grew up in the twentieth century, after the homo/
hetero divide—the mass dissemination of a new, gender-divided, erotic
system called homosexuality and heterosexuality. Under that epochal,
new ordering and naming of sexuality (within that same-sex/different-sex
arrangement of eros) human-beast intercourse and the anal intercourse
of humans were thought of as essentially different sorts of acts. The
nineteenth-century distinction between procreative and nonprocreative
closely linked its bestiality cases to those involving men's sexual relations
with human males, females, and children.

The linking of human-beast contacts with the anal intercourse of men
with men, women, and boys, was accomplished, in part, by a mobilization of language. The same words were used to describe both kinds of
acts. As a Louisiana appeals court judge concluded in 1882, the "crime
against nature" prohibited by statute was also "known in the common
law by the convertible and equivalent names of . . . 'sodomy,' and 'buggery.' "[12] Those three terms all referred, interchangeably, to human-beast
intercourse *and* to the anal intercourse of human males with men,
women, and boys.

The construction of "sodomy" as, specifically, human-beast intercourse was exemplified in a case that occurred in Van Buren County,

Iowa, in the 1860s. There, Mary Cleveland sued Cynthia Detweiler for slander, claiming that Detweiler had publicly declared, "When you see Mary Cleveland, say dog, howl or whistle, and that will make her drop her feathers" (that is, her drawers). Mary Cleveland had "been caught in the act with the dog," Detweiler had explained—adding ominously, "the dog had died from the effect of it." Cleveland's murderous "sexual intercourse" with a dog had caused Detweiler to warn neighbors: "You had better not let your children go to Cleveland's, nor associate with them," for they are "not creditable folks."[13]

The court's term "sodomy" equated a woman's dropping her drawers and copulating with a canine with the anal intercourse of men with men, women, and boys. Men's sexual acts with men, my focus in this book, existed in nineteenth-century America among a larger group of criminalized behaviors, from which they took on particular historical meanings.

Eighteen of the 105 case reports mentioning sodomy, buggery, or the crime against nature referred to sexual acts of men or women with animals, or the accusation of such acts.[14]

Nineteenth-century bestiality required one party to have a penis, the other a vagina. There was no such thing as penisless bestiality—no bestiality between a human female and a female animal. Penisless sexual acts were never mentioned in any of these cases; women's and girls' sexual acts with women or girls were never discussed as sodomy. That silence speaks worlds: If an act did not employ a penis, it was not copulation, it was not worth adjudicating, and it did not legally exist.

The age's improper, nonreproductive, and antireproductive acts included masturbation (mutual or singular), abortion, and the use of birth control. Improperly reproductive acts included a woman's alleged birthing of "pups," adultery, penis-vagina intercourse outside of marriage ("free love"), and sex with a prostitute. All were defined and judged according to the single nineteenth-century standard of proper coition: The "penetration" of a wife's vagina by a husband's penis for the purpose of reproduction. Sodomy, buggery, and the crime against nature existed among a specific historical constellation of desecrated acts.

In eight cases people were indicted for slander for publicly accusing a neighbor of sexual intercourse with animals (as Cleveland charged Detweiler).[15] Two other cases involved extortion employing the *threat* of charging someone with a beast connection.[16] No slander or extortion cases involved charges of a man's sodomy with another man or youth.

In Missouri, for example, in the 1840s, McCutchen charged that Edgar had publicly accused him of "carnal knowledge of a mare," and had used "the word 'fuck'" to convey that imputation.[17] Edgar tried to halt

McCutchens's suit by arguing that the "word used to convey the slander is unknown to the English language," is therefore "not understood by those to whom it was spoken," and is therefore not slanderous. The state's high court sensibly responded: "Because the modesty of our lexicographers restrains them from publishing obscene words," it "does not follow that they are not English words, and not understood." Everyone knew what "fuck" meant, the judges concluded, upholding Edgar's conviction.

Judges concurred about the widespread carnal knowledge of Americans: "The crime of sodomy is too well known to be misunderstood," declared the Maryland judge in 1810, concerning Davis's alleged attempt on a male.[18] "Ninety-nine persons out of an hundred" understood that the expression "has been with a sow" charged "a criminal and unnatural connexion," said a New York judge in 1824.[19] "Every person of ordinary intelligence understands what the crime against nature with a human being is," asserted a California judge in 1881.[20]

But the same judges sometimes disagreed among themselves about what specific acts were included in or excluded from sodomy, buggery, and the crime against nature. Some said that sodomy included human-beast contacts; others disagreed.[21] Some questioned whether the emission of seed was required to constitute sodomy, or whether penetration was sufficient.[22]

Though the particular acts included in or excluded from sodomy, buggery, and the crime against nature shifted over this century, as we will see, there was, I stress, no confusion at all between the two kinds of acts traditionally criminalized: human-beast intercourse and the penis-anus intercourse of men with men, women, boys, or girls. The legal universe exhibited no failure to name and know, no genteel conspiracy of silence about those acts.

To be sure, sodomy and the crime against nature were spoken of, in the traditional way, as "the abominable crime not fit to be named among Christians."[23] But that phrase was, curiously, almost always immediately followed or preceded by one of the names not fit to be named: sodomy, or the crime against nature.

That Christian injunction not to name, violated immediately and typically by the act of naming, expressed deeply conflicted emotions about human-beast contacts and anal intercourse. Those acts were, simultaneously, too "disgusting" *and* too alluring to name. Though regularly condemned as "abominable," that ritual denunciation was required precisely because those acts were so dangerously attractive to sin-tempted humanity—that is, to everyone. The special repulsion and allure of sodomy and the crime against nature was reflected in the repeated Christian injunction not to name it, a command unique to sodomy and the crime against nature—the order not to name is linked to no other crimes.

The injunction not to name anal intercourse and human-beast copulation suggested that, if Christians heard those acts named, they would learn of them (or be reminded of them), try them, like them, and try them again—and again. (The same idea was expressed in New York's sporting press). An urge to perform sodomy was not thought of as restricted to a particular, small minority of Americans: it was considered a general propensity of all fallen humans. The traditional injunction not to name expressed a domino theory of sodomy, in which naming necessarily led to knowing and knowing inevitably led to doing. Sodomy, buggery, and the crime against nature were among the century's best-known prohibited sexual acts.

Specifically nineteenth-century American meanings of human-beast intercourse and anal intercourse were hinted at in another bestiality/slander case, this one in Miami County, Indiana. Here, Eli Ausman and his wife, Mary, charged a man fittingly named Veal with starting the conflict on June 27, 1857.[24] That day, Veal had supposedly informed neighbors that Mary Ausman had given birth to two half-human, half-dog "pups in *Ohio,* and it can be proved. She had two pups by a haystack." Having given birth to pups, Mary Ausman was, by implication, "guilty of bestiality, or the crime against nature."

Some Americans of this era may have believed that sexual connections between humans and other species could result in mixed, beastlike progeny. But whatever their conscious beliefs, the mingling represented by Mary Ausman's pups expressed a deep-seated fear of losing one's carefully cultivated humanity and becoming one with the beasts of the field.

"Civilization is separated from barbarity by a film that is diaphanous," declared an appeals court in the case of a stepfather's incest with two stepdaughters, a decision hinting at some even "more hideous bestiality."[25] Anal intercourse also threatened a disconnection from civilization, a reversion to Ignoble Savage. In this still largely agricultural but fast-industrializing economy, human-animal intercourse and anal intercourse threatened to return gentility-aspiring Americans to the beast natures they were all striving desperately to disown, divest, and leave behind. All sexuality was animalistic and bad. Even the "natural" intercourse of human males and females had to be redeemed by marriage and procreative necessity.

Human-beast intercourse and anal intercourse were linked, then, as the improper opposites of proper reproductive intercourse: penis-in-vagina-coitus-for-reproduction within marriage. By criminalizing human-beast intercourse and anal intercourse, that third kind of act—married, reproductive coitus—was actively legitimated by legislators and judges officiating for the state.

Although that marital, reproductive norm usually went unstated in these appeals reports, it became explicit in a bestiality/slander case in the 1850s in Parke County, Indiana. There, William Harper of Sugar Creek township sued his neighbor, Jonas Delp, for publicly announcing that Delp's son Erial had passed the Harper farm and seen "a young man a ravishing a cow"—meaning that "the crime of bestiality and buggery . . . had been committed."[26]

Delp's declaring publicly that Harper "was a young married man" whose "wife had no children, and not like for any," had further implicated Harper as the cow ravisher. There "was no other young married man in the neighborhood whose wife had no children," Harper explained. Under the terms of a powerful reproductive norm, Harper's failure to multiply, even though married, made him a good target for a cow-ravishing charge.

The age's moral condemnation of human-beast intercourse rebounded, via the sodomy/bestiality connection, to its partner in crime, anal intercourse between humans. When, in 1842, sodomites were dubbed "beastly" in New York's sporting press, that epithet had a particular historical resonance.

Though sodomites (men identified by their act of sodomy) appeared in the sporting press in 1842, no person defined by their sexual acts with animals or humans is identified in the appeals cases; we find no references to a "bugger" or "sodomite." The law punished acts, not kinds of people. But a "person of unnatural passions" did emerge casually in one of the bestiality/slander cases as a possible, ascribed, contingent American identity.

In Utica, New York, in the early 1820s, Issachar H. Goodrich charged Charles Woolcott with telling neighbors that he, Goodrich, "has been with a sow."[27] Goodrich protested that the allegation caused him "to be suspected" of being "a person of unnatural passions and appetites," a person "guilty of the abominable and detestable crime against nature," a person "capable of committing," and a person who "had committed," that crime. Goodrich was consequently "abhorred and shunned as a person unfit for, and unworthy of all society."

In this case, decided in 1824, a temporary, assigned sexual identity (founded on "unnatural passions and appetites") made a brief appearance in the American legal arena, though the passions and appetites of that person were focused on a beast, not a human. By the end of the century, however, this mode of attributing identity would become common. It would be taken up by men and women who thought themselves defined by their sexual desire for men or women. That identity would also be appropriated by psychiatrists to define a new type, a "person of unnatural passions"—the men or women whose psychological or biological constitution fated them, supposedly, to be sexually attracted to their own sex. Persons so attracted then found it useful to unite with others of their kind for the defense of the identity for which they were all condemned.

In the nineteenth century, when human-beast contact and anal intercourse were both condemned as "against the order of nature," nature was conceived as the ordered bulwark against chaos.[28] Practicing anal intercourse or bestiality, a person fell from the order of nature into a twilight zone—the threatening, unpredictable world of the unnatural.[29] A moral opposition between "natural" and "unnatural" sexual acts ruled nineteenth-century thought, though the "natural" was only a relative, ambiguous signifier of the good. (The "normal" and "abnormal," never mentioned in these legal reports, were, significantly, the terms of a later, medical vocabulary.)

Society was said to be seriously threatened by crimes against nature. To violate nature by anal intercourse or human-beast intercourse was, allegedly, to attack those natural laws followed by right-thinking, rational humans. By threatening the supposedly natural social order, sodomy and bestiality also attacked "the peace, government, and dignity of the state," and thus constituted a sort of treason.[30]

These old bestiality appeals cases clearly provide us insight into the nineteenth-century response to sexual relationships between human males, one focus of this book. If present-day researchers of "gay history," "homosexuality," or "same-sex sexuality" ignore these cases as irrelevant, as did I and another researcher when we first looked at them in the 1970s, they overlook a trove of revealing documents. If we reject these bestiality cases because they appear, according to our present understanding, to have nothing to do with erotic or affectionate relationships between men, we blind ourselves to a different society's linking of those acts.[31]

The anal intercourse of these reports was, I stress, not then exclusively an act of men with men, nor, precisely, a same-sex act (implying acts of women with women). I argue here not just about words, ideas, or meanings. What is at issue is the place of particular acts within a specific, institutional structuring of sexuality—in this instance, a legal structure.

The specification of age plays a special role in the appeals case reports. Some of the sodomy cases did involve an adult man or a boy in what is now called "child abuse," and such cases were much more likely to have been prosecuted and reported than those involving voluntary acts between lustful adults. In the early 1890s, in Texas, sodomy was allegedly committed "in a child's mouth."[32] About 1894, a "boy under 14 years of age" was tried in Georgia for "sodomy committed upon a child."[33]

But age was *not* the contested legal issue in the ten appeals case reports in which a man was accused of a sexual act with a "boy" or "youth."[34] That age specifying, though it was not legally at issue, helped to construct a public image of sodomy as, stereotypically, the act of an older perpetrator and younger victim—the same stereotype detailed in New York's sporting press.

Cases involving a physical assault were, also, more likely to be prosecuted than cases involving consenting partners. A physical "assault" is mentioned in nine of the twenty-five appeals cases explicitly involving sex between human males.[35] In 1810, in Maryland, Davis was charged with using "force and arms" to "beat, wound, and ill-treat" a youth, "assaulting" him and "attempting to commit *Sodomy*."[36] In 1898, in Washington, Frank Romans was charged with an "assault" on Harley Morgan, a crime against nature, and buggery.[37]

But "assault" was almost always considered integral to anal intercourse, whether or not the act had involved force or coercion. In one case a judge disagreed with that tradition, ruling that an "assault may or may not be an element in the felony designated as 'sodomy.'"[38] The reference to "assault" in the formal, standard language of the indictment for the crime against nature tells us nothing at all about what actually occurred in many cases.[39]

Force or coercion was specified in eight attempted or completed acts of sexual intercourse between human males, and force was, of course, sometimes employed.[40] Starting in 1857, Nathaniel W. Sowle, master of a whaling ship departing from New Bedford, Massachusetts, does seem to have obsessively pursued a cabin boy, Manuel Enos. Finally, "by threats and his physical powers," he committed sodomy upon Enos. Later, he apparently successfully attacked another cabin boy, Manuel Vieira.[41] In January 1860, George W. Lambertson may well have committed forcible buggery on Peter Cohen in Brooklyn, New York.[42] In December 1885, Robert Foster and two other men probably did force sodomy on Christian Ramsayer in Butler County, Ohio.[43] And in 1895, in St. Louis, a police officer did apparently attempt forcible sodomy between a sixteen-year-old male's thighs.[44]

But in at least one case of attempted sodomy in which force was charged, it seems doubtful that force was used. In Merced County, California, in the 1890s, George Ryan charged James Wilson with an attempted crime against nature while both were "inmates of the county jail . . . and occupied the same cell and same bed."[45]

One night, Ryan testified, Wilson "solicited" Ryan's "consent" to a "crime against nature." When refused, Wilson said, "I won't make you do it; I never make any boy do it if he don't want to." The next night, after Wilson's solicitation was again rejected, he "grabbed hold" of Ryan "and tried to roll him over." To this grabbing and rolling, Ryan "resisted and made some noise," and Wilson "did nothing after that," apart from telling Ryan "to say nothing" about the incident.

Prompted by a prosecutor, Ryan later testified that Wilson "was trying to force me by coaxing and everything." Convicted of an *attempted* crime against nature employing force by coaxing, Wilson was sentenced to five years in California's Folsom Prison.

Even when no force or assault was specified, and both parties clearly consented to sodomy, that intercourse was still referred to in these reports as forcible and assaultive. Even if twelve-year-old Angelo Mascolo "consented to the act" of "buggery" with fifteen-year-old Achillo Montesanto, as the Connecticut appeals court said in 1891, even if he "submitted without resistance, still the act was done by force."[46] All anal intercourse was, by definition, forcible and assaultive, a kind of rape.

"Sodomy" was analogous to "rape," implied a Maryland judge in 1810. The identification of rape (a human male's forcible intercourse with a human female), anal intercourse (consented to or not), and human-beast contacts held in several appeals cases.[47]

"Penetration alone constitutes the crime of rape as well as sodomy," said a Virginia court in an 1812 bestiality case. In the case of Mack Cross's sodomy with a mare, as in rape, penetration had to be proved "but to no particular depth," said the Texas appeals court in 1885. The U.S. Supreme Court, in 1892 and 1895, twice cited a New Jersey provision associating "arson, rape, sodomy, robbery or burglary."

Courts might recognize that consent to anal intercourse occurred in practice, but an Ohio court declared in 1886 that consent was of no *legal* relevance to this crime: "In sodomy cases, the question of consent of the party with whom the act is committed, is not a material one. The crime is complete in either case" (with or without a consenting party).[48] The Illinois appeals court agreed in 1897: Lloyd Kessler was an "accomplice" in a crime against nature with Charles Honselman, "committed between two persons both of whom consent."

Consent to anal intercourse *did* become an explicit and serious legal issue in some cases, because an accusation made by a consenting sexual partner generally required corroboration. The corroboration of a consenting partner was at issue in 1873 in Suffolk County, Massachusetts, in the trial of James A. Snow. He was accused of "sodomy" with Willard A. Smith, the prosecution's lead witness.[49]

On Sunday, August 20, 1871, between twelve and one o'clock, Smith testified, he was passing the building where Snow had his rooms, and Snow "asked him to come up." Smith did so, and Snow "committed the act charged" (sodomy).

While "in the act," Smith heard "a loud rapping at the outside door," and Snow went down and let in a Mrs. Morse, the third-floor tenant. Smith evidently remained in Snow's room waiting for the sodomy to continue. Smith admitted not only to the act with Snow but to "various other acts of a similar nature," claiming "that all these acts were against his will and resistance."

Sixteen days after Snow's alleged sodomy with Smith, a Dr. Bean testified that he was called "to attend Smith for having taken poison." Feeling remorse, evidently, Smith had tried to punish himself—before turning on his sexual partner, Snow.

That evening, Snow had called on Dr. Bean, asking if Smith "would die" and if Smith had said why he had poisoned himself. (He had not.) Two additional times Snow had asked Dr. Bean if Smith had confessed why he had poisoned himself.

Seven days after Snow's alleged sodomy with Smith, a youth named Emerson testified that Snow "attempted to commit the same offence" with him, saying "it would not hurt [me], and that he had done it with other boys."

The prosecutor's lead witness, Willard Smith, claimed that his act with Snow was "against his will and resistance." But even the prosecutor admitted that "substantially Smith acquiesced." As "a confederate" in sodomy, Smith's testimony therefore "required corroboration." It was the jury's job to decide, ruled the judge, whether Snow's reputed admission—that "he had done it with other boys"—corroborated Smith.

A local jury found that Smith's testimony was corroborated and that Snow was guilty of sodomy. Snow then appealed to the Massachusetts high court, which, in 1873, also found Smith's testimony corroborated, upholding Snow's conviction.

The corroboration of a consenting partner was also at issue in a case of 1878 in the Montana Territory, where Mahaffey was charged with a "crime against nature" with B, a "boy" of fourteen, tried as an adult.[50] Fourteen was apparently the legal age of consent.

When, a year after the alleged crime, Mahaffey was charged, the youth testified that Mahaffey had "committed the offense with his consent," on "various occasions," at a hotel and at Mahaffey's ranch. B also reported a dispute with Mahaffey, who had "called him a boy prostitute and threatened to put him in the penitentiary."

On his way to jail, Mahaffey told a deputy sheriff, "it would be one of the most interesting cases ever in court, and that B was a boy prostitute." Mahaffey and B "went to bed" in a room shown them by a clerk at a hotel in Deer Lodge. The accused Mahaffey testified that the boy came to Deer Lodge to get his pay, and that they then "went to the Scott House and slept together." Mahaffey "paid for the bed and had nothing to do with the boy," he claimed. The jury disagreed, finding Mahaffey guilty of a crime against nature.

Mahaffey then appealed to the Montana high court, which ruled in 1878: Though the boy was an accomplice in the crime, his testimony was corroborated by other evidence. The lower court's guilty verdict against Mahaffey was affirmed.

Consent was at issue in these cases, I stress, *not* because of questions about a reasonable age of consent, or because consenting to sodomy made it a questionable crime, but because the accusation of an accomplice required corroboration.

∼

These appeals court decisions reflect substantial changes in American society and morality over the course of the nineteenth century. The appeals cases mentioning bestiality or anal intercourse *increase strikingly* in numbers, from the rare, occasional case in the first half of the century, to four cases in the 1850s, nine in the 1860s, seven in the 1870s, fifteen in the 1880s, and sixty-two in the 1890s, when the policing of sexualities became extremely intense. In the last decades of the century, sex was bustin' out all over. And the eros police tried to keep it underground.

Not until the century's end did physicians of the mind begin to gain authority as arbiters in the legal realm. In 1899, the Vermont appeals court cited a text on medical jurisprudence to legitimate a sodomy decision, a first in these cases. Sodomy was just then being reconstructed by the medical profession as pathology.[51] In striking contrast, earlier in the century, two Ohio libel and slander decisions had explicitly distinguished sodomy *from* a "loathsome disease."[52] By 1895, however, an Ohio court was linking sodomy, the "unnatural practices" of a husband with a beast, and a wife's "apprehension of . . . disease."[53]

Over the century, explicit references to "God" and "the Devil" were replaced by judgments founded on a secular, "natural law" theory—a phi-

losophy asserted, not rationally argued. Referring to oral-genital acts between two men, the Illinois appeals court in 1897 declared: "The method
employed in this case is as much against nature, in the sense of being unnatural and against the order of nature, as sodomy or any bestial or unnatural copulation that can be conceived."[54] Such blatantly circular reasoning reflected a judiciary unchecked by any higher, countervailing
power, or protest movement.

Most influentially, perhaps, within the world of these appeals decisions, until the 1890s an extremely narrow definition of sodomy, buggery, and the crime against nature strictly limited these offenses to anal intercourse and human-beast copulation. That restrictive, traditional
definition of illicit coitus is fundamental to our understanding of how
wide a range of erotic acts then lay *outside* the realm of legally constructed
crimes. The mutual masturbation of two men, for example, was not penetrative, and so was not regulated by the law, though it was subject to
powerful extralegal prohibitions.

Only in 1879 did oral-genital contacts emerge in a Pennsylvania
sodomy/buggery statute, which became the first American law to crimi-
nalize any man or woman who permitted or perpetrated the "penetrat-
ing" of a mouth (by a penis, presumably).[55] Only in the 1890s did oral-
genital intercourse emerge in the appeals cases as a subject of legal
discussion, judicial decision, and state regulation. During that decade,
lawyers and judges argued whether oral-genital acts were criminalized
under sodomy, buggery, crime against nature laws, or other statutes.
Oral-genital acts were the topic of a new, intense, end-of-the-century legal debate.

The first appeals case referring to oral-genital contacts dates to the
early 1890s in Wichita County, Texas, where Charlie Prindle was convicted of "sodomy" committed "in a child's mouth."[56] Claiming that pe-
nis-mouth contact was not included in the crime of sodomy, Prindle appealed to the state's highest court. This ruled in 1893 that, to constitute
the offenses of sodomy and the crime against nature, the "act must be in
that part where sodomy is usually committed," implicitly, the anus,
though that word is not in the published record. An "act in a child's
mouth," however "vile and detestable," did "not constitute the offense."
Prindle's original guilty verdict was overturned. The Texas appeals court
was not yet ready to sanction the broadening of the traditionally narrow
sodomy prohibition.

But the following year, 1894, the Massachusetts appeals court heard
the case of Rufus L. Dill, who had been convicted under a state law crim-

inalizing "an unnatural and lascivious act with another person" (not a "sodomy" law).[57] Though Dill's act was unspecified in the published record, it probably involved oral-genital contact.

Dill protested that his act did not fall within the state's traditionally narrow prohibition of sodomy as anal intercourse. In response, the court ruled that the new state law against "an unnatural and lascivious act with another person" was intended to "punish any mode of unnatural copulation not coming within the definition of sodomy, as usually understood." The Massachusetts appeals court affirmed Dill's conviction for "an unnatural and lascivious act with another person."

The terms sodomy, buggery, and crime against nature each came into use with epochal shifts in the social ordering of sexuality, power, and property, as several researchers have maintained.[58] Likewise, the naming and outlawing of a new "unnatural and lascivious act with another person" (and other laws like it) advanced the late-nineteenth-century surveillance and criminalizing of sexual acts. In London, under a similar, new, and broad "gross indecency" act (*not* a sodomy law), Oscar Wilde was convicted in 1895.[59]

The criminality of American oral-genital acts next arose in the case of a Texas man named Lewis, who received fifteen years' imprisonment for "sodomy" (anal intercourse) with a woman and with "copulating in the mouth" of the same woman. In 1896, Lewis appealed his conviction, and the court found: "To constitute the crime of sodomy the act must be in that part of the body where sodomy is usually committed." The Texas appeals court was not yet ready to include Lewis's oral-genital act under the crime of sodomy.[60]

Oral-genital acts were next debated in the late 1890s, in Tulare County, California, after Edward Boyle was found guilty of an attempted "carnal assault . . . in the mouth of a boy."[61] Appealing his conviction in 1897, Boyle argued that his act did not constitute the offense prohibited in California as a crime against nature—implicitly, anal intercourse (again, the act is not specified in the published report).

Countering Boyle's argument, the state's attorney asserted that the crime against nature "ought not to be confined to" the traditional definition (anal intercourse) "but should be construed to cover any form of unnatural carnal knowledge with any part of the human frame"—an innovative widening of the traditionally narrow prohibition.

But the California appeals court was not yet ready to allow that broadening. Ruling in 1897 that Boyle's attempt at oral copulation did not constitute a crime against nature, it reversed his conviction and remanded his case for a new hearing. Here, as in the 1893 Texas case, a state appeals court restrained, temporarily, the innovative broadening of the traditional sodomy proscription.

In the last nineteenth-century case to raise the issue of oral-genital acts, Charles Honselman was convicted in Piatt County, Illinois, of making use of his mouth "upon and with" Lloyd Kessler's penis. In this case the fellated Kessler was the accuser in what all parties admitted had been a consensual act.[62]

The court ruled in 1897 that the state's criminal code *did* indeed proscribe "other forms" of the "crime against nature" than "sodomy or buggery." The crime of putting a penis in a mouth, the court then enthusiastically and expansively added, "may even be committed by husband and wife." Such judicial broadening of existing sodomy, buggery, and crime against nature statutes, combined with new laws against oral-genital acts, continued to gain acceptance in the early twentieth century, criminalizing an ever wider variety of sexual pleasures.[63]

❧

The tales told in these appeals case reports were lust stories, not love stories. The America of these reports was not crowned with brotherhood. Any affection or intimacy hinted at was amity gone awry, familiarity soured. These lust tales asserted the essentially evil, unnatural, abusive character of anal intercourse between humans and intercourse between humans and beasts. Something much more fundamental than a bad public image was constructed here. The essential character of sodomy, buggery, and the crime against nature was asserted—and it was found to be extremely bad. The legal indictments for sodomy, buggery, and the crime against nature, prosecuted nationwide and reported, sometimes, in the press, put a horrifying public face on anal intercourse between men, and, later, on oral-genital contacts. But the narrow, specific idea of sodomy that existed for most of the nineteenth century meant that a range of other sexual acts did not fall within that worst-of-all category.

When Walt Whitman, in the 1856 *Leaves of Grass,* refused to deny "the felon," he also implicitly included those accused of the particular felony called sodomy, buggery, and the crime against nature.[64] That Whitman repeatedly dared to explicitly name and defend the "onanist" and "prostitute," but never the "sodomite," provides one measure of the abject terror linked then with that demonized sexual character.

6   *The Man Monster*

The nineteenth century's narrow conception of sodomy constructed a wide-open category of other, not-quite-so-bad erotic acts and desires. Not-sodomy might even be a source of jest, as it was in the revealing letters, written in 1826, by the twenty-two-year-old Thomas Jefferson Withers—later, a lawyer, politician, and judge in the South Carolina court of appeals. Withers addressed his nineteen-year-old friend James H. Hammond—later, a prominent governor of South Carolina, a congressman, and a famous defender of slavery.[1]

On May 15, Withers wrote to Hammond and wondered "whether you yet sleep in your Shirt-tail, and whether you yet have the extravagant delight of poking and punching a writhing Bedfellow with your long fleshen pole—the exquisite touches of which I have often had the honor of feeling."

Withers and Hammond had shared a bed, it seems, and Withers had felt more than one poke of his bedfellow's erection. Since Withers considered this a subject for levity, probably no penetrative prodding had occurred.

Warning Hammond that "unless thou changest former habits in this particular, thou wilt be represented by every future Chum as a nuisance," and

> for good reason too. Sir, you roughen the downy Slumbers of your Bedfellow—by such hostile—furious lunges as you are in the habit of making at him—when he is least prepared for defense against the crushing force of a Battering Ram. Without reformation my imagination depicts some awful results for which you will be held accountable—and therefore it is, that I earnestly recommend it. Indeed it is encouraging an assault and battery propensity, which needs correction—& uncorrected threatens devastation, horror & bloodshed, etc.

Despite the final allusion to the destruction of Sodom and Gomorrah, and thus, to sodomy, Withers's tone was remarkably jocular, suggesting that Hammond's penile poking remained safely distinct in both youths' minds from the legally prohibited, heavily punished, strongly condemned, and horrifying anal intercourse. Withers signed his letter: "With great respect I am the old Stud, Jeff," reasserting his own masculine and erotic position. Poking fun at Hammond, Withers returned in kind Hammond's earlier prodding.

On September 24 of the same year, Withers continued his sexual kidding, fancying, "Jim, that your *elongated protuberance*—your fleshen pole . . . has captured complete mastery over you—and I really believe, that you are charging over the pine barrens of your locality, braying, like an ass, at every she-male you can discover." Hammond's acts were "prostituting the 'image of God,'" Withers even joked, warning, "the flaming excess of your lustful appetite may drag down the vengeance of supernal power."

Excessive appetite was the primary evil here, though the reference, again, was to Sodom and Gomorrah. But Withers's tone was still comic, as he envisioned his friend's pursuing "every she-male"—a startling type for us to find inhabiting the imagined pine barrens of the American South in the 1820s. Though an effeminate male was the imagined object of Hammond's desire, and sodomy the imagined act, Withers clearly distinguished this comical, fanciful sodomy from the serious, real thing.

ॐ

Acts not called sodomy played a large part in the records kept by Phillip Van Buskirk, whose diaries provide a rich source of clues to the language, the conceptions, and the erotic and affectional interactions of American sailors in the 1850s and 1860s.[2] Van Buskirk, born in 1834 into a southern, Catholic, middle-class family, was catapulted out of his class by his father's bankruptcy and suicide, to land at age twelve in the U.S. Marines. There, he became a meticulous diarist and participant-observer in the affectional and sexual lives of sailors. His diaries indicate that many sailors rejected, in practice if not in theory, the dominant reproductive ethic that condemned sexual relations between males.

In 1853, the judgmental but fascinated Van Buskirk asked Old White, an experienced mainmast man, "What's your opinion of those men who have to do with boys? If you were King, wouldn't you kill every one of 'em?" To which the old salt answered: "Every feller that lives ashore and does *that,* I'd shoot him." But Old White applied a different standard to sailors: "What can a feller do? three years at sea—and hardly any chance to have a woman. I tell you . . . , a feller *must do so.* Biles and pimples and corruption will come out all over his body if he don't."[3] Sailor folklore stressing the disease consequences of erotic abstinence justified for Old White the unspecified sexual acts of men and boys, conceived as a substitute for the real thing. Here, a popular health model *justified* sex between older and younger males.

Writing in the early 1850s, Van Buskirk reported that men and boys seeking unspecified erotic encounters found them under the boom cover that protected stored masts. This interaction was so common it had a name, the "boom cover trade."[4] The junior partners in erotic relations between sailors, Van Buskirk reported, were called "chickens," and the relation was dubbed "chickenship"—also suggesting a common, institutionalized practice.[5]

But what kind of practice was this? The nineteenth-century hierarchy of infractions between human males placed a variety of acts in the category of the not-quite-so-bad-as-sodomy. Mutual masturbation constituted just such an act, as Van Buskirk made clear.

In 1855, this marine's diary reports, a military man called Rio Grande spent evenings with young sailor boys, telling them about "the mysteries of *having to do with women and doing for yourself.* He explained . . . how by masturbation . . . all of the pleasure that a woman yields by her embrace [could be obtained]. It was this man's wont to practice masturbation on himself in the presence of all the smaller boys in order to teach them the *modus operandi.*"[6] In another case, in 1846, when the twelve-year-old Van Buskirk enlisted in the marines and became a drummer, a fellow boy-percussionist, Dorell, also publicly practiced masturbation, teaching it by example.[7] Publicly demonstrating on themselves, these early sex educators provided an experience that we can view as an erotically charged relationship of males.

In a second kind of act that sailors called "going chaw for chaw," men or boys joined in simultaneous, mutual masturbation.[8] Whatever the sex of their *imagined* partners, whatever their *imagined* acts, we can view this as sex involving males with males. To these men, however, the biological sex of their partners was probably less significant than the nonreproductive, "wasteful" character of their acts, however pleasurable.

A third kind of act that Van Buskirk considered a form of "self-abuse" involved one man actively using a man or boy for his own pleasure. When Van Buskirk was ten, in 1844, an old soldier named Scott persuaded him to stand against a tree and (in Van Buskirk's later description) used him for "the abusing of himself" (probably, by rubbing). Van Buskirk regarded Scott's act as masturbation, though we can view it as a same-sex erotic act.[9] Neither characterization is more or less correct. Seeing this as "masturbation," or as a "same-sex act," simply constructs it according to a different age's way of making meaning.

In a fourth kind of act perceived by its participants as masturbation, one man offered to "do it" for another, or asked to have it done, without necessarily doing it for himself. In 1852 the censorious Van Buskirk charged a sailor, Andrew Milne, with masturbating. To which Milne indignantly replied: "I acknowledge doing it for other men, but, 'pon my

word, I haven't done it to myself since I been on the ship but once."[10]
Milne's phrasing suggests that he considered "doing it for other men"
much less of an offense than doing it to himself.[11] The moral hierarchies
of other ages often surprise. Milne's sexual rating system distinguished
not between acts performed with a same or different sex, but between
acts performed on oneself or on others.

In another case, around 1855, a sailor named Charley Evans spread
gossip that Van Buskirk had asked him for a "yankum"—nineteenth-
century sailor slang for today's "hand job."[12] The rhetoric of onanism
provided an important language for categorizing and identifying what
we can now regard as "same-sex" erotic relations. But Van Buskirk
and other nineteenth-century sailors distinguished those acts from
sodomy.

Recalling his navy life, Van Buskirk boasted that he had not "once consented to participate in sodomy with any one"—a unique achievement,
he explained: "No boy or man can ever remain a year on board of an
American man-of-war without being led or forced to commit this crime
(which, by the way, is not regarded as a crime in a man-of-war)."[13]

In 1855, referring to youths in a dormitory at Marine Headquarters,
in Washington, D.C., Van Buskirk said: "There is so much sodomy carried on . . . I felt it my duty to sleep there to prevent or restrain the
spreading of the contagion by every means in my power."[14] His era's conceptual segregation of carnal urges from spiritual motives allowed him to
believe that his sleeping with the boys was motivated by duty, not desire.[15]

The same year, 1855, Van Buskirk warned fourteen-year-old Charley
Evans to avoid brandy, chewing tobacco, smoking, lying, and associating
with "noted sodomites."[16] Van Buskirk also reported that "ninety per cent
of the white boys in the Navy of this day . . . are . . . blasphemers and
sodomites."[17] Men's participating in sodomy made them into sodomites,
according to Van Buskirk. His rhetoric solidified an act into an attributed
identity. He also pointed to a perceived distinction between the sexual
cultures of whites and blacks.

༚

In striking contrast to the New York City antisodomite, antisodomy crusade of 1842 was a sensational story that appeared six years earlier, in the
city's popular penny press. In this story the term "sodomy" never, significantly, appeared.

About ten o'clock on the night of Tuesday, June 11, 1836, in New
York City, a master mason named Robert Haslem, a white man, was

walking home after a liaison with a woman he had picked up earlier that evening, as the *New York Herald* later reported.

On Bleeker Street, Haslem met a black woman, Mary Jones, dressed "elegantly and in perfect style," with white earrings and a gilt comb in her hair.[18] The *Herald*'s rival, the *New York Sun,* added that Mary Jones also went by the names "Miss Ophelia," "Miss June," and "Eliza Smith."

Haslem or Jones initiated a conversation—the newspapers differed. Haslem then asked Jones, "Where are you going my pretty maid?" and volunteered to go with her. Before they set off "on this tour of pleasure," said the *Herald,* she "lovingly threw her arms around him and strained him to her heart." Then, "these delicate preludes having ended, they proceeded onwards, until they arrived at an alley in Greene Street [known then as a site of prostitution], which having entered *****" Here, a series of asterisks in the *Herald*'s report suggest, as clearly as the missing words, a sexual act.

Haslem and Jones "had some further conversation" in an alley, said the more reticent *Sun,* "where the prisoner again had his arms about complainant."[19] Afterward, on his way home, according to the papers, Haslem discovered that his wallet and ninety-nine dollars were missing. In their place he unaccountably found the wallet of a man he did not know, with a bank order for the then large sum of $200.

Haslem sought out the man who, at first, denied ownership of the wallet, but then admitted he had had his pocket picked the previous evening, under the same circumstances as Haslem. He had been "too wise," however, "to expose himself" by reporting the theft to the police. Next morning the determined Haslem confessed his story to a Constable Bowyer who, that evening, set out to find Mary Jones. Around midnight, on the Bowery, Bowyer passed a black woman and, according to the *Herald,* "thinking that this might be the one he sought," and assuming the right to his gaze, looked at her face and "made up his mind that he was right."

"Where are you going at this time of night?" he asked. "I am going home, will you go too?" she answered. He agreed, and "she conducted him to her house in Greene Street, and invited him in."

He declined, "with great regret," but later walked her to an alley where she asked him, as the *Herald* put it, "to reenact the scene of the previous evening" with Haslem. She then "proceeded to be very affectionate," and Bowyer arrested her.

"A tussle ensued," the *Sun* reported, during which the prisoner allegedly took two wallets from her bosom and threw them away. One turned out to be Haslem's. On the way to the watch house, Jones allegedly tried to ditch another wallet but was caught. With Jones locked up, the constable took her key, searched her apartment, and found, allegedly, a number of other wallets.

Constable Bowyer then searched Mary Jones, and, said the *Sun,* "for the first time discovered that he [Jones] was a man." Until that time, said the paper, Bowyer had had no doubts about Jones's sex.

The papers suggested that the complainant, Haslem, had not reported, or had not known that Jones was a man.[20] Can we believe this? Might Haslem have recognized a cross-dressing prostitute but not cared about his sex? Or, could Haslem have sought sex with a cross-dressed woman-man? The known documents do not tell us.

"Bowyer also discovered," said the *Sun,* that the prisoner, "to sustain his pretension, and impose upon men"—here seventeen words in clumsy Latin complete the sentence. Translated, the phrase says that the woman impersonator "had been fitted with a piece of cow [leather?] pierced and opened like a woman's womb ["vagina" is the intended word], held up by a girdle."[21] Educated, Latin-reading, upper-class men could apparently contemplate such details without harm; women and lower-class persons of either sex could not.

On June 16, five days after Haslem's fateful meeting with Jones, the prisoner, charged with grand larceny, was tried for stealing Haslem's wallet and money. He was not prosecuted for "sodomy," apparently because he had not participated in anal intercourse.

The accused appeared in court, the *Sun* reported, "neatly dressed in female attire, and his head covered with a female wig," seemingly his outfit when arrested. Did the prisoner choose to be tried in drag? His costume was probably the court's doing.

The spectacle of a cross-dressed black man, and of the victimized Haslem, the *Herald* reported, provided "the greatest merriment in the court, and his Honor the Recorder, the sedate grave Recorder laughed till he cried." During the trial, the *Sun* reported, someone in the audience, "seated behind the prisoner's box, snatched the flowing wig from the head of the prisoner." This "excited a tremendous roar of laughter throughout the room."

Do not we sense here a note of hysteria, suggesting submerged anxieties about sexuality, gender, and race, each highly charged emotionally and politically? Then, as now, the combination of eros, gender, and race made an explosive mix.

A legal transcript of the prisoner's examination recorded the words he uttered in his own defense; a brief, rare, first-person voice from America's sexual past. Certainly, though, the situation of his interrogation skewed his words.[22]

Asked his age, place of birth, business, and residence, he answered: "I will be thirty three Years of age on the 12th day of December next, was born in this City, and get a living by Cooking, Waiting &c and live No. 108 Greene St."

"What is your right name?" he was asked. "Peter Sewally—I am a man," he answered.

Asked "What induced you to dress yourself in Women's Clothes?" he answered: "I have been in the practice of waiting upon Girls of ill fame and made up their Beds and received the Company at the door and received the money for Rooms &c and they induced me to dress in Women's Clothes, saying I looked so much better in them and I have always attended parties among the people of my own Colour dressed in this way—and in New Orleans I always dressed in this way—."

He added: "I have been in the State service"—his military duty was offered, apparently, as plea for the jury's forbearance.

Asked if he had stolen Mr. Haslem's wallet and money, Sewally answered: "No Sir and I never saw the Gentleman nor laid eyes upon him. I threw no Pocket Book from me last night, and had none to throw away, and the Pocket Books now Shown me I never Saw before —." Not knowing how to write, Sewally signed his statement with the letter *X*.

The following day, June 17, the *Herald* and *Sun* both carried detailed stories of the case. The *Herald* was fairly open about the sexual activity associated with the prisoner's cross-dressing and pickpocketing: "Sewally has for a long time past been doing a fair business, both in money making, and *practical* amalgamation, under the cognomen of *Mary Jones*." The word "amalgamation" was used often in the nineteenth-century United States to refer to sexual contacts between different races.

During the daytime, added the *Sun,* Sewally "generally promenades the street, dressed in a dashing suit of male apparel, and at night prowls about the five points and other similar [poor, disreputable] parts of the city, in the disguise of a female, for the purpose of enticing men into the dens of prostitution, where he picks their pockets if practicable, an art in which he is a great adept." Combining a daytime career as a dashing man and nighttime work as a cross-dressed woman was certainly unusual in the paper's view. But it made no overt link between Sewally's cross-dressing and his erotic intercourse with men. He was presented as an eccentric, not a "sodomite," nor was he identified by any other such label.

"Numerous complaints of robberies so perpetrated by him had been made at the police office at sundry times," says the *Sun*, "but owing to the scruples of the complainants against exposing themselves in the Court . . . , on trial, they have generally abandoned their complaints, and their stolen money, watches, &c."

This echoed earlier comments in the sporting press that men innocent of sexual activity with men, when blackmailed by sodomites, were too fearful of any public association to prosecute them in open court. Large sums were alleged to be carried by Haslem and the other victimized man. If those sums were typical, those who were robbed and who made no complaint must indeed have had *strong* scruples about exposing themselves to public scrutiny.

But what, exactly, were such men embarrassed about? Were they ashamed to be exposed as the patrons of a female prostitute, or a black female prostitute? Or were they ashamed of having had intercourse with a cross-dressed man, or, specifically, a black men—or all of these? The answer is not clear. As the *Sun* stressed of Haslem: "On this occasion, however, the complainant, to recover his money, mustered courage enough to stand the brunt of the trial." What made Haslem unafraid to go public with his accusation? We do not know.

The *Herald* reported that the jury, "after consulting a few moments, returned a verdict of guilty of grand larceny." Sewally was sentenced to five years in the state prison.[23]

A week or so after Sewally's trial and sentencing a lithograph of him dressed as a woman, and titled " 'The Man Monster,' Peter Sewally, alias Mary Jones," was published in New York City. Despite the "monster" status invoked by its title, the print portrayed Sewally as a rather ordinary-looking and unthreatening black woman in a clean white dress with small blue flowers. The prosaic, even genteel, image countered his alleged monster status. The lithograph and newspaper accounts suggested that Sewally's cross-dressing, theft, and sexual conduct were sensational in 1836. But these behaviors were by no means as threatening in 1830s New York as they would have been in, for example, the early 1700s.

Nine years later, on August 9, 1845, a New York paper, the *Commercial Advertiser,* reported that "a notorious character, known as *Beefsteak Pete,* was arrested on Thursday night, perambulating the streets in woman's attire." His object, the newspaper judged, was of a "villainous character." (The name "Beefsteak" apparently defined Sewally by his mode of sustaining the illusion of femaleness during sexual intercourse with men.)

The following year, on February 15, 1846, the *New York Herald* carried an item about "Pete Sevanley, alias 'beef steak Pete,' a notorious black

THE MAN-MONSTER,

Peter Sewally, alias Mary Jones &c&c.

Sentenced 18th June 1836. to 5 years imprisonment at hard labor at
Sing Sing, for Grand Larceny.

Published by H.R. Robinson, 48. Courtlandt St. N.Y.

Peter Sewally/Mary Jones, 1836. © Collection of The New-York Historical Society, negative number 40697. ❧

rascal, who dresses in female attire and parades about the street."[24] Liberated from Blackwell's Island on the previous Sunday, this Sevanley had been arrested again for "playing up his old game, sailing along the street in the full rig of a female." He was sent back to prison "to finish some blocks of stone for the next six months."

Sewally's court testimony of 1836 provides us the earliest American evidence of a supportive link between female prostitutes and a man who, at least sometimes, had sex with men. The newspaper reports of that time also documented the judge and jury's response to Sewally. They punished him quite severely for a theft accomplished via a masquerade, and they had a good laugh at his and his white victim's expense. The paper's need to maintain a respectable level of discourse meant that Sewally's sex acts with men were given less explicit coverage than were his cross-dressing and theft.

In these documents, the exact character of Sewally's own desire remains ambiguous, though his pecuniary motive seems clear. But his unusual, defiant, long-term cross-dressing and streetwalking surely suggest a personal proclivity. His story provides evidence of a man appropriating for his own use a particular model of illicit womanhood, the female prostitute, or "Girls of ill fame." The tales of Peter Sewally and of Sally Binns (discussed in chapter 4 above) show that "acting like a woman" was one option available to men in the nineteenth century who, for whatever reason, desired sexual contact with men.[25]

The story of Sewally's arrest and trial also shows us an African-American man working the race, class, sexuality, and gender systems to appropriate for himself a little of the wealth of white men. Did Sewally rob white men, in particular, because they were more likely to carry larger amounts of cash than black men? Or did his robbing of white men also indicate a specifically racial animosity? He certainly suggested, defensively, that the black community of New York and New Orleans had never found his cross-dressing problematic. White people, he implied, were less tolerant. Sewally's testimony provides the earliest account of African-American parties in New York City and New Orleans attended, without incident, apparently, by a cross-dressed black man interested, for whatever reason, in sex with men. Black people accepted Sewally's cross-dressing, and, perhaps even his sex with men, his testimony suggested, hinting at relationships among blacks that varied substantially from those among whites and blacks.

And the white man, Haslem, did he seek a black woman, or a black male cross-dresser, in particular, as a paid sexual partner? Or did he undertake intercourse with Mary Jones just because she was available, whatever her race and whatever her sex? The reports leave many questions unanswered.

Affectionate *and* sexual, loving *or* erotic relations between white men and men of color have a long, emotionally fraught American history, as Leslie Fiedler long ago pointed out.[26] Focusing on the intimacy between Mark Twain's Huck Finn and his black friend Jim and the intimacies between white and Indian men in the novels of James Fenimore Cooper, Fiedler analyzed these adventures as fantasies of escape from marriage and manly responsibilities. Such stories were sometimes tales of comradeship and desire—expressing a yearning to reach across the chasm of difference—sometimes tales of conflict and exploitation.

⁓

In the last decades of the nineteenth century, the clear distinction between sodomy and not-sodomy began to blur, as sodomy statutes were reinterpreted and other new laws and judicial decisions expanded the realm of the criminal to include oral-genital acts and a variety of other, more vaguely defined erotic contacts.

The earliest American reference to oral-genital contact that I know of appeared in 1849, but it was unusual.[27] In Herman Melville's *Redburn,* the title character's friend, handsome Harry Bolton, leads him upstairs in a London den where there hang "mythological oil paintings" of lewd character: "Such pictures as Martial and Suetonius mention as being found in the private cabinet of the Emperor Tiberius." Other obscene pictures are also described vaguely. William Gilman's study, *Melville's Early Life and Redburn* (1951), showed that only one of those mythic pictures referred to an actual historical work: Suetonius did mention a painting that Tiberius kept in his bedroom. In a modest note Gilman said this pictured "Atalanta performing a most unnatural service for Meleager." My own research, with the late John Boswell's expert translation, indicates that the exact act referred to was oral sex. (The original Latin verb translates literally as "to gratify with the mouth.")[28]

The new, increased, late-nineteenth-century concern about oral-genital acts is documented not only in that era's legal appeals case reports but also in American medical books and articles, a tourist's memoir, and another, more famous novel.

An early example of this concern is explicit in 1871, in Dr. Mary Walker's popular medical treatise warning Americans against the belief (evidently, a common bit of sexual folklore) that the "eating of semen by women and the sipping of the exudations of women by men, will promote health, prolong life, and promote beauty."[29] Walker pointed to what she perceived as a problem in male-female relations.

The popularity of oral-genital contacts between men in the nineteenth century is hinted at in an anonymous German tourist's explicit, first-person testimony.[30] Half a year after this fellow's return from duty in the Franco-Prussian War (1870–72), he reported, "I went to North America to seek my fortune." In America (probably in the United States), he sought, in addition, numerous sexual encounters with men—and found them in abundance. Fifteen-or-so years later, he sent his self-authored sexual story to a sexologist who published it as a case history, in a German book on legal medicine.

This witnesss, born on May 8, 1835, the son of a "high official," at seven felt "a lively attachment" for a nine-year-old schoolmate. He "was satisfied when I could be as close as possible to him," and "lay my head near his genitals," or "when he lay on top of me, as if he was the man, and I the woman" (body positions were routinely thought of then as biologically sexed; the "male" position was top, the "female," bottom).

In his teens, shortly after his First Communion, he started to drink men's urine, and he loved men to sit on his face, but he had his own, definite sexual standards. He made it clear that he never engaged in "real pederasty" (in context, anal intercourse). He was most satisfied performing oral-genital sex on men—one of the rare first-person nineteenth-century accounts of this particular sexual act.

His idea that "real pederasty" did not include oral-genital contact was common then, and this belief is mirrored in American sodomy appeals case reports. The exclusion of oral-genital connections from "sodomy" meant that a good way to avoid that most execrated act was by participating only in oral copulations. Oral was definitely better than anal on this century's scale of deviations, at least until late in the era.

Referring to his oral-genital encounters in North America, and, probably, to other acts (excluding anal intercourse) the German declared: "This unnaturalness is an everyday occurrence there even more than here, and I was able to pander to this passion of mine more openly and with less risk of punishment than here. The American man loves this cult in the same way I worship it, and I had the experience of always being quickly recognized as a fellow member of the faith."

He lacked the "ability to recognize others immediately by sight," he said, explaining: "I become aware and arrive at certainty only after rather lengthy observation: by staring firmly, my eyes roving to the area where the sexual member reposes, and by a certain bearing of the personality."

> If I am seized by fervent passion toward a man [it is] essential that he be
> an attractively built, educated person who is well groomed. Then the
> proofs of my love know no bounds; it is the greatest bliss for me to kiss
> his hands, his feet, his behind; I can lie at his feet for hours, placing them
> on my face and kissing them over and over again; I would term it a
> fawning, cringing love, and this satisfies me entirely—I feel happy and
> content. I had this in America many times. In such moments the entire
> outer world disappears for me entirely.

Quantities of American men evidently enjoyed being fawned upon by
this German.[31]

In the 1880s and 1890s, American doctors' interest in oral-genital acts
began to be expressed in medical journals, reflecting a new professional
concern about proper and improper sex. In 1889, Dr. A. B. Holder called
the "sexual perversion" practiced by the Native American *bote* "the most
debased that could be conceived of."[32] The "practice of the bote among
civilized races is not unknown to specialists, but no name suited to ears
polite, even though professional has been given to it." The lack of a medical name suggests the newness of the doctors' concern, and Holder felt
it necessary to explain: "The practice is to produce the sexual orgasm by
taking the male organ of the active party in the lips of the bote, the bote
probably experiencing the orgasm at the same time."

In 1892, Irving C. Rosse, a medical doctor given to flowery prose and
confident denunciations, called oral-genital sex "a hideous act that marks
the last abjection of vice," and "the 'nameless crime' that moves in the
dark."[33]

Bram Stoker's vampire tale, *Dracula,* first published in *Lippincott's
Magazine,* in Philadelphia, in 1897, speaks metaphorically to the same
late-nineteenth-century concern about oral-genital connections.[34] In the
novel, Mina Harker describes Dracula's initial seduction: "He pulled
open his shirt, and with his long sharp nails opened a vein in his breast.
When the blood began to spurt out, he took my hands in one of his . . .
and with the other seized my neck and pressed my mouth to the wound,
so that I must either suffocate or swallow some of the —— Oh, my God,
my God! What have I done?"

These vampires' "dietary indiscretions" (as literary critic Christopher
Craft called them) reveal Stoker's and other men's anxiety, not about sexuality in general, but, specifically, about oral consumptions.[35] Reference
to such consuming desires, and the blood/semen analogy pointed out by
Craft, were not unique to Stoker. In 1855, Walt Whitman's first edition
of *Leaves of Grass* had referred to "You my rich blood, your milky stream
pale strippings of my life," and to "prurient provokers stiffening my

limbs, / Straining the udder of my heart for its withheld drip." (Whitman and his *Leaves* were an important influence on Stoker, who visited the poet and wrote him a long, confessional love letter.)[36]

By century's end, oral-genital acts were rising to the surface of consciousness. "Come to me, Arthur," called one of Stoker's "languorous, voluptuous" female suckers: "Leave those others and come to me. My arms are hungry for you. Come, and we can rest together. Come, my husband, come!"[37]

Elsewhere in *Dracula,* that archetypal sucker, the Count himself, asserted his male prerogative, driving his women vampires away from Jonathan Harker and admonishing them: "How dare you touch him, any of you? How dare you cast eyes on him when I had forbidden it? Back, I tell you all! This man belongs to me."[38]

ॐ

The world of not-sodomy, like that of sodomy, stood separate from the world of asexual, sentimental love. The world of sodomy depicted in the appeals case reports, in a few sensationalistic newspapers, and in an occasional novel, made no reference to romantic, spiritual love—the dominant genteel ideal. And the world of pure, true love included no mention of sodomy or sodomites. Romantic lovers and sodomites inhabited separate, parallel universes, leaving a great unmapped space between. This was a site in which Walt Whitman began to explore the erotic intimacy of men and to invent a new language to express it.

Valt Whitman, probably 1854. Courtesy Library of Congress. ⟨⟩

PART III

Coming Together, Coming to Terms

Voices of Sexes and Lusts

W alt Whitman's unpublished notes on language, written between the early 1850s and the early 1860s, reveal his profound, persistent concern about the lack of words to express men's deep feelings for men. The same problematic language lack complicated Lincoln's and Speed's feelings for each other—they had no adequate, affirmative words with which to talk of them. Albert Dodd pondered privately about the nature of his feelings and how to name them. Whitman, however, pondered how to talk publicly of such emotion. Before and after his *Leaves of Grass* gave poetic voice to a startling new vision of erotic love between men, his need to find words was urgent, his impulse to speak was strong.

"Among the young men of these states," said Whitman in a notebook, there exists "a wonderful tenacity of friendship, and a passionate fondness for their friends, and always a manly readiness to make friends." And yet these men "have remarkably few words . . . for the friendly sentiments." The words Whitman did use—"friends" and "friendship," "friendly sentiments" and "passionate fondness"—were, for him, inadequate to express the intense emotions and relations they named.

Terms for friendship, Whitman complained, "do not thrive here among the muscular classes, where the real quality of friendship is always freely to be found." Whitman pointed, in particular, to "friendship" among working men. The words available to those men did not express, for Whitman, such men's experienced intensity of feeling. Working men, Whitman stressed, even "have an aversion" to naming their friendly feelings for each other: "They never give words to their most ardent friendships."[1]

Whitman, in contrast, felt it imperative to give words to his ardent intimacies. This naming was for him, and for a few other men of his time, an affirmative action, a way of asserting the value of such intimacies. Whitman's naming countered the social practice that institutionalized romantic love and reproductive sexual intercourse between married men and women exclusively and that condemned sex between men as "sodomy" or "mutual masturbation." Giving words to men's "ardent friendships" with men, Whitman affirmed his own profound feelings; he was writing for his life.

Commenting on "the blank left by words wanted, but unsupplied,"

Walt Whitman, July 1854 (the engraving appears in the 1855 and 1856 editions of *Leaves of Grass*). Courtesy Library of Congress. ❧

Whitman mentioned the lack of words for "the act male and female" and mused vaguely about "other words wanted"—words for the act male and male? He made no reference to the erotic desires of women for women and no reference to a same-sex desire that included such feelings.

When language is needed, said Whitman optimistically, "the words will surely follow." He predicted his own eloquent coming to terms. His prediction encouraged him to make this a self-fulfilling prophecy.

The "lack of any words," Whitman declared, "is as historical as the existence of words." He explained: "As for me, I feel a hundred realities, clearly determined in me, that words are not yet formed to represent." Language had not yet caught up with his experience, he suggested. But Whitman's "not yet" again anticipated the future formation of the missing words. Emotions were clearly bubbling in this writer, desires for which there were, as yet, no adequate words—or only condemnatory words.

Whitman was confident that men and women "like me . . . will gradually get to be more and more numerous,—perhaps swiftly, in shoals;— then the words will also follow, in shoals."[2] His others "like me" imagined men and women as frustrated as he was by the lack of words to express their affectionate and erotic feelings for men or women.

Those others "like me" did *not* refer just to men attracted to men, but to all those whose strong feelings could not be expressed within the tepid, clichéd vocabulary of the sentimental romance. Whitman predicted his own and those others' breakthrough into expressive speech. Human beings make new words and use words in new ways, he suggested, when the old words do not convey their strong, new emotions.

༄

In July 1855, in Whitman's first *Leaves of Grass,* the words did begin to follow in shoals. Here, and especially in the next two revised editions of his book, the poet began to speak up for his own, heretofore obscure, feelings. Whitman initiated a talking cure, formalized a half century later in Sigmund Freud's private sessions with a voluble woman patient and later published case histories and theories. Whitman's talking was also public, as well as poetic, lyrical, and dazzling.

Walt Whitman's poems were narrated in the first person by a character sometimes called "Walt Whitman," but that virtual character was not identical to the bricks and mortar author. To recognize this distinction between the two Walts is not to deny any similarity at all between the author and his alter ego. There is a close resemblance, but it is complex and creative—literary, not always literal.

In his new book, Whitman's speaker almost gasps for words, the hesitations in his lines conveying his struggle to transmute feeling into speech, words into poetry. (The ellipses here, and in following selections, are Whitman's unless marked with square brackets):

> There is that in me. . . . I do not know what it is. . . . but I know it is in me.
> Wrenched and sweaty. . . . calm and cool then my body becomes; I
>   sleep. . . . I sleep long.
> I do not know it. . . . it is without name. . . . it is a word unsaid,
> It is not in any dictionary or utterance or symbol.
> Something it swings on more than the earth I swing on,
> To it the creation is the friend whose embracing awakes me.
> Perhaps I might tell more[. . . .] Outlines! I plead for my brothers and
>   sisters.³

His mysterious, unnamed emotion, Whitman's narrator concluded, "is happiness."

Here, Whitman adapted to his own expressive purpose a politically loaded, peculiarly American term. For, just seventy-nine years earlier in the Declaration of Independence, England's rebellious colonists had guaranteed all citizens the right to the pursuit of "happiness." Whitman's antipuritanical validation of this-world enjoyments—of sensual joys and physical pleasures—became his poetic mission.

In *Leaves of Grass,* Whitman began, consciously and explicitly, to speak the unspeakable, to discuss experiences and use words unmentionable in polite, middle-class parlance. Almost alone in his time, he spoke up publicly, explicitly, and unequivocally for sexual desire:

> Through me forbidden voices,
> Voices of sexes and lusts. . . . voices veiled, and I remove the veil,
> Voices indecent by me clarified and transfigured.⁴

Against the era's reticence about and censure of sensuality, Whitman's narrator named "unnameable ardors" and the "prodigal" with whom he shared "unspeakable passionate love."⁵ The most famous "prodigal," the Bible's, was, specifically, a son, so Whitman alluded here to "passionate love" between metaphorical fathers and sons, or older and younger males. Naming that "unspeakable" love, Whitman, paradoxically, made it speakable—and most eloquently so.

Speaking the unspeakable, Whitman also countered the condemnatory tradition represented in the Maryland indictment of Davis for that "detestable crime . . . among christians not to be named." Whitman's public speaking took on that "not to be named," that powerful injunction to silence contained in the stock theological condemnation of sodomy. Breaking that silence, Whitman found ways to give words to his own and other men's unspoken erotic desire for men.

Whitman spoke in *Leaves of Grass* for "prostitutes" and, more generally, for "the rights of them the others are down upon." Appropriating the democratic rhetoric of "rights" to defend sexual outcasts, Whitman did *not* explicitly include sodomites among those put-down persons. Even this daring poet feared to defend that particular abused group or utter that particular freighted word. He did speak many others, however.

As numbers of shocked nineteenth-century reviews reveal, unwary genteel readers who casually picked up Whitman's *Leaves of Grass* were seriously dismayed to read of "soft-tickling genitals," a "phallic procession" dancing through the streets, "libidinous prongs," "a spirt of my own seminal wet," "limitless limpid jets of love hot and enormous," "unspeakable passionate love," and "onanists." They were not happy to encounter references to opium smoking, venereal disease, and celebrations of the author's penis, testicles, and semen, as well as the sexual desire of women for men, men for women, and their "copulation." The rare, particularly sensitive reader also sensed erotic desire irradiating, subtly, Whitman's references to love relations between men.

Fourteen years earlier, in "The Child's Champion," Whitman had counted on the dominance of the sentimental pure-love ideal to dampen his story's powerful sexual overtones. But, in 1855, the love that Whitman depicted was then, consciously and explicitly, suffused with eroticism. The emotion he celebrated was now a sexual love far different from that purely spiritual love idealized by respectable, middle-class Americans. Whitman wrote against the idea that fleshly love was separate and distinct from spiritual love or any less worthy. He wrote against the genteel culture and for the sexual culture.

In Whitman's book, love between men was first linked affirmatively to the erotic, along with the love of women for men, men for women, and, even, self-love, the love of nature, and the love of God. Whitman thereby risked readers' perceiving that men's love for men also contained, according to respectable values, a deeply disturbing sensual element, a touch of what was called the "unnatural," a hint of what was sometimes termed the "sodomitical."

All of Whitman's evocations of male-male eros therefore contain escape clauses that could be invoked should he be charged with celebrating sodomy or the sodomy-like. Whitman employed a variety of deniability devices to avoid detection: he designed clever ways to simultaneously speak and deny speaking of sex between men.

First, the narrator of *Leaves of Grass*—identified in the text as "Walt Whitman," thirty-six years old, six feet tall, "disorderly fleshy and sensual"—talks in several poems, warmly and evocatively, of men as the objects of *women's* sexual desire.[6] In the most lusty of such scenes, "twenty-eight young men bathe by the shore," observed secretly and yearningly by a "lonesome" lady in a "fine house." From behind her window she watches the "friendly" young men "and loves them." While the lady is "richly drest," the flesh of the young male bathers is naked to her gaze. As she watches, "The beards of the young men glistened with wet, it ran from their long hair, / Little streams passed all over their bodies."

In her fantasy, this woman reaches out, her hand following the wet streams over youthful male flesh: "An unseen hand also passed over their bodies, / It descended tremblingly from their temples and ribs." As she observes, "The young men float on their backs, their white bellies swell to the sun," a floating that exposes other swelling parts.

She watches, unobserved, and increasingly aroused: These young men "do not ask who seizes fast to them, / They do not know who puffs and declines with pendant and bending arch, / They do not think whom they souse with spray."[7] Thanks to Whitman's remarkable new powers of evocation, his readers vicariously participate in this woman's voyeuristic fantasy.

But the participants in this mental orgy are not all created equal. The young men are objects of sexual desire, the female observer is not. Whitman and his readers look over her shoulder, as it were, at the unclothed, white, young men's bodies with which she so amorously connects. Her rich dress and fine house contrast with and set off their bodies, free of clothes and class markers. The whiteness of those young bellies evokes other parts usually hidden in mixed, genteel society, as well as a sex-marked, race-coded desire.

The poet, Walt Whitman, wrote here in the person of "Walt Whitman": a man who identifies with a woman who desires a man—well, actually, twenty-eight naked young men. (If we count the writer Walt Whitman, his narrator "Walt Whitman," the woman, and one reader, there are actually thirty-two participants in this orgy.) For Whitman, lust was democratic and equalitarian, the province of women as well as men— a daring, courageous breach of the age's genteel ideal of the "pure," asexual true woman. Portraying this woman's erotic desire for men, Whitman hid behind her back, in effect. Whitman here identified with and transposed himself into a woman in order to express his own erotic feelings for men.

Posing as women, metaphorically or literally, was one way that some nineteenth-century men connected erotically with men, as we have seen. Recall "Sally Binns," described in the sporting press's attacks on sodomites, and the newspaper accounts of Peter Sewally/Mary Jones.

Another sexy scene in this first *Leaves of Grass* portrays a desiring woman who "blushingly" urges a "limber-hip'd man" by a garden fence to "come nigh to me," and (suggestively) to "give me your finger and thumb." She tells him to "fill me with albescent [whitish] honey," and to "rub to me with your chafing beard . . rub to my breast and shoulders."[8] This eagerly desiring woman actively pursues the male object of her lust, her unconstrained behavior again daringly challenging the dominant, respectable ideal of true womanhood. While a woman once more takes the sexual lead, the poet again cast a male as the *object* of a pressing erotic urge.

In another scene, the poet wrote from the viewpoint of a woman who has recently welcomed her "truant lover" into her dark room and bed: "His flesh was sweaty and panting, / I feel the hot moisture yet that he left me."[9] Though the scene involves a woman and a man, the male poet's identification with the woman places him in a sexual relation with a man.

As many critics have commented, Whitman generally described men in much more erotically charged words and physically detailed language than he did women. Although Whitman dared to imbue his women with strong sexual desires, presenting them as actively desiring *subjects,* rarely, if ever, did he present them convincingly as *objects* of erotic desire.

Another scene starts with the male poet "drawn" to "the female form," but quickly moves on to a "bridegroom-night of love" in which the bride is all but forgotten, and the sex of the lusting parties is obscured in the thrill of vividly pictured copulation. This deniability device focuses on acts, obscuring the sexes of the copulating parties:

> Ebb stung by the flow, and flow stung by the ebb. . . . loveflesh swelling
>   and deliciously aching,
> Limitless limpid jets of love hot and enormous. . . . quivering jelly of
>   love. . . . white-blow and delirious juice,
> Bridegroom-night of love working surely and softly into the prostrate
>   dawn,
> Undulating into the willing and yielding day,
> Lost in the cleave of the clasping and sweetfleshed day.[10]

The sex of one or both partners to an erotic encounter was not always specified by Whitman. This strategic ambiguity left to readers' imaginations the sex of the lusting parties. In another famous *Leaves* passage, the body of Whitman's male persona submits passively and ecstatically to erotic play with an active soul of unspecified sex:

> I mind how we lay in June, such a transparent summer morning;
> You settled your head athwart my hips and gently turned over upon me;
> And parted the shirt from my bosom-bone, and plunged your tongue to
>   my barestript heart,
> And reached till you felt my beard, and reached till you held my feet.[11]

This delirious mating of the narrator's male body with an ambiguously sexed soul climaxes with the speaker experiencing a mystical revelation of "peace," "joy," and "God." Here again in Whitman the flesh and spirit are intermingled, defying the age's separation of body and spirit.

A desire oblivious of the sex of its object is several times depicted: "Whichever the sex," imagined Whitman, the man with "the passkey of hearts" is welcomed universally—"The person he favors by day or sleeps with at night is blessed."[12]

The poet spoke often of "some man or woman I love,"[13] but his narrator's alleged desire for both women *and* men rings a bit hollow. His men are hot objects of yearning, his women hot only in pursuit of the same. The poet's oft proclaimed democracy of desire operated as a cover—another deniability device—as if Whitman was saying, "You see, men aren't my only love interest."

Invoking another escape clause, Whitman's narrator focuses on a sexy male body—his own. (Sodomy, after all, requires two bodies.) The narrator's erotic relationship to his own body is one sort of male-male sensuality that Whitman did, daringly, depict. His male narrator boasts, charmingly: "I dote on myself. . . . There is that lot of me, and all so luscious." He declares: "If I worship any particular thing it shall be . . . the spread of my own body."[14] This affirmation of a loving, pleasurable relationship between the male narrator and his own male anatomy was extremely rare in nineteenth-century America. The perils of self-abuse, onanism, or masturbation were decried. Even Whitman elsewhere spoke judgmentally of "onanists" and the "depravity of young men."[15]

Whitman's sometimes guilty laments reveal that even this rebellious writer continued to battle his society's antisexual strictures. But, in transforming private guilt into public confession, Whitman began to say no to sexual shame. His articulate, published confessions transmuted guilt into verbal gold. And, by publicly confessing, Whitman beat any future puritanical critics to the draw, anticipating their charges of shameful, guilty acts. If accused, he could always plead, "But I've already confessed!"—another escape clause.

Whitman's narrator sometimes castigates his bodily urges and, specifically, his penis, for betraying him to seducers "hardly different from myself":

> Treacherous tip of me reaching and crowding to help them,
> My flesh and blood playing out lightning, to strike what is hardly different
>   from myself,
> On all sides prurient provokers stiffening my limbs,
> Straining the udder of my heart for its withheld drip,
> Behaving licentious toward me, taking no denial,
> Depriving me of my best as for a purpose,
> Unbuttoning my clothes and holding me by the bare waist.[16]

But even before giving in to his seducers, the narrator confesses, "I went myself first to the headland. . . . my own hands carried me there."[17] Submitting to those who strain "the udder of my heart" suggests, specifically, agreement to another's request to perform oral sex. Though Whitman was definitely pushing the limits here, oral-genital connections then fell outside the legally banned sodomy. Oral sex may, in 1855, have also fallen outside of everyday popular speech and even most people's consciousness. That mental and verbal void made Whitman's allusion less risky. An act without a name lacked a clear set of condemnatory judgments.

Whitman's narrator often lyrically extolls his own beloved parts, including his metaphorically invoked penis. "Root of washed sweet-flag," he called it, the common name for *Acorus calamus,* a plant with long leaves, a long-flowering spike, and a pungent, aromatic root. (*Calamus,* the Latin name for sweet-flag, will later suggest to Whitman a way of naming and affirming men's sexual desire for men. But, in 1855, "sweet-flag" was still just a plain old phallic symbol.)

In 1855, the poet's penis was also represented as a "timorous pond-snipe" (a long-billed bird), his testicles as a "nest of guarded duplicate eggs," and his semen as the "Trickling sap of maple, fibre of manly wheat." The common names of plants, birds, and trees were already suggesting to Whitman original, charming, even sweet, *nature-derived* metaphors for his sexual organs and fluids. Linking his pleasurable parts with nature and the natural, Whitman countered the accusation that nonprocreative sexualities were "against the order of nature" or a "crime against" it. His new poetic vocabulary permitted him to express and to affirm his smoldering erotic desires.

From the worship of his own natural organs, Whitman's narrator moved on to affirm his erotic intimacy with nature. Though this nature was coded, specifically, as male, Whitman could, if challenged, once more deny that he was writing about eros between men:

> Winds whose soft-tickling genitals rub against me it shall be you,
> Broad muscular fields, branches of liveoak, loving lounger in my winding paths it shall be you,
> Hands I have taken, face I have kissed, mortal I have ever touched, it shall be you.[18]

Whitman had originally considered using the live oak as a central symbol for a series of twelve poems on the erotic love of a man for a man. But here "live oak" was just a sexy stand-in for a particular man-lusting man.

In another erotic encounter with a force of nature marked as male, Whitman's narrator imagined riding a "gigantic beauty of a stallion, fresh and responsive to my caresses." As the narrator's "heels embrace him," the stallion's "well built limbs tremble with pleasure."[19]

This evocation of a beast's pleasure is astonishing, for at the time, as we have seen, neither pleasure nor hints of bestiality were in good repute. In 1855, the interchangeable legal terminology of sodomy, buggery, and the crime against nature associated man's anal intercourse with man and men's carnal congress with animals. So it is all the more remarkable that Whitman dared here to make a man's physical "embrace" of a pleased, trembling stallion serve as metaphor for the unspeakable, equally controversial, erotic intimacy of man with man.

In one brief scene the narrator imagines grass to be "the beautiful uncut hair of graves," as well as the hair growing from the chests of young men, and he fantasizes:

> Tenderly will I use you curling grass,
> It may be that you transpire from the breasts of young men,
> It may be if I had known them I would have loved them.[20]

In those few lines, a nature that is male and sexual threatens to revert momentarily from the metaphorical to the literal, from grass to the hair on young men's chests, to the young men loved by the poet's narrator, to the young men loved by the poet.

Invoking the idea of a natural goodness, Whitman's narrator speaks up affirmatively for his body, its urges and acts:

> I do not press my finger across my mouth,
> I keep as delicate around the bowels as around the head and heart,
> Copulation is no more rank to me than death is.

> I believe in the flesh and the appetites,
> Seeing hearing and feeling are miracles, and each part and tag of me is a
>   miracle.[21]

Celebrating "flesh" as "miracle," Whitman again countered the common religious condemnation of the body at the expense of the spirit.

Writing specifically of a young man, Whitman's narrator positioned himself as an older admirer: "The young fellow drives the express-wagon. . . . I love him though I do not know him."[22] If challenged, Whitman could defend this as spiritual love, though his book's strong, central focus on sexual/spiritual love undermined such a defense.

Whitman's narrator is "enamoured of growing outdoors," and "Of men that live among cattle or taste of the oceans or woods." How the narrator knows and came to love men's "taste" is not explained, though he boasts that he can "eat and sleep with" men "week in and week out."[23] That eating and sleeping hint at other sensual satisfactions shared (specifically oral satisfactions, which are several times hinted at throughout *Leaves of Grass*). This deniability device employs vagueness as cover.

In another scene Whitman's male narrator encounters a Supreme Being who is also a man and an affectionate bedmate: "God comes a loving bedfellow and sleeps at my side all night and close on the peep of day," leaving "baskets covered with white towels bulging the house with their plenty."[24] Those bulging baskets may evoke male genitals, and those white towels may evoke the public baths visited regularly by Whitman. God provided the deniability device in this poem. If eyebrow were raised, Whitman was picturing a religious communion. He was, in fact, but one also deeply, affirmatively sensual.

Switching from the first person to the safer, distanced second person (another escape clause), the poet's narrator speaks of "you" admiring a male body (making the reader an active coconspirator in his attraction): "The expression of the wellmade man . . . is in his limbs and joints . . . / The strong sweet supple quality he has strikes through the cotton and flannel. . . . / You linger to see his back and the back of his neck and shoulderside."[25] You do indeed.

For Whitman's narrator, love is various, suffocating, and empowering, lust free and lustful, sad ("the sobbing liquid of life")[26] as well as joyful. His love objects are men, women, himself, nature, and God; his love is simultaneously genital-love, body-love, sensual-love, and spirit-love. His proclaimed love is often indifferent to the sex of its object, a passionate affection *not* yet officially divided between a same-sex or different-sex object. But, in practice, his love is often focused strongly on a particular sex: men.

ॐ

In Whitman's 1855 *Leaves of Grass* a strong tide of erotic feeling for men began to find original, explicit, deeply felt expression. But only one contemporary review of Whitman's *Leaves* recognized this particular, startling aspect of his book. During most of Whitman's lifetime, it was almost always his evocations of male-female sexuality that threatened *Leaves of Grass* with being banned. For most of the nineteenth century, sexuality was not perceived as permeating the intimacies of men. This is important; not until the last decade of the nineteenth century, and the last years of Whitman's life, did his portrayals of male-male eros begin to be perceived as such and publicly condemned.

"It is impossible to imagine how any man's fancy could have conceived such a mass of stupid filth," declared a review of *Leaves of Grass,* published anonymously by Rufus Wilmot Griswold in *The Criterion,* in November 1855.[27] This reviewer, who claimed to have studied theology and to have become a Baptist minister before going into journalism, was unusually astute about the male-male eros haunting Whitman's *Leaves.*[28] Griswold had been an owner and chief editor of the *New World* when, in 1841, Walter Whitman's "The Child's Champion" was published in that New York literary weekly and thus may have been alerted then to the sex circulating surreptitiously in Whitman's writing.[29] Whitman worked at the time in the *New World* printing office, and the poet in 1855 personally sent Griswold a review copy of *Leaves of Grass.*[30]

Griswold's religious training and his journalistic career perhaps made him especially alert to the possibility of men lying with men. Perhaps, also, some personal experience or unresolved desire opened him to the eros in Whitman's work. Just a year after castigating Whitman's *Leaves,* Griswold was party to a sensational divorce suit, suggesting that his own personal relations with one woman, at least, were deeply problematic.[31]

The author of *Leaves of Grass,* charged this reviewer, was guilty of the "the vilest imaginings and shamefullest license," a "degrading, beastly sensuality." But only gradually did Griswold specify the exact character of that voluptuousness.

Griswold bemoaned the immorality of the day, the lustfulness of the age: "There was a time when licentiousness laughed at reproval; now it writes essays and delivers lectures. Once it shunned the light; now it courts attention, writing books showing how grand and pure it is, and prophecies from its lecherous lips its own ultimate triumph." Whitman was not alone among salacious authors, Griswold complained.

The reviewer left "this gathering of muck to the laws which . . . have the power to suppress such gross obscenity"—a clear expression of his belief that legal prosecution was in order. Unable to describe Whitman's book "without employing language that cannot be pleasing to ears polite," Griswold concluded: the "records of crime show that many monsters have gone on in impunity, because the exposure of their vileness was attended with too great indelicacy." Griswold's "monsters" echoes the denunciations of sodomites that had appeared in the sporting press eighteen years earlier.

The reviewer exposed this particular monster by ending with a warning, phrased in Latin: "Peccatum illud horribile, inter Christianos non nominandum" (that horrible sin, among Christians not to be named), the stock phrase long associated with Christian condemnations of sodomy. In 1855, Griswold was alone in publicly linking the act of sodomy with Whitman's celebration of men's erotic desire for men; Griswold alone pointed to the male-male eros growing wildly among Walt Whitman's *Leaves.*

ॐ

The second edition of Whitman's *Leaves of Grass,* published in August 1856, contained twenty new poems, a number of which talked more explicitly of sexuality than the author had previously dared. In "Bunch Poem" (later, "Spontaneous Me"), Whitman spoke more directly than ever before about an erotic encounter between its male narrator ("Walt Whitman") and a young man.[32]

This poem, suffused with sensuality, begins quietly enough, with the narrator and "the friend I am happy with" alone in the country. This natural, pastoral setting soon provides a welcome to eros, moving, by free association, to "real poems" to "poems of the privacy of the night, and of men like me" (the speaker's sexual parts). Whitman's narrator here identifies affirmatively with other men, and, perhaps, with other men interested in sex with younger men. He then moves, startlingly, to the poem of the poet's penis:

> This poem, drooping shy and unseen, that I always carry, and that all men carry,
> (Know, once for all, avowed on purpose, wherever are men like me, are our lusty, lurking, masculine poems,) . . .

This leads to an ecstatic, escalating evocation of carnal love in action, a love directed at both sexes and the earth:

Love-thoughts, love-juice, love-odor, love-yielding, love-climbers, and the
    climbing sap,
Arms and hands of love—lips of love—phallic thumb of love—breasts of
    love—bellies, pressed and glued together with love,
Earth of chaste love—life that is only life after love,
The body of my love—the body of the woman I love—the body of the
    man—the body of the earth, . . .

And this leads to the graphically pictured copulation of a hirsute male
bee with a mature female flower: "The hairy wild-bee that murmurs and
hankers up and down—that gripes the full-grown lady-flower, tight upon
her till he is satisfied." Here, the trite image of bees and flowers—one of
the most clichéd, sentimental metaphors of that era's genteel literature—
is newly minted, electrified by the sexy language: "hairy," "wild," "hankers
up and down," "gripes," "tight upon her." Whitman's word power makes
his man-bee a representative male, and (again) an enticing sexual object,
as well as an active sexual subject aggressively pursuing his pleasure. (The
lady-flower's satisfaction with her hairy friend's hankering and griping is
not mentioned.)

The poem then moves toward its central sequence, the erotic consorting of "Walt Whitman" and a partner called, alternately, a "boy"
and "young man." In this surprisingly sexual and explicit version of a
nineteenth-century bed-sharing scene the male narrator is "stung" by
sense impressions (like the lady-flower "griped" by the man-bee), testicles touch tenderly in brotherly communion, and semen is effused:

The wet of woods through the early hours,
Two sleepers at night lying close together as they sleep, one with an arm
    slanting down across and below the waist of the other,
The smell of apples, aromas from crushed sage-plant, mint, birch-bark,
The boy's longings, the glow and pressure as he confides to me what he
    was dreaming,
The dead leaf falling its spiral whirl, and falling still and content to the
    ground,
The no-formed stings that sights, people, objects, sting me with,
The hubbed sting of myself, stinging me as much as it ever can any one,
The sensitive, orbic, underlapped brothers, that only privileged feelers may
    be intimate where they are,
The curious roamer, the hand, roaming all over the body—the bashful
    withdrawing of flesh where the fingers soothingly pause and edge
    themselves,
The limpid liquid within the young man,
The vexed corrosion, so pensive and so painful,

> The torment, the irritable tide that will not be at rest,
> The like of the same I feel, the like of the same in others, . . .

The poem ends (climaxes, actually) with the narrator's "wholesome relief, repose, [and] content," as he joins without shame in the erotic play, plucking a bunch of semen-flowers from himself, to "toss it carelessly to fall where it may."[33] This particular scene set a nineteenth-century American record for the affirmative, public, poetic depiction of sexual relations between males.

The sexy, manly hairiness of the wild-bee returns, in the 1856 *Leaves of Grass,* in several admiring references to "the beauty of wood-boys and wood-men, with their clear untrimmed faces," and to the "roughs, beards, friendliness, combativeness, the soul loves."[34] In contrast, Whitman associated a man's "shaved face" with physical disability.[35] By 1854, the poet had grown a short beard and had himself photographed as the manly rough into which he had self-transformed. This bearded bard replaced the earlier beardless dandy of his 1840s photos, as Whitman actively embraced the virile sensuality his poetry associated with "manhood."

A particularly bold narrator recalls loving men of few words "saying their ardor in native forms." He commands them to "take what I have then . . . , take the pay you approached for, / Take the white tears of my blood, if that is what you are after."[36] Those "white tears" are semen, and the white blood offered signals a sexual favor granted.[37] Like the speaker of the 1855 poem, who granted a provoker the "udder of my heart," the narrator here is also situated on the giving end of an oral-genital act. Saying his ardor in native forms—giving verbal expression to his society's native forms of desire—was exactly what Whitman was up to.

In another new poem, the narrator refers to the past, recalling his "lust," and the "hot wishes I dared not speak." He also recalls that he was once "a Manhattanese, free, friendly, and proud!" Then, he was one

> called by my nighest name by clear loud voices of young men as they saw
>   me approaching or passing,
> Felt their arms on my neck as I stood, or the negligent leaning of their flesh
>   against me as I sat,
> Saw many I loved in the street, or ferry-boat, or public assembly, yet never
>   told them a word.[38]

The narrator's feelings are completely clear to him, though undeclared to his beloved young men. Whitman's poems, however, eloquently disclose that undisclosed love.

In this *Leaves of Grass,* Whitman talked for the first time in his published poetry of "adhesiveness." This is a term he borrowed from the phrenologists, the pop psychologists of his day, who measured areas of people's heads to adduce the quantities of the various emotions they contained. Whitman began here to reconstruct "adhesiveness" as a word specifically for what he also called "manly love"—the love of men for men. "Here is adhesiveness," his poetic persona says, "it is not previously fashioned, it is apropos." Apropos of what? By way of answering, Whitman's narrator asks: "Do you know what it is as you pass to be loved by strangers? / Do you know the talk of those turning eye-balls?"[39]

Here, Whitman records the eye contact of male strangers as they pass each other in a city street—already, evidently, a customary urban mode of meeting and mating.

Adhesiveness is further illumined as the poet asks: "These yearnings, why are they? / these thoughts in the darkness, why are they? / Why are there men and women that while they are nigh me the sun-light expands my blood?"

His questions continue later in this poem:

> What is it I interchange so suddenly with strangers?
> What with some driver as I ride on the seat by his side?
> What with some fisherman, drawing his seine by the shore, as I walk by, and pause?[40]

The "hot wishes" Whitman's persona "dared not speak" and those erotic desires of which he did openly talk evoke a universe of yearning. This was set, implicitly, against the world of acts constituted by legal language, the sphere of sodomy, the crime against nature, and the detestable and abominable crime of buggery.

Whitman's 1856 *Leaves of Grass* also included one of nineteenth-century's America's major sex manifestos, a passionate prose plea for the open treatment of sexuality in the nation's literature.[41] This appeared in an open letter to Ralph Waldo Emerson who, in a rhapsodic private letter to Whitman, had praised the writer's first edition—then found his private communication reprinted, without permission, in Whitman's second edition. (Whitman, an unembarrassed self-promoter, also wrote and published several glowing reviews of his own *Leaves*.)

The "lack of an avowed, empowered unabashed development of sex," charged the no-nonsense Whitman, was responsible for the "remarkable non-personality" of current "books, art," and "talk." The sex-talk taboo resulted, he complained, in biographies of men and women portrayed as if they were of "the neuter gender." In "orthodox society today, if the dresses were changed, the men might easily pass for women and the women for men," said Whitman. He took a swipe here at feminine men and masculine women as prime defenders of the antisex, genteel culture. Whitman was a sexual rebel, but no defender of gender benders. He did not see sexual freedom as linked to gender democracy. His defense of sexuality was couched in terms of the full development of manly men and womanly women. Whitman, like his society, did not yet link unorthodox sexuality with gender nonconformity.

Borrowing religious language for his prosex cause, Whitman argued that it was in women's interest, as much as men's, that there should be "perfect faith" in sexuality, not "infidelism." In his argument, he broke again with the pure, good woman ideal.

By keeping silent about sex, he said, "poets, historians, [and] biographers . . . have long connived at the filthy law" that the "manhood of a man" was never discussed. Whitman's ideal of manhood emphatically included "sex," and this "sex" included, along with reproductive behavior, a large measure of the "lusty." He complained: "Sex, womanhood, maternity, desires, lusty animations, organs, acts, are unmentionable and to be ashamed of, to be driven to skulk out of literature." That "filthy law," he reiterated, "has to be repealed—it stands in the way of great reforms."[42]

The "tepid wash" called "love," Whitman declared—the asexual, "diluted deferential love" presented in his era's sentimental songs and fiction—"is enough to make a man vomit." Whitman's love emphatically included lust as a central component, another dissent from the dominant, asexual love ideal.

Whitman then added: "As to manly friendship, everywhere observed in The States, there is not the first breath of it to be observed in print." (His private complaint about unnamed male friendships broke here into published prose.) He compared the "manly friendship" of men with men and the bodily "love" of men and women, upholding both kinds of love.

Shall American poets express "the inherent nastiness of sex," asked Whitman, or should the nation's bards "celebrate in poems the eternal decency of the amativeness of Nature, the motherhood of all"? Whitman's "amativeness" was another borrowing from the phrenologists. He used the word to signify a natural, sexual love of men and women for each other. His amativeness was associated with creativity, but *not* necessarily with creating new humans—breaking with the era's dominant *reproductive* ethic.[43]

The culture of America, Whitman stressed, "stagnates in its vitals, cowardly and rotten, while it cannot publicly accept, and publicly name, with specific words, the things on which all existence, all souls, all realization, all decency, all health, all that is worth being here for . . . depend." Sexual love, in its many varieties, needed to be named and described, he urged. American culture must discuss "all of woman and of man" and "all friendship," he stressed.

"The courageous soul, for a year or two to come, may be proved by faith in sex, and by disdaining concessions," concluded Whitman. He was overly optimistic, unfortunately, about how long it would take to create a new, sexually free America. Now, more than a hundred years after his manifesto's publication, though public sex-talk is an everyday commodity, Americans still struggle to realize the free world of eros he envisioned.

&

Whitman's sexual poems had a seductive and unnerving effect on Henry David Thoreau. With Bronson Alcott (the writer Louisa May Alcott's father) and Sarah Tyndale, he trekked in 1856 to visit the poet in New York in order to confront the daring word worker in his native habitat.

"That Walt Whitman . . . is the most interesting fact to me at present," Thoreau wrote privately to a friend a short time later. "I have just read his 2nd edition (which he gave me) and it has done me more good than any reading for a long time."[44]

But Thoreau was also alarmed: "There are 2 or 3 pieces in the book which are disagreeable to say the least, simply sensual. He does not celebrate love at all. It is as if the beasts spoke. I think that men have not been ashamed of themselves without reason." Thoreau's use of the negative obscures a point he had trouble expressing directly: when sensuality is the subject, *men have been ashamed of themselves with reason.* When sex acts are the topic, even eloquent men become tongue-tied.

Thoreau was, indeed, referring to sex *acts:* There have "always been dens where such deeds were unblushingly recited," he added, "and it is no merit to compete with their inhabitants. But even on this side, he [Whitman] has spoken more truth than any American or modern that I know. I have found his poems exhilarating encouraging."

As for the "sensuality" of Whitman's book, "& it may turn out to be less sensual than it appeared—I do not so much wish that those parts were not written, as that men & women were so pure that they could read them without harm, that is, without understanding them." Thoreau wished for misunderstanding. He hoped that readers' insensitivity to the sensuality of Whitman's poems would prove their unfamiliarity with lust. The implication? That readers who comprehended the sensuality of these poems were dirty minded and, perhaps, even dirty acting. But what did this imply about Thoreau, who understood Whitman's sensuality with crystal clarity? The New Englander admitted: "Of course . . . if we are shocked, whose experience is it that we are reminded of?"

Thoreau concluded of Whitman: "We ought to rejoice greatly in him. He occasionally suggests something a little more than human. You cant confound him with the other inhabitants of Brooklyn or New York. How they must shudder when they read him! He is awefully good." Thoreau subdued his own shudders to affirm Whitman's poems.

During their visit, Thoreau "did not get far in conversation" with Whitman, he explained, "two others being present" (Alcott and Tyndale).[45] Whitman's hot and bothersome poems had *not* been discussed, and the uneasy standoff between Thoreau and Whitman was confirmed by Alcott: "Each seemed planted fast in reserve, surveying the other curiously,—like two beasts, each wondering what the other would do, whether to snap or run; and it came to no more than cold compliments between them." Alcott and Thoreau had said good-bye to Whitman, leaving Mrs. Tyndale with Brooklyn's "savage sovereign of the flesh."[46]

ॐ

The intimacies of men with men were the subject of forty-five eloquent new poems gathered under the title "Calamus" in Whitman's third *Leaves of Grass* (1860).[47] These man-love poems were distinguished from another section of fifteen, mostly new poems on the mutual love of men and women, collectively titled "Enfans d'Adam" (later titled less pretentiously in English as "Children of Adam").

Whitman published thirty more poems about the love of men for men than about the love of men and women, reversing his society's usual prioritizing and suggesting the relative importance of man-loving in his life. His man-woman, Enfans d'Adam section, in fact, came to Whitman as an afterthought, as indicated by his notebook: "a Cluster of Poems the same *to the Passion of Woman-Love* as the 'Calamus-Leaves' are to adhesiveness, manly love. / Full of animal fire, tender, burning."[48]

That notation posed man's love for man and man's love for woman as similar, *not different, not opposed*. Whitman viewed these loves as parallel, equally animalistic, equally "burning" and "tender." Man's love for man, and the love of man and woman for each other, were not yet set against each other as antagonistic, or exclusive; one did not yet rule out the other.

Neither was the distinction between man's love for man and the love between man and woman posed as an opposition between a "same-sex" versus "different-sex" love. The poet's Calamus and Enfans d'Adam poems make no reference to a same-sex love of women for women. Same sex/different sex was a later distinction.

Several of the fifteen Enfans d'Adam poems, ostensibly about man-woman love, focus most expressively on the love of males for each other, further evidence of the central place of man loving in Whitman's emotional constitution. For example, included in the new section on *man-woman love* is "Spontaneous Me," Whitman's old, renamed "Bunch Poem" of 1856, in which, in one scene, a man and youth consort, testicles touch, and semen is effused. None of the new Calamus poems pictured the orgasmic intercourse of males as candidly.[49]

In another case, wily Whitman actually changed the sex of the male narrator's beloved, a man in the original manuscript of "Once I passed through," to a woman in the published version. As published among Whitman's man-woman-love poems, a male narrator recalls visiting a city and remembers "only a woman I casually met there, who detained me for love of me." But the original manuscript has the male speaker recall

> only the man who wandered with me there, for love of me,
> Day by day, and night by night, we were together.
> All else has long been forgotten by me—I remember, I say, only one rude and ignorant man, who, when I departed, long and long held me by the hand with silent lips, sad and tremulous.[50]

Changing the beloved's sex allowed Whitman to place this poem in the anemic Enfans d'Adam section, providing it a necessary beefing up.[51]

If the Walter Whitman who published "The Child's Champion" in 1841 was unconscious of the male-male eros just below the surface of his text, the Walt Whitman of 1860 was completely aware of this particular sexuality. He was even carefully monitoring and manipulating its overt manifestations. Between 1841 and 1860 Whitman became increasingly conscious of sexuality in general, and male-male sexuality in particular; increasingly he made it his explicit, valued subject. American society trudged slowly along after the poet, protesting all the way. Whitman's valuing of sensual pleasure made him a premature sexual modernist, an advance man for the erotic revolution of twentieth-century America.

In another poem included in the new *man-woman-love* section, Whitman's narrator commands:

> Give me now libidinous joys only!
> Give me the drench of my passions! Give me life coarse and rank!
> Today, I go consort with nature's darlings—to-night too,
> I am for those who believe in loose delights—I share the midnight orgies of young men,

> I dance with the dancers, and drink with the drinkers,
> The echoes ring with our indecent calls,
> I take for my love some prostitute—I pick out some low person for my
>   dearest friend,
> He shall be lawless, rude, illiterate—he shall be one condemned by others
>   for deeds done.[52]

Though that "dearest friend" is explicitly male, the beloved prostitute's sex is ambiguous. If they are one and the same, however, this whore is male. Whitman's ambiguity is always strategic, always carefully calculated both to permit his speech and to protect his words from their "worst" implications. He was already anticipating criticism of the male-male eros that suffused his poems, already plotting how to evade it.

This narrator "will play a part no longer," he boasts, asking, "Why should I exile myself from my companions?" Whitman now explicitly wrote for and spoke to other sexual nonconformists. Addressing "you shunned persons," the narrator vows, "I will be your poet."[53] These "shunned persons" certainly included "loose" women; but sharing "the midnight orgies of young men" clearly delighted this speaker most. This poem displays strong Calamus tendencies, though it is not found in Whitman's Calamus section. ("Orgies," by the way, did not then have the specifically sexual meaning that would develop in the eroticized twentieth century.)

Several poems not included in either the Calamus section or the Enfans d'Adam group also contain striking references to men's love for men or youths. The poet's love for men breaks out all over this edition—he could not or would not limit its expression to the one Calamus section.

In the 1860 edition's first piece, the new "Proto-Leaf" (later, "Starting from Paumonok"), Whitman's evangelist of eros promises to write of "sexual organs and acts," determined "to prove you illustrious." He immediately adds: "I will sing the song of companionship," showing "what alone" must compact the disunited American states (this was published shortly before the Civil War). The narrator believes these states

> are to found their own ideal of manly love, indicating it in me; I will
>   therefore let flame from me the burning fires that were threatening to
>   consume me,
> I will lift what has too long kept down those smouldering fires,
> I will give them complete abandonment,
> I will write the evangel poem of comrades and love,
> (For who but I should understand love, with all its sorrow and joy?
> And who but I should be the poet of comrades?)[54]

The first poem of the new Calamus section constructed "comrades" as Whitman's major, approving name for men who loved men. Henceforth, says this poem's narrator, alone at a pond, the "calamus-root" shall "be the token of comrades," because at such a place "I last saw him that tenderly loves me—and returns again, never to separate from me." The narrator's personal love story generates a public love symbol.

Here, Whitman explicitly appropriated Calamus, the plant and the name, for the special use of men who love men and for his poems about such men. The narrator commands a group of "youths" to interchange this calamus love token "with each other!" He orders: "Let none render it back!"[55]

Whitman's narrator imagines himself heading a band of young men desirous of exchanging love tokens with other men and youths. In the poet's mind, at least, and probably in his life, men-loving men were already a collective reality. Whitman's knowing a group of like-loving, like-lusting men encouraged him to imagine himself their spokesman, and to create his man-love poems.[56]

Five years earlier, in the first *Leaves of Grass,* Whitman had referred to "sweet-flag" (the common name for the plant calamus).[57] Constructed in his first edition as phallic symbol, the poet's sexually charged sweet-flag reappeared in the 1860 edition, though *not,* significantly, in the new Calamus section. Whitman's segregation of his passionate Calamus poems and his phallic sweet-flag reference discouraged the interpretation of his Calamus love as at once passionate *and* phallic. Both references remain, however, scattered among his 1860 *Leaves,* indicating that his Calamus love was simultaneously passionate *and* sexual.

The narrator of the first Calamus poem explicitly rejects "all the standards hitherto published," the "pleasures, profits, conformities, / Which too long I was offering to feed my Soul." "Clear to me now," he affirms, "standards not yet published—clear to me that my Soul, / That the Soul of the man I speak for, feeds, rejoices only in comrades."[58] The values he rejects are implicitly those institutionalized by judges in law courts, by politicians in statutes, by ministers in church sermons. He rejects those ideals of sexuality, affection, and love that discourage, condemn, prohibit, and prosecute men's intense, erotically expressed intimacies with men. Going public in this poem with his new Calamus ideal, Whitman actually published a new standard "not yet published." Coming together with other like-feeling men, and writing for them, he was rapidly coming to terms.

"Resolved to sing no songs to-day but those of manly attachment," this narrator bequeaths to the world "types of athletic love." Whitman gave numbers of different names to what he called "athletic love," "robust love," and "manly love"—men's love for men.[59] Countering the Christian injunction not to name, naming became one of Whitman's most pressing tasks.

"Love" was the word by which Whitman most often named the Calamus feeling of man for man. His speaker gives his calamus-root "only to them that love, as I myself am capable of loving."[60] He proclaims "the flames of me, consuming, burning for his love whom I love!" dedicating his words to "love, for friendship, for you."[61] He memorializes Manhattan's "frequent and swift flash of offering me love."[62] He praises "the dear love of comrades."[63] He conjures "a youth who loves me, and whom I love"; he teaches "robust American love."[64] And, sometimes, he confesses, "I fill myself with rage, for fear I effuse unreturned love."[65]

In the hands of this master word worker, the sentimental, asexual love of the century's mainstream romance was radically remade. One poem demands men "with sweet and lusty flesh . . . choice and chary of its love-power."[66] His love included erotic desire—specifically, that of men for men, as well as that of men and women.

In a future love land, Whitman dreamed, "The most dauntless and rude shall touch face to face lightly."[67] Men kiss men passionately in numbers of Calamus poems: Two males, "by stealth," seek a wood, or the "back of a rock, in the open air," or a "high hill—first watching lest any person, for miles around, approach unawares." Only after a private place is found do these two commence a "long-dwelling kiss," a "new-husband's kiss"—a passionate kiss indeed.[68] Another poem memorializes the man on a pier who "passionately kissed" the friend he leaves behind.[69] Another looks forward to a future America in which "the departing brother or friend shall salute the remaining brother or friend with a kiss."[70] Here, Whitman audaciously transmutes a "salute," more often the sign of a military, masculine patriotism, into a kiss, a physical, passionate connection between males. A salute is also transmogrified in a poem in which a "Manhattanese . . . ever at parting, kisses me lightly on the lips with robust love, / And I, in the public room, or on the crossing of the street, or on the ship's deck, kiss him in return; / We observe that salute of American comrades, land and sea."[71] Whitman's kiss-salute is a cheeky metaphor.

Men holding men's hands is another physical connection repeatedly imagined in the Calamus poems. "He ahold of my hand has completely satisfied me," reports one narrator. The speaker of another is happiest, "he and another, wandering hand in hand, they twain, apart from other men."[72] An affectionate youth, loved by the narrator, approaches in another poem to "hold me by the hand."[73]

These hand-holding men sometimes signify self-sufficient couples, seemingly oblivious to others. But numbers of Calamus poems imagine and endorse a future, collective hand holding: "There shall be countless linked hands."[74] Another offers "you friendly boatmen and mechanics" a "leaf for hand in hand!" This ends with the "wish to infuse myself among you till I see it common for you to walk hand in hand."[75]

Men put their arms around men in many Calamus poems. In one, "spirits of friends" lovingly "embrace my arms or neck."[76] Another envisions America's cities united "with their arms about each other's necks."[77] Another presents a man "who oft as he sauntered the streets, curved with his arm the shoulder of his friend—while the arm of his friend rested upon him also."[78] Another pictures "we two boys together clinging"— and "dancing," and "loving." And in one of Whitman's deepest-felt man-love poems, the male narrator is happy because the man he loves most lies beside him at night, "and his arm lay lightly around my breast."[79]

Men sleep with men in several Calamus poems, an interaction that is sometimes physical and sensual. One narrator, longing for passing strangers, imagines a bygone, intimate merging: "I ate with you, and slept with you—your body has become not yours only, nor left my body mine only."[80]

Bodily contact—touching—becomes a deep source of shared joy in the same Calamus poem: "You give me the pleasure of your eyes, face, flesh, as we pass—and take of my beard, breast, hands in return."[81] Touching bodies are eroticized as the poet imagines his loving reader "thrusting me beneath your clothing, / Where I may feel the throbs of your heart, or rest upon your hip." Here, the poet asks his lover-reader to "carry me when you go forth over land or sea; / For thus, merely touching you, is enough—is best, / And thus, touching you, would I silently sleep and be carried eternally."[82]

Men eyeing men in the city streets was another sexually suggestive act hailed under the flag of Calamus. Whitman's poems point to several other locations where men can meet—like a workingmen's bar—and others where they can consummate erotic desire: at night on an empty beach, behind a rock in the open air.

And, as we have seen, a Calamus poem celebrating the rewards of the senses refers to a joyous "Calamus taste"—an ambiguous allusion hinting at oral satisfactions.[83] The Calamus poems are, quintessentially, about men's *physically enacted, erotic love* for men.

Whitman's Calamus poems portray a wide range of intimacies between men and various responses to such intimacies, from fear of losing oneself, to anger, envy, jealousy, and unrequited yearning, to joy, contentment, ecstatic bliss, and celebration. Whitman's poems look deep into the problems and promise of human intimacy. This poet-proselytizer of man-love launches no banal, positive images campaign.

The narrator's deep need for a man-friend is clear in his identification with a live oak growing alone and "lusty" in Louisiana, "Without any companion." A "curious token," he calls it, "it makes me think of manly love." But though that tree utters "joyous leaves all its life, without a friend, a lover near," he concludes, "I know very well I could not."[84] To create his own *Leaves,* Whitman's stand-in needs the presence, actual or imagined, of friends and lovers. That poem's joining of "manly love" approvingly with the "lusty" was, for its time, a daring union—"lusty" was not often employed then to designate a good sort of feeling, much less a good sort of carnal love between men.[85]

The live oak was another of the names and symbols that Whitman appropriated from the mainstream vocabulary to express the "manly love" of men for men. A twig from a live oak is among the tokens that one Calamus narrator gives "only to them that love, as I myself am capable of loving."[86] As noted, before settling on his Calamus symbol, Whitman had considered using the live oak as his main emblem of manly love.

Another confesses the narrator's intense, unspoken feelings for a friend: "As I walk by your side, or sit near, or remain in the same room with you," this narrator warns, "little you know the subtle electric fire that for your sake is playing within me."[87] Once again, Whitman's speaker gives voice in a poem to an emotion he cannot declare directly to a beloved.

Men "of earth-born passion" are demanded in one poem.[88] "Passion" is another of the words that Whitman appropriates to name men's intense, sensual feeling for men.

Intimacy eagerly anticipated is recounted by a narrator who awaits the arrival of "my dear friend, my lover." After that arrival, he hears the water and sand (nature) "whispering, to congratulate me, / For the one I love most lay sleeping by me under the same cover in the cool night, / In the stillness, in the autumn moonbeams, his face was inclined toward me, / And his arm lay lightly around my breast—And that night I was happy."[89] This may well be the nineteenth century's most eloquent public evocation of loving men bedding down together.

A quiet, satisfied intimacy is glimpsed in a workingmen's barroom, described by a narrator who tells "of a youth who loves me, and whom I love, silently approaching, and seating himself near, that he may hold me by the hand." Amid the "drinking and oath and smutty jest, / There we two, content, happy in being together, speaking little, perhaps not a word."[90]

Contented, peaceful intimacy is also pictured in another Calamus poem: "When he whom I love travels with me, or sits a long while holding me by the hand," relates the narrator, then he is "silent—I require nothing further. . . . He ahold of my hand has completely satisfied me."[91] Whitman's words paradoxicallly describe a simple act supplanting the need for words.

The difficulty of speaking freely and publicly of "manly attachment" and "types of athletic love" is stressed in several Calamus poems. Whitman made poems about his struggle to speak.

In one of these, an evangelist of comrade love threatens to drop his Calamus-leaf metaphor in order to speak directly: "Emblematic and capricious blades, I leave you—now you serve me not." His punning "blades" are at once his poems, the comrades who are their subject, and the comrades to whom they are addressed. He adds: "I will say what I have to say, by itself, / I will escape from the sham that was proposed to me, / I will sound myself and comrades only—I will never again utter a call, only their call." He "will give an example to lovers, to take permanent shape and will through The States."[92]

In another poem, the "bleeding drops" issuing from the narrator (the words issuing from the poet) are urged to flow freely:

> From my breast—from within where I was concealed—Press forth, red
>   drops—confession drops,
> Stain every page—stain every song I sing, every word I say, bloody drops,
> Let them know your scarlet heat—let them glisten,
> Saturate them with yourself, all ashamed and wet.[93]

The difficulty of speaking about such powerful, explosive, tabooed emotions is stressed by the narrator who addresses the earth, his likeness. He suspects

> there is something fierce in you, eligible to burst forth;
> For an athlete is enamoured of me—and I of him,
> But toward him there is something fierce and terrible in me, eligible to
>   burst forth,
> I dare not tell it in words—not even in these songs.[94]

The narrator's own words "expose me more than all my other poems," he warns in one of the last entries in the Calamus section.[95]

Several of Whitman's Calamus pieces speak exclusively to men who love men. Others, however, present men's love for men as a unifying force benefiting all denizens of his day's Disunited States. On the eve of the American Civil War, Whitman presented men's love for men as the glue that could keep the union intact. These explicitly political poems also envision a future society in which men's love for men is openly encouraged. Whitman publicly and audaciously linked the full, free development of men's erotically charged love for men with the fate of America.

Addressing "The States," the narrator of one such poem names a special, unifying Whitman friendship. He asks: "Were you looking to be held together by the lawyers? / By an agreement on a paper? Or by arms?" Instead, the poet offers "a new friendship—It shall be called after my name, / It shall circulate through The States, indifferent of place, / It shall twist and intertwist them through and around each other." "Affection," he adds, optimistically, "shall solve every one of the problems of freedom."

Another Calamus speaker rejects the "timid models of the rest, the majority," and offers specifically, the model of the man who always "kisses me lightly on the lips with robust love." The narrator offers the model of himself, one who publicly kisses his man-friend in return. He offers the model of these two "natural and nonchalant persons."[96]

Whitman here mobilizes democratic rhetoric to question the ideals and values of the "majority," thereby implicitly affirming the models of a men-friends minority. He places men-loving-men within the democratic republic.

For Whitman and many others of his day, America was exemplary in its embrace of democratic ideals, a practical model for the world. (The eventual freedom of African-Americans and civil equality of women was assumed by the progressive Whitman, though he was certainly vague and complacent about the means of liberation and the timing.) Whitman daringly extended American ideals to include a democracy of "manly affection" expressed in kisses.

Another of his narrators promises to establish in every American state the "institution of the dear love of comrades."[97] Comrade-love, Whitman here innovatively proposed, constituted an "institution," a socially structured organization of men and emotions, relationships and acts. Not until a hundred years had passed would Kate Millett and other U.S. feminists discuss personal relationships as ordered within a power-stratified social institution.[98]

Another narrator presents himself as a secular preacher, promising "to teach robust American love," for he knows "that I and robust love belong among you."[99] Men's intense love for men is *not* foreign to Americans, Whitman asserted, countering the stereotype of sodomite as alien. Whitman imagined himself a teacher, a propagandizing prophet of a vigorous new American sex-love.

Considering his own, unique contribution to America, Whitman concluded: "Only these carols, vibrating through the air, I leave, / For comrades and lovers"—all comrades and lovers.[100] Whitman envisioned an affectionate-erotic utopia, celebrating in advance great changes in the social organization of intimacy and sexuality.

"I dreamed in a dream," reports another speaker, that

> I saw a city invincible to the attacks of the whole of the rest of the earth,
> I dreamed that was the new City of Friends,
> Nothing was greater there than the quality of robust love—it led the rest,
> It was seen every hour in the actions of the men of that city,
> And in all their looks and words.[101]

"I believe the main purport of These States," declares another crusading narrator, "is to found a superb friendship, exalté, previously unknown, / Because I perceive it waits, and has been always waiting, latent in all men."[102]

Whitman's latency theory suggested that all men experience a deep, sometimes erotic love for men. All men could, therefore, express this love in a variety of ways. The idea anticipated Sigmund Freud's theory of a universal bisexuality, though Whitman did not talk about a love of women for women, which would logically be included within the bisexual. Encouraging this dormant affection—making the latent blatant—was the patriotic contribution Whitman imagined he made to his nation.

⁓

The narrator of the first Calamus poem ends by precisely dating his vow to write, publish, and proselytize for comrade-love: "Afternoon, this delicious Ninth Month, in my forty-first year, / I proceed, for all who are, or have been, young men, / To tell the secret of my nights and days, / To celebrate the need of comrades."

Whitman might have actually written this poem earlier than the specified date, but his time specifying established his narrator's resolve to celebrate men's need for men as a memorable moment in American history. Specifying that date also linked the narrator's biography with Whitman's. For the poet had turned forty on May 31, 1859, and in September was living through his forty-first year; that fall he was indeed preparing his new *Leaves* for publication. Whitman's narrator thus coincides in age exactly with the author.[103]

The last Calamus poem mirrors the first in specifying the year in which its narrator is speaking and the age of its author, "Walt Whitman."[104] "Full of life, sweet-blooded, compact, visible, / I, forty years old the Eighty-third Year of The States," Whitman wrote, "To one a century hence, or any number of centuries hence, / To you, yet unborn, these, seeking you." Whitman was forty in 1859, the eighty-third year after the American Revolution—so the age of the book's narrator and that of its author again coincide.

Whitman's specifying of dates in his first and last Calamus poems stressed the author's identification with his narrator; it proclaimed Whitman's desire to mark his dedication to "the dear love of comrades."[105] The original, singular character of that commitment, and its expression in poetry, was clear to its author, as it is now in retrospect to many readers.

In addition to the artistic achievement of the 1860 *Leaves of Grass,* it is one of an extraordinary decade's amazing man-love manifestos. It is the plain-speaking, poetic, American equivalent of the twelve prose pamphlets published in Germany between 1864 and 1879 by the lawyer and classicist Karl Heinrich Ulrichs and the open letter to the Prussian minister of justice, issued in 1869, by the journalist Karoly Maria (Kertbeny) Benkert.[106]

Ulrichs's pamphlets called for the decriminalization of "unnatural vice" between men (acts between women were not criminal). He defended those persons he termed "Urnings" (biological men born, he said, with a female soul) and "Uraniads" (biological women born, he said, with a male soul). Such persons should not be persecuted for desires which, he alleged, were inborn, and for which they were not responsible. Kertbeny's letter called on the officer of the state to oppose the adoption throughout a unified Germany of a new law against "unnatural fornication by two persons of the male sex or by people with animals."[107]

Employing the medium of poetry, Whitman's *Leaves of Grass* also spoke publicly, in its own, unique, powerful voice, for the sexual-spiritual love of men for men and, by extension, for all "comrades and lovers." As Whitman's correspondent Fred Vaughan found out, however, the poet-advocate of manly love had an independent streak that made him, in practice, a difficult catch.

In Boston, in March 1860, forty-one-year-old Walt Whitman was preparing his third revision of *Leaves of Grass* for the press; at the same time, he was receiving distraught letters from a disappointed pursuer, twenty-three-year-old Fred Vaughan.[1] The proof sheets that Whitman had earlier promised to send Vaughan, and that he failed to send, contained, ironically, two new poems warning pursuers that "Walt Whitman" was an ornery cuss, not the affable, available fellow he appeared.

"Whoever you are holding me now in hand," the poet's speaker cautioned, "I am not what you supposed, but far different." He who signed himself "a candidate for my affections" would "have to give up all else—I alone would expect to be your God, sole and exclusive." Whitman's narrator promised his pursuer no equivalent, "exclusive" worship in return, no restriction of his own roving eye.[2]

The narrator's warning signaled no final rejection, however. His message was definitely mixed. If the pursuer persisted and insisted, Whitman's seductive alter ego was willing to cooperate: "just possibly with you on a high hill—first watching lest any person, for miles around, approach unawares . . . / Here to put your lips upon mine I permit you, / With the comrade's long-dwelling kiss, or the new husband's kiss, / For I am the new husband, and I am the comrade."[3]

Though that new husband's kiss promised ardor, no mere peck on the cheek, that fervor was apparently momentary, for the narrator again cautioned his pursuer: "I will certainly elude you, / Even while you should think you had unquestionably caught me, behold! / Already you see I have escaped from you." Being caught or escaping, it seems, were the only two alternate responses to an avid pursuer's proffered love. Only a few "candidates for my love" will prove victorious, this difficult narrator added, finally urging his pursuer to "release me, and depart on your way."[4]

In another poem, the "new person drawn toward me" was urged to "take warning," for "I am probably different from what you suppose." Stressing his unreliability, this narrator asked, rather belligerently:

> Do you suppose you will find in me your ideal?
> Do you think it so easy to have me become your lover?
> Do you think the friendship of me would be unalloyed satisfaction?
> Do you suppose I am trusty and faithful?
> Do you see no further than this facade—this smooth and tolerant manner
>   of me?

> Do you suppose yourself advancing on real ground toward a real heroic
> man?

His loving image may be an "illusion," he warns, and "the next step may precipitate you!"

The narrator cautions that the present pursuer was not the first: "O let some past deceived one hiss in your ears, how many have prest on the same as you are pressing now, / How many have fondly supposed what you are supposing now—only to be disappointed."[5] However unreliable this narrator, this particular warning of his sounds quite reliable indeed.

These lines reveal that the "Walt Whitman" who narrated the 1860 *Leaves of Grass* viewed his own ardent pursuers as threatening to attach themselves and to adhere like leeches. Intimacy, in his view, was a kind of banding, clinging, or tying—a merging in which the narrator lost his valued independence, even his sense of a separate self. Fear of such oppressive bonding was one of the many different responses to men's intimacy with men pictured in Whitman's 1860 *Leaves*. But, by the time Fred Vaughan had a chance to read these particular Whitman poems, it was too late for him to heed their warning. He had already fallen for the poet.

Vaughan's letters several times refer nostalgically to living with Whitman, or near him, on Classon Avenue, in Brooklyn. This places Vaughan's earlier relationship with Whitman sometime between May 1856 and May 1859 when the poet, in his late thirties, lived with his family on that avenue. Vaughan's comments suggest that he either boarded with Whitman and his family, or he lived nearby.

During the years that Whitman was living on Classon Avenue he was writing some of his most heartfelt poems on the joys and tensions of man's "manly love" for man. This was an erotic love that, as we have seen, included a full range of satisfactions and discontents. It is possible that a romantic and sexual relationship with Vaughan, then between nineteen and twenty-two years old, inspired some of Whitman's Calamus poems, though there is no direct evidence of this, either in Vaughan's correspondence or elsewhere. But twelve of the poems included in Whitman's 1860 Calamus section had been arranged in their original manuscript version to tell the tale of the narrator's love for a man who soon contented himself elsewhere. That story could have mirrored Whitman's relationship with Vaughan a few years earlier.[6] Had Vaughan earlier rejected Whitman, and was he now profoundly regretting it? Had Whitman earlier pursued Vaughan, only to renounce the intimacy when Vaughan contented himself with another? Or had Vaughan pursued Whitman from the start, as he was doing in 1860? We do not know.[7]

In his first extant letter to Whitman, Vaughan wrote from New York City on March 19, 1860, reporting that he had tried, unsuccessfully, to see the poet before Whitman's departure for Boston. Vaughan said he had dropped in, two nights in a row, at Pfaff's, the basement tavern on the corner of Bleecker and Broadway, where Whitman was often found with other writers, artists, and actors. Vaughan's "sorry I could not see you" reproached Whitman for leaving town without a good-bye. In this relationship, at this time, Whitman was the ambivalent pursued, Vaughan the avid pursuer.

Despite Whitman's waning interest, Vaughan's attention to the poet and his work seems to have flattered the writer, and he did answer Vaughan's first note with a letter. (This is now lost or destroyed, like all of Whitman's letters to Vaughan, which may suggest that they contained something the poet wanted to hide. Whitman kept copies of many of the letters he wrote, and it is unusual for a whole set of correspondence to be missing.) Vaughan, in his response to Whitman on March 21, hopes that the poet "will continue to write often"—anticipating, it seems, the opposite. He was already feeling the chill in Whitman's response.

The "folks up town," said Vaughan, will be glad to hear that Whitman's new publication is proceeding well; he referred several times to his and Whitman's mutual acquaintances. Vaughan also offered introductions to a couple of his own friends in Boston. If Whitman wanted to meet any of that city's stagecoach drivers, Vaughan explained where to go and whom to ask for. He told Whitman: "introduce yourself as my friend." *Friend* was one of his most freighted words. Vaughan was still trying to claim—or reclaim—Whitman as his intimate.

Vaughan, a bachelor, was then sharing rooms with a Robert and "Mrs. Cooper," probably Robert's mother. "Robert is drinking tea," Vaughan reported in one letter, and, "as usual," Mrs. Cooper was "ready to wait upon Bob even before he needs it."

Whitman had evidently joked in an earlier letter about proposing to Mrs. Cooper—possibly because her attentive care of Robert suggested that she would take good care of him. Vaughan had relayed Whitman's proposition to the lady, and he now reported: "Mrs. Cooper says if you will make love to her you had better do so personally next time you call, as she cannot put much faith in a profession made in a letter to an outside party."[8] "To make love to" then meant "to court," not "to have sex with," as it came to mean in the eroticized twentieth century.

In a long recent walk in Central Park, Vaughan and Robert had talked "much of you," Vaughan told Whitman. Anticipating future walks with Whitman, Vaughan and Robert had taken other "long, long strolls together in Central Park this summer." This March reference to the past summer suggests that Vaughan had not seen Whitman for six months or more.

Central Park made Vaughan think of Boston's famous green, and he ended with a query: "By the way, what do you think of the common?" Was there sexual innuendo in Vaughan's question? Were Central Park (opened a year earlier) and Boston Common already cruising areas for men interested in sex with men? No evidence is now available.

Whitman replied again, and Vaughan answered on March 27 that he was glad the poet liked Boston, though that city was "a little too straight-laced for such free thinkers as you and I are." Vaughan's criticism of Boston affirmed his own unlaced morals. He obviously prided himself on his and Whitman's relaxed values, which might have licensed men's sexual connections with men.

"You tell me," said Vaughan, that Ralph Waldo Emerson "came to see you and was very kind." Whitman had told Vaughan in a private letter about his now-famous encounter on Boston Common, on March 17, with the influential Emerson. This was the meeting during which, as Whitman later reported, Emerson spent two hours trying every conceivable argument to get the poet to cut or tone down his most explicit, provocative "Children of Adam" poems—his poems of sexual love between men and women.[9]

Whitman's new Calamus poems may also have been discussed by Emerson, though Whitman never mentioned this. The sensitive Emerson may have been one of those rare early readers who, like Rufus Griswold, saw sex in Whitman's man-love odes. Just a few days after Emerson's 1860 meeting with Whitman, *men's intimacies with men were definitely on Emerson's mind,* as a comment by Fred Vaughan to Whitman indicates. Emerson had lectured in New York City on March 23 and Vaughan had been there, listening carefully to the talk, Vaughan wrote to Whitman in this letter of March 27.[10] Though the critical Vaughan was "very much pleased with the *matter,* I did not at all like [Emerson's] delivery. It appeared to me to be strained." Vaughan added: "But Walt, when I looked upon the man, & thought that it was but a very few days before that he had been so kind and attentive to you . . . my heart warmed towards him very much. I think he has *that* in him which makes men capable of strong friendships."

Whatever *that* was, which motivated men's "strong friendships," Vaughan rightly intuited Emerson's deep feelings about the intimacies of men with men. As a Harvard University student, forty years earlier, the New Englander had become obsessed with a fellow student, Martin Gay,

"The men's cottage" (toilet), Central Park, 1860 (note man in doorway).
Stereopticon card courtesy Herbert Mitchell; photograph by Dwight
Primiano. ❧

and the two had exchanged long, profound stares, with Emerson playing cat in his unsuccessful pursuit of mouse Gay.[11]

In March 1860, with Vaughan listening intently, Emerson had actually touched in his talk on the theme of intense male intimacies, declaring (reported Vaughan) "that a man whose heart was filled with a warm, ever enduring *not to be shaken by anything* Friendship was one to be set on one side apart from other men, and almost to be worshiped as a saint." The emphasis on "*not to be shaken by anything*" may be read as Vaughan commenting, ironically and pointedly, on Whitman's faltering interest in him.

Emerson's words, said Vaughan, applied specifically to men like himself and Whitman: "There Walt, how do you like that? What do you think of them setting you & myself, and one or two others we know up in some public place, with an immense placard on our breast, reading *Sincere Friends*!!!"[12] Vaughan added: "Good doctrine that," but "I think the theory preferable to the practice." This sounds to me like yet another dig at the gulf between Whitman's warm poetic celebration of men's intense friendships with men and his then cool practice of friendship with Vaughan.

Vaughan's "*Sincere Friends*!!!" referred to an especially genuine and deep intimacy. Sincerity of feeling was an oft reiterated value in nineteenth-century America, one that Vaughan turned here against Whitman's faltering affection.

Vaughan's reference to "one or two others that we know" is extremely important—it indicates that he and Whitman were in contact with a small group of other sincere men friends—a network of such friends was already in place. In Vaughan's mind, this group already went by a collective name, "*Sincere Friends*"—a self-defined group identity was in the making—or made. Whitman was writing specifically for such "comrades and lovers" in his 1860 Calamus poems, as we have seen, and his sense of appreciative readers must have encouraged those poems' creation.

Whitman had earlier offered to send Vaughan the first proof sheets of the newly revised *Leaves of Grass*, but he had not done so, and Vaughan now hoped that Whitman would not forget his promise. Vaughan wanted the proofs to prove to him Whitman's continuing regard. If he did eventually read Whitman's newest *Leaves of Grass*, Vaughan may have discerned a bitter irony: The proofs he pleads for warned pursuers that "Walt Whitman" was difficult to have and hold. Whitman's failure to provide the proof sheets showed the poet to be actively distancing himself from his demanding, aggressively dependent friend.

Sensing Whitman's cooling interest, Vaughan's letter of April 9 was even more demanding: "How is this, Walt? I have written to you twice since I heard from you. Why won't you answer? How about them proof sheets?"

On April 30, anticipating the poet's return to New York, the insistent Vaughan commanded Whitman to be "sure and make it your business to call and see me. Do not neglect it please Walt, for I want to see you very much."

In a letter of May 7, Vaughan was again angry: "What the devil is the matter? Nothing serious I hope.—It seems mighty queer that I cannot succeed in having one word from you.— I swear I would have thought you would be the last man in this world to neglect me.—But I am afraid." Whitman had once evidently declared his undying affection, or so Vaughan recalled.

Vaughan concluded with a plaintive cry: "Lizzie is married! Johnny is dead! Walt has forgotten." It is easy to imagine that Whitman found Vaughan's pathetic pleading intolerable.

Vaughan's intense need for Whitman meant that he could not stay angry for long. His next letter, on May 21, was at once flattering and insistent: "Walt, I hope you will be home soon. I want to see you very much indeed. I have never thought more frequently about you than during the time you have been in Boston. Make it your business to call and see me as soon as you arrive in New York, and we can make an appointment to pass some hours together. As I have much, very much to talk to you about." It seems unlikely that Whitman contacted Vaughan when he returned to New York.

The next extant note from Vaughan to the poet is dated exactly two years later, May 1862. In this brief memo Vaughan abruptly announced: "I am to be married tomorrow." He listed the address of the church, and declared, "I shall have no show!"—"I have invited no company." This was followed by the underlined command: "*I want you to be there*"—at once imperious and pleading. He then added, pitifully: "Do not fail please, as I am very anxious you should come."

Six years later, in May 1870, when Whitman was trying to restrain his own overwrought feelings for Peter Doyle, he wrote in a notebook: "Depress the adhesive nature / It is in excess—making life a torment . . . Remember Fred Vaughan."[13] Whitman was thinking either of Vaughan's romantic obsession with him, or his own earlier obsession with Vaughan.

Vaughan probably had not seen Whitman for twelve years when he wrote to him on August 11, 1874, attempting to reopen communication. He enclosed "one of the very many letters I write to you"—letters he admitted he did not send. For, as Vaughan revealed, "I have written to you at least once a week for the past four years . . . and I often keep them months before I destroy them." Vaughan had written Whitman more than 200 unsent letters!

Though unmailed, the letters, Vaughan affirmed, "are all real to me." His many letters clearly kept alive for Vaughan his past intimacy with Whitman, a relationship he still clung to stubbornly, despite Whitman's rejection.

In this 1874 letter, Vaughan recalled Whitman's "*presence*" years earlier, when they had ridden together on a Broadway stagecoach or lounged together on the deck of a ferry from Manhattan to Brooklyn. Was Whitman's famous "Crossing Brooklyn Ferry" inspired by a trip with Vaughan?

Vaughan asked Whitman to acknowledge his note, but was prepared for no response: "If you cannot, I shall still keep writing in my own way." He was still demanding *and* pathetic.

With this letter Vaughan enclosed a prose mood piece that mentioned his loafing on a pier, watching a sailor on a nearby ship, and hearing "the laugh and wrangle of the boys in swimming"—all of which bring back the "remembrance of thee dear Walt." And all of which may provide clues to Vaughan's and Whitman's interest in sailors, swimming boys (naked, no doubt), and piers (famous as sites of illicit assignations).[14]

Then Vaughan's mood changed. He complained: "Walt my life has turned out a poor miserable failure." He had no identity of his own: "I am not a drunkard nor a teetotaler—I am neither honest or dishonest"—neither one thing nor another. He had never "robbed, cheated, nor defrauded . . . and yet I feel that I have not been honest to myself—my family nor my friends."

Vaughan perceived himself as possessing a "self" to which he had been untrue. But what sort of self? He did not specify. However, Vaughan's reference to "Sincere Friends," and his long, unyielding romantic attachment to Whitman suggest that his sense of self may have centered on that feeling. But, did Vaughan's particular feeling for Whitman extend to other men? And, if so, was Vaughan conscious of his feeling extending to men in general? His letters raise many questions. If his feelings did extend to other men, did he understand that attraction as founding his sense of self? Did he see himself as a man-loving man? And was that the self to which he felt untrue? If so, Vaughan was an early example of a self-identified man-loving man. If his feeling and identity did focus primarily on men, he differed significantly from many other men of his century. Many, possibly most, could then fall in love with a man and even have sexual encounters with a man without developing a sense of self centered on those desires and acts.

At the end of 1874, on November 16, Vaughan wrote again to Whitman, still reminiscing. Years before, Vaughan said, his "father used to tell me I was lazy" and his mother had "denied it." Vaughan, in turn, had told Whitman's mother that "you was lazy and she denied it." But although Whitman had asserted himself, noted Vaughan, "I have confirmed my Father." Vaughan referred to his lack of economic success, to his excessive drinking, and, seemingly, to other troubles.

"O, Walt, what recollections will crowd upon us," said Vaughan, listing some of his own: "Marriage . . . Babies—trouble. *Rum,* more trouble—more *Rum*—estrangement from you. More *Rum.*—Good intentions, sobriety. Misunderstanding and more *Rum.* . . . The innate manly nature of myself at times getting the best of it and at other times entirely submerged." He did not specify the troubling "it" with which his "innate manly nature" was at war. Did "it" refer simply to a dependence on rum? Or, did "it" refer to an *unmanly sexual nature* with which his "manly nature" warred?

Vaughan now found himself "possessed of a wife and four boys" and "no money, no friends." Lack of friends was an especially poignant deficiency, given Vaughan's earlier encomium to sincere friends. He and his family were living once again near Classon Avenue, in Brooklyn, and Vaughan had "been down past our old home several times this summer," taking his son, Freddie, on this journey of remembrance.

Vaughan confessed, "There is never a day passes but what I think of you." He added: "My love my Walt—is with you always." He ended with a request: "Walt—please do not criticize my grammar, nor phraseology—it was written too heartfelt to alter."

෯

At different times in Vaughan's life he worked as a sailor, a stagecoach driver, an elevator operator, a clerk for an express company, and a conductor on a freight train. His letters to Whitman have the slightly formal quality of a self-taught writer, a formality contrasting oddly with the intimate relationship they assume. Vaughan's letters, carefully preserved first by Whitman, then by Whitman's ardent archivists, are rare records of one nineteenth-century American working man's deep feeling for another male.

Vaughan's vocabulary suggests that he was a reader, and his manner of expression was clearly influenced by his poet-friend. Though his spelling and grammar were erratic, his letters show him to have been intelligent, sensitive, and extremely needy.

Whitman's notebooks indicate that his contact with Vaughan continued, sporadically, until the end of the poet's life. In 1876 Vaughan called on Whitman at least twice. In May 1890, two years before Whitman's death, he again recorded a visit from Vaughan.[15]

What kind of intimacy was this? Vaughan's letters of 1860 assume an earlier, special intimacy with Whitman, though the poet's feeling for Vaughan appears to have cooled. These letters display Vaughan's strong and continuing romantic attachment to—even fixation on—Whitman. Whether or not theirs was ever an overtly sexual relationship, Vaughan's letters do express his deeply felt, passionate devotion.

Whitman's own, earlier feeling for Vaughan may have inspired some of his most deeply felt man-love poems. But, in 1860, this is the relationship of an ardent, pitiful pursuer and a mostly indifferent pursued. For Vaughan, his past intimacy with Whitman and his continuing, unshakeable attachment probably constituted the most intense, meaningful love of his life. For many other men, the U.S. Civil War provided a special incitement to intense intimacy, encouraging their closest relationships with men.

Affectionate Union soldiers, 1860s. Daguerreotype courtesy Herbert Mitchell; photograph by Dwight Primiano.

Specifically *sexual* relationships between men are documented during the Civil War era thanks to the United States Navy. On April 21, 1865, William Anderson, a sailor, and Henry Smith, a petty officer on the USS *Shamrock,* docked in North Carolina, were charged with "holding improper indecent intercourse."[1]

The *Shamrock* was evidently a busy place, for two days later, on April 23, John C. Smith and Louis Jerut of the same ship were charged with "improper and indecent intercourse with each other." A witness to this act, Daniel Nevels, testified that he saw Smith do to Jerut something "indecent, immoral and a violation of nature." When Smith was tried, he pleaded guilty, while Jerut, according to navy records, "endeavored to extricate himself of the imputation but only gave conclusive evidence of his guilt."

In another case recorded by the navy, on October 30, 1865, after the war's end, Captain George M. Danson, of the ship *Muscoota,* docked at Key West, Florida, sent seaman Henry Williams and ordinary seaman William Stewart to trial for "an unnatural crime" (unspecified).

The terms "unnatural crime," "indecent intercourse," and "violation of nature" inhabited a vague, threatening region of the age's consciousness, haunting, in particular, men who desired sex with men. How often the Civil War era provided opportunities for sexual contacts between men awaits further research. For now, the fragments of evidence are suggestive, our questions many.

Between 1861 and 1865, during the American Civil War, thousands of young men left behind the regulating gaze of families and local communities. They joined others in a mobilization that fostered new kinds of intimacy between and among men, challenging their established values. In particular, the Civil War's mobilizations and extremely bloody battles encouraged a suspension of traditional sexual morality and, evidence suggests, inspired various connections between men. Many men experienced this war as horrifyingly destructive of human life and as conducive to sometimes affectionate, sometimes carnal intimacies with other men.[2] Sometimes these intimacies were affectionate *and* carnal.

༄

John King, a Confederate soldier held as a Union prisoner, recalled prison balls at which a number of men "would be selected to represent ladies," and these, "to distinguish them from the men, would run strings through the center of their blankets and tie these around the waist."[3] King's text, published in 1904, implies that such balls were completely devoid of illicit, sexual innuendo. But, why, then, were such dances stopped in American prisons by the mid-twentieth century? Were prison dances free of eros in the nineteenth century and full of eros in the twentieth? It is possible, and it is also possible that nineteenth-century Americans were simply unconscious of the eros hovering over prison dances.

Another all-male ball is described in a letter that Union soldier John J. Willey, of the First Massachusetts Infantry Regiment, quartered in Brandy Station, Virginia, wrote to his wife on March 20, 1864.[4] The "privates of our brigade had a ball Thursday night," Willey reported, adding that "sixty young fellow[s] got women[']s closes [clothes] and dressed up and some of the real women went but the boys girls was so much better looking they left." The boy-girls, Willey suggested casually to his wife, were more attractive to men than were actual women.

The ball was a "splendid afair," added Willey, and "everything passed of[f] the same as if they had been real ladies." He was sorry not to have attended. He had "supposed it would be a rough old time but it was [a] very quiet afair and no one could hav told wich of the party had fell on a *hatchet*" (which, that is, were women with a "gash," and which were men passing as women). Willey's use of "fell on a hatchet" indicates that the century's genteel vocabulary coexisted with a popular, male-defined language of female body parts.[5]

But Willey's letter says more. At the ball, he heard, "a Major fell in love with a boy [who] belongs to Comp D. of our Regiment who was the bell[e] of the evening." This boy-belle was a "young fellow and fair and no one could hav told him from a hansome girle." The "Major was introduced to him as a girle from Culpeper and was realy smitten after *her* or him all the evening." But when the entranced major pursued this girl to a drawing room, Willey reported, the cross-dresser pulled up his dress, showed his parts, and "asked the Major how he liked the looks." The major's response was not mentioned. Willey thought it "must hav ben fun," and ended by telling his wife to "kiss the little darlings for me" (their babies), sending love from "your affectionate husband." How Willey's wife responded to his mixture of sexual reportage and romantic sentiment is not known.

Mistaken sex and misplaced amour was the surface subject of this story about a major, circulated as a funny tale among the men of Willey's unit and retold for the entertainment of a soldier's wife. But just below this story's surface lurked another story in which a man "fell in love with a boy," amorously pursuing this "young," "fair," and "hansome" male. A man's falling in love with a boy and pursuing him romantically was certainly imaginable to these Union troops. In this case, the age difference between man and boy was marked as male and female, masculine and feminine, and this sex and gender difference was eroticized.

Willey's reference to cross-dressed boy-girls suggests a romantic transgression as well as a gender infraction, so it is relevant to note that "boy-girl" is recorded in mid-twentieth-century America as prison slang for the sex partner of a man. "Girl-boy" was used in the nineteenth century and earlier to refer to effeminate males and, specifically, effeminate males interested in sex with men.[6]

Just a few weeks later, on April 3, 1864, from a military camp near the same busy Brandy Station, Virginia, another Union soldier, Oscar Cram, of the Eleventh Massachusetts Infantry, wrote to a correspondent named "Ellen," telling her of "another Ball in our hall this week," and that he had "had a very good time." He added: "For ladies we had boys in ladies clothes & some of them looked almost good enough to *lay* with & I guess some of them did get layed with. I know I slept with mine." He bets that Ellen could not have distinguished the little drummer boys "from girls if you did not know them."[7]

Did Cram's letter mean in 1864 what it seems to mean more than a hundred years later? Is it really possible that Cram so openly and enthusiastically wrote to a woman friend, relative, or lover about his own sexual encounter with a little drummer boy dressed as a girl? Did Cram and Ellen honor an antigenteel ethic in which a man's casual sexual encounter with a boy dressed in woman's clothes was just that—casual—not an event signifying any extreme moral lapse? Could it be that Cram's behavior just did not signify, specifically, sexual intercourse?

"To lie with" was well known in nineteenth-century America as a Biblical term for sexual intercourse. "To sleep with" then sometimes meant "to be sexually intimate with."[8] So Cram's "good enough to *lay* with," and his "slept with," certainly suggest an erotic act, not just a sleeping arrangement.

But was it possible that Cram's and other soldiers' reported lying with cross-dressed boys implied an erotic, genital encounter, but *not* that most tabooed act of all, sodomy? Perhaps. The era's focus on sodomy, defined narrowly as anal intercourse and bestiality, left oral-genital contacts, mutual masturbation, and other varieties of "lying with" outside the realm of the banned. The fragmentary evidence is tantalizing.

&

Male prostitutes and the men buying their services were characters in a drama that became prominent in the nineteenth century's last decades. But on May 13, 1862, the *Richmond Daily Dispatch,* in the Confederate capital, reported a large increase in "prostitutes of both sexes." The Virginia paper denounced those "cyprians" (prostitutes) who had gathered in the city, as well as loose males of the most abandoned character [who] have been disporting themselves extensively on the sidewalks and in hacks, open carriages, &c. . . . , to the amazement of sober-sided citizens compelled to smell the odors which they exude, and witness the impudence and familiar vulgarity of many of the shame faced of the prostitutes of both sexes. [These indulge in] smirks and smiles, winks, and . . . remarks not of a choice kind, in a loud voice.

Responding to many complaints, the major, determining "to enforce the vagrant law," had arrested "one lewd character," a female, and the paper hoped that she would not be the last.[9]

Until the end of the nineteenth century in the United States, the term "male prostitute" usually referred to men who bought sex from women, pimped for women, or who seduced and extorted money from women.[10] So, does this reference to "prostitutes of both sexes" refer to men who sold their sexual services to men, or simply to men associated with female prostitutes? Future research may tell.

ॐ

James J. Archer, a Confederate general captured at Gettysburg, was held prisoner at Johnson's Island, in Lake Erie, Ohio, in the winter of 1863–64, when the temperature plunged to well below zero. But Archer evidently found ways to keep warm. The diary of a North Carolina captain, Robert Bingham, another Confederate prisoner, notes: "We had a jolly party in our room tonight. Captain Taylor got some whiskey in a box under other things and so not noticed." Bingham added: "We had General Archer down and they all got drunk together and got to hugging each other and saying that they had slept together many a time." Captain Taylor "hugged" General Archer, and "cursed at every word," much to an old chaplain's discomfort.[11] Exactly what this hugging and sleeping together signified is not clear, but Captain Bingham, presenting himself as a non-participant, found it "jolly."

ॐ

In 1865, George McClaughtery, a Confederate private in Captain Thomas A. Bryan's company of the Virginia Artillery, reported to his sister: "The boys . . . rode one of our company on a rail last night for leaving the company and going to sleep with Captain [William M.] Lowry's black man."[12]

Why would a Southern, white soldier have left his company to go and "sleep with" his captain's black servant? There could have been many reasons. But tying a soldier to a rail, carrying him off, and publicly humiliating him may suggest a greater transgression than leaving one's quarters, socializing—even across race and class lines—and breaking military rules. Does the phrase "to sleep with" suggest a sexual act? Would a Confederate soldier's "leaving the company" and bedding down with the captain's black servant, by themselves, call for such strong retribution? If McClaughtery's letter to his sister did refer, even indirectly, to sex between men, and, specifically, to interracial sex, we need to radically revise our idea of what was casual, permissible speech in nineteenth-century America.

∽

The sleeping arrangements of Civil War military life made it easy for men interested in sex with men to realize their desires. "The cavalryman," recalled a former Union cavalryman, John McElroy, in a memoir published in 1879, "always sleeps with a chum."[13] "Chum," a nineteenth-century word for a close companion, sometimes served double-duty—in sailor slang, for example—as a term for a sexual partner.[14]

Two cavalry chums, McElroy explained, constructed their shared bed by gathering

> enough small tufts of pine or cedar to make a comfortable, springy, mattress-like foundation. On this is laid the poncho or rubber blanket. Next comes one of their overcoats, and upon this they lie, covering themselves with the two blankets and the other overcoat, their feet towards the fire, their boots at the foot, and their belts, with revolver, saber and carbine, at the sides of the bed. It is surprising what an amount of comfort a man can get out of such a couch.[15]

Deep romantic friendships between military men—ongoing, emotionally committed relationships—are documented in a number of nineteenth-century sources. McElroy, describing his fifteen months' captivity in Confederate prisons, detailed several such love affairs between men that may or may not have included carnal activity—McElroy's 1879 memoir, published in Toledo, Ohio, is, typically for its time, silent about sexuality, even deaf to the possibility of eros between men. In McElroy's time, sex was usually consigned to a nighttime procreative order, outside the daytime world.

In the hospital of Andersonville prison, McElroy related, "I saw an admirable illustration of the affection which a sailor will lavish on a ship's boy, whom he takes a fancy to, and makes his 'chicken,' as the phrase is." McElroy was either feigning lack of knowledge, or had not heard that "chicken" was nineteenth-century American sailor slang for the younger party in a specifically sexual relationship between seafarers.[16]

McElroy explained that, when the Union sloop *Water Witch* was captured after a battle and her crew brought to the prison, one of "her boys—a bright, handsome little fellow of about fifteen—had lost one of his arms in the fight." Taken to the prison hospital, "the old fellow whose 'chicken' he was, was allowed to accompany and nurse him."

"This 'old barnacleback,'" McElroy added,

> was as surly a growler as ever went aloft, but to his "chicken" he was as tender and thoughtful as a woman. They found a shady nook in one corner, and any moment one looked in that direction he could see the old tar hard at work at something for the comfort and pleasure of his pet. Now he was dressing the wound as deftly and gently as a mother caring for a new-born babe; now he was trying to concoct some relish out of the slender materials he could beg or steal from the Quartermaster; now trying to arrange the shade of the bed of pine leaves in a more comfortable manner; now repairing or washing his [boy's] clothes. . . . This "chicken" had a wonderful supply of clothes, the handiwork of his protector who, like most good sailors, was very skillful with the needle. He had suits of fine white duck, embroidered with blue in a way that would ravish the heart of a fine lady, and blue suits similarly embroidered with white. No belle ever kept her clothes in better order than these were. When the duck came up from the old sailor's patient washing it was as spotless as new-fallen snow.[17]

McElroy wrote as if the sexual potential of this protector-chicken relationship never entered his or his readers' minds. That was only possible in a society not preoccupied with sexuality, a society that had relegated eros to some other, obscure place.

McElroy himself waxed eloquent about another youthful prisoner in Andersonville, "a bright, blue-eyed, fair-haired little drummer boy, as handsome as a girl." As "well-bred as a lady," this particular drummer was called Red Cap because of his "jaunty, gold-laced, crimson cap."

"Ordinarily," reported McElroy, "the smaller a drummer boy is the harder he is, but no amount of attrition [association] with rough men could coarsen the ingrained refinement" of this youth of thirteen or fourteen. Red Cap was the "most popular person in the prison," said McElroy, assuming that all the boy's "old admirers share my great interest" in his postprison fate.[18] Most striking to modern eyes is McElroy's lack of fear that readers might spot sexual innuendo in his text.

McElroy also related the romantic tale of John Emerson and John Stiggal of his company, "two Norwegian boys, and fine specimens of their race—intelligent, faithful, and always ready for duty." Their affection for each other "reminded one of the stories told of the sworn attach-

Sailor and chicken. McElroy, *Andersonville,* 361. ❧

ment and the unfailing devotion that were common between two Goth warrior youths."

Arriving at the already-overfull Andersonville prison, John Emerson and John Stiggal had "established their quarters at the base of the hill, near the Swamp. There they dug a little hole to lie in, and put in a layer of pine leaves. Between them they had an overcoat and a blanket. At night they lay upon the coat and covered themselves with the blanket. By day the blanket served as a tent."

"The hardships and annoyances that we endured made everybody else cross and irritable," McElroy reported. "Even the best of chums would have sharp quarrels and brisk fights, and this disposition increased as disease made greater inroads upon them." But Emerson and Stiggal, said McElroy, "never quarreled with each other. Their tenderness and affection were remarkable to witness."

Then, these two "began to go the way that so many were going; diarrhea and scurvy set in; they wasted away till their muscles and tissues almost disappeared, leaving the skin lying flat upon the bones; but their principal solicitude was for each other." Each seemed jealous if anyone else did his friend a favor.

"I met Emerson one day," related McElroy, "with one leg drawn clear out of shape, and rendered almost useless by the scurvy. He was very weak, but was hobbling down towards the Creek with a bucket made from a boot leg." When McElroy offered to carry the bucket, Emerson wheezed out: "No; much obliged. . . . My pardner wants a cool drink, and I guess *I'd* better get it for him." Stiggal "died in June," McElroy reported, "one of the first victims of the scurvy."[19]

A third male couple described by McElroy included Ned Johnson, "a young Englishman," whose "fist was readier than his tongue," and his "chum," Walter Savage, "of the same surly type." These two "had come from England twelve years before and had been together ever since."

When Savage was killed in battle, "Ned could not realize for a while that his friend was dead. It was only when the body rapidly stiffened in its icy bed, and the eyes . . . glazed over with the dull film of death, that he believed he was gone from him forever."

The rest of that day, McElroy recalled, Ned fought furiously, heading every assault, and "cursing the Rebels bitterly." When his regiment finally surrendered, Ned threw down his revolver belt and "sat apart, his arms folded, head hung upon his breast, brooding bitterly upon Walter's death." But when a Confederate officer rode up, "Ned sprang to his feet, made a long stride forward, snatched from the breast of his overcoat the revolver he had been hiding there, cocked it and leveled it at the Rebel's breast." Before he could fire, however, he was disarmed by his fellow Union soldiers.[20]

&

A novel by Frederick Wadsworth Loring, titled *Two College Friends,* published in 1871, is set at Harvard University and, later, during the Civil War.[21] A combined school and war novel, this nineteenth-century buddy fiction, by an author too young to have served in the recent conflagration, began to mythologize the Civil War as an extreme situation in which one man could prove his passionate love for another. Loring dedicated his story to his Harvard friend and classmate, William Wigglesworth Chamberlin, suggesting that the chums of the novel paralleled these chums in life.

At the novel's start, the "graceful" Ned, a Harvard freshman, is "jealous," thinking that his friend and roommate, the beautiful Tom, a junior,

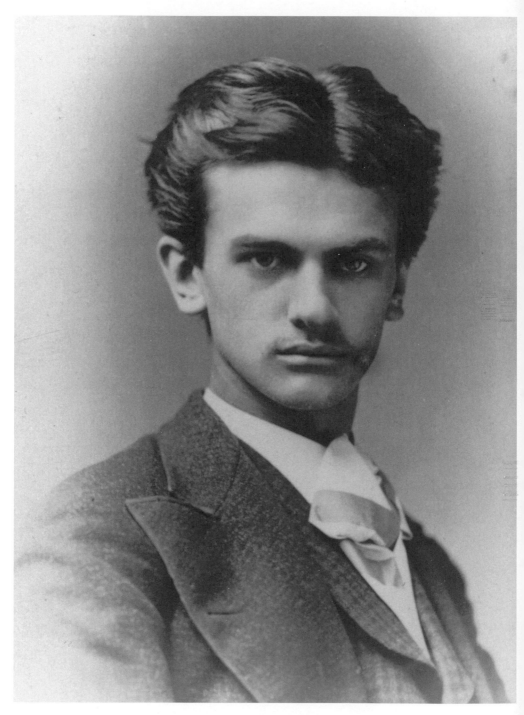

Fred Wadsworth Loring, Harvard, 1870. Courtesy Harvard University Archives. ❧

William Wigglesworth Chamberlin, Harvard, 1870. Courtesy Harvard University Archives. ❧

"has fallen in love" with a girl. For Ned has seen Tom glancing at a mysterious photograph.[22] He is "morbid upon the subject of Tom," a bachelor professor friend warns Ned, who admits: "I have neither father nor mother; I have no one except Tom. I care more for him than for any one else in the world."[23] Thinks Ned at one point, "I wonder if I shall ever care for any woman as much as I do for Tom."[24]

Ned is also jealous of a "big Western friend" of Tom's, the ruddy-faced Blodgett, nicknamed "Blush Rose," who Ned believes had introduced Tom to the girl. Some Harvard boys of this era evidently called each other girlish names, but such gender inversions did not yet usually signify erotic inversion.

Ned's jealousy is relieved only when it turns out that the photograph is of Tom dressed as a "dear little peasant girl" for a Harvard play; it is actually a present for Ned. After seeing this photograph, the boys' professor friend exclaims: "What a mistake nature made about your sex, Tom."[25] "Sex" deviance did not yet overtly imply "sexual" deviance.

Ned and Tom present another photograph of themselves to their bachelor professor friend. This depicts Tom standing behind a chair in which Ned is sitting, and Tom's "whole attitude, as he leans over his companion, is full of that quaint grace of boyish tenderness so indefinable and so transitory."[26] Ned's face is more contradictory, "now all love, now disfigured by scorn."[27] Photographs circulate in this fiction and this culture as material emblems of men's deep feeling for men. Photography was popularized in the 1850s and 1860s, the time during which this novel is set, allowing Tom to endow a permanent image of Ned with his own deep feelings.

In his junior year at Harvard, Ned sees "a good deal" of a young woman who asks about the initials Ned has engraved on a locket. "Is she pretty?" asks the young woman. To which Ned replies, "It isn't any girl; it's my chum, Tom." Ned plans to give the locket to Tom as a token of affection.[28]

When war starts, the president of the United States calls on men to help him save the country, and Ned immediately joins the Union Army, followed by Tom. In battle, Tom saves Ned's life, later forgoing a visit home to stay with his wounded friend. Hearing of Tom's sacrifice, Ned wants "to die for" Tom.

Ned worries, however, about the long-term staying power of Tom's affection: "When this war is over, I suppose Tom will marry and forget me. I never will go near his wife—I shall hate her."[29] Ned and the author feel no need to hide such thoughts. This is *not* a world in which a jealous man-friend is suspected of erotic attraction. But the fictional Ned's fantasy about Tom's future wife reminds us of Lincoln's real-life response to Speed's financée.

Tom is wounded in battle, he and Ned are captured, and the Confederate general, Stonewall Jackson, allows Ned to stay with his friend until Tom can be moved—if Ned swears that he will not try to escape. Ned so swears, and Stonewall Jackson comments that Tom "is a handsome boy"—a non sequitur unless General Jackson recognizes Ned's attraction to Tom's beauty.[30]

Ned and Tom are guarded by a rough Confederate soldier who threatens Ned, "I could just chaw you up in no time. I should kinder like to have a gouge at you, anyway"—a sexual threat?[31]

But the threat is idle: this "Virginia barbarian" turns out to be good hearted as well as aware of Tom's and Ned's special intimacy. Earlier, by coincidence, while lying wounded in a Union hospital, the Virginian had observed Tom's tender ministrations to Ned. "You care for him about as you would for a gal, don't you?" asks this extremely observant soldier, adding his own opinion of Tom's good looks: "Well, he's pootier [prettier] than any gal I ever seen anywhar."[32] This friendly Confederate then suggests an escape route, and Ned, breaking his vow to Stonewall Jackson, carries Tom to freedom. In this novel, love between men trumps antagonism between Union and Confederate. Had author Loring been reading Whitman?

Safe among Union forces, Ned orders that "no one enter" their room, and, alone with his friend, "threw himself down beside Tom," who, drugged, is "sleeping restlessly." Ned "looked at him, laid his hand upon his forehead, and then bent over and kissed his hot face."

This is their last meeting, Ned tells the unconscious Tom: "O my darling, my darling, my darling! please hear me. The only one I have ever loved at all, the only one who has ever loved me." Ned hopes that Tom, when recovered, will remember Ned's embrace and his declaration of love. "O Tom, my darling! don't forget it. If you knew how I love you, how I have loved you in all my jealous, morbid moods, in all my exacting selfishness,—O Tom!" Tom's photo "will be with me when they bury me," asserts Ned. When the war is over, Ned commands Tom: "You won't forget Ned, darling; he was something to you; and you were all the world to him."

Ned again kisses "the flushed face of his friend," rushes out, and returns behind Confederate lines, honoring his oath to Stonewall Jackson, who orders Ned to be shot. As Ned puts it, "having sinned, I accepted the penalty." Ned pays with his life for loving Tom. Romantic friendship was losing its old ease and innocence. Is there erotic innuendo in Ned's sense of sinning and paying the price for it?

As the novel ends, the war is over, "the country is intact," and the wife of the healthy, fertile Tom suggests that they call their new son Ned— marriage, fatherhood, and fatherland triumph.[33] Walt Whitman was not the only man who imagined finding love among the ruins during America's Civil War.

Walt Whitman, mid-1860s. Courtesy Library of Congress. ❧

On April 18, 1861, six days after Confederate forces fired on Fort Sumter and initiated the Civil War, Walt Whitman vowed in his diary to initiate a new bodily regime: "to inaugurate for (myself) a (pure)(perfect) sweet, cleanblooded (robust) body by ignoring all drinks (but) water and pure milk—and all fat meats [and] late suppers—a great body—[a] purged, cleansed, spiritualised invigorated body."[1]

Whitman's aspiration to a "pure," "spiritualized" body has been interpreted as a vow of sexual chastity (suggesting, incidently, an earlier devotion to carnal expression).[2] But Whitman, after all, rejected the genteel opposing of spirit and body. So his dedication to the spiritual was also, at the same time, a desire for, as he said, a newly "robust," "invigorated" body—a body ready for spiritual service *and* amorous action.

In the months following his vow, Whitman's letters to his male drinking buddies and dinner companions suggest that he did not devote himself entirely to water and milk or avoid all "late suppers."[3] During the first year of the war, he did, however, dedicate himself to the spiritual/bodily work of visiting and comforting sick young men in New York's Broadway Hospital, and to several new bodily (and spiritual?) connections.

A flirtatious love note to the poet, dated March 25, 1862, from a pseudonymous someone signing herself "Ellen Eyre," asks Whitman "to renew the pleasure you afforded me last p.m."[4]

Whatever that "pleasure," Whitman's diary records that he discussed Eyre with one of the strangers (all men) he picked up in New York City's streets: Frank Sweezey—"brown face, large features, black mustache (is the one I told the whole story to about Ellen Eyre)." The "whole story" of Eyre, recounted by the talkative Whitman, created a shared intimacy between himself and Sweezey, who, Whitman recorded, "talks very little."[5] Sharing the "whole" Eyre story *only* with Sweezey, apparently, Whitman made this passing stranger a confidant. Once again, a woman cemented the intimacy between men. Whitman's telling Sweezey a tale of romantic or sexual adventure with a woman may well have been his way of raising the subject of sex with this working man and stimulating his erotic imagination.

Two months later, on May 29, 1862, Whitman's diary tersely records his meeting the "rather feminine" Daniel Spencer, on the corner of Fifth Avenue and Forty-fourth Street: "told me he had never been in a fight and did not drink at all." Spencer had joined the Second New York Light Artillery, deserted, and then returned to his regiment. Three months after Whitman's and Spencer's first meeting, beside the date "Sept 3d," in the margin of this diary, the poet recorded: "slept with me."[6] Despite Whitman's many, repeated accolades to the "manly," Spencer's "feminine" features did not keep the poet from bedding down for a night with this soldier.

A month after this bed sharing, on a Saturday, Whitman recorded a Brooklyn meeting with *"David Wilson*—night of Oct. 11, '62, walking up from Middagh—slept with me—works in blacksmith shop in Navy Yard—lives in Hampden st.—walks together Sunday afternoon & night—is about 19."[7]

In this case Whitman was definitely not just providing a homeless young man a place to stay for a night, for Wilson "lives in Hampden st.," within easy walking distance of Middagh, where they met. Wilson's home on Hampden Street, in Brooklyn, was also within walking distance of Whitman's home on Portland Avenue, the first house north of Myrtle Avenue. So there was no obvious *practical* reason why Wilson *had* to spend that night with Whitman.[8] If their bed sharing took place in Whitman's Portland Avenue home and if a reason was required in those days for such bed sharing, his poet's creative imagination no doubt furnished his mother a convincing rationale for the stranger's nocturnal visit. The walk that Whitman and Wilson took the day after their night together suggests that the two shared some interest in each other as well as a bed.

Whitman's beddings of men continued. Just a few weeks later, on October 22, Whitman's diary records his meeting Horace Ostrander, "about 28 yr's of age," from Otsego County, New York, sixty miles west of Albany. Ostrander "was in the hospital" visiting a friend. Ostrander told the poet that, when he was about twenty-one, in about 1855, he had sailed "on a voyage to Liverpool" and related "his experiences as a greenhand." (Melville's novel, *Redburn,* the tale of a young American's virgin sail to Liverpool, includes hints of various sexual encounters, which may suggest some of the experiences Ostrander shared with Whitman.)[9] Whitman met Ostrander again on November 22, and a few weeks later reported: "slept with him Dec. 4th '62."[10]

Spencer, Wilson, and Ostrander are three of the four casual pickups that Whitman's diary notes he "slept with." Although nineteenth-century males often casually shared beds, Whitman's bedding down for a night with men met, by chance, in the city streets, certainly revealed an active search for short-term, male bed mates. It also most probably expressed his desire for whatever sort of bodily coupling seemed possible with each, whether hugging, kissing, or some act more genitally or orgasmically oriented.

Whitman's noting the occasions on which men he picked up in the streets slept with him distinguished those encounters from dozens of others in which he simply noted a meeting. New York's sporting press, and other evidence I have offered, suggests that in the nineteenth century the streets of America's larger cities provided anonymous spaces in which men could meet and, unobserved, initiate sexual contacts with other men. Industrialization drew men to cities, and urbanization provided anonymous cover for sexual encounters between previously unacquainted males—encounters not sanctioned by the sex-only-in-marriage-with-a-woman ideal.

Spencer, Wilson, and Ostrander are just three of the many men whom Whitman's diary records his meeting in the city streets. For example, Whitman's jottings of 1862 note: *"Mark Ward*—young fellow on fort Greene—talk from 10 to 12"; *"Wm Miller* 8th st (has powder slightly in his face)" (gunpowder or face powder?); *"Aaron B. Cohn*—talk with— . . . appears to be 19 years old—fresh and affectionate young man— spoke of a young man named *Gilbert L. Bill* (of Lyme, Connecticut) who thought deeply about Leaves of Grass, and wished to see me"; "Theodore M Carr . . . met on Fort Greene forenoon Aug. 28—and came to the house with me—is from Greenville Green County 15 miles from Coxsackie left Sept 11th" (after spending two weeks with Whitman?); "Tom English, has been some at sea, married young, has three children living— good looking . . ."; "James Sloan (night of Sept 18 '62) 23d year of age . . . is an only son . . . plain homely, American."[11] Whitman's listing the names and a bit about these numerous, passing, male strangers indicates that he desired to recall these brief encounters and, in some sense, at least, treasure them.

∽

On December 16, 1862, two weeks after Whitman's night with Ostrander, the poet and his family read a newspaper report suggesting that brother George Washington Whitman, a Union soldier, had been wounded at the battle of Fredericksburg.[12] Walt immediately left Brooklyn for the South, to try to locate and aid his sibling. After miraculously locating George and finding his wound safely healing, Walt stayed in the South, dedicating himself, heart and soul, to wartime volunteer work, visiting hospitals and comforting wounded soldiers. This was a ministry specifically to men and, equally, to ill bodies and needy spirits.

At the Lacy House, an army hospital in Virginia, on December 22, one of the first sights Whitman encountered, "at the foot of a tree, immediately in front," was "a heap" of amputated "feet, legs, arms, and human fragments, cut, bloody, black and blue, swelled and sickening." In "the garden near," he saw "a row of graves . . . a long row of them."[13]

The horrors of war alternated, in these years, with alluring new intimacies. Three months later, on March 19, 1863, from Washington, D.C., Whitman wrote New York friends that he had "struck up a tremendous friendship with a young Mississippi captain (about 19) that we took prisoner badly wounded at Fredericksburg." The poet had first met the captain at the Lacy House, "his leg just cut off, and cheered him up." The "poor boy, he has suffered a great deal, and still suffers."[14] Whitman wrote this to Nat Bloom and Fred Gray, the leading figures in a group with whom the poet had often drunk, dined, and caroused at Pffaf's and other establishments catering to New York's sporting men and bohemians.

The Mississippian "wears his confederate uniform, proud as the devil," added Whitman, his attraction to the youth's spirit conquering the poet's dislike of his cause. The captain "has eyes bright as a hawk, but face pale." Whitman continued: "our affection is quite an affair, quite romantic— sometimes when I lean over to say I am going, he puts his arm around my neck, draws my face down, &c." It is "quite a scene," added Whitman, "for the New Bowery."[15] The staged kiss of hero and heroine on the boards of this popular New York City theater served Whitman as an ironic model for kissing the captain. Calling this physical exchange of affection an "affair" and "romantic," Whitman presented the young captain as the active kisser, himself as the passive kissed. Evocatively picturing this embrace, Whitman recreated his old intimacy with his New York men friends, presuming their interest in his bussing.

While visiting Washington's Civil War hospitals, Whitman then continued, altering his tone: "The sick and dying soldiers . . . begin to cling to me." These "American young men, badly wounded, . . . pallid with diarrhea, languishing, dying with fever, pneumonia, . . . open a new world somehow to me, . . . exploring deeper mines than any yet, showing our humanity."[16]

Reference to sickness, wounds, and death alternate in Whitman's Civil War letters with banter about romance and hints of eros. When they met again, Whitman told his New York friends, "I have some curious yarns I promise you, my darlings and gossips, by word of mouth."[17]

Whitman three times bestows the title "darlings and gossips" on Bloom and Gray, and this arch man talk of 1863 may well have been the, as yet unnamed, forerunner of twentieth-century homosexual camp talk. Addressing the members of his bohemian circle, Whitman employed an urban lingo and expressed a jocular, ironic, sophisticated side of himself far different from the earnest, maxim-spouting, paternal persona he showed to his less educated soldier friends and the serious poet-prophet face he presented to his literary acolytes.

In March 1863, at the time that Whitman wrote to Bloom and Gray about "curious yarns" to be privately related, he had probably already conceived an obsessive romantic interest in and fantasy about sergeant Thomas P. Sawyer and a less intense interest in private Lewis Kirk Brown, both of whom he had met and nursed in Washington hospitals.

Sawyer, a soapmaker from Cambridgeport, Massachusetts, had been wounded on August 29, 1862, at the second battle of Bull Run.[18] Brown, a resolutely pro-Union soldier from Elkton, Maryland, had been wounded in the left leg on August 19, 1862, and had lain, injured, on a battlefield for four days. He had then been brought to a Washington hospital where Whitman probably met him in February 1863.[19] Brown was about twenty, Sawyer about twenty-one, when they met the forty-four-year-old Whitman. The poet typically found himself attracted to men half his age.

On April 21, 1863, Whitman wrote to Sawyer about kissing their mutual friend Brown: "Lew is so good, so affectionate—when I came away, he reached up his face, I put my arm around him, and we gave each other a long kiss, half a minute long."

A man's kissing a man for thirty seconds was evidently unusual in Civil War hospitals. Describing that kiss to Sawyer, Whitman was trying to provoke a little jealousy in this soldier, whom Whitman perceived as insufficiently responsive.

"We talked about you," Whitman told Sawyer, adding, "Tom, I wish you was here. Somehow I don't find the comrade that suits me to a dot—and I won't have any other, not for good."[20]

Lewis Brown did not fill the bill, Whitman made clear to Sawyer, but Sawyer could be his "comrade," and "for good." Whitman here pitted Sawyer against Brown, attempting to capture Sawyer's affection and to make him comrade number one.

Before the Civil War, Whitman had used "comrade" to name a man's intimate male friend, giving that term a specifically sexual connotation.[21] During the war, Whitman's "comrade" retained its hint of eros, but took on the new sense of male intimacy formed, specifically, in battle.

"Dear comrade, you must not forget me, for I never shall you," Whitman implored Sawyer: "My love you have in life or death forever."

Whitman spelled out his forever fantasy: "I don't know how you feel about it, but it is the wish of my heart" to come together again after the war, "in some place where we could make a living, and be true comrades and never be separated while life lasts—and take Lew Brown too."[22] The poet's domestic dream starred Thomas Sawyer and himself, with Lewis Brown as walk-on. He told Sawyer: "My soul could never be entirely happy . . . without you," calling him his "dear darling comrade."[23]

Sawyer responded to Whitman's heart-on-sleeve outpouring by engaging a professional letter writer to devise a cool, formal response ("I fully reciprocate your friendship . . . it will afford me great pleasure to meet you after the war.")[24] Sawyer's agreeing to a postwar meeting probably fed Whitman's fantasy, but the soldier's passionless reply could not have pleased him.

"Lewy Brown had received two letters [from you]," Whitman whined to Sawyer on April 26—Whitman was still waiting for a response to his own letter. The jealous Whitman begrudged Sawyer's correspondence with Brown.

Whitman was also "sorry" that Sawyer "did not come up to my room to get the shirt & other things you promised to accept from me . . . when you went away"—Whitman mentioned "a good strong blue shirt," and "a pair of drawers & socks." If Sawyer had accepted his presents, said Whitman, "I should have often thought now Tom may be wearing around his body something from *me*."[25]

Getting close to Sawyer, physically and metaphorically, was clearly Whitman's obsession. But Sawyer was not interested in the drawers or the shirt and socks, casually spurning the seductive presents."[26]

"Not a day passes, nor a night but I think of you," Whitman told Sawyer, his "dearest comrade." He hoped (actually, prayed) that "God will put it in your heart to bear toward me a little at least of the feeling I have about you. If it is only a quarter as much I shall be satisfied." This was clearly a lie—the unsatisfied Whitman virtually begged for Sawyer's affection,[27] playing the same humiliating pursuer role that Fred Vaughan had played earlier with him.

A month later, on May 27, Whitman again chided Sawyer, his "dear brother," for failing to write, while Whitman's own "thoughts are with you often enough." When Lewis Brown was discharged, Whitman told Sawyer, he planned to "share with Lewy whatever I might have—& indeed if I ever have the means, he shall never want." The hint of financial support was aimed here, seductively, at Sawyer.

"I cannot, though I attempt it, put in a letter the feelings of my heart," Whitman told the still unresponsive Sawyer. Whitman supposed "my letters sound strange & unusual to you as it is."

For the first time in these letters, Whitman recognized that his yearning for Sawyer far exceeded the feeling associated, usually, with friendship; he was clearly anxious about Sawyer's response. But since "I am only expressing the truth . . . , I do not trouble myself on that account," said the obviously troubled Whitman.

Whitman repeated: he did not expect Sawyer "to return for me the same degree of love I have for you"—another pitiful plea for Sawyer's affection.[28] This was not the first time that Whitman himself had played the unrequited lover—simultaneously smitten, rejected, and humiliated—as an earlier Calamus poem hints.[29] Nor was it the last time.

෴

Three months later, on August 1, 1863, Whitman first wrote to the soldier Lewis Brown, thanking him for a letter and adding that, if Brown "& one other person [Thomas Sawyer] & myself could be where we could work & live together, & have each other's company . . . I should like it so much—but it is probably a dream." Finally, perceiving that his yearning for a live-in arrangement with Sawyer was only a fantasy, Whitman's interest now focused, opportunistically, on Brown. He assured the soldier: "your letters & your love for me are very precious." He sent his love to his "dear son and comrade"—positioning himself as Brown's "father," one nineteenth-century way of naming the intimacy of older and younger males.[30] Whitman repeatedly called Brown and Sawyer "son" and "boy."

Unlike Sawyer, Brown responded warmly to Whitman's declarations of affection. When the poet mentioned stopping his daily hospital visits, the unlettered Brown wrote to him: "The boys . . . could ill spare you, if you are as good to them as you wer to me. I shal never for get you for your kindness to me while I was a suffering so mutch." How "mutch I would like to see you," Brown said.

Whitman should not chastise him for "writing so much foolishness," Brown added, "for you know that I am young and foolish" (how Brown was "young and foolish" he did not say). Brown closed with "love" from "your ever faithful friend & companion."[31] Brown's "friend" augmented his "companion," "companion" amplified "friend." Qualifiers typically characterized friendships more intense than ordinary.

In August 1863, Whitman complained, yet again, to Thomas Sawyer: "I cant understand why you have ceased to correspond with me"—he was still pining after the silent soldier. Lewy Brown's "leg has not healed, gives him trouble yet," Whitman added, and Brown "goes around on crutches, but not very far."[32]

The same month, Whitman urged Lewis Brown, his "darling boy," not to worry about the literary quality of his letters—what counts was "the *man* & the *feeling*."[33] What counted for Whitman were certainly men and feelings.

༄

The "amputated, sick, sometimes dying soldiers cling & cleave to me . . . as a man overboard to a plank," Whitman wrote on September 5, 1863, to Nathaniel Bloom, his New York friend. Whitman mentioned "the perfect content they have if I will . . . sit on the side of the cot awhile . . . & caress them." Whitman admitted: "It is delicious to be the object of so much love & reliance, & to do them such good."[34] The poet's nursing work was unabashedly self-interested *and* profoundly comforting to its soldier recipients, as their many letters to him testify.[35]

"I believe no men ever loved each other as I & some of these poor wounded, sick & dying love each other," Whitman wrote to his mother on September 8.[36] His deep "love" for men was recounted without fear of raising a maternal eyebrow—"love" had no conscious sexual connotation.

But a month later, Whitman allowed his love for men some sort of physical expression. In a diary entry of October 9, 1863, he noted that Jerry Taylor, from New Jersey, of the Second District Regiment, "slept with me last night" (his fourth "slept with" notation). Whitman immediately added: "weather soft, cool enough, warm enough, heavenly." Was "heavenly" a comment on the weather, or on Whitman's night with Taylor?[37]

༄

How much Elijah Douglas Fox missed Whitman's "cheerful smiling face," his "kiss of friendship and love," and his "kind 'good night,'" wrote this soldier from a Washington hospital on November 7. Signing himself "your own Adopted Douglass," Fox employed another model of intimacy between older and younger men—the adopted son.[38]

"Lew, I wish you was here with me, & I wish my dear comrade Elijah Fox in Ward G was here," Whitman wrote to Lewis Brown on November 8 and 9—the poet had now transferred to Fox some of his unrequited affection for Sawyer. But Whitman's pursuit of Sawyer also continued. Whitman urged Brown to tell Sawyer, "he is the one I love in my heart, & always shall till death, & afterwards too."[39]

Whitman sent this long, multipage letter to Brown, asking him to have it read by "all my dear comrades in the hospital." Whitman's nonexclusive affection for particular men expanded here, beyond the twenty soldiers cited by name, to include male humanity in general. Whitman judged none of the endearments he directed to particular soldiers too personal for public consumption.[40]

But one of the hospital's women nurses, Amanda Akin, from an upper-class New York family, sensed something bothersome in Whitman's "very ludicrous" letter "to his 'fellow comrades,' as he called the soldiers." Akin wrote her sister that Whitman's "love" for the soldiers "was repeated in many incoherent sentences." Whitman "took a fancy to my fever boy," this possessive, perceptive nurse protested in another letter. Whitman "is a poet," she explained, "and I believe has written some very queer books about 'Free Love.'" This poet was "an odd-looking genius," she added, "with straggling hair, and very *pink* rims to his eyes. When he stalks down the ward I feel the 'prickings of my thumbs.'" She concluded: "With all his peculiar interest in our soldier boys he does not appeal to me."[41] Akin's half-spoken condemnation of the eros in the air around Whitman and his boys anticipates the criticism of the poet that emerged much more often in the later nineteenth century.

Elijah Fox addressed Whitman as "Dear Father" on November 10, 1863, asking: "You will allow me to call you Father wont you[?]" Both of Fox's parents were dead, he reminded Whitman, and "now Walt you will be a second Father to me wont you, for my love for you is hardly less than my love for my natural parent." "Father" and "son" reappeared here (with "natural") as a young man's way of understanding his love for an older man.

But the intensity of his feeling for Whitman struck Fox as unique: "I have never before met with a man that I could love as I do you." This man-love made Fox nervous, for he had to reassure himself: "Still there is nothing strange about it for 'to know you is to love you.'" That "nothing strange" suggests the opposite, that Fox's intense feeling for Whitman indeed felt "strange" to him. Fox then pacified his anxiety with a maxim, "to know you is to love you," and concluded: were it not for his "great love" for his wife, he would wait in Washington for Whitman. "What a vacancy there would be in my affections were I to be deprived of your love and your company," Fox told Whitman.[42]

Though Whitman's romantic fantasy now included Fox, he was still dreaming of Thomas Sawyer, complaining to him by letter once again on November 20: "I do not know why you do not write me." This time, however, Whitman stated his own worst fear: "Do you want to shake me off?" The poet then, again, seductively assured Sawyer that as long as he, Whitman, had "a meal, or a dollar," or a "shanty," no one "will ever be more welcome there than Tom Sawyer."[43] Whitman yet again offered

Sawyer material enticements to intimacy. The poet's romantic obsession made him desperate.

The next day, November 21, Whitman's yearning turned back to Fox, to whom he admitted: "I cannot bear the thought of being separated from you—I know I am a great fool about such things, but I tell you the truth, dear son." Recently, while attending "the gayest supper party, of men," in New York City, Whitman told Fox, "I would see your face before me . . . & I would realize how happy it would be if I could leave all the fun & noise & the crowd & be with you."[44] The comrade at a distance often looked better to Whitman than the comrade at hand. "You are so much closer to me than any of them," Whitman told Fox. He disparaged the "artificial accomplishments" of his urban men friends in comparison to Fox's "manly & loving soul."[45] When romantic obsession reared its head, Whitman's loyalty to his casual men friends wavered.

Whitman's Fox fantasy soon met the reality principle, however. Two weeks later, on December 9, the soldier wrote to Whitman from Illinois, where he had gone to be with his wife and to go into business with his brother. "Since coming here," Fox confessed, "I have often thought of what you told me when I said to you I am certain I will come back to Washington." A great many "boys had said the same but none had returned," Whitman had told Fox. This soldier's dedication to business and family once again defeated Whitman's dream of domesticity with a man.

Seven months later, Fox reasserted his tie to Whitman: "If you could see your other child" (Fox's daughter), Whitman would "like her better than you did me." Fox signed himself "your Son and Comrade."[46] Whitman's progeny were already growing.

∾

At the end of December, 1863, another soldier, Alonzo S. Bush, responded to Whitman from Maryland, where he was stationed.[47] Bush told "Walt" that he was "glad to know that you are once more in the Noted City of Washington So that you can go often and See that Friend of ours at Armory Square [Hospital], L. K. B. [Lewis K. Brown] The fellow that went down on your BK, both So often with me. I wished that I could See him this evening and go in the Ward Master's Room and have Some fun for he is a gay boy."

Bush's letter, one of several suggestive missives that survive among Whitman's correspondence, seems to say that he and Lewis Brown had both often performed oral sex on Whitman in the privacy of the ward master's room in Armory Square Hospital. But was "to go down on" used then to signify oral-genital contacts? No evidence has yet surfaced, but it is difficult to imagine what else Bush could mean. Oral-genital contacts between men *are* documented in the nineteenth-century United States, though the most explicit references date to about a decade after this.

Bush calling Lewis Brown a "gay boy" was consistent with the nineteenth-century use of "gay" to refer to someone (a female prostitute, usually) who could be induced to perform oral sex, or other acts considered disreputable for a proper wife.[48] Bush's calling Brown a "gay boy" thus may have named a young man willing to perform oral sex on a man. It did *not* name men interested, generally, exclusively, or even predominantly in sex with men. (The earliest known unambiguous use of "gay" to refer to men interested in sex with men dates to the late 1920s.)[49]

Bush's "BK" may be a coded reference to "buck," nineteenth-century American slang for penis. At the very least, Bush's use of the encrypted "BK," and the initials "L. K. B.," indicate references requiring some measure of secrecy.[50]

The cryptic character of Bush's wartime letter then shifted abruptly, and he ended on a somber note—a reference to Lewis Brown: "I am very Sorry indeed to here [hear] that after laying So long that he is about to loose his leg." Sudden swings in tone, from lighthearted to serious, reflect abrupt shifts in the wartime lives of Civil War soldiers.

"Today, after dinner, Lewy Brown had his left leg amputated five inches below the knee," Whitman confided to his diary on January 5, 1864. "I was present at the operation, most of the time in the door." After Brown came out of the ether, said Whitman, his leg started bleeding, and the doctors "thought an artery had opened." They had to reopen the wound, then suture it a second time, and "Lew felt every one of these stitches." Whitman "could hear his cries sometimes quite loud, & half-coherent talk & caught glimpses of him through the open door. At length they finished, & they brought the boy in on his cot."

"I sat down by him," added Whitman, and Brown "talked, quite a good deal. His face was very pale, his eyes dull. He asked often about me. He remained very sick, opprest for breath, with deathly feeling, in the stomach head, &c. & great pain in the leg. As usual in such cases he could feel the lost foot & leg very plainly. The toes would get twisted, & not possible to disentangle them. About 7 o'clock in the evening, he dozed into a sleep. . . . The rest of the night was very bad. I remained all night, slept on the adjoining cot. (The same the next night.)"[51]

Lewis Brown did eventually recover from that operation. He became a clerk in the United States Treasury Department, and, in 1880, sixteen years after the operation, was appointed chief of the Paymaster's Division, a job he held until retiring in 1915.[52] Married and widowed three times, he raised a son who became a lieutenant colonel in the United States Marines.[53]

Reminiscing in 1867, two years after the war's end, Whitman reported to a former soldier: "Tom Sawyer, (Lewy Brown's friend), passed safe through the war—but we have not heard from him now for two years."[54] Sawyer was still the man who got away.

ॐ

On June 24, 1865, one month after the capitulation of the last Confederate forces, a Union soldier, Nicholas Palmer, wrote to "Mr. Whitman" from an army camp near Louisville, Kentucky. Palmer was wondering how he was going to make a peacetime living.[55]

Commanding, "talk Plain to me Mr. Whitman," Palmer said: "I have been over the world more Perhaps than you would imagine," and the world, he had concluded, offered a great many "cruel turns," and "a variety of ways of making a living. Leaving hard work out of the Books." Although his "Education is limited," he knew "there are bigger fools than me making a living very Easy."

Name "any thing you Please," Palmer told Whitman, "and If I do not Propose to accept: that is as far as it will Go." No fear of blackmail here, he indicated, stressing: "I will *blow* on no one." He would not, that is, "blow the whistle" on Whitman if the poet acceded to his sexual come-on.[56]

This soldier did have sex in mind, for he then immediately and abruptly asked: "What about Such houses as we were talking about?" Palmer evidently recalled discussing with Whitman whorehouses that procured male prostitutes for male clients.

If it "Could be made agreeable for me" (that is, financially remunerative) to "take up Lodgeing in Close Proximity with yours," Palmer said, he "Should be Pleased in the Superlative Degree."[57] This bold bawd ended by asking again for advice, "no matter what Sort," and signed himself "your Friend as Ever."

A note written by Whitman on June 28, 1865, on the envelope of this letter, had future readers in mind as it affected surprise at the soldier's query: "I have rec'd many curious letters in my time from one & another of those persons (women and mothers) who have been reading 'Leaves of Grass' " as well as "some singular ones from soldiers—but never before one of this description—I keep it as a curiosity." Whitman positioned himself for posterity as archivist of the unusual, not specifically of the sexual.

Whitman's note continued, explaining to the future that Palmer "was one of the soldiers in Sherman's army," and "one of the hundred I talked with & occasionally showed some little kindness to—I met him, talked with him some." Whitman then, belatedly, confessed that Palmer "came one rainy night to my room & stopt with me." The ever cagey poet then inserted "rainy" between "one night," thereby supplying a practical, non-sexual reason for Palmer to have stopped with him. Whitman's insertion is astonishing, anticipating and trying to obstruct the future investigation of his sexual history. As early as 1865, then, Whitman was clearly expecting posterity's research into his intimacies with men. Whitman was already anticipating that his papers would be scrutinized for clues to his erotic life and sexual poetry.

"Stopt with me" was obviously Whitman's euphemism for "slept with me"—and Palmer was clearly another of those young men who accepted Whitman's bed for a night. Whatever occurred in that bed, Palmer afterward judged Whitman to be a man to whom he could safely offer his sexual services. The material support that Palmer sought from Whitman was not entirely unlike the material support that Whitman had twice seductively offered Thomas Sawyer.

Whitman's note professed to be "completely in the dark" about Palmer's reference to "such houses as we were talking about." But, surely, Whitman, an old New York City newspaper man, and one of his day's prominent sex radicals, knew exactly what kind of houses Palmer had in mind. (Houses that procured male prostitutes for men were mentioned in several contemporary sources.) The poet's protestation that he was "completely in the dark" is so unbelievable it constitutes indirect evidence of his knowledge—and direct evidence of his desire to deny that compromising knowledge.

Whitman ended his note on Palmer's letter: "Upon the whole not to be answered—(& yet I itch to satisfy my curiosity as to what this young man can have really taken me for)." On the most obvious level, Whitman's claim not to understand Palmer seems completely premeditated, calculated to confuse future readers who, like Palmer, suspected the poet of having a sexual interest in men.

But, less obviously, Whitman was probably extremely curious to know exactly what Palmer took him for—the range of available identities was not large. "Sodomite" (and, perhaps, "bugger") were among the few available terms. "Cocksucker" and "fairy" apparently originated later in the century, as we will see. Whitman does seem fascinated that Palmer thought of him as a man so interested in sex with men that he would pay for it. In 1865, it was still rare for a man to be so identified.

Whitman himself probably favored free erotic exchanges between men and considered the bartering of sex for money a violation of a "natural," spontaneous connection. So why did he not simply burn Palmer's letter, as he did destroy other, too revealing, too personal documents?[58] He preserved this letter, I suggest, because he understood it to be a rare, precious, even historic document, one that illuminates men's erotic life with men in his time. That was a sensual life that Whitman savored and considered central to his nation's future.

Ten years earlier, in 1855, the unusually perceptive Rufus Griswold had first publicly pointed to the sodomitical implications of Whitman's *Leaves of Grass,* first alerting Whitman to that particular charge against his book. But Whitman and his publisher had not then felt much threatened by Griswold's accusation, even reprinting it in an advertising pamphlet designed to draw attention to *Leaves of Grass.* By June 1865, however, Whitman was becoming more circumspect.

ക്ക

Whitman also preserved another sexual document of the war years. Twenty-four years after the Civil War, on March 14, 1889, Whitman told his friend Horace Traubel that his brother, George Whitman, had visited that day. Traubel asked: "Was he injured by his imprisonment in the War?"[59] (George had been captured and held for months in several Confederate prisons.)[60] Traubel's question excited Walt, Traubel relates, and the poet exclaimed: "Those Southern prisons were hells on earth! hells on earth!"

Later that day, Whitman handed Traubel a letter addressed by an anonymous "Private of the 5th Pa. Cavalry" to United States Attorney General James Speed (the brother, incidentally, of Lincoln's friend, Joshua Speed). Whitman had probably acquired this letter when he worked as a document copyist in the attorney general's office.

The letter, dated "Aug. 1865," charged that a commission investigating "the conduct of the war" had publicized "a scandalous and most infamous" example of "the 'cruelties' of the Confederates towards our [Union] prisoners."[61] The investigators had exhibited drawings, claimed the writer, illustrating a "disgusting disease of the feet!" Rejecting the idea that the disease was caused by unhealthy conditions in Confederate prisons, the writer blamed Union soldiers for their disease. Speaking, specifically, of the Union prisoners in Andersonville, the writer claimed: "Had it not been for the unnatural and criminal practices of those worse than brute men, they would not have been so afflicted. Sodomy was the cause of their disgusting condition, and the Committee disgraces themselves by their miserable attempt to irritate the people against the South by such infamous exhibitions."[62]

Once again, "sodomy" was the root of all evil (even foot disease). The writer exonerated Confederate officials of responsibility for the Union prisoners' disease, blaming it on their "sodomy." The writer also blamed Union leaders for their "heartless disregard" of Union prisoners' welfare in failing to quickly initiate prisoner exchanges.

Discussing this letter with Traubel, Whitman admitted: "prisoners are real—pigpens are real." But he questioned the writer's charges without coming to any firm conclusion about their accuracy. A "disgusting disease of the feet" allegedly caused by "sodomy" was not, certainly, how Whitman recalled the intimate relationships of men with men during the war years.

෴

Twenty-three years after the war, on September 23, 1888, Whitman's intimate, Traubel, was reading through the poet's old correspondence and exclaimed: "These letters of yours to the soldiers are the best gospel of comradeship in the language"—"better," said Traubel, even than *Leaves of Grass.*

This inspired Whitman to reply: "Comradeship—yes, that's the thing: getting one and one together to make two—getting the twos together everywhere to make all: that's the only bond we should accept and that the only freedom we should desire: comradeship, comradeship."[63]

Twenty-four years after the Civil War, on January 20, 1889, Traubel again read aloud one of Whitman's letters to a soldier. Whitman replied: "My letters, sent to the boys, to others, in the days of the War, stir up memories," both "painful and joyous."

His ministry to the soldiers, said Whitman, "was the sort of work I always did with most relish." He reiterated: "There is nothing beyond the comrade—the man, the woman: nothing beyond; even our lovers must be comrades: even our wives, husbands: even our fathers, mothers: we can't stay together, feel satisfied, grow bigger, on any other basis."

The seventy-year-old Whitman, aged and ill, told Traubel that he had sacrificed his health to his hospital work. Then he asked, rhetorically, "What did I get for it?" He answered: "Well—I got the boys, for one thing: the boys; thousands of them: they were, they are, they will be mine. I gave myself for them: myself: I got the boys: then I got Leaves of Grass." But for the boys, he claimed, "I would never have had Leaves of Grass—the consummated book."

This was Whitman's old-age hyperbole. The third edition of *Leaves of*

Grass had preceded Whitman's Civil War nursing, even his New York hospital visits. The central, inspiring role of "boys" is clear, however, in his life and poetry.

"You look on me now," added the poet, "with the ravages of that experience finally reducing me to a powder. Still I say: I only gave myself: I got the boys, I got the Leaves."[64]

The twenty-one-year-old Peter Doyle and the forty-five-year-old Walt Whitman first met one night in 1865, sometime between January and March, on the Washington, D.C., horsecar where the Irish immigrant worked as conductor.[1] Interviewed thirty years later, Doyle described the encounter: "You ask where I first met him? It is a curious story. We felt to each other at once."

"The night was very stormy," Doyle remembered, the "storm was awful. Walt had his blanket—it was thrown round his shoulders—he seemed like an old sea-captain. He was the only passenger, it was a lonely night, so I thought I would go in and talk with him." He initiated the meeting, the younger man recalled: "Something in me made me do it and something in him drew me that way. He used to say there was something in me had the same effect on him. Anyway, I went into the car. We were familiar at once—I put my hand on his knee—we understood. He did not get out at the end of the trip—in fact went all the way back with me."[2]

❧

In May 1895, three years after Whitman's death and a month after Oscar Wilde's trials were first reported in the American press, Whitman disciples Richard Maurice Bucke and Horace Traubel interviewed Peter Doyle about his intimate friendship with the poet. Doyle presented this intimacy as loving and supportive, though not without conflict. At the same time, reports of the Wilde case were presenting intimacy between men as newly sexual and suspect. On April 4, for example, in Utah, headlines in the *Salt Lake Herald* advertised: "One of the Most Peculiar Cases Ever Heard. LOVE LETTERS TO A BOY. . . . Accused of Intimacy with Lord Alfred Queensbury." The headline, unusually explicit for its time, referred to Wilde's novel *The Picture of Dorian Gray:* "Book Wherein Sodomy Appears to Be Justified." On May 26, the paper reported that Wilde was sentenced to two years in prison, its headline concluding: "Poetry and Bestiality Were Synonymous."[3]

The intimacies of men with men were just then being linked publicly with sexuality, though Doyle's relationship with Whitman still generally passed as spiritual. It was in this heated, historic context that Doyle was asked to recall his relationship with America's most notorious poet. Uninformed, apparently, of the newly suspect status of men's intimacy with men, Doyle answered: "Yes, I will talk of Walt, nothing suits me better."

Peter Doyle, 1868. Courtesy Director and University Librarian, the John Rylands University Library of Manchester. ❧

Traubel carefully transcribed Doyle's words, as he had Whitman's, and Doyle edited the transcript, published in 1897, as *Calamus,* a collection of Whitman's letters to Doyle, edited by Bucke.[4]

৯৯

Peter Doyle was born in Limerick, Ireland, probably on June 3, 1843. He sailed to America with his mother and brothers, landing in the United States in May 1852, just shy of his ninth birthday. During this voyage, Doyle later told Whitman, "the sailors took to him a good deal, as sailors do." The good-looking Doyle was probably especially adorable as a child, and his recollection of the sailors' response records an early affectionate relationship with men.

Reuniting with Doyle's father, a blacksmith who had migrated to America earlier, the family first settled in Alexandria, Virginia, where young Peter may have attended a Jesuit school. With the start of the Civil War, Doyle, then seventeen, enlisted in the Confederate Army. His military induction papers describe him as five feet, eight inches tall, with blue eyes, a light complexion, and light-colored hair. The young Doyle is strikingly handsome in several existing photos from that time. Twice wounded, Doyle deserted the army, made his way north, and was captured by Union forces. He was imprisoned in Washington, D.C., then released after swearing not to aid the rebellion. In Washington, Doyle worked as a blacksmith's helper, then as a horsecar conductor.

৯৯

Three years into Doyle's and Whitman's intimacy, in September 1868, they experienced their first separation when Whitman left Washington for Brooklyn and New York City to oversee a new printing of *Leaves of Grass.*[5]

He "could not resist the inclination to write," Doyle admitted to Whitman after a week, as if he had tried to resist but failed. (The same day Whitman also wrote, but the drafts of his first letters to Doyle are, suspiciously, lost.) It "seems more than a week since I saw you," Doyle told Whitman, and "hardly anything of interest transpired since you went away." With Whitman around, Doyle's life was exciting. "I am very impatient to hear from you," Doyle confessed.[6]

After receiving a note from Whitman, Doyle responded, "i cant explain the Pleasure i experience from your letters"—there were mysteries for him in this intimacy. He called Whitman "my good & true friend," and signed himself "Pete the Great." He was feeling good.[7]

"Walt you cant think [how] much pleasure i derive from our letters,"

Doyle repeated in his next note, "it seems to me Very often that you are With me and that i am Speaking to you."[8]

Writing to and receiving letters from one another was, for Doyle and Whitman, a deeply satisfying, uncomplicated form of intimacy. Doyle's signature, in some of his letters, is followed by "xx"—a symbol of two kisses.[9] Whitman later referred to their kissing and embracing.[10]

"Dear Boy" and "friend," Whitman called Doyle on September 25, 1868, in his first extant letter, confessing: "I think of you very often, dearest comrade, & with more calmness than when I was there." In Doyle's presence, evidently, Whitman was troubled. "I find it first rate to think of you, Pete," added Whitman, "& to know that you are there, all right, & that I shall return, & we will be together again. I don't know what I should do if I hadn't you to think of & look forward to."[11] Doyle at a distance evoked less perturbed feelings in Whitman than Doyle in the flesh—Whitman valued the serene pleasure of their new, long-distance relation.

One of Whitman's lost letters to Doyle had recounted a story in which a young woman praised Whitman's sexual prowess, and, as the writer intended, Doyle had passed this letter around to their Washington, D.C., men friends. Sex-talk about women charged these men's intimacy with each other, as Lincoln's dirty stories had electrified his male circle.

In response, Doyle reported to Whitman in September 1868, that one of their friends, Jim Sorrell, a railroad worker, "sends his love & best respects . . . but the most thing that he don't understand is that young Lady that said you make such a good bed fellow."[12]

Now, why would Sorrell *not* understand Whitman's making a "young lady" a "good bedfellow"? Among this group of Washington working men did Whitman have a reputation for sexual abstinence or restraint? Doyle may have thought of Whitman that way, for in 1895, as we will see, he claimed that sexual thoughts about women "never came into" Whitman's head. Or, was Whitman known among these men for his lack of sexual interest in women? Or, was he known to be sexually interested in men—or men as well as women? If so, were other of these men friends also known to be so interested? The present evidence is inconclusive.

The sex-talk of Whitman and these working men does contrast, strikingly, with the following month's scandalized middle-class response to the sex-talk in *Leaves of Grass*. He had run into trouble printing a new *Leaves* in New York City, Whitman told Doyle in October 1868: "There is a pretty strong enmity here toward me," and toward the book, "among certain classes." Not only was the book considered "a great mess of crazy talk & hard words, all tangled up, without sense or meaning." (That was also Doyle's judgment, Whitman reminded his friend.) But some people "sincerely think that it is a bad book, improper, & ought to be denounced & put down, & its author along with it."[13] Until late in the century, as I have noted, objections to *Leaves of Grass* commonly referred to its poems of male-female sex-love, not, significantly, its man-love poems.

"Yes, Walt often spoke to me about his books," Doyle confirmed in 1895.[14] He added: "I would tell him 'I don't know what you are trying to get at.' And this is the idea I would always arrive at from his reply. All other peoples in the world have had their representatives in literature: here is a great big race [Americans] with no representative. . . . It was also his object to get a real human being into a book."

From Providence, Rhode Island, Whitman wrote to Doyle again in October 1868: "I have made . . . a change of base, from tumultuous, close-packed, world-like N.Y., to this half-rural, brisk, handsome, New England, third-class town." He added: "Pete, your old man is in clover." At the houses he visited, "we have plenty of ripe fresh fruit and lots of flowers. Pete, I could now send you a bouquet every morning, far better than I used to, of much choicer flowers."[15] In the nation's capital, the "old man" had *daily* sent his young man a flowery token of affection—a token that probably had no conscious connotation, for Doyle, of Whitman's sexual interest.

A day later, Whitman wrote to Doyle: "I went by invitation to a party of ladies & gentlemen—mostly ladies." He "made love to the women" (flirted with them, in that day's parlance), and "flatter myself that I created at least one impression—wretch and gay deceiver that I am." (No evidence suggests that "gay deceiver" was a secret code, or that "gay" was used then as it is today.)

Among these "young & jolly" women, Whitman added, "the way in which this aged party comes up to the scratch & cuts out the youthful parties & fills their hearts with envy is absolutely a caution. You would be astonished, my son, to see the . . . capacity of flirtation & carrying on with the girls—I would never have believed it of myself." Pursued by these women, said Whitman, "there is nothing left for me—is there—but to go in." Then, immediately repudiating the sexual connotations of "going in," he assured Doyle that his "going in amounts to just talking & joking & having a devil of a jolly time . . . that's all." Sex was on Whitman's mind as he wrote to Doyle that day, though it may not have been on Doyle's mind, or their society's. And, once again, sex-talk about women triangulated an intimacy between men.

Whitman concluded, charmingly: "Fortunate young man, to keep getting such instructive letters—aint you?"[16]

"I never knew a case of Walt's being bothered up by a woman," Doyle told his interviewers in 1895, revealing his own Roman Catholic ideas about sex between the sexes. Whitman's "disposition," Doyle recalled, "was different": "Woman in that sense never came into his head. Walt was too clean, he hated anything which was not clean." A man's sexual intercourse with a woman outside of marriage was dirty, Doyle suggested. "No trace of any kind of dissipation in him," Doyle added. "I ought to know about him those years—we were awful close together."

Doyle stressed Whitman's lack of sexual feeling for women as he talked of his and Whitman's intimacy without any self-consciousness. It did not occur to Doyle that Whitman's lack of sexual interest in women suggested a sexual interest in men. Doyle had no idea of a sexual orientation that pressed for expression, toward one sex rather than another.

"Towards women generally," Doyle assured his interviewers, "Walt had a good way—he very easily attracted them. But he did that with men, too. And it was an irresistible attraction. I've had many tell me—men and women. He had an easy, gentle way—the same for all, no matter who they were or what their sex."[17]

Recalling life with Whitman in Washington, Doyle emphasized his friend's energy: "He was an athlete—great, great. I knew him to do wonderful lifting, running, walking." In the afternoon, after Whitman finished work as copyist in the attorney general's office, Doyle recalled: "We'd stroll out together, often without any plan, going wherever we happened to get. This occurred days in and out, months running."

"We took great walks together," Doyle reiterated: "We went plodding along the road, Walt always whistling or singing. We would talk of ordinary matters. He would recite poetry, especially Shakespeare—he would hum airs or shout in the woods. He was always active, happy, cheerful, good-natured. Many of our walks were taken at night. He never seemed to tire. When we got to the ferry opposite Alexandria I would say to myself, 'I'll draw the line here—I won't go a step further.' But he would take everything for granted—we would cross the river and walk back home on the other side." Doyle recalled: "Walt knew all about the stars. He was eloquent when he talked of them."[18]

Whitman confirms their stargazing in a letter to Doyle: "Dear son, I can almost see you drowsing & nodding," and "I am telling you something deep about the heavenly bodies—& in the midst of it I look around & find you fast asleep, & your head on my shoulder like a chunk of wood—an awful compliment to my lecturing powers."

Whitman concluded this letter gently: "Good night, Pete—Good night, my darling son—here is a kiss for you, dear boy—on the paper here—a good long one." He ended: "I will imagine you with your arm around my neck saying Good night, Walt—& me—Good night, Pete."[19]

Many of Whitman's letters called Doyle his "darling son." Kinship terms—father-son, uncle-nephew, brother-brother—provided nineteenth-century males several ways to name and define intimacies between otherwise unrelated men and youths. Throughout Whitman's correspondence, diaries, and essays, such terms repeatedly designate his intimacies with younger men.

❧

In August 1869, Whitman was about to leave Washington—initiating his and Doyle's second separation—when his young friend startled him with a dramatic threat. Doyle was depressed, ostensibly about a skin irritation, but, probably, about their parting. He announced to Whitman that he was thinking of suicide. This dramatic confession, on the eve of Whitman's departure, provoked the expression of concern that Doyle desired.

While still in Washington, Whitman scolded Doyle, then, later, apologized by letter, saying: "You must forgive me for being so cold the last day & evening. I was unspeakably shocked and repelled from you by that talk & proposition of yours." It seemed to Whitman "that the one I loved, and who had always been so manly & sensible, was gone, & a fool & intentional murderer stood in his place." Whitman appealed to Doyle's Catholic strictures against suicide, taking his threat seriously.

Doyle's distress then drew from Whitman the reassurance the young man was seeking: "My darling, if you are not well when I come back I will get a good room or two in some quiet place, . . . and we will live together, & devote ourselves altogether to the job of curing you, & rooting the cursed thing out entirely. . . . I have had this in my mind before, but never broached it to you." Whitman stressed: "My love for you is indestructible." He called Doyle "dear son, my darling boy, my young & loving brother" (kinship and age terms again did double duty). Playing paternal, Whitman sternly warned Doyle: "Don't let the devil put such thoughts in your mind," for they were "wickedness unspeakable," and suicide would mean "death & disgrace here, & hell's agonies hereafter."[20]

❧

Whitman returned to Washington in September 1869, after about a month away from Doyle. But living in the same city as the young man proved difficult for him. While Doyle longed, seemingly, for some more explicit expression of Whitman's devotion, Whitman apparently looked to Doyle for a more committed, live-in arrangement, like the domesticity he had dreamed of earlier with Thomas Sawyer. So what was the problem?

Doyle's letters to Whitman show him to be deeply and openly devoted to the poet, even dependent on him, so it is clear that Whitman wanted some *other* expression, something more than evening walks and stargazing. Whitman, it seems clear to me, yearned for sex with Doyle and feared that expressing this desire would forever alienate his Catholic friend. Would it have? We do not know. In any case, the unspeakableness of both men's desires twisted Doyle's and Whitman's romance into a tangled, complex knot.

Nine months later, on June 17, 1870, Whitman finally decided to break emotionally with Doyle, vowing in his diary: "*It is* IMPERATIVE, that I obviate & remove myself (& my orbit) *at all hazards,* from this incessant *enormous* & *abnormal* PERTURBATION." The "PERTURBATION," it is clear, was Doyle. "Abnormal" referred to excessive feeling, and, in the late nineteenth century, was often linked with medical writings. (He did not call his feelings "unnatural.") Rereading that entry on July 15, Whitman pronounced it "Good!"

That same July, Whitman vowed again "To GIVE UP ABSOLUTELY & *for good, from the present hour, this* Feverish, FLUCTUATING, *useless* UNDIGNIFIED PURSUIT of PD." Then, feeling a need to disguise the cause of his perturbation, Whitman erased "PD" and wrote "16.4," a simple code for *P* and *D,* the sixteenth and fourth letters of the alphabet. Whitman felt an impulse to code his intense feelings for Doyle, but the simplicity of the code also suggests that Whitman wanted the code broken, his perturbation understood.

The pursuit of Doyle, Whitman added, had been "*too long, (much too long)* persevered in,—so humiliating." The break, he wrote, "*must come at last* & had better come now—*(It cannot possibly be a success).*"

Whitman urged himself: "LET THERE FROM THIS HOUR BE NO FALTERING, NO GETTING [here, he erased a revealing word] *at all henceforth,* (NOT ONCE, UNDER *any circumstances*)—*avoid seeing him, or meeting him—or any talk or explanations*—or ANY MEETING WHATEVER, FROM THIS HOUR FORTH, FOR LIFE."[21]

Later, Whitman amended the last diary entry, writing "her" over each original "him," disguising the sex of the perturbing party. Inverting those sex signifiers, Whitman clearly felt a need to conceal, even in his private diary, the male source of his perturbation. His desire for Doyle, Whitman knew, was socially impermissible, not to be spoken about—because his desire was for sex with a man.

Whitman then sketched in his diary his ideal "of a superb calm character," a man whose "emotions &c are complete in himself, irrespective of whether his love, friendship, &c are returned or not." Doyle clearly returned Whitman's "love" and "friendship," so it was the poet's mysterious "&c" that signaled the unspeakable for which he pined.

In a following diary entry Whitman warned himself: "Depress the adhesive nature / It is in excess—making life a torment / All this diseased, feverish disproportionate adhesiveness." The striking, pathologizing adjective, "diseased," here refers to "excess" of emotion, not, generally, to "adhesiveness," one of Whitman's major, affirmative terms for the sexual love of man for man. Whitman then revealingly urged himself to "remember Fred Vaughan." That earlier one-sided love affair, was, apparently, recalled by Whitman as deeply humiliating in the end to Vaughan, and, possibly, to himself.

Whitman also recalled the case of Jenny Bullard, a story he had evidently heard about the romantic obsession of a New Hampshire woman for another woman. This is important as the one place in Whitman's writing that he consciously linked the love of man for man with the love of woman for woman. By 1870, then, Whitman was newly conceptualizing, specifically, a same-sex love.[22] His earlier idea of love had posited only the love of men for men and of men and women for each other.

A few weeks later, Whitman left Washington and, back in Brooklyn, wrote to Doyle on July 30, 1870, acknowledging in words a new stage in their relationship: "We parted there, you know, at the corner of 7th st. Tuesday night. Pete, there was something in that hour from 10 to 11 oclock (parting though it was) that left me pleasure & comfort for good—I never dreamed that you made so much of having me with you, nor that you could feel so downcast at losing me. I foolishly thought it was all on the other side. But all I will say further on the subject is, I now see clearly, that was all wrong."[23]

Had Whitman really "thought it was all on the other side"—that his love for Doyle far outweighed Doyle's for him? Doyle had expressed his strong devotion, directly and indirectly, in many ways, many times. The certain important something that Whitman had missed in this relationship could not have been devotion.

Whitman and Doyle's physical separation instituted a flurry of letter writing in which Whitman then regularly called Doyle "dear son" and "my darling son," and himself Doyle's "father"—those kinship terms now shifting in meaning to connote a lust-free "natal love"—a kind of love named in the first *Leaves of Grass*.[24] Whitman evidently attained the serenity to which he aspired in his new relationship with Doyle. Their new intimacy-by-letter, punctuated by occasional visits, lasted until Whitman's death twenty-two years later.

Light is thrown on Doyle and Whitman's intimacy by a letter that the poet wrote to Doyle in September 1870; he relates that he had taken up again in New York with some of his prewar, single, men friends (the "Fred Gray association"), though of that circle "some are dead—& some have got married." Death and marriage both bespoke desertion. Some of these friends "have grown rich," said Whitman, and the night before he had dined with one of these (Charles H. Russell), in "a big house on Fifth avenue . . . every thing in the loudest sort of style, with wines, silver, nigger waiters, &c. &c. &c. But my friend is just one of the manliest, jovialist best sort of fellows—no airs—& just the one to suit you & me—no women in the house—he is single—he wants me to make my home there—I shall not do that, but shall go there very frequently—the dinners & good wines are attractive—then there is a fine library."[25]

With his casual reference to "wines, silver" and "nigger waiters," Whitman was positioning himself and the Irish Doyle as whites who enjoyed the good life. In his reference to women, he was positioning himself and Doyle as men who preferred socializing only with men. The waiters served by their presence; the women served by their absence. But both served Whitman's linking of Doyle, himself, and his host in a chummy comradeship of single, superior, white men. Whitman probably played here to that day's Irish, working-class prejudiced view of blacks, and against the national prejudice that derogated Irish workers as nonwhite. America publicly professed equality and daily practiced inequality. Like his nation, Whitman's publicly professed democratic ideals were sometimes contradicted in private (not, of course, a contradiction limited to men who loved men). Whitman's mixed feelings about the rich are also suggested here by the strong whiff of opportunism in his plan to eat his friend's dinners, drink his wines, and use his library, while maintaining his own, independent abode.[26]

When Whitman suffered a stroke in 1873, Doyle returned briefly to act as his nurse. But both men then understood that theirs was not a live-in love.

⁙

Whitman's dream of a domestic, sexual relationship with Doyle was not to be, but the poet-prophet continued to envision a future world that would welcome such intimacies between men. In 1871, Whitman published "Democratic Vistas," an essay suggesting that, even before the bicentennial of the American Revolution arrived in 1976, "much that is now undream'd of, we might then see established."

America's future, Whitman hoped, would include the full expression of "intense and loving comradeship, the personal and passionate attachment of man to man—which, hard to define, underlies the lessons and ideals of the profound saviours of every land and age." Associating male-male intimacy with religion, Whitman resisted the Christian linking of sodomy with the devil.

The "passionate attachment of man to man," Whitman stressed, "seems to promise, when thoroughly develop'd and recognized in manners and literature, the most substantial hope and safety of the future of these States." In a footnote Whitman added one of the most remarkable comments made in the nineteenth century on the implications for a money-mad society of passionate intimacies between men: "It is to the development, identification, and general prevalence of that fervid comradeship . . . that I look for the counterbalance and offset of our materialistic and vulgar American democracy, and for the spiritualization thereof." Whitman's "fervid comradeship," he explained, referred to "the adhesive love [between men], at least rivaling the amative love [between men and women] hitherto possessing imaginative literature, if not going beyond it."

"Many will say it is a dream, and will not follow my inferences," Whitman continued, "but I confidently expect a time when there will be seen, running like a half-hid warp through all the myriad audible and visible worldly interests of America, threads of manly friendship, fond and loving, pure and sweet, strong and life-long, carried to degrees hitherto unknown."

The full development of "manly friendship" would not only give "tone to individual character," making it "unprecedently emotional, muscular, heroic, and refined." Such friendships would also have "the deepest relations to general politics. I say democracy infers such loving comradeship, as its most inevitable twin or counterpart, without which it will be incomplete, in vain, and incapable of perpetuating itself."[27]

American democracy required sexual equality, Whitman argued, forging an embryonic concept of erotic politics. The politics of the sexual did not gain serious national attention again in the United States until the second wave of feminism and the founding of the militant gay and lesbian liberation movement in the late 1960s and early 1970s.

❧

Numbers of Washington, D.C., laboring men are mentioned in Doyle's and Whitman's letters of the late 1860s and early 1870s. "Give my love to Johnny Lee, my dear darling boy, I love him truly," Whitman wrote to Doyle.[28]

In 1870, both Doyle and Whitman wrote to Edward C. Stewart in Nova Scotia, Canada. Stewart answered on February 25, requesting a "double" photo—he evidently considered them a couple and desired a visual keepsake of their union. Whitman and Doyle had two such double photos made.

Stewart also supposed "there is gay times" in Washington at two variety halls, the Metropolitan Rooms and Canterbury Hall.[29] He added, "Moses but I wish I was there with you old Covies." The slang term "covey" was used in nineteenth-century America as "guy" is today. But "covey" also referred to a company of boys, a group of girls, or a brood of birds, specifically, a mother bird with her brood of chicks. So Stewart's "you old Covies" may be hinting that Doyle, Whitman, and their group of men friends are not the manliest.[30] Is this another early example of working-class camp talk? Possibly. The story of John Safford Fiske, recounted later, indicates that camp was being talked in London just three months after Stewart wrote this letter.

In Nova Scotia, Stewart told Whitman, he had "a grand chance . . . with some Lady whose Pa happens to have some spare cash." Stewart, a man on the make, bragged that he was moving "among the Elite." Though "a Lager beer imbiber," Stewart reported that he had even joined the "Sons & Sisters of Temperance," and delivered, cynically, a rousing talk against alcohol. He had considered reciting, instead, "that familiar old piece of Pete's" about a man "who could not get his chimney up high Enough" to keep his neighbor's cats from putting out his fire. But "the girls up this way are very modest."

The man in Doyle's story who could not get it up reveals, once again, that working-class men casually exchanged ribald tales that would have horrified defenders of the day's middle-class Christian culture. The sex-consciousness and sex-tolerance of some working-class men of this time distinguished them from men of the respectable middle class.

Stewart said he had received valentines from some young lady, but as they "came from [the] wrong quarter why I didn't accept." Did the gold-digging Stewart mean that his valentines were sent by girls too poor for him? Or, did the "wrong quarter" mean the "wrong" sex? We do not know.

Stewart also reported "driving in a Sleigh with 'Her'" and having a "gay time"—the quotes around "Her" strongly suggesting some coded meaning. Could "her" mean "him"—another early example of camp talk? Whitman did substitute "her" for "him" in order to code his diaries and poetry, so the possibility of Stewart doing so is not far-fetched.

Peter Doyle and Walt Whitman, about 1869. Courtesy Library of
Congress. ❧

Stewart signed his letter suggestively: "Yours Infernally" (punning, devilishly, on "Yours Eternally").[31] Camp talk certainly seems aborning.

᠊ᡇ᠊

In 1895, near the end of Richard Bucke and Horace Traubel's interview with Peter Doyle, this working man went to his closet, pulled out Whitman's old overcoat, and said: "I have Walt's raglan here. . . . I now and then put it on, lay down, think I am in the old times. Then he is with me again. It's the only thing I kept amongst many old things. When I get it on and stretched out on the old sofa I am very well contented. It is like Aladdin's lamp. I do not ever for a minute lose the old man. He is always near by. When I am in trouble—in a crisis—I ask myself, 'What would Walt have done under these circumstances?' and whatever I decide Walt would have done that I do."

In the last three or four years of Whitman's life, said Doyle, he saw "little" of his friend, though Whitman "continued to write to me." Pulling out a few of Whitman's postcards, Doyle said, "you will see that they show the same old love." Doyle said he had had "a mad impulse" to go and nurse his friend: "I was his proper nurse—he understood me—I understood him. We loved each other deeply." But something had stopped Doyle. He still regretted it, he said, "but it is all right. Walt realized I never swerved from him—he knows it now—that is enough."

Doyle ended the interview. "I have talked a long while," he said, offering Bucke and Traubel a beer: "You gentlemen take the glasses, there; I will drink right from the bottle. Now here's to the old man and the dear old times—and the new times, too, and every one that's to come."[32]

Charles Warren Stoddard. Courtesy The Bancroft Library, University of California, Berkeley. ❧

O n February 8, 1867, Charles Warren Stoddard, a twenty-four-year-old journalist, aspiring essayist, and poet, first wrote from San Francisco to Walt Whitman, beseeching him for an autograph.[1] Whitman did not respond. But two years later, on March 2, 1869, the determined Stoddard wrote again, this time from Honolulu. Stoddard justified his persistence with Whitman's own come-on, quoted from *Leaves of Grass:* "Stranger! if you, passing, meet me, and desire to speak to me, why should you not speak to me? And why should I not speak to you?"[2]

"So fortunate to be traveling in these very interesting Islands," Stoddard continued. In Hawaii, "I have done wonders in my intercourse with these natives." For the first time "I act as my nature prompts me." This "would not answer in America," he said, "not even in California, where men are tolerably bold."[3] Tolerably bold was not bold enough.

But how, exactly, did Stoddard's "nature" prompt? To what kind of "intercourse" did he refer? At dusk, he wrote, he reached "a few grass huts by the sea or in some valley." The "native villagers gather about me. . . . Superb looking, many of them. Fine heads, glorious eyes that question, observe and then trust or distrust with an infallible instinct. Proud, defiant lips, a matchless physique, grace and freedom in every motion." Romanticized beyond the human, Stoddard's natural men were the idealized obverse of immoral, uncivilized primitives, and as much a white man's fantasy.

The gaze of the native, in Stoddard's letter, centers on the white man, whose eyes focus on a sentimentalized, eroticized youth, eager to oblige: "I mark one, a lad of eighteen or twenty years, who is regarding me. I call him to me, ask his name, giving mine in return. He speaks it over, manipulating my body unconsciously, as it were, with bountiful and unconstrained love."

After the lad's loving manipulations, apparently enacted without embarrassment before the entire village, Stoddard said, "I go to his grass house, eat with him his simple food, sleep with him upon his mats, and at night sometimes waken to find him watching me with earnest, patient looks, his arm over my breast and around me." Stoddard echoed one of Whitman's most eloquent Calamus poems: "And his arm lay lightly around my breast—and that night I was happy."[4] In the morning, continuing on his travels, Stoddard held the youth in memory, as he fancies the youth recalled him.

"You will easily imagine, my dear sir," Stoddard told Whitman, "how delightful I find this life." He added: "I read your Poems with a new spirit, to understand them as few may be able to." His night with the Hawaiian, and nights with other men, Stoddard hinted, placed him among a special, small group able to decipher meanings in Whitman's poems that are inaccessible to the many. His sexual interest in men, Stoddard rightly suggested, provided special insight into Whitman's verse.

If Whitman would send him just a few lines, begged Stoddard, the poet's "personal magnetism" would recharge Stoddard's own. A photo of the poet would even more revitalize him, reenergizing him for new adventures, Stoddard suggested.

On June 12, 1869, from Washington, D.C., Whitman responded positively to Stoddard's call for a bit of the poet's magnetism: "I cordially accept your appreciation, & reciprocate your friendship." He took Stoddard's erotically charged travelogue in his stride. Identifying with Stoddard, Whitman admitted that he, too, liked to meet people, so Stoddard's "tender & primitive personal relations away off there in the Pacific Islands . . . touched me deeply." Confessing his own empathetic response to Stoddard's romantic "relations," Whitman obligingly sent a photograph of himself, urging the young man to visit. The poet was clearly fascinated by Stoddard and even curious to meet him. Stoddard never arranged a meeting, despite Whitman's repeated invitations. For Stoddard, the idealized Whitman-in-a-letter was preferable to the warts-and-all Whitman in-the-flesh.[5] But the seductive give and take of their mutual fan letters constituted a long-distance romance by correspondence.

Three months later, in September 1869, Stoddard, encouraged no doubt by Whitman's response, published "A South Sea Idyl," an account of his Hawaii visit, in the popular San Francisco magazine *The Overland Monthly,* which was edited by the well-known western writer Bret Harte.[6]

The "Idyl" Stoddard published takes place on an unnamed South Sea island and pits a judgmental white man, "the Doctor," against the first-person narrator, a hedonistic white man whom most readers probably assume to be Stoddard. This narrator, a pleasure advocate, explicitly warns readers that premature moralizing may deprive them of "fun," urging them to do whatever they want, "then be sufficiently sorry to make it all square [right]."[7] *Fun now, sorry later,* was precisely Stoddard's motto, the ethic that justified his acting on his sexual desires. His sense of sinning subsidized his sensual expression; his penance paid for—and permitted—his active pursuit of unorthodox pleasures. In this he was not alone, as Claude Hartland's story will confirm. Making a doctor the agent of mainland morals, Stoddard anticipated the medical professions' later role as arbiter of sexuality.

In the tropical valley in which he had arrived, says Stoddard's narrator, "there were no temptations which might not be satisfied." Within ten minutes of his arrival, in fact, the narrator meets a beautiful androgynous youth, Kana-ana, and knows he is "to have an experience with this young scion of a race of chiefs"—an experience spelled out in surprisingly suggestive detail.[8]

Kana-ana, readers are told, is sixteen—a few years *younger* than the unnamed native described in Stoddard's letter to Whitman. Either Stoddard intended his story to be even more provocative than the private tale, or he lowered the youth's age in an attempt to desexualize him. The youth had a "round, full, rather girlish face; lips ripe and expressive—not quite so sensual as those of most of his race." (Sensual, but "not quite so sensual"—Stoddard typically had it both ways. His comments on nonwhite races were typical of his time.) Kana-ana's smile "was of that nature that flatters you into submission against your will."[9] But the narrator's will needed little flattering before submitting. Kana-ana announces that the narrator is to be "his best friend, as he was mine"; he commands the visitor to "come at once to his house, and there live always with him." The obliging narrator ingenuously asks the reader, "What could I do but go?"[10]

In the published story the narrator immediately leaves with the moralistic doctor on a week's trip. Only on their return does the narrator tactfully inform the puritanical medical man of his plan to stay with Kana-ana: " 'There was a dear fellow here,' I said, 'who loved me, and wanted me to live with him; and his people wanted me to stop, also: his mother and his grandmother had specially implored me to stay a little.' "[11]

Invoking the mother and grandmother is intended to counter any suspicions the doctor (and reader) may have about the character of Kana-ana's proposition and the white man's friendship with him. "The Doctor looked very grave," the narrator reports: "I knew that he misunderstood me—placed a wrong interpretation upon my motives; the worse for him, I say."[12] That "wrong interpretation," though not spelled out, clearly sees sex in the offing.

The doctor tried "to talk me over to the paths of virtue and propriety," says the narrator, "but I wouldn't be talked over." After this, "The Doctor," readers are told, "never spoke again, but to abuse me." Finally the doctor rode off angrily, leaving the narrator "actually hating civilization—feeling above the formalities of society"—and resolving "to be a barbarian."[13] Affirmations of the "barbarian" and "primitive" are ways some nineteenth-century American white men certified their sex acts with darker-skinned Others.

Stoddard's introduction of the doctor character cleverly answers any questions that eros-conscious readers may have about the narrator's carnal interest in luscious Kana-ana and the native's reciprocal interest in him. Without explicitly stating his sexual suspicions, the doctor expresses the vague thoughts that may have passed through some readers' minds, permitting the narrator to answer them with a denial. In the person of the doctor, Stoddard's text contains its own accuser—and, in the person of its narrator, its own, built-in defender.

Left with his comely South Sea Islander, the narrator was "taken in, fed and petted in every possible way, and finally put to bed, where Kana-ana monopolized me, growling in true savage fashion if any one came near me." Stoddard's "comic" exaggeration of the animalistic, savage stereotype here cools any suspicion of eros, though his narrator remains both warm *and* supposedly innocent of sexual desire: "I didn't sleep much, after all," he admits, "I think I must have been excited."[14] The ironic understatement evokes its opposite: Stoddard's narrator is excited indeed.

With his "bosom friend," says the narrator, "hugging me like a young bear," the two "lay upon an enormous old-fashioned bed with high posts," hung with shawls, "so that I might be dreadfully modest behind them." No particular modesty possesses Kana-ana, however, for readers learn, indirectly, that he sleeps naked next to his visitor. In the morning, we are informed, he "resumed his single garment."[15] Read from our viewpoint in the present, this two-guys-in-bed scene now seems almost explicit in its sexuality.

The "seductions of nature" (and, by implication, of Kana-ana, the natural man) are such that the narrator became "as natural as possible in three days." But "as natural as possible" was not natural enough. The narrator, unable to free himself from Christian strictures, added: "The prodigal lived riotously and wasted his substance"—hinting strongly at seminal spendings. Readers learn that Kana-ana hypnotized the narrator "into a most refreshing sleep with a prolonged and pleasing manipulation."[16]

The narrator's lingering ties to Christian civilization finally trump his prodigal tendencies, however. He feels he must "escape" his tropical paradise, though he fears a big fuss if he warns his trusting native friend of his impending departure. Abruptly leaving Kana-ana behind, the narrator returns to civilization and, significantly, to his father. Then, safely home and now provocatively honoring his prodigal tendencies, he tells his dad, "*If* I have sinned against Heaven and in thy sight, I'm afraid I don't care much." He will, if necessary, renounce his patrimony for "that dear, little, velvet-skinned, coffee-colored Kana-ana . . . because he hates business, and so do I"—and because "above all others, and more than any one else ever can he loved your Prodigal."[17] The father's response is not reported.

෴

The mystery for today's readers is how such a manifestly erotic, first-person account of sexual intimacy between an adult male narrator and a South Seas male teenager could be published openly, without scandal, in a mainstream American periodical in the nineteenth century. This was possible, in part, because Stoddard used the same words to convey, simultaneously, different meanings, writing at the same time for two separate sets of readers: "respectables" and men with an interest in erotic relations with men. By the time his essay was published in 1869, Stoddard could envision such men as a discrete set of readers. Men-loving men had become a collective presence, an audience, as they had for Whitman by 1860. But knowledge of such men was not yet widespread. Stoddard could still count on the respectables to live in a world that lacked an everyday awareness of men-lusting men. The respectables inhabited a social and mental universe in which sexual intimacy between men and male youths was seen as affection, not sex, and sodomy was a narrowly defined act.

Because respectable readers did not see the sex Stoddard put in his text, there was no need for it to be hidden. "Closeted" is misleading as a descriptor for Stoddard's writing, for he hardly conceals the sex at all. In his published essays the sex between men is almost as explicit as in his private letters to Whitman. Stoddard simply counted on respectable readers not to see it. He even republished this story in 1892 in a book of his travel pieces.

Stoddard's letters and published writings (like many of Whitman's poems) spoke sex to some readers, nonsexual love to others. Simultaneously saying and not-saying was Stoddard's (and Whitman's) typical mode of speech.

෴

On April 2, 1870, seven months after publishing his "South Sea Idyl," Stoddard sent this youth-love document to Whitman with a letter.[18] His note opened with an imperious command: "In the name of CALAMUS listen to me!" The capitalized "CALAMUS" emphatically established Stoddard's interest in men-loving men as the particular link between them, a link Whitman could not have missed.

Stoddard was thinking of "sailing for Tahiti in about five weeks." Civilization, even San Francisco civilization, had again proved inhospitable:

> I know there is but one hope for me. I must get in amongst people who are not afraid of instincts and who scorn hypocrisy. I am numbed with the frigid manners of the Christians; barbarism has given me the fullest joy of my life and I long to return to it and be satisfied.

If Whitman replied within the month, said Stoddard, seeking the blessing of this counterauthority figure, he would "then go into the South Seas feeling sure of your friendship and I should try to live the real life there for your sake as well as for my own." Stoddard here clearly and unambiguously sought Whitman's blessing for a second sexual adventure in the South Seas. He got Whitman's approval in an extremely encouraging, remarkably forthright response.

On April 23, 1870, Whitman answered, saying that he had just reread Stoddard's "Idyl" and found it "soothing & nourishing"—his alimentary metaphor is striking. Whitman then significantly added: "As to you, I do not of course object to your emotional & adhesive nature, & the outlet thereof, but warmly approve them."[19]

Whitman here clearly understood, and heartily, *unequivocally supported* Stoddard's man-loving desire, "& the outlet thereof"—his sexual activity. Whitman's was, in fact, one of the most explicit private statements supporting the active sexual expression of a man-lusting man written in the nineteenth-century United States. I stress Whitman's explicit, unqualified approval of Stoddard's active sexual expression. For, as we will see, Whitman's better-known, later response to John Addington Symonds has often been understood to condemn men's sexual acts with men.

Whitman then continued with a question: Did Stoddard know "how the hard, pungent, gritty, worldly experiences & qualities in American practical life, also serve? how they prevent extravagant sentimentalism? & how they are not without their own great value & even joy?"[20] Without discounting Stoddard's past sexual acts with men and without discounting his support for Stoddard's future pursuit of such acts, Whitman here suggested an emotionally fulfilling "American" alternative.

Whitman had, after all, just half a decade earlier, found that he could stroll around New York City and pick up and "sleep with" a variety of men. What his "slept with" entailed exactly, we do not know. But Whitman, unlike Stoddard, had not found it necessary to travel halfway around the world to find "real life."

When, at the end of April 1870, the fifty-one-year-old Whitman wrote this letter, he may also have been hinting at the satisfaction he hoped to find in inactive, platonic, and therefore less emotionally taxing erotic relationships with men. Just two months later, on June 17, Whitman would admonish himself in his notebook to "remove myself . . . from this incessant *enormous* & *abnormal* PERTURBATION" (a reference to Peter Doyle). In any case, Whitman's depreciation to Stoddard of "extravagant sentimentalism" (his implicit extolling of a cool practicality) was offered as an *alternative* way of relating, by no means *instead of, or as moral condemnation of,* Stoddard's active pursuit of sex with men.

Whitman was, in fact, "comforted," he told Stoddard in April 1870, that "young men dwell in thought upon me & my utterances—as you do"; and again he expressed his hope to meet Stoddard. He had obviously been seduced by Stoddard and this journalist's self-dramatizing essays and letters, as well as fascinated by his active, cross-cultural search for sexual and emotional satisfaction.

ৎ

In July 1870, three months after receiving Whitman's encouraging letter, Charles Warren Stoddard left San Francisco for what, right from the start, became another sexually instructive adventure. On July 7, boarding the *Chevert,* a French training ship bound for Tahiti, Stoddard found himself "In a Transport." That is how he punningly and campily titled his published account of his maiden voyage to Tahiti, published in December 1873 in a volume of his travel writings.[21] If Stoddard's actual adventures were only half as stimulating, this was an exciting trip indeed.

The erotic shenanigans to follow were anticipated as Stoddard's narrator (clearly his alter ego) made his way at night to the docks, passing "one or two shadows . . . groping about . . . , making more noise than a shadow has any right to make."[22] The crew of the ship was also described suggestively: forty "bold sailor-boys," dressed in "blue flannel with broad collars—skipping about in the most fantastic manner," as if in a "ballet."[23] Stoddard's feminizing of the crew suggested sexual nonconformity to readers in the know, though most nineteenth-century readers would not have seen any link between gender and erotic deviance.

At the ship, the narrator was immediately greeted by a "little French *aspirant de marine,* with an incipient mustache" named Thanaron, who "embraced me when I boarded the transport . . . , treated me like a long-lost brother all that afternoon, and again embraced me when I went ashore." Thanaron's embracings are so "impulsive and boyish" that the narrator "immediately returned his salute, and with considerable fervor, feeling that kind Heaven had thrown me into the arms of the exceptional foreigner."[24]

Heaven had indeed done its work; the narrator does soon fall, literally, into the arms of "Thanaron, my foreign affinity" ("affinity" being another nineteenth-century term for an intimate partner).[25] As the narrator's ship sailed toward Tahiti, the atmosphere aboard grew "warmer every day" and something "unmanned us; so we rushed to our own little cabin and hugged one another, lest we should forget how when we were restored to our sisters and our sweethearts, and everything was forgiven . . . in one intense moment of French remorse." If this was not explicit enough, Stoddard's narrator asked: "Who took me in his arms and carried me the length of the cabin in three paces . . . ?" Thanaron, of course.[26] The embracing turned promiscuous as Thanaron's admirers among the crew suddenly appeared on the scene without explanation. They "nearly squeezed the life out of him in the vain hope of making their joy known to him."

Who looked upon this orgy, wondering what was coming next? The narrator, of course. Assuring us that "we kept doing that sort of thing [squeezing of some kind] until I got very used to it," he confessed, "by the time we sighted . . . Tahiti, my range of experience was so great that nothing could touch me further."[27]

Another day, after a mock military battle, the sailors "rush into our little cabin and regale themselves with copious droughts of absinthe, and I am pressed to the proud bosom of Thanaron, who is restored to me without a scar to disfigure his handsome little body."[28] The "warlike beard" of the ship's first officer, we are told, is belied by "very soft dark eyes" and "long lashes." This officer is said to be "the happy possessor of a tight little African, known as Nero, although I always looked upon him as so much Jamaica ginger." (That is, Nero is Jamaican. "Tight," in this context, most obviously meant either that Nero was close with his master or that he was a rare prize; but it may also have suggested an anal constriction satisfying to the master.)

The first officer, we learn, "loved with the ardor of his vacillating eyes, yet governed with the rigor of his beard," one minute torturing Nero with work, the next publicly and emphatically praising the loyal and "faithful Nero." Once, even, readers are told, the officer, "took Nero by the throat and kissed him passionately upon his sooty cheek . . . with an expression of virtuous defiance that was calculated to put all conventionalities to the blush."[29]

The casual racism is much less surprising than the casual, public display of kisses between a white man called "master" and a black man called, figuratively, a "slave." Stoddard pointed to, but made light of, the abusive, obsessive character of this domestic arrangement between social unequals.

After thirty-three days at sea, the ship approached Tahiti. At twilight the air was "fragrant" and "fruity" as its passengers prepared for shore, and the narrator muses: "O Thanaron, my Thanaron, with your arms about my neck, and [the chief officer's] arms about you, and Nero clinging to his master's knees—in fact, with everybody felicitating every other body," all are "literally in a transport!" Stoddard's pun transmutes that age's tradition of camp talk into campy published prose. "Felicitating," indeed! Fellating, more like it! In this published account of his trip to Tahiti, Stoddard's narrator found the sexual encounters that Stoddard had hoped for, and that Whitman had encouraged him to seek. If Stoddard's published travelogue reproduces even just a bit of his actual experience, this was a successful trip for him indeed.[30] Stoddard, like Whitman, was starting to go public about man-loving. And he was not alone as an international, cross-cultural sexual explorer.

John Safford Fiske, Yale, 1863. [Fiske], *History* (1905). Courtesy Yale University Library. ∼

In August 1867, J. Mullin, a local politician in Watertown, New York, wrote to United States Secretary of State William H. Seward, recommending John Safford Fiske for the position of United States consul at Leith (now Edinburgh), Scotland.[1] Mullin praised Fiske as "a young man of unblemished character," and of "unquestionable ability," who "intends devoting himself to literature," and who "seeks a place abroad with the aim of extending his knowledge of man." Fiske's appointment, Mullin added, "will do no discredit to the department or the country," and "aid a young man who is destined to do honor to both." Though Fiske was faultless in the matter, this was *not* how things turned out. This young man did, however, extend his knowledge of man.

John Safford Fiske had been born in Ashtabula, Ohio, on January 18, 1838, and had prepared for college at Williston Seminary, in Easthampton, Massachusetts; he entered Yale College in 1859. Graduating in 1863, he worked as a deputy clerk in the New York State Senate in Albany from 1863 to 1864, then spent 1865 as a private tutor with a family near New York City. Over the next two years he wrote for the monthly magazines.[2] In August 1867, Fiske applied for and was awarded the consul job in Scotland.[3]

In October 1868, two Englishmen—Ernest Boulton, son of a London stockbroker, and Frederick Park, son of a superior court officer—traveled to Edinburgh where they met the new United States consul. The American Fiske became enamored of the British Boulton, and when Boulton returned to London, fascinated Fiske attempted to sustain the romance by mail. Fiske's letters proved fateful for all concerned.

On April 18, 1870, the thirty-two-year-old Fiske wrote to the twenty-two-year-old Boulton, "wishing . . . a hundred times each day" that his "darling Ernie" were "to be here." The American desired Boulton's physical presence, not just his memory and his photographs, however alluring.[4]

Boulton and his friend Park were fond of dressing as elegant, enticing women, and they appeared in public in amateur theatricals and had their pictures taken. Fiske collected Boulton's portraits: "I have eleven photographs of you (and expecting more tomorrow) which I look at over and over again." Photographic portraits circulated often among nineteenth-century men friends, the images giving physical form to memories and fantasies of distant bodies and souls. Fiske also kept "four little notes" from Boulton, "which I have sealed up in a packet," and, he added, wistfully, "I have a heart full of love and longing."

Fiske missed Boulton in the flesh: the photographs, notes, and "my memory is all that I have of you." "When," he asked, "are you going to

Ernest Boulton, acting a woman and acting a man. Courtesy Essex Record Office. ❧

Frederick William Park, acting a woman and acting a man. Courtesy Essex Record Office. ❧

give me more?" What more, exactly, did Fiske desire? Ordinary Fiske imagined offering the extraordinary Boulton a mundane, steady love. He asked Boulton, rhetorically, when he was going to write that "all the world is over head and ears in love" with him? And when was Boulton going to report that he was "so tired of adoration and compliments" that he was ready to turn to his "humdrum friend as a relief?"

"Believe me, darling," said Fiske, probing for a response, "a word of remembrance from you can never come amiss." He threatened not to write his "darling" a long letter again if Boulton did not send an encouraging note.

The American then tried to pique Boulton's interest with a tease: "Adventures do turn up, even in Edinburgh. Perhaps you would envy me for five whole minutes if I were to tell you of one that I've had since you left." Fiske did not ask more than five minutes' envy from Boulton hinting obliquely, it seems, that longer concentration would challenge Boulton's attention span. Fiske's adventure, he said, would keep for Boulton's "own ear when very likely you try after the same happiness." The American either expected Boulton to pursue similar "adventures" with others or with Fiske himself. The details of such adventures, Fiske already intuited, were dangerous to commit to writing.

Then Fiske mentioned yet another romantic interest: "Robbie Sinclair" was coming to Edinburgh, with "his smiling face" and "clear grey eyes and vivid roses." The consumptive Robbie's rosy cheeks provided the flowery metaphor. Fiske's prose transformed a life-threatening disease into a sentimental figure of speech.

Fiske wondered if his and Boulton's mutual friend Louis Hurt (a surveyor for the Scottish post office department) would like Robbie Sinclair: "I hope not—at least not too much." For Fiske himself was "getting fond of Louis, and as I am fond of Robbie too, I don't want them to take too violently to each other." Fiske was clearly acquainted with a circle of like-minded, like-loving, like-lusting men, whose value system and psychology permitted the simultaneous pursuit of several romantic adventures. Walt Whitman was not alone in spreading his adhesiveness around.

"But what are these fancies," asked Fiske grandiloquently, compared "to the devotion with which I am yours always?" Fiske's letter called his desire for Boulton "devotion," "love," and "longing." He ended this letter with a last line in French, addressed (in translation) *To an angel named Ernie Boulton, London.*

The American's precious literary style suggests that a group of men were, by 1870, already constructing a distinctive, still secret, subcultural mode of speech, now known as "camp." That word itself was actually used in a letter that Boulton's cross-dressing friend, Frederick Park, wrote in November 1868 to Boulton's "husband," Lord Arthur Clinton. In this missive, Park hoped that he will live to "a green old age," but bemoaned the great amount of make-up it would then take "to hide that very unbecoming tint." Park then immediately complained that his "campish undertakings are not at present meeting with the success they deserve." This is the earliest-known use of "campish" among men-lusting men.[5] The word's historical documentation helps to bring a formerly hidden subculture to the light.

The explicit emergence, in London, of the word "campish" supports my suggestion that in America, too, we may also have discovered some early examples of the campish. I refer to the arch letters of Walt Whitman to his New York City friends Bloom and Gray (in 1863), the playful letters to Whitman from the soldiers Alonzo Bush (in 1863) and Edward Stewart (in 1870), and the double entendre travel writing of Charles Warren Stoddard (starting in the late 1860s).[6]

Fiske and friends were also already using the word "drag" to refer to men dressing in women's clothes. On March 20, 1870, from the United States consulate in Edinburgh, Fiske wrote again to Boulton, saying that he had received a "charming" letter from their friend Louis Hurt, reporting that Boulton, in London, was "living in drag"—one of the earliest documented uses of that term.[7] Within this Anglo-American male culture there was already a name in use for dressing as the other sex. If Boulton was now indeed "living in drag," his cross-dressing had shifted from an occasional theatrical appearance to a full-time occupation.

Fiske was definitely intrigued by Boulton's sartorial and gender shift, exclaiming: "What a wonderful child it is!" Fiske's "child" and his "it" ironically referenced Boulton's ambiguous manhood. The American told Boulton that he had "three minds to come to London and see your magnificence with my own eyes." But then reality intervened, and he wondered: "Would you welcome me?" He answered himself: "Probably it is better I should stay at home and dream of you. But the thought of you— Lais and Antinous in one—is ravishing." Fiske was ravished by the idea that Boulton, in drag, combined the charms of Lais (soon after called "one of the most famous prostitutes in antiquity") with the attractions of Antinous (soon after called "a male prostitute").[8] Boulton's mingling of the feminine and masculine clearly piqued Fiske's interest and inspired his admiration.

The American then solicited Boulton's advice: "A young lady," a "charmingly-dressed beautiful fool with £30,000 a year," was on her way to Edinburgh, and "I have reason to believe that if I go in for her I can marry her." Another tease to rouse Boulton's interest? It seems not, for Fiske immediately assured Boulton: "You know I should never care for her; but is the bait tempting enough for me to make this further sacrifice to respectability?" The American consul already felt he had conceded enough to propriety.

Yet the pressure to marry was strong, and Fiske seemed to be seriously considering a wedding. He mused out loud: "Of course, after we were married I could do pretty much as I please." He explained: "People don't mind what one does on £30,000 a year, and the lady . . . hasn't brains enough to trouble herself about much beyond her dresses, her carriage, etc." Nasty comments about the lady's interest in dresses cannot have endeared Fiske to Boulton, who also troubled himself a great deal about dresses. "What shall I do?" inquired Fiske. Though Boulton had still not written to Fiske, the smitten American ended "with all the love in my heart," declaring himself "yours."

On April 28, 1870, just eight days after Fiske wrote his second note to his beloved, the cross-dressed Ernest Boulton and Frederick Park were leaving the Strand Theatre in London when they were arrested. Boulton and Park were first charged simply with outraging public decency by dressing publicly as women, and were taken to the Bow Street station house and held overnight.[9]

At a public hearing the next day, Boulton, known to friends as "Stella," or "Lady Stella Clinton," the companion of Lord Arthur Clinton, member of Parliament, was still wearing the clothes of the night before: a cherry-colored silk evening dress, trimmed with white lace, bracelets, a wig, and a braided chignon. Frederick William Park, known as "Fanny Winifred," was adorned in a low-necked, dark green satin dress with black lace trim, a black lace shawl, white kid gloves, and blond curls.[10]

The police had, it turned out, for a year been following the movements of Boulton and Park as they migrated beyond appearances as women in amateur theatricals to cross-dressed promenades in London's public markets, arcades, restaurants, taverns, balls, and theaters. Flirting and perhaps seeking romantic and sexual adventures with men, Boulton and Park had sought to expand their freedom of movement and expression, while the officers of the state had sought to restrict the public sites open to these nontraditional gender performances. The cross-dressers had unknowingly contested the state over the use of public, urban space.

The morning after Boulton and Park's arrest, the story goes, the police superintendent had met a friend, James Paul, a medical doctor, and, by way of harassing the cross-dressers, had asked him to examine the prisoners.[11] But the doctor had been studying French medical writings on

"La Pédérastie." On his own, he decided to examine the prisoners' anuses for the alleged physical signs of participating, on the receiving end, of anal intercourse. Sure enough, he found the anuses he sought. He reported his findings to the police, and these officials then significantly expanded the charge, accusing Boulton and Park of the "detestable and abominable crime of buggery not to be named among Christians," an act punishable by ten years to life imprisonment. Just a decade earlier in England, buggery had been punishable by death.

With the new charge, the crime of Boulton and Park had escalated from a relatively minor violation of gender norms and laws into a much more serious breach of sexual standards and statutes. In this case, the historical, cultural, and public linking of gender bending with, specifically, sexual deviance—the construction of a new, sexual *and* gender inversion—can be observed as it happened. But, since police investigators could find no witnesses to Boulton and Park's alleged buggery, the revised charge, for which the two cross-dressers were finally tried, was "conspiracy" to commit buggery.

After the arrests, the police searched Boulton's and Park's apartments and confiscated quantities of photos and correspondence, including the two letters from John Safford Fiske to his inamorato. Thanks to this zealous police work and the subsequent prosecution, we possess the texts of Fiske's two authentically campish letters, written before any hint of legal trouble, as well as many wonderful photos of Boulton and Park, in drag and out.[12]

A series of a well-publicized preliminary hearings began to proceed slowly through the English legal system. On May 18, 1870, Louis Hurt, in London, wrote the first of several notes to John Safford Fiske, in Edinburgh, warning him "that the worst letter" held by the prosecution "is yours."[13] Hurt referred to Fiske's second letter (March 20, 1870), the one that mentioned Lais and Antinous. Fiske's literary references and flowery writing style had suddenly become prime evidence of a conspiracy to commit a serious crime. Fiske's literary allusions now threatened to send men to jail for years. The word wars had intensified.

The police were "anxious" for Fiske to come to London, Hurt told the American, "and I really believe it would be your best course." Fiske's "name must appear" in the proceedings, Hurt reasoned, so the American might as well cooperate with the authorities. But Hurt also encouraged a little resistance: "E [Ernest] begs you will destroy any letters from him you may have in your possession." Fiske did destroy Boulton's "four little notes."

Later, Hurt wrote to Fiske that he had seen a copy of one of the American's letters to Boulton: There "is nothing indecent" in it, "of course, but it is the most high-flown language."[14] Fiske's campish letters had become a dangerous liability.

Another letter from Hurt to Fiske, on June 3, 1870, again urged the American to come to London and explain to the police "what utter nonsense your letters were."[15] The literary interpretation of Fiske's language and meaning—what academics call the hermeneutics of his literary style—suddenly had serious, real-life consequences. The analysis of his literary efforts could send him and others to jail for ten years to life.[16] In the eyes of the police, Fiske's unmanly literary style was evidence of the conspiracy to commit buggery.

Six days later, on June 9, Fiske was visited in Edinburgh by a Detective Holland, who searched his apartment for evidence of the American's involvement with Boulton and Park. In addition to Hurt's recent letters, Fiske (intimidated and frightened, evidently) produced from behind a bedroom grate an album containing "a number of photographs, beautifully executed, of Boulton in female attire"—one showed "Stella" in "an attitude of prayer."[17]

Later in June, when Fiske finally traveled to London to see the police, he was arrested and charged, along with Boulton, Park, Hurt, and four others, with conspiracy to commit buggery. One of the accused, the member of Parliament, Lord Arthur Pelham Clinton (Ernest Boulton's London boyfriend), died suddenly and mysteriously on June 18, and may well have committed suicide or been driven to a heart attack. Three of the accused were never apprehended. On June 24, John Safford Fiske, facing a scandalous upcoming court case, wrote to the United States Department of State, voluntarily resigning his post as consul, to avoid tarnishing that government office, though maintaining his innocence.[18]

Almost a year later, on May 9, 1871, the case of *The Queen v. Boulton and Others* began before a jury guided by a famous English lord chief justice, Alexander Cockburn, and numbers of prominent attorneys. The campish letters from the American, John Safford Fiske, were among the chief evidence offered of his and the others' involvement in an international conspiracy to commit buggery.[19]

A government clerk, Donald Sinclair, testified in Fiske's defense. He had known the American since 1868, when the consul first mixed in Edinburgh society. Fiske had "sought the society of ladies a great deal," Sinclair offered. He meant, obviously, to suggest Fiske's attraction to women (*not*, certainly, to hint that Fiske identified with women's erotic interest in men). Fiske was a man of culture and a good musician, testified Sinclair, who said he had dined often with the accused in his rooms. (If Sinclair

was himself a man-lusting man, his testimony was all the more courageous.)

At one dinner party, Sinclair had asked to meet Ernest Boulton, of
whom he had heard favorable things, and Fiske had immediately sent a
note to "Darling Ernie," asking him to come by that night, adding,
"Everybody is too drunk to mind." Boulton had appeared that night, Sinclair testified, in formal men's apparel, and not the slightest impropriety
had occurred. (One man's impropriety was, of course, another man's bit
o' fun.)

Cross-examined by the prosecution, Sinclair denied that anyone had
been drunk; Fiske's phrase, "too drunk to mind," referred to Boulton's
formal clothes (not his feminine appearance and sodomitical character, as
the prosecution suggested).

Fiske's landlady, Eliza Corner, testified that she had known him for
two-and-a-half years, and that he had not been absent from her house for
one night. Fiske did not stay out all night carousing, her supportive testimony implied.[20]

A clerk in the Edinburgh courts, Charles Doeg, testified that he knew
Fiske intimately, and that the American was well bred, well educated, and
liked musical and literary society, though his words were sometimes romantic and exaggerated. Doeg regarded Fiske as a man of high moral
character, "remarkably sensitive to the feelings of others."[21] (Was Doeg
the "adventure" Fiske had mentioned to Boulton? If so, his testimony
was also incredibly courageous.)

There was no evidence against Fiske, just his acquaintance with Boulton, and a couple of letters, argued the American's lawyer, Henry
Matthews.[22] If Fiske had *not* been conscious of his complete innocence he
could have fled to America, the lawyer pointed out. But, instead, Fiske
had even traveled, voluntarily, to London to give evidence, at which time
he had been accused and arrested.

The lawyer did not "attempt to justify the execrable taste, the indelicacy of penning such letters" as Fiske had sent to Boulton. Manly men did
not write letters like this to other men, Fiske's attorney conceded. But the
jury should not read buggery into Fiske's feminine language, the lawyer
implied—these were simply notes "addressed to an effeminate lad; a
dainty and pleasing boy, who was generally treated as a young girl, and
who was so addressed by Fiske." The lawyer directed his words to a jury
unlikely to link gender nonconformity with sexual crime.

Matthews argued against reading Fiske's highflown words as evidence
specifically of buggery: "It is inconceivable that two Christians in the
nineteenth century, having towards each other the relations that are im-

puted to the two young men, should express their mutual attachment in language savoring of sentiment, refinement or of respect."[23] Expressions of Christian intimacy were one thing, buggery another. That is important—the respectable virtues, sentiment, refinement, and respect, existed in a universe completely apart from the world of buggery. The lawyer's argument revealed the dominant consciousness of his time. This is one of those rare moments in history when particular evidence illuminates the worldview of an age.

Defending Fiske's reference to Robbie Sinclair's "vivid roses," Matthews asked the jury to recognize "what peril an innocent man may be put because he uses foolish and vile phrases." The barrister exclaimed: "Good heavens, gentlemen! Are expressions of that sort to be twisted into expressions of unnatural affection?" Matthews asked: "Is it in this way that persons committing unnatural crimes express themselves?" Buggers did not talk like this, he suggested. The struggle of Whitman, Fiske, and other men for an eloquent language of love between men countered such assertions.

The prosecutor, in turn, asked if Fiske's reference to Boulton as Lais and Antinous was "the language of friendship or . . . love, or . . . guilty desire?" Friendship and love were one thing, guilty desire another. The defense and prosecution debated the meaning of Fiske's words, just as historians of sex, a hundred years later, debate the meaning of old letters—though without dire legal consequences for the correspondents.

Near the trial's end, Judge Cockburn instructed the jury that Fiske and Hurt did not even live in the same country as their cross-dressing friends. They "had nothing to do with the conduct of Boulton and Park in going about in women's dresses." The judge upbraided the police for searching Fiske's and Hurt's lodgings "without any authority."[24]

The only evidence against Fiske was his own letters, which did "excite very ugly suspicions" that he "had in his mind some unnatural love for this young man." Fiske's love, his lawyer had suggested, may have been "entirely spiritual," a love like that between "persons of the opposite sex" in which "no sensual thought existed." That is a most revealing comment on the age's dominant view of love between men and women as asexual. No heterosexual hypothesis here. The judge concluded: Whatever the meaning of Fiske's letters, the prosecution had not proved them to contain more than romantic expressions of personal admiration and affection.

The judge declared: a "gross injustice" had been done to Fiske and Hurt. They "ought never to have been put upon their trial in this court." He left it to the jury, he said, to decide if Fiske's and Hurt's letters supported the charge of a conspiracy to commit buggery.[25]

On May 15, 1871, the jury retired and returned to the courtroom in fifty-three minutes, finding Boulton, Park, Fiske, and Hurt not guilty on every count. The verdict was received in court with "Loud cheers, and cries of 'Bravo!'" Ernest Boulton fainted and had to be revived with water.[26]

In London, in the early 1870s, the charge that cross-dressing and an unmanly literary style were hallmarks of anal intercourse was found to be unproved. Within twenty years, however, the link between gender non-conformity and sexual crime would be assumed, customarily.

෴

In 1878, 1889, and 1905, the autobiographies that John Safford Fiske sent to his alma mater, Yale, to be published in his class chronicles, are silent, not surprisingly, about his harrowing brush with British law.[27] After his consulship in Edinburgh, Fiske wrote, he went to Düsseldorf, Germany, and painted architectural subjects—inanimate buildings were safer to savor than cross-dressing youths. In 1873, Fiske returned to the United States for three years, publishing a translation of the historian Hippolyte Taine's *A Tour through the Pyrenees*. In 1874, Fiske again left the United States, living in Constantinople, Germany, and France. There, Fiske said, he took a house near Paris "with an English friend," a hint that Fiske perhaps found the lover for whom he yearned.[28] Fiske settled, finally, in 1882, in Alassio, on the Italian Riviera. Italy had a history as refuge for American and English men-loving men.

During these years, Fiske published journalistic reports from Sweden, Russian, Germany, Turkey, Greece, and Italy in various newspapers, and he contributed cultural and political reports to *The Nation* in New York and the *Princeton Review*. In 1893, Fiske reported on the Columbian Exhibition in Chicago. He also wrote articles for the *Dictionary of Architecture*, edited by a well-known architect, Russell Sturgis. In 1893, Fiske lectured on art and architecture at Hobart College, in Geneva, New York, and in 1897 received an honorary degree from that institution.[29]

In 1905, the fifty-five-year-old Fiske wrote from Alassio to his Yale classmates, summing up his life: "With advancing years I have gradually abandoned painting and even drawing"; now he divided his time between reading, writing, and horticulture. "I have a large and beautiful garden" in a region "where the rose blooms the whole winter," and, as he sold his flowers, the garden paid for itself. He was at home, he reported, "on a coast famous all the world over for beauty, happy in its climate, frequented by pleasant people from every quarter of the globe." Having "congenial employments that occupy without driving, I think I may

John Safford Fiske, about 1879. [Fiske], *History* (1905). Courtesy Yale University Library. ♌

claim that, in an unpretending way, I have shaped for myself a life that is agreeable enough in the living."[30]

When Fiske died in 1907, he left 4,000 books, cataloged in three large, carefully handwritten volumes, to Hobart College. Among these are John Addington Symonds's multivolume history of Italy, Oscar Wilde's *Picture of Dorian Gray,* and an English edition of Walt Whitman's poems.[31]

A memorial to Fiske, by his friend Joseph Hetherington McDaniels, a Hobart professor of Greek language and literature, reveals that Fiske had guided historian Edward Augustus Freeman in his travels and research for a book on Sicily, and "had been the intimate companion of the scholar and diplomatist, Eugene Schuyler, in voyages through the Levant and the Aegean sea." Fiske, Freeman, and Schuyler had constituted a "brace of comrades."[32] McDaniels had visited Fiske's villa in Alassio, and recalled his "bewitching garden which he opened hospitably and freely to his friends" and the many "pictures which were mostly mementos of beloved artist friends."[33]

McDaniels mentioned the effort Fiske had made to visit "and cheer the solitary hours of an imprisoned friend," claiming that this effort had brought on Fiske's final illness.[34] That most tantalizing reference was not further explained.

Fiske "craved relations of mutual helpfulness and affection," made friends in all classes, and cherished "the recollections of a life full of the most varied sympathies and friendships." McDaniels called Fiske "a sweet soul that gave much and asked no praise, but affection. And that affection he certainly had."[35]

By 1874, the American travel journalist Charles Warren Stoddard had given up on the South Seas to pursue his erotic destiny in Italy. There in romantic, legendary Venice at the end of the year, "a young man quietly joined me" in a box at the opera during intermission, Stoddard recalled. "We looked at each other and were acquainted in a minute. Some people understand one another at sight, and don't have to try, either." Stoddard's recollection of this meeting was published in Boston's *National Magazine* in 1906.[1]

Stoddard's new friend was the American artist Francis Davis Millet. The two had heard of each other, but never met. Stoddard was thirty-one in 1874, and Millet was twenty-eight. During the Civil War, Millet's father, a Massachusetts doctor, had served as a Union army surgeon, and in 1864, the eighteen-year-old Frank Millet had enlisted as a private, serving first as a drummer boy and then as a surgeon's assistant. Young Millet graduated from Harvard in 1869, with a master's degree in modern languages and literature. While working as a journalist on Boston newspapers, he learned lithography and earned money enough to enroll in 1871 in the Royal Academy, Antwerp. There, unlike anyone before him, he won all the art prizes the school offered and was officially hailed by the king of Belgium. As secretary of the Massachusetts commission to the Vienna exposition in 1873, Millet formed a friendship with the American Charles Francis Adams, and then traveled through Turkey, Romania, Greece, Hungary, and Italy, finally settling in Venice to paint.[2]

At the opera, as Stoddard recalled, Millet immediately asked, "Where are you going to spend the Winter?" He then invited Stoddard to live in his eight-room rented house. "Why not come and take one of those rooms?" the painter offered, "I'll look after the domestic affairs"—is this another Stoddard double entendre? Stoddard accepted Millet's invitation, recalling that they became "almost immediately very much better acquainted."[3] Did Stoddard go home with Millet that night?

The two lived together during the winter of 1874–75, though Stoddard did *not* take one of the extra rooms. Millet's romantic letters to Stoddard indicate that the men shared a bed in an attic room overlooking the Lagoon, Grand Canal, and Public Garden.[4] Lack of space did not explain this bed sharing, and Stoddard's earlier and later sexual liaisons with men, his written essays and memoirs, and Millet's letters to Stoddard, all strongly suggest that their intimacy found active affectionate and erotic expression.

Charles Warren Stoddard. J. N. Katz/Roger Austen Collection. ৯৬

Francis Davis Millet, photograph given to Stoddard in February 1875. Courtesy Syracuse University Library. ❧

Though Stoddard's erotic interests seem to have focused exclusively on men, Millet's were more fluid. In the last quarter of the nineteenth century, Millet's psychic configuration was probably the more common, Stoddard's exclusive interest in men the less usual. In any case, the ranging of Millet's erotic interest between men and women was not then understood as "bisexual," a mix of "homo" and "hetero."

Another occupant of the house was Giovanni, whom Stoddard called "our gondolier, cook, chambermaid and errand-boy."[5] His use of "maid" and "boy" hint at gender doubling, and, perhaps, at sexual nonconformity. (Giovanni's last name, not mentioned, is lost to history, typical in masters' accounts of servants.) That winter, Millet taught Giovanni to prepare two classic New England dishes, baked beans and fish balls, and during the cold months, Stoddard recalled, he and Millet dined Massachusetts style in their warm Italian kitchen.[6]

From the window of this kitchen in warmer weather, Stoddard recalled, they watched "the supple figures of half-nude artisans" working in an adjoining shipyard. It was "no wonder that we lingered over our meals there," said Stoddard, without explaining.[7] Visual, alimentary, and erotic pleasures are repeatedly linked in Stoddard's and Millet's writings, as we will see.

During the daytime, Millet painted in their home's courtyard while Stoddard dozed, smoked, and wrote columns about Venice and other Italian cities for the *San Francisco Chronicle*. They dined early and took gondola rides at sunset. In a newspaper column that Stoddard published early in his relationship with Millet, the journalist wrote of "spoons" with "my fair," an unnamed *woman*, in a gondola's covered "lovers' cabin," and of "her memory of a certain memorable sunset—but that is between us two!"[8] Stoddard here changed the sex of his fair one when discussing "spooning" (kissing) in his published writing. Walt Whitman was not alone in employing such literary subterfuge.

In February 1875, Stoddard, seeking new cities to write about for the *Chronicle,* made a three-week tour of northern Italy, revising these memoirs twelve years later for the Catholic magazine *Ave Maria,* published at Notre Dame University. Stoddard wrote that his unnamed painter friend accompanied him as guide and "companion-in-arms," a punning name for his bed mate—the companion in his arms.[9] The definitely intended pun allowed Stoddard to imply more about this companionship than he could say directly. A variety of other, barely coded references lace Stoddard's writing with allusions to eros between men.

In Padua, for example, Stoddard wrote that he and his companion were struck by views of "lovely churches and the tombs of saints and hosts of college boys."[10] Casually including "hosts of college boys" among the "lovely" religious sights of Padua, and substituting "hosts of . . . boys" for the proverbial "angels," Stoddard's sacrilege-threatening run-on sentence suggested that, to these two tourists, at least, the boys looked heavenly.

In another case, on the train to Florence, Stoddard and his companion noticed a tall "fellow who had just parted with his friend" at a station. As "soon as they had kissed each other on both cheeks—a custom of the country," Stoddard explained to nonkissing American men, the traveler was "hoisted into our compartment." But "no sooner did the train move off, than he was overcome, and, giving way to his emotion, he lifted up his voice like a trumpeter," filling the car with "lamentations." For half an hour "he bellowed lustily, but no one seemed in the least disconcerted at this monstrous show of feeling; doubtless each in his turn had been similarly affected."[11]

Suggesting, slyly, that bellowing "lustily" was common among parting men friends and represented the expression of a deep, intense, and by no means unusual feeling, Stoddard pointed to a ubiquitous male eros, *not* one limited to men of a special, unique, man-loving temperament. Typically keeping a sharp eye out for the varieties of physically expressed attachment between males, he also invoked Walt Whitman's poem on the tender parting of men friends on a pier: "The one to remain hung on the other's neck and passionately kiss'd him, / While the one to depart tightly prest the one to remain in his arms."[12] That poem, and Stoddard's essay, suggest that parting provided, in the nineteenth century, a public occasion for the physical expression of intense love between men, a custom that had special resonance for men, like Stoddard, attracted to men.

Among the statues that Stoddard admired in Florence were "The Wrestlers, tied up in a double-bow of monstrous muscles"—another culturally sanctioned icon of physical contact between, in this case, scantily clad men.[13]

In Genoa, Stoddard recalled seeing a "captivating" painting of the "lovely martyr" St. Sebastian, a "nude torso" of "a youth as beautiful as Narcissus"—yet another classic, undressed male image suffused with eros. The "sensuous element predominates," in this sculpture, said Stoddard, and "even the blood-stains cannot disfigure the exquisite lustre of the flesh."[14]

In Sienna, Stoddard recorded, he and his companion-in-arms slept in a "great double bed . . . so white and plump it looked quite like a gigantic frosted cake—and we were happy." The last phrase directly echoes Stoddard's favorite Whitman Calamus poem in which a man's friend lies "sleeping by me under the same cover in the cool night"—"and that night

I was happy."[15] Sleeping happily with Millet in that cake/bed, Stoddard again linked food and bodily pleasure.[16]

Back in their Venice home in spring 1875, Stoddard recalled one day seeing "a tall, slender and exceedingly elegant figure approaching languidly." This second American artist, A. A. Anderson, appeared one Sunday at Millet's wearing a "long black cloak of Byronic mold," one corner of which was "carelessly thrown back over his arm, displaying a lining of cardinal satin." The costume was enhanced by a gold-threaded, damask scarf and a broad-brimmed hat with tassels. In Stoddard's published memoirs, identifying Anderson only as "Monte Cristo," the journalist recalled the artist's "uncommonly comely face of the oriental-oval and almond-eyed type."[17] Entranced by the "glamor" surrounding Monte Cristo, Stoddard soon passed whole days "drifting with him" in his gondola, or walking ashore.[18]

Invited to dinner by Monte Cristo, Stoddard and his friend (Millet) found Monte occupying the suite of a "royal princess, it was so ample and so richly furnished."[19] (Monte was a "princess," Stoddard hints.) Funded by an inheritance from dad, Monte had earlier bought a steam yacht and cruised with an equally rich male friend to Egypt, then given the yacht away to an Arab potentate. Later, while Stoddard was visiting Paris, he found himself "at once in the embrace of Monte Cristo," recalling: "That night was Arabian, and no mistake!"[20] Stoddard's reference to *The Arabian Nights,* a classic text including man-love scenes, also invoked a western mystique of "oriental" sex.[21]

After the beautiful Anderson left Venice, Stoddard, the perennial rover, found it impossible to settle down any longer in the comfortable, loving domesticity offered by Millet. The journalist may also have needed new sights to inspire the travel writing that supported him. He therefore set off for Chester, England, to see Robert William Jones, a fellow with whom, a year earlier, he had shared a brief encounter and who had since been sending him passionate letters.[22] Stoddard's flight, after living with Millet for about six months, marked a new phase in their relationship. Millet now became the devoted pursuer, Stoddard the ambivalent pursued.

From Venice, Millet wrote affectionately to Stoddard on May 10, 1875, calling him "Dear Old Chummeke"—explaining, "I call you chummeke," the "diminutive of chum," because "you are already 'chum' but have never been chummeke before. Flemish you know." "Chum" and its variations constituted, as we have seen, a common, positive name among nineteenth-century male intimates, one of the terms by which they affirmed the special character of their tie.

Claiming he had not much to say because he "let out" so much in his first letter (not extant, significantly and unfortunately) Millet reported that he had a new pet. He had told their mutual friends, the Adamses, that he had "named the new dog Charles Warren Stoddard Venus," though "it wasn't that kind of a dog" (not, that is, a dog of mixed, ambiguous sex). To Stoddard, Millet certainly referred to Stoddard's large admixture of the feminine and perhaps to Stoddard's sexual interest in men. To the Adamses, Millet may have seemed to refer only to Stoddard's effeminacy. The dog's name "was not a question of sex," Millet had stressed to the Adamses, "but of appropriateness."

The dog's—and Stoddard's—ambiguous masculinity had obviously been the subject of some lighthearted banter between Millet and the Adamses. But Millet's reference to Stoddard's effeminacy probably did not then bring erotic infractions to this Adams family's mind, nor is it likely to have suggested to them the sexual aspect of the relationship between these men. Gender deviance and erotic nonconformity were not yet linked as they would be after the installation of homosex and heterosex.

Another dog, Tom, "sleeps in your place now and fills it all up, that is, the material space he occupies, crowding me out of bed very often." Stoddard's body was absent, but his spirit lingered on.

"Miss you?" Millet asked. He answered: "Bet your life. Put yourself in my place. It isn't the one who goes away who misses, it is the one who stays. Empty chair, empty bed, empty house." Millet's desire for Stoddard's bodily presence is palpable in his words.

"So, my dear old cuss," Millet ended warmly, "with lots of love I am thine—as you need not be told." He had obviously declared his love many times earlier.

He was working on a painting that called for two boy models, "posing two small cusses—the naked ones—together," Millet wrote to Stoddard on May 26 (again, the talk was of nude male flesh). But the hot, dust-laden, dry wind of Venice, lightning flashes, and "the mercurial little cusses" made him feel that he had "nearly ruined what good there was on the canvas." Millet wished Stoddard was present to "make me feel that I have not done so awfully bad work today."

"No gossip to speak of," Millet reported, except that a mutual male friend "does no work but spoons with Miss Kelley." "Spoon" appeared repeatedly in Millet's letters and in Stoddard's published journalism, with varying degrees of romantic and sexual intimation.[23]

Spooning reminded Millet that he had had "a squaring up" with Charlotte ("Donny") Adams, the eighteen-year-old daughter of their good friends.[24] Millet had told Donny "exactly what I thought of her going off with one fellow and coming home with another." In response, she had tried to "put it all on to me," saying "I alone was touchy." But Millet had told her Stoddard agreed with his criticism, "and then she seemed very anxious to beg my pardon etc. which was not granted."

Millet's high-handed objection to what he considered Donny's breach of dating etiquette shows him identifying with a man done wrong, supposedly, by a woman. Criticizing Donny's inconstancy in ditching one man for another, Millet may have applied to her the same standard to which he held himself. He was certainly constant in his romantic devotion to Stoddard, despite the journalist's inconstancy. Stoddard, off with Monte Cristo and Robert William Jones, clearly applied a less rigid rule to his own liaisons.

Donny Adams had ended this confrontation by reporting one of her men friends' suggestions: Millet was gaining weight that winter "because I liked her and did not care to see another fellow go with her." Donny and her man friend did not perceive that Millet's romantic-erotic interest was focused then on Stoddard. Men's erotic romances with men were invisible because at this time in the public consciousness, there was only one kind of erotic-romantic attraction—toward the other, different sex.

Millet asked Stoddard to meet him in Belgium in July. Then, for the first time in his letters, he acknowledged the imbalance in their need for each other: "My dear old Boy, I miss you more than you do me." He wondered "constantly—after dark," he confessed, "why should one go and the other stay. It is rough on the one who remains"—a repeated refrain.

"Harry" (another dog) "sends a wave of her tail and a gentle swagger of her body"—"Charles/Venus" was not the only mixed-sex dog name. "Tom," Millet added, "sends you his brightest smile and Venus wags his aimless tail in greeting."

He had not "passed one good night" since they parted, Millet admitted to Stoddard on May 30, and he was "completely played out from want of sleep and rest." He had not mentioned it before, "and I don't dare tell you why I haven't."

What was it, exactly, that Millet dared not say? Was it simply that he missed Stoddard too much and was depressed? Or did he believe, possibly, that he had exhausted himself, in Stoddard's absence, from voluntary or involuntary seminal emissions? Or, did Millet believe, perhaps, that he received from Stoddard's physical presence some spiritual, or material, vitality-enhancing substance? We cannot know for sure. But other evidence that we will consider supports a sexual interpretation.

Whatever Millet did not say, he was also probably worrying again about their unequal need for each other and about coming on too strong to Stoddard. We have already heard Stoddard's reference to two men friends' "monstrous show of feeling." Displays of emotion were evidently threatening, as well as intriguing, to Stoddard.

Millet had supposed for a while that it "was our old attic chamber that made me restless," and he had ordered Giovanni to move his bed elsewhere in the house. He had not "been into our attic room since and don't intend to go"—strong feelings about their old bedroom. But the "change of room does not cure me."

"What is the matter?" asked Millet, struggling to understand the source of his distress: "I know I miss you, my old chummeke, but isn't it reasonable that my other self misses you still more and cant let me sleep because he wants your magnetism! I think it must be so."

Millet was two-sided, he suggested, and one of his sides lacked the vital force provided by Stoddard's physical, bodily presence. "Magnetism" was a common nineteenth-century name for an individual's power to attract, his force of personality, and his energy.[25]

Was it possible that Millet missed, specifically, the vivifying ingestion of Stoddard's spirit via oral sex? This is not as far-fetched as it may sound. Three years after Millet wrote to Stoddard, in 1878, Dr. Mary Walker warned readers of her popular medical manual not to believe the common folklore that women's ingestion of men's semen, and men's ingestion of women's vaginal secretions, promoted health, life, and beauty.[26] As we will see, the benefits of an older man ingesting a younger man's semen was extolled by the English sex reformer Edward Carpenter to an American visitor with whom he tested the practice in the early twentieth century.

Mrs. Adams "is spooney on you, you know," Millet told Stoddard. But the roaming Stoddard was not thinking about Mrs. Adams, however affectionate their relationship. At long last, Stoddard admitted that he missed Millet, who was extremely pleased to hear it: "Bet your life, dear Boy, that it soothes me to learn that I am not the only one who misses his companion in arms." ("Companion-in-arms" appears here, again, as these bedfellows' private, affectionate name for each other.)

Millet sent Stoddard "much love," declaring himself "yours to put your finger on"—he was still available for the taking. Millet played Penelope, stay-at-home wife, to Stoddard's wandering Odysseus.

"Since I got your last letter," Millet reported on June 9, "I have passed two good nights dreamless and waking only in the morning." Reassured of Stoddard's love, he slept: "I reckon it was the influence of the letter, or the prayer."

Stoddard was still much on Millet's mind, however: The Adamses "say I am always thinking of you," and Millet did not deny it. But Mr. and Mrs. Adams probably did not understand Millet's infatuation as sexual.

Earlier, Millet and Stoddard had conspired with Donny Adams for her to meet a young woman she idolized from afar, Julia ("Dudee") Fletcher, an androgynous, aspiring writer (later, the author of the novel *Kismet,* the source of the musical).[27] But Donny had decided that she was afraid to meet Dudee at home—to "beard the lion in his den," as Millet put it (Julia, the lion, is an intriguing, sex-mixed metaphor). So Millet had arranged to introduce Donny to Dudee on some neutral ground, and, he reported, "Donny at last has met her idol!!" He hoped that Donny "has not created too exalted an ideal." The Donny/Dudee introduction, in fact, proved a bust. A few weeks later Millet reported to Stoddard that Donny "has given up the study of girls and is going to devote herself to the law. A profitable change, I think."

What, exactly, "the study of girls" meant to Donny is not clear. But Donny's "interest in girls" *and* in men again suggests a historical fluidity of libido that only later hardens into an exclusive, either/or devotion to girls or boys. In 1875, neither Millet, Stoddard, nor Donny seem surprised at her shift in interest from men to women.

Millet ended this letter playfully, sending Stoddard "more than the sum total of the whole with a sandwich of love between the slices," bidding him, "Eat & be happy." Millet's love sandwich echoed Stoddard's earlier linking of food and sensual satisfaction. "Yours with all my heart," Millet signed himself.

But Millet's needy heart now sometimes bled for his wandering loved one. A note that the artist wrote the next day concluded with a drawing of a heart dripping blood, an arrow through it, and the slang query "How high is that?"—meaning What do you think of that?[28]

A few weeks later, however, on June 18, Millet was telling Stoddard: "You can't imagine what pleasure I take in anticipating our trip in Belgium and Holland. Don't fail to come, old chummeke, and we'll have a busting time."

But, true to Millet's anxious premonition, his slippery, intimacy-shy friend failed to appear in Belgium. And by the summer of 1875, Millet had run out of money and had returned to America, writing to Stoddard, first from Boston, then from his parents' home in East Bridgewater, Massachusetts, where he had a studio. In the States, Millet sought writing and illustration work as a journalist, as well as commissions for painted portraits.

In Massachusetts, Millet reported on August 13, he was "bored to death" and felt himself "the prey of a thousand vulturous individuals who suck the vitality out of me in ten thousand different ways." This draining of his vitality was the exact opposite of the vitality provided by Stoddard's "magnetism," and Millet's sucking metaphor may hint again at an aspect of their energy interchange.

A letter from Stoddard had "brought an odor of the old country with it that was refreshing in this desert," a gloomy Millet reported on August 15, from East Bridgewater, a place he detested: "If there ever was a soul killing place this is it. Crowds of people . . . swoop down upon me and bore me to death."

If Stoddard, his "dear old fellow," was with him, Millet imagined, "we could be happy a few months and do some good work." Only his own death, or his father's, could keep him in America, Millet declared dramatically, adding, "I hope for a long life for both of us yet." Intimations of mortality.

"You know that I only feel whole when you are with me," Millet now confessed, admitting for the first time his full, profound need for Stoddard. Millet then referred, again, to Stoddard's "magnetism of the soul that can not be explained and had better not be analyzed." Close analysis of Stoddard's magnetism was dangerous for Millet. Stoddard's magnetic attraction led Millet to a humiliating pursuit of an unavailable beloved, perhaps even a loss of self.

His and Stoddard's "Venetian experience is unique," declared Millet, summing up their former romance at its height. He hoped for as good an experience in the future, "if not a similar one." He still seemed to be expecting a similar future intimacy with Stoddard, whom he urged to join him on his travels through Europe (and, implicitly, through life): "We can do the world if you keep up your courage."[29]

Millet ordered Stoddard, jokingly, to "Tell Mrs Swoon" (Mrs. Adams, no doubt) that he would send his photograph. But, in the meantime, he enclosed for Stoddard "a crumpled proof of one as Juliette." The faded proof of Millet in a long, curly, blond wig is still enclosed in his letter. Playing with sex inversions was not, among these friends, limited to dogs' names.

Stoddard had written earlier that if Millet did not return to Europe soon, he would find a new "boy"—his tease simultaneously expressed desire for Millet and suggested that he was replaceable. Once again, "boy" and "man" name the partners in a nineteenth-century intimacy of males, though, in this case, the actual age difference was slight. Millet was Stoddard's "boy" only metaphorically, and temporarily, for the younger Millet usually acted the active, pursuing "man," the older Stoddard, the hard-to-get "boy."

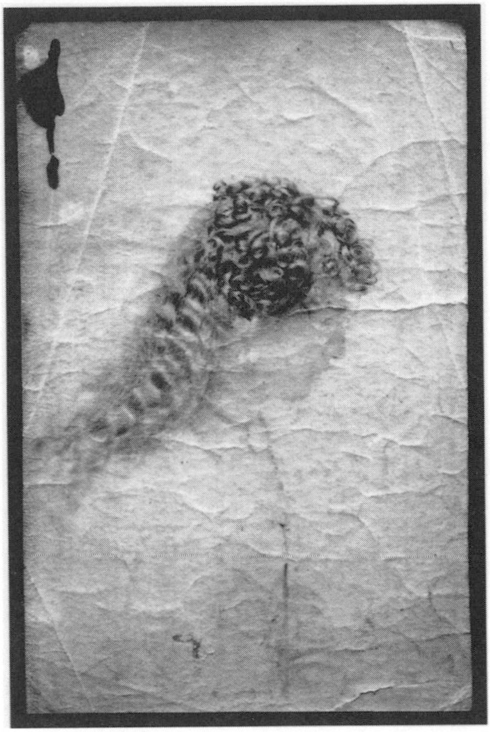

Frank Millett as Juliette. Courtesy Syracuse University Library.

The ever-traveling Stoddard was impossible to pin down. Millet finally understood, admonishing his flighty friend: "I see indications of butterflying in your threat to try another boy if I wont come back." "Butterflying" was slang then for "fickleness," "inconstancy in love," or "sexual unfaithfulness"; only later did the butterfly come to symbolize effeminate, men-lusting men.[30]

"Go ahead!" (Try another boy!) Millet urged Stoddard, "You know I'm not jealous, if I were I should be of Bob [Robert William Jones]. Anyone who can cut me out is welcome to. Proximity is something but you know I'm middling faithful."

Millet's faithfulness was now, for the first time, qualified, but his devotion was still steady. Millet promised to write "pretty often," so that the straying Stoddard "may not entirely forget me." He called Stoddard "my windward anchor," declaring himself "thine."

There is a "glorious sunset" but he "cannot enjoy it," a disgruntled Millet complained to Stoddard on August 25, blaming his unhappiness on the "the absence of the only one of my sex (or any other sex) with whom I could enjoy any beauties of nature or of art without the feeling that one or both of us was a porcupine with each quill as sensitive as a bare nerve."

The sex of his soulmates was not important, Millet indicated, only their sharing an appreciation of nature or art. However prickly their present relationship, Millet still looked to Stoddard for contentment: "If you were here Charlie, I could perhaps, be happy." He employed another food/affection metaphor: "Hungry: I'd give all I possess if you were here to lie down under the pines at the river side and yawn with me for a season."[31] He ended, "With very much love," and "I am always yours."

He had spent the afternoon with Stoddard's brother Fred, Millet reported on September 6, adding that Fred was a "dear fellow, wonderfully like you." This resemblance, Millet knew, Charles was *not* happy about, for the wastrel, alcoholic Fred represented the drifting Charles's worst fears about his own future.[32] Millet reassured Charles that his brother had "changed very much since you saw him."

Fred, Millet again insisted, "certainly resembles you in a remarkable degree in more ways than one"—Millet intimates that Fred, like Charles, was interested sexually, and perhaps exclusively, in men.

Insistently reminding Charles that he resembled Fred, Millet got his own back against his long-courted, long-fleeing friend. He even tried to incite a little jealousy: He and Fred "embraced," then spent the "whole afternoon . . . together," Millet reported.

Millet was still hoping "to have you for myself for a season in the only country in the world"—Italy.[33] He was fantasizing about collecting a little money, and buying a small house in Venice, making "an artistic place of it," where Stoddard could stay, even if he was not a convert to "Bohemia."[34] The terms "artistic" and "Bohemia" included sexual nonconformity within the iconoclasm they invoked. Millet would like to "live and die in Venice," he said later.[35]

Stoddard had reported quarreling with Mrs. Adams and her daughter Donny, and Millet now commanded: "You had better make it up again and spoon as before." He called Stoddard a "Don Juan" (in this context, a man feminized by associating too closely with women). And, Millet added, "it is plain that you need masculinizing a little—association with an active broad-shouldered large-necked fellow will do it." He continued: "I'm not that, but will do as a substitute in a pinch and would gladly serve if you would only come in my way." Millet here played aspiring butch to Stoddard's retiring femme.

Millet eagerly anticipated reconnecting with Stoddard in Europe, but warned him, in a letter of September 9, not to "go skimming way off somewhere where I can't come to." Just as he was returning to Europe, Millet worried, "you will be on the move."[36] He was "starving" for a letter, he said, again looking to Stoddard for metaphorical sustenance.

But Stoddard was busy that September, visiting Ostend, Belgium, and a secluded beach called, appropriately, "Paradise," where, as he reported to the *San Francisco Chronicle,* the bathers, "mostly males," walk "to and fro in the sunshine naked as at the hour of their birth." He had also spied "one or two unmistakable females trip down to the water-line in Godiva-habits," as well as "two Italians—lovers possibly, and organ grinders probably," who, "guileless, olive-brown, sloe-eyed, raven-haired, handsome animals, male and female, hand-in-hand, strode on the sand," then loosened their clothes, and "with the placid indifference of professional models . . . stepped forth without so much as a fig-leaf for shame's sake— a new Adam and Eve."[37] Given Stoddard's past practice of sex-reversal, it is not difficult to imagine that this Italian Adam and Eve were actually Adam and Steve, two male "lovers" and "organ grinders." To "grind" had meant to "copulate with" since the 1600s, so Stoddard's "organ grinders" certainly signified copulating lovers.

"If you are within grabbing distance," Millet wrote on September 27, imagining a hands-to-body connection, "I shall get my paws upon you suddenly, you bet!"[38]

He had attended a "country cattle fair," and "a great ball," where he had found "lots of stunning girls but none strong enough to anchor me to this country, you may write your people." Stoddard was evidently charged with informing their friends of any romantic adventures that might delay Millet's return, and Millet's interest in girls was apparently unremarkable to this group. But Millet's ship was still tied to Stoddard, his "windward anchor."

He would never have enough money to buy a house in Venice, Millet despaired: "Such tight times I never experienced," he complained on October 19. Stoddard's brother also wrote to say that he, "like many others," was "out of employment."

The panic of 1873, caused by unregulated speculation in railroads and the overexpansion of industry, agriculture, and commerce, had weakened the United States economy, which was eroded further by the contraction of European demand for American farm products. The effect of this crisis was still being experienced in 1875.[39]

For the first time in his letters, Millet expressed anger directly at the elusive Stoddard, swearing on November 15: "You D.B. [damn bastard?

deadbeat?],[40] you haven't written me for ages you know you haven't and why? Two weeks in Munich spooning! Spooning! SPOONING! and couldn't find time to write me[.] *Che diavolo!*"

Millet complained to Stoddard about a demanding visitor whose three-week stay had left him "in agony." He added: "We'll have to take an extra spoon to make up for all this," and confessed his own faithfulness, "I haven't spooned a bit since I got back, you know I haven't but you, you [here, he pasted a butterfly on the paper] you have had one solid spoon with the Adamseseseseses and that's why I envy you." Millet's spooning with Stoddard, and Stoddard's spooning with the Adamses, apparently implied different sorts of spoons.

Jokingly, Millet directed his anger at Stoddard's lack of reciprocal feeling, threatening him: "Now then you butterfly if you don't write more I'll cut your ———— off so you won't flutter about anymore." The missing word is clearly "cock," "dick," "prick," or some other slang term for penis, and the slang suggests how the two may have talked sometimes when alone. He could not speak freely in a letter, Millet several times told Stoddard. Millet's threat also shows that he understood Stoddard's straying as, specifically, sexual. The missing word also strongly, though indirectly, suggests the sexual character of their own past relation.

"Do come up to Paris, chummeke!" Millet urged Stoddard on December 2; *"Come and work!"* he pleaded, begging, "Come up, Charlie, do! Come and spoon and . . . produce something! We will live again the old Bohemian [life] in a different way." They would travel together, "and live as artists should in Paris. Do come!"

Millet was then assisting the artist John La Farge in the decoration of Trinity Church in Boston ("The romantic and picturesque details of this enterprise I shall take keen delight in elaborating to you when we meet.")[41] In addition, Mark Twain, a mutual friend of his and Stoddard's, had come into the church and had "asked me to come to Hartford and paint his portrait."[42] Millet's artistic career was beginning to take off, and he became, in a few years, a well-known artist of his day.

In his next letter, on January 15, 1876, Millet was fantasizing once more about his and Stoddard's return to Venice: "If we could pass another season there together I think I would not begrudge any sacrifice." Financial sacrifice was Millet's obvious meaning, but emotional sacrifice was implied. His feeling for Stoddard was frustrated and painful, as well as sustaining.

Ending this letter with a postscript, Millet reported: "People here think I am insane about a chum of mine and wonder why I don't find a female attachment." The unnamed people did not expect that Millet's openly expressed, overwrought, persistent attachment to a male pre-cluded the more common attachment to a female. But even this new dec-laration of Millet's affection provoked only silence from Stoddard, who did not write again for about seven months.

The wandering Stoddard was having a jolly time. In "gay Paris," on New Year's Eve, 1876, with a group of young men friends, as he reported to the *San Francisco Chronicle,* he attended a masked ball. There, those who had come only "to renew our feeble but I trust virtuous indignation at such sights, turn at last from the girls in boys' clothes; from the jaunty sailor girl-boy who has just ridden around the room on the shoulders of her captain; from the queen of darkness who swept past us in diamonds and sables, and never so much as suffered her languishing eyes to rest for a moment on any one of us." Stoddard stayed at a hotel "like a great boys' boarding school," where he and the other boy-guests had pillow fights while "robed in the brief garments of our sleep." With these friends he hied himself to "gay halls where sin skips nimbly arm in arm with inno-cence and verdancy," and the noisy carousers later attracted the attention of a "brace of gendarmes, the handsomest and most elegant fellows in Paris." Stoddard's "gay," "girl-boy," and "queen" are certainly sexual in implication, but I do not believe they yet had the specifically "homo-sexual" meanings they did two decades later.[43]

In March of the following year, 1877, Millet was in Paris, and Stod-dard was somewhere else. On March 11, the persistent Millet was still urging Stoddard to come and "occupy a room with me. I dare say I can so arrange it with William who now is my bedfellow and roommate."[44]

On April 24, Millet again urged: "My bed is very narrow but you can manage to occupy it I hope." If Stoddard did not want to share that bed, "we can fix things in the study."

In the summer of 1877 Millet was employed by several newspapers as a journalist and illustrator to cover the Russian-Turkish war. On June 29 he wrote to Stoddard: "I've seen two battles and thirst for more." "Hu-man nature," he added, "is incomprehensible, it adapts itself much too easily to circumstances." His comment applied to his affection, as well as his aggressive urges. "I am quite warlike now. You wouldn't know me," he later told Stoddard.

For the first time in his letters to Stoddard, Millet mentioned a new love interest: "I am spooning frightfully with a young Greek here in Oltenitza. He is a first rate fellow."

Back in London on May 7, 1878, after receiving medals for services rendered to Russia, Millet for the last time addressed Stoddard as "My dear Chummeke." That change in address marked the end of Millet's fantasy of live-in domesticity with Stoddard, though the two remained friends for life.

Just eight months later, on February 19, 1879, Millet wrote friends about his forthcoming marriage to Elizabeth ("Lily") Greely Merrill, an accomplished musician and the sister of a successful newspaper editor, William Bradford Merrill. Describing his love for Elizabeth, Millet joked that he was suffering from a "malady that doesn't let go very soon when it has once taken hold and the more it attacks one the more he wants." This "contagion" he had caught "very badly some time ago," and "on the Eleventh of march next I am going to marry Miss Merrill."[45] Millet clearly felt for Elizabeth the same strong, constant, romantic infatuation that, just a few months earlier, he had still felt for Stoddard. On the appointed date, in Paris, Mark Twain and the foremost American sculptor of the time, Augustus Saint-Gaudens, served as witnesses for the groom, and showman Phineas Taylor Barnum stood as a witness for the bride. In time, Millet and his wife produced three children: Kate, John Parsons, and Lawrence.

Five years later, Millet fulfilled a dream, founding a Bohemian colony with the painters John Singer Sargent, Alfred Parsons, and Edwin Austin Abbey in the little old town of Broadway in England. In addition to working as a journalist and an illustrator, in 1887 Millet published a translation of a Tolstoy war novel (read and praised, incidentally, by Walt Whitman), wrote a book about his own seventeen-hundred-mile canoe trip down the Danube (1891), a book of short stories (1892), and his report of the United States military expedition in the Philippines (1899).[46]

In 1893, Millet was appointed Director of Decoration and Functions for the World's Columbian Exhibition, in Chicago, on the grounds of which he got the visiting Stoddard a room next to his own.[47] Millet received major commissions for murals for the state capitols of Minnesota and Wisconsin, the Baltimore Customs House, and the Cleveland Trust Company. He served on the American Federation of the Arts, the National Commission of Fine Arts, and as director of the American Academy in Rome, which he helped to found.

In 1912, Millet and his close friend and Washington, D.C., roommate, the bachelor Major Archie Butt, aide to President William Howard Taft, booked steamer passage to the United States.

From Southampton, Millet mailed a letter to the artist Alfred Parsons describing their steamer's accommodations: "I have the best room I ever had in a ship and it isn't one of the best either."

Millet added: "Queer lot of people on the ship," in particular, "a number of obnoxious ostentatious American women, the scourge of any place

they infest and worse on shipboard than anywhere. Many of them carry
tiny dogs and lead husbands around like pet lambs. I tell you when she
starts out the American woman is a buster. She should be put in a harem
and kept there."[48] Millet's comment seems as much a critique of class ar-
rogance and the relations of men and women as a misogynistic statement
on human females, and he probably did not mean this to be his last word
on the subject of women.

Three days after writing that letter, on the night of April 14, 1912,
Millet was reportedly last seen encouraging Italian women and children
into the lifeboats of the *Titanic,* on which he, age 60, and Butt, age 46,
lost their lives. A joint monument to Frank Millet and Archie Butt, designed by the sculptor Daniel Chester French and architect Thomas
Hastings, in President's Park, Washington, D.C., is described as a tribute
to friendship.[49]

ॐ

Millet's wonderful, loving letters to Stoddard were among Stoddard's papers when he died in 1909, three years *before* Millet's death. Millet's letters were then sold to Charles E. Goodspeed, a Boston dealer in books
and literary manuscripts, who seems to have held them off the market for
years because they were love letters from one man to another, and because
Millet, and, later, his wife, and immediate descendants were still alive.
The letters were again sold, finally, to another dealer in literary manuscripts, from whom they were purchased by the library of Syracuse University, which today preserves these precious documents.

I Wish You Would Put the Ring on My Finger Again

Harry Stafford, about 1876. Courtesy Library of Congress. ❧

Early in 1876, the intense, wild-eyed, eighteen-year-old Harry Stafford met the fifty-seven-year-old Walt Whitman in the office of the *New Republic,* a newspaper in Camden, New Jersey. Stafford was employed at simple tasks around the office, and Whitman was supervising a new printing of *Leaves of Grass.*[1]

Despite the thirty-nine years between them—or perhaps because of it—Stafford quickly took to Whitman and the poet to him. By April 1, a few months after their meeting, Stafford was bringing Whitman home to his family's farm near Timber Creek, New Jersey, about a mile from the village of Kirkwood, a dozen miles from Whitman's Camden residence.[2] On the Stafford farm, Whitman sunbathed nude in the woods, recuperating from a stroke that had felled him in 1873.

Harry's siblings and his parents, George and Susan Stafford, welcomed Whitman, and he grew fond of them. The parents approved their teenage son's close relationship with the older man, and Susan Stafford hoped that Whitman would employ Harry or help him get work in an office—her son did not like farmwork, she explained to "Mr. Whitman," a few months after they met.[3]

In September 1876, about eight months into Whitman and Stafford's relationship, the poet's diary records that he had talked privately with the young man and had given him a ring. Their intimacy was modeled on an engagement or a marriage. Whitman later took the ring back and then gave it to the youth again—a mysterious, on-off ritual to which Stafford acceded several times during the years of their intimacy.[4]

On November 1, for example, Whitman's diary reports another talk with Stafford, and says: "Gave him r again." The abbreviation "r" suggests that Whitman felt a need to hide his ring giving from prying eyes, even in his private diary. But Stafford wore the ring in a formal portrait (almost a wedding photo) for which he and Whitman posed around 1876, so the ring cannot have been that secret.[5] Perhaps Stafford only wore the ring when he was with Whitman, as a sign of their physical proximity, their bodily presence in each other's lives. Though this on-again off-again ring is difficult to interpret, it must have symbolized a special tie recognized by both men.

The heart-to-hearts continued: in November Whitman recorded an especially "memorable talk with HS—settles the matter."[6] A month later Whitman reported a "serious inward rev[elatio]n." He saw "clearly . . . what it really meant—very profound meditation on all," and he was "happy & satisfied at last about it—singularly so." He ended with the parenthetical hope "(that this may last now without any more perturbation)."[7] "Perturbation" was the word Whitman had used eleven years ear-

Harry Stafford and Walt Whitman, about 1876 (the ring is on Stafford's right hand). Courtesy Sheffield Archives, Carpenter Collection Box 8/76. ❧

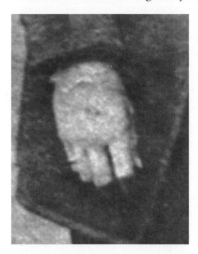

Stafford's ring ॐ

lier about his out-of-control feelings and humiliating pursuit of Peter Doyle. With Stafford, Whitman's calm did last—young Stafford was the perturbed party in the early years of this relationship.

A few weeks after Whitman's revelation, on December 13, 1876, the poet wrote to a friend, a New York City jeweler, John H. Johnston, thanking him for offering his home for a week's stay. Whitman added: "My (adopted) son, a young man of 18, is with me now, sees to me, & occasionally transacts my business affairs, & I feel somewhat at sea without him."[8]

Whitman again employed a familial son/father metaphor as a way of naming and characterizing the relationship between a younger and older man. Whitman asked Johnston if he could bring this "son" with him, "to share my room."[9] The son was Harry Stafford.

Six days later, on December 19, the forgetful Whitman wrote again to Johnston: "My nephew & I when traveling always share the same room and bed, and would like best to do so there. I want to bring on a lot of my books . . . (& that is what my young man is for.)"[10] What Johnston made of Whitman's son/nephew confusion—and bed sharing—is not recorded, but Johnston, his wife, and children continued for years to befriend the poet.[11]

The next day, Whitman felt free enough about his relationship to write to the jeweler yet again, this time to order a gold watch, "middling showy in appearance," as "a Christmas present for a young man" (probably Stafford).[12]

ॐ

Early in Stafford's association with Whitman, in May 1876, the young man introduced the poet to a farmhand friend, Edward Cattell, and the poet and the twenty-five- or twenty-six-year-old Cattell also developed a special intimacy. Whitman's love was not restricted to one youth at a time. The ring he gave Stafford did not promise unqualified faithfulness, at least to Whitman.

Cattell and Whitman experienced a noteworthy, though unspecified, interaction on the night of June 19, 1876, "at the front gate by the road." Two days later, Whitman noted "the swim of the boys," including "Ed. C. & Harry."[13] The swim of those no-doubt naked boys suggests that Whitman shared the erotic fantasy of the woman in his poem who secretly watched the male bathers, making love to them in her mind.

By January 24, 1877, Harry Stafford was extremely jealous of Whitman's friendship with Ed Cattell. This is clear from a note that Whitman sent Cattell: "Do not call to see me any more at the Stafford family, & do not call there at all any more—Don't ask me why—I will explain to you when we meet. . . . There is nothing in it that I think I do wrong, nor am ashamed of, but I wish it kept entirely between you and me."[14]

Whitman added: "As to Harry you know how I love him. Ed, you too have my unalterable love, & always shall have. I want you to come up here & see me. Write when will you come."

Whitman continued to see Ed Cattell, evidently without Stafford's knowledge. The poet's diary of 1877 mentions multiple romantic rendezvous: "Sept meetings [plural] Ed C by the pond at Kirkwood moonlight nights."[15] A month later Whitman's diary records: "Ed. Cattell with me."[16] Juggling several, simultaneous, potentially conflicting intimacies must have appealed to Whitman despite the drama sometimes caused by such balancing acts.[17] Throughout Stafford's and Whitman's relationship, each sometimes teased the other with jealousy-inspiring references to others.

❧

On the evening of Saturday, April 21, 1877, Harry Stafford, practicing his writing, recorded a peaceful domestic scene: "Mr. Whitman and I are sitting in the room together; he is reading the New York Herald, and I am writing these lines for exercise."

The next day Stafford, still testing his writing skills, reported: "It is a beautiful morning and you are feeling well and hearty. My friend and I, he says, have had a happy night and morning."[18] It is a touching picture.

But a few weeks later, on May 1, Stafford wrote to Whitman to ask his "forgiveness." The youth had suffered a fit of "temper" and had quarreled angrily with Whitman for a day or so—as he had earlier. "Can you forgive me," Stafford asked again, "and take me back and love me the same. I will try by the grace of God to do better. I cannot give you up"—the words of a distraught lover. Stafford must learn to control his temper, he agreed, "or it will send me to the States Prison or some other bad place." He signed himself, "Your lovin, but bad-tempered, Harry."[19]

What was Stafford so angry about? Could he have been jealous at the impending visit of Whitman's ardent English admirer Edward Carpenter,

who arrived for a first meeting with the American on May 1, the day that
Stafford begged Whitman's forgiveness? Carpenter stayed with Whitman
for a whole week, in the Camden, New Jersey, home of the poet's brother,
and Whitman took Carpenter to visit the Stafford farm, where Carpenter
took special notice of handsome Harry.[20]

On May 21, 1877, the tension between Stafford and Whitman was
continuing, and Stafford wrote: "You may say that I don't care for you,
but I do. I think of you all the time. I want you to come up to-morrow
night."[21] Stafford said he could not sleep "fore thinking of you." He asked
Whitman "to look over the past," and added: "You are all the true friend
I have and when I cannot have you I will go away some ware, I don't
know where."

But other friends, Stafford hinted, were waiting in the wings. He told
Whitman that Edward Carpenter "has been to see me *Several* times since
I was away and he lef me a book and a letter." After Carpenter's return to
England he continued to inquire after fair Harry.[22]

Whitman's fatherly and physical feelings for Stafford are evident in a
letter the poet wrote to the young man in June 1877: "Dear son, how I
wish you could come in now, even if but for an hour & take off your coat,
& sit down on my lap."[23] The image of nineteen-year-old Stafford sitting
in Whitman's lap provides a telling snapshot of their relationship.

"I cannot get you off my mind somehow," Stafford told Whitman a
month later, adding: "I should like to come up to Camden next week, and
stay all night with you."[24] Spending the night with Whitman was a special treat, mentioned several times in these letters. Is "stay all night" code
for sexual desires and acts? It seems probable.

Stafford was thinking of Whitman "and the plesant time we had Saturday," he told the poet in August, adding: "I will be up to see you on
Thursday to stay all night with you, don't want to go any wares then,
want to stay in and talk with you, did not get time to say anything to you
when I saw you, did not have time to say scarcely anything."[25]

A couple of weeks later, Stafford was writing from Woodbury, New
Jersey, eager to visit Whitman "and have a good time, for I don't let myself out here." The townspeople "are too mild for that."[26]

In October, Stafford again yearned to visit: "I want to come bad don't
know how I will stay away. I want you to have some place to go when I
come down someplace where there is plenty of girls. I want to have some
fun when I come down this time."[27] Stafford's interest in girls was not
precluded by his tie to Whitman.

That same October, Stafford told Whitman about wrestling a young
man, stressing "the fun I had last night, it was with a fellow that has been

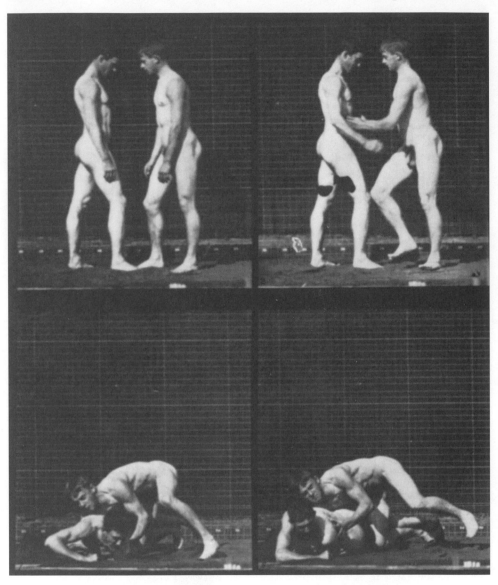

Wrestlers, photograph, Eadweard Muybridge, late nineteenth century. Courtesy George Eastman House. ∝

thinking for a long time he could throw me." Stafford told the fellow he was welcome "to try his hand, so we bucked in." The two fighters "pulled around for a short time and then I let loose on him and down he went." A similar vision of naked male bodies intertwined in fight was photographed, sketched, and painted by Thomas Eakins, and photographed

by Eadweard Muybridge.[28] In a note to Stafford, Whitman's English friend Edward Carpenter asked Harry "to teach me wrestling."[29] Wrestling was one way of justifying the physical mixing of male bodies.

Stafford was spending lots of time, he said, planning how to get ahead, and "when I am not thinking of my business I am thinking of what I am shielding." Stafford had some secret, confided earlier to Whitman. (Was it "solitary vice," "mutual masturbation," or a nonsexual secret? Again, the evidence is only suggestive.) Stafford added: "I want to try to make a man of myself, and do what is right if I can do it."[30] Constructing his manhood did not come easily to Stafford.

A week later, Stafford told Whitman that Herbert Gilchrist, a young, artistic, middle-class friend of Whitman's (whom Harry, unsurprisingly, detested) was visiting the farm. Stafford's mother told her son that if Harry did not want to sleep with Herbert, Harry "could go somewhere else for she was not going to keep a bed for me by myselfe."[31] The farm's usual sleeping arrangement placed a guest in Stafford's bed, a system to which Stafford and Whitman had never objected.

ॐ

In October 1877, while Stafford was writing to Whitman, Whitman was writing to Edward Cattell, asking the young farmhand to visit him in Camden. Cattell responded that he was "glad to hear from you my loving old friend." Cattell positioned himself as Whitman's loving young friend. Cattell added: "i would Com up To see you But i Cant get of[f] a day now we are so Bisse [busy] now husking Corn!"

Cattell reported: "i went with Some Boys up [to] the Pond to day and i seen your old Chir [chair] floting down the Strem [stream]." Cattell added: "i think of you old man think of the times down on the Creek. i did Want to Com up to Camden on Wensday to G.B."

What took place up in Camden and down on that creek? The pioneering provocateur of Whitman research, Charley Shively, speculates that "to G.B." meant "to get blown," and that Cattell wanted to be the recipient of oral stimulation, given, probably, by Whitman. As we will see, Whitman *was* similarly presented as a giver of oral sex in Gavin Arthur's memoir of sex and sex-talk with Edward Carpenter, an account probably produced with no knowledge of Cattell's letter. But no direct evidence demonstrates that "to blow" was used in nineteenth-century America in a sexual sense.[32]

Cattell hoped to visit Whitman in a week or so: "i would like to See you and have a talk. I love you Walt and all ways will." Cattell's "love" named his special feeling for his "old man."

This untutored letter writer ended on a formal, but heartfelt, note: "May God Bless You is my prayer, from a young frand [friend], Edward P. Cattell."[33] If Cattell's intimacy with Whitman was sexual, as seems probable, this farmhand had clearly found a way to integrate his religion and his libido.

In November, Cattell wrote to Whitman again: "Would love to see you once moor [more] for it seems an age Since i last met with you down at the pond and a lovely time We had of it to[o] old man." Cattell added: "i would like to Com up Som Saterday afternoon and Stay all night With you. . . . i love you Walt and Know that my love is returned." Cattell's letter ended: "i think of you in my prayers old man Every night and Morning."[34] Cattell again wished well to his beloved old man. Cattell's repeated stress on his youth, and Whitman's years, suggests that he, like Stafford, perceived their age difference as constituting a defining aspect of their intimacy, and, probably, an erotic and affectional charge between them.

෨

That same November 1877, Harry Stafford also wrote to Whitman. From the Western Union telegraph office at which he was working, Stafford said: "I wish you would put the ring on my finger again, it seems to me there is something that is wanting to compleete our friendship when I am with you. I have tried to studdy it out but, cannot find out what it is. You know when you put it on there was but one thing to part it from me and that was death."[35] For Stafford, at least, the ring recalled the traditional pledge of spouses: "Till death do us part." For him, the ring marked his marriage to Whitman, a model other male intimates also adapted.

"I cannot enjoy myself any more at home," Stafford complained to Whitman in January 1878, for, upstairs in his room, "the first thing I see is your picture, and when I come down in the sitting room there hangs the same, and whenever I do anything or say anything the picture seems to me is always looking at me." Stafford had made Whitman his goad to self-improvement.

The young man told Whitman of a woman, "a good and true friend," with whom he "had many good times . . . , but none that hangs [stays] with me like those you and I have had."[36] His intimacy with Whitman bested the male-female intimacy required by society. Such comparisons, explicit or implicit, are found in Dodd's diary, in Lincoln's letters to Speed, and other documents.

Later that month Stafford again complained to Whitman: "You did not give me what you said you was going to"—another reference, apparently, to the ring. The young man wondered if Whitman's failure of giving was due to Stafford's having accepted a ring from his cousin Lizzie. If so, said Stafford, he would give Lizzie back her ring.[37] Whitman might experience Stafford's intimacy with Lizzie as rivaling their tie, the youth suggested.

"I have thought of you almost constantly," Stafford assured Whitman in March, reminding him of a promise: "I have been thinking of the suit of clothes which I am to have like yours: I have had myself all pictured out with a suit of gray, and a white slouch hat on about fifty times, since you spoke of it; the fellows will call me Walt then. I will have to do something great and good in honor [of] the name."[38]

Stafford formally asked "Mr. Whitman" in July if he thought that he could study and become "an educator." Stafford wanted to "be something," he stressed. His self-making was still incomplete, he perceived. He thought how he could work together with Whitman for the "times have become settled, and our love sure (although we have had very many rough times to-gather but we have stuck too each other so far and we will until we die, I know. . . .)."[39]

Advising Stafford about his health and eating habits, Whitman, in 1879, added parenthetically: "(I tell you Harry, it is the *stomach, belly* & liver that make the principal foundation of all *feeling well—with one other thing*)." The penis, Whitman coyly suggested, was another foundation of good feeling.[40] Here, clearly, Whitman played teacher to Harry's student, a pedagogical relation that, for both men, included a decided eros.

Two years later, in February 1881, Whitman was "a little surprised" that "Hank" was taking to *Leaves of Grass* "so quickly." They had known each other five years, but Stafford had taken up Whitman's book only recently. Their years together, said Whitman, had "been *preparing & fixing the ground*" for Stafford's appreciation of his poems. *Leaves of Grass,* Whitman told Stafford, tried to make "every fellow *see himself,* & see that *he has got to work out his salvation himself.*"[41] What Stafford made of Whitman's man-love poems we do not know.

Later that same February, Whitman was still recalling the years of his and Stafford's intimacy: "Of the past I think only of the comforting soothing things of it all—I go back to the times at Timber Creek beginning most five years ago, & the banks & spring, & my hobbling down the old lane—and how I took a good turn there & commenced to get slowly but surely better, healthier, stronger."[42]

Whitman added: "Dear Hank, I realize plainly that *if I had not known you*—if it hadn't been for you & our friendship & my going down there summers to the creek with you—and living there with your folks, & the kindness of your mother, & cheering me up—I believe *I should not be a living man to-day.*" Whitman reiterated: "I think & remember deeply these things & they comfort me—*& you, my darling boy, are the central figure of them all.*"

The poet stressed: "Of the occasional ridiculous little storms & squalls of the past, I have quite discarded them from my memory—& I hope you will too—the other recollections overtop them altogether, & occupy the only permanent place in my heart—as a manly loving friendship for you does also, & will while life lasts."[43]

In April 1881, Stafford told Whitman: "I have a new *gal* and a mighty nice little thing she is too; Just such a one as you would like." The two had discussed gals, and Stafford counted on Whitman to endorse his choice.[44] Three years later, in 1884, the twenty-six-year-old Stafford married, and Whitman accompanied him to the civil ceremony.[45] Until Whitman's death, Stafford and his wife visited the poet, and Whitman kept in touch with them.[46]

⁂

In 1882, a year after Stafford's meeting his new gal, and two years before Stafford's marriage, Whitman wrote to him, wishing that the younger man "could all your life come in & see me often for an hour or two—You see I think I understand you better than any one—(& like you more too)—(You may not fancy so, but it *is* so)." Whitman, in effect, made his own last bid for Stafford's hand, trying to hold on tightly to their own alliance. He did not make it easy for Stafford to focus his affections on his gal.

"I believe, Hank," added Whitman, "there are many things, confidences, questions, candid *says* you would like to have with me, you have never yet broached—me the same."

Whitman then asked Stafford if he had read about Oscar Wilde, who was touring America: "He has come to see me & spent an afternoon—He is a fine large handsome youngster—had the good sense to take a great fancy *to me!*" Playing man-loving admirers against each other was a trick Whitman and Stafford both indulged.[47]

The following year, 1883, Stafford ended a letter to Whitman: "With lots of love and a good old time kiss I am ever your boy Harry."[48]

PART IV

Going Public

John Addington Symonds, 1864, soon after his marriage. Courtesy University of Bristol. ❧

16   *He Cannot Be Oblivious of Its Plainer Meanings*

In 1866, a twenty-six-year-old Englishman, John Addington Symonds, first heard a poem of Walt Whitman's read aloud by a friend at Cambridge University. The experience was mind and life altering.

The poem, from Whitman's Calamus section of *Leaves of Grass,* described the narrator's giving up his faith in knowledge, heroes, and the grandeur of "The States," to "go with him I love, / It is enough for us that we are together—We never separate again."[1]

From then on, reported Symonds in his *Memoirs,* Whitman's *Leaves of Grass* "became for me a sort of Bible." The American's poems helped Symonds achieve a more forgiving response to his own, strong sexual attraction to men—particularly working-class men. He learned from Whitman's work "a strong democratic enthusiasm, a sense of the dignity and beauty and glory of simple healthy men." Reading Whitman's man-love poems, Symonds's desires grew "more defined" and "more daring."[2] Whitman's proselytizing poetry did its real-life, sexual work.

It also did its political work. Symonds went on to become one of Britain's earliest defenders of sex between men. Whitman's influence on Symonds thus became central to the personal and political history of sex between men in the United States and England in the nineteenth century. Symonds wrote man-love poetry and researched the history of man-love, finally going public with that writing, an early form of resistance to the sexual establishment.

In 1866, and for many years afterward, Symonds was still struggling mightily to accept the erotic in his love for men and to act on it without a deep sense of sin. The son of a straitlaced, well-off physician, Symonds's ties to conventional Christian morality clashed violently with his sexual desire for men.

Thanks to Symonds's intimate *Memoirs*—begun by March 1889 when he was fifty—as well as the detailed sexual history he wrote at about the same time, we know the precise desires he was struggling with when he first discovered Whitman in 1866.[3]

"Sexual consciousness," wrote Symonds in his third person, anonymous case history, "awoke before the age of 8 (1848). Then, his attention was directed to his own penis" by a nursemaid who told him "that when little boys grow up" their penises "fall off." The "nurse-maid sniggered,"   235

Symonds recalled, "and he felt that there must be something peculiar about the penis."[4] The class revenge of British nannies took odd forms.

"About the same time," related Symonds, he began to have "curious half-waking dreams" in which "he imagined himself the servant of several adult naked sailors." He had observed sailors on the streets of Bristol, England, his hometown. And sailors had long played a prominent role in the erotic fantasies of men-lusting men.[5]

In his reveries young Symonds "crouched between" the sailors' thighs "and called himself their dirty pig" as they ordered him to perform "services for their genitals and buttocks which he contemplated and handled with relish." A mix of desire and guilt typically colored Symonds's desire.[6]

"Between the ages of 8 and 11" (1848–51), he recalled, when sleeping with a cousin, he twice took the cousin's penis "into his mouth"—perhaps the earliest, first-person, nineteenth-century report of oral-genital contact. While sleeping with another male cousin, Symonds put his hands on his relative's buttocks. With five male cousins he played a game in which, sitting in a circle, they exposed their penises; one cousin was punished by having to go around the room on his knees and take each penis in his mouth. At school, he observed a boy playing with his penis, and this gave Symonds "a powerful uneasy sensation."[7]

Until the age of thirteen (1853), Symonds "had frequent opportunities of closely inspecting the sexual organs of girls, his playfellows," but these "roused no sexual excitement." His complete lack of sexual response to girls and women was several times mentioned by Symonds. Seeing a schoolfellow "copulating with a little girl," Symonds experienced "a sense of mystical horror."

As a boy, he "showed no effeminacy in his preferences for games or work," Symonds stressed, though he did mention his strong dislike of boys' competitive, physical games.[8] By the end of the nineteenth century, when Symonds was writing, he and others felt it important to repudiate the association of men's gender deviance and men's sexual desire for men, a link increasingly asserted.

In his reading as a boy, Symonds was attracted to certain male characters, and also "wished he had been Venus," the object of Adonis's adoration in Shakespeare's *Venus and Adonis*.

Young Symonds was also "very curious" to know why the Roman emperors "kept boys as well as girls in their seraglios," as well as what the male gods in Greek and Roman myths "did with the youths they loved." What people actually *did* sexually remained a subject of profound curiosity to Symonds, as he struggled to accept his own sexual desires and behaviors. His early curiosity about ancient Greek and Roman sex later resulted in pioneering historical research on those sexualities.

When, at thirteen, Symonds went to Harrow, the preparatory boarding school, he was "provoked" by other boys "to masturbate." But "though he often saw the act in process it only inspired him with a sense of indecency."

At age fifteen (1855), Symonds experienced "nocturnal emissions," and began to masturbate about once a week for eight months, always with the feeling that the act was "repulsive." Confiding in his physician father and, following his advice, Symonds "entirely abandoned onanism," but this caused "very frequent and exhausting" emissions. These were "medically treated by tonics" that only increased his anxiety.[9] Believing that semen expenditures greatly depleted his bodily energy seems to have caused exhaustion.

In his dreams the teenage Symonds now "enjoyed visions of beautiful young men and exquisite Greek statues." He then began to dream of "the large erect organs of naked grooms or peasants," but these "gross visions offended his taste and hurt him." The "seminal losses" accompanying these dreams "were a perpetual source of misery."[10]

In January 1858, a gossipy, boastful, and irresponsible Harrow classmate, Alfred Pretor, wrote to Symonds that the head of the school, Charles Vaughan, a married clergyman, had begun "a love affair" with Pretor. The youth found the affair amusing and enclosed some incriminating letters from Vaughan for Symonds's entertainment. Deeply troubled by this active expression of illicit sexuality by an older authority figure, Symonds kept it to himself for a year and a half.[11] In March 1858, at age eighteen, Symonds first read Plato's *Phaedrus* and *Symposium* and a "new world opened." He "felt that his own nature had been revealed."[12]

The next month, in church on his Easter vacation, Symonds saw Willie Dyer, a beautiful fifteen-year-old choirboy, and arranged to meet him alone on April 10, an encounter to which Symonds later dated his "birth." During the four years of the ensuing romance, contact with Dyer caused Symonds "erection, extreme agitation and aching pleasure, but not ejaculation." For Symonds, orgasm distinguished very bad sexual activity from the not-so-bad. He never saw Dyer naked, he stressed, or even "touched him pruriently," and "only twice kissed him." But "these two kisses were the most perfect joys he ever felt."[13] He recalled those kisses more than a quarter of a century later.

Symonds told his father about his attraction to men and youths, and the doctor warned his son of "the social and legal dangers attending his temperament."[14] Symonds promised his father to stop seeing Willie Dyer, but continued to do so secretly for several years—his only direct resistance to his father's unsympathetic advice. In the autumn of 1858, Symonds began Balliol College at Oxford University, where he met numbers of classmates and teachers who provoked him to think more deeply about, and judge more tolerantly, the love of men for men and youths. Oxford, in fact, presented Symonds with a large cast of talkative, articulate sexual nonconformists. For example, he met Edward Urquhart, a Scotsman of "High Church proclivities" who ran after choristers and developed "a violent personal affection" for Symonds, who then broke off the connection.

He also met Claude Delaval Cobham, an Oxford student, who in 1861 professed himself "an '*anderastes*'" (probably something like "man enthusiast") and remained one for the rest of his life.[15] Making up names for men's sexual love for men was, in these years, a preoccupation of men in England, Germany, and America. Walt Whitman was not alone in appropriating "Calamus" and "adhesiveness" for the use of men-loving men.[16] Symonds knew that Cobham had "a passion for soldiers," and enjoyed "the most licentious pleasures to which two men can yield themselves" (unspecified, unfortunately). Cobham's imagination "was steeped in a male element of lust," and he "disliked women." But in all other ways, said Symonds, Cobham was "sympathetic, warm-hearted, ready to serve his friends, successful in society, cheerful, and not devoid of remarkable intellectual gifts."[17]

John Conington, a "scrupulously moral" professor, sympathized "with romantic attachments for boys." He gave Symonds a volume of verse by William Johnson that told the "love story" of the author, an Eton master, and the "pretty" Charlie Wood of Christ Church, who had been his pupil.

Symonds wrote to Johnson asking for advice about his own feelings and, remarkably, received in return "a long epistle on paiderastia in modern times, defending it and laying down the principle that affection between people of the same sex is no less natural and rational than the ordinary passionate relations" (Symonds's later summary). In the 1860s, other men than Whitman, Ulrichs, and Benkert were starting to distribute resistant defenses of man-loving. But beneath Johnson's bold defense Symonds sensed a note of "wistful yearning sadness" due to "forced abstention."[18]

"One hot afternoon" in the summer of 1859, Symonds was discussing with Conington what Symonds then called "Arcadian love"—another new name for sex-love between men and a term he had adapted from the ancient Greek historian Herodotus. Symonds's talk with Covington then turned to "unrecognized passion between male persons," and Symonds blurted out the story of Vaughan and Pretor's affair. Conington advised Symonds to tell his father about it, young Symonds did, and the elder Symonds used the threat of exposure to force the resignation of Vaughan as Harrow's head and later to prevent Vaughan from accepting a desired bishopric. Symonds was torn over his role in the ruin of Vaughan for acting on the same feelings he himself was trying to suppress. (The ethics of a teacher's romance with a student does not seem to have been the source of Symonds's conflict in this case.) But Symonds's ties to his father and conventional morality justified his actions.[19]

At Oxford in 1861 Symonds fell "violently in love with a cathedral chorister," Alfred Brooke, a "passion" Symonds experienced as "more intense, unreasonable, poignant," and "sensual" than his feeling for Willie Dyer. Brooke had "the most beautiful face I ever saw and the most fascinating voice I ever heard." His passion for the seductive Brooke made it more difficult for Symonds to resist acting upon his sexual impulses, but resist he did. The two exchanged not a single kiss.[20]

In November 1862, a vindictive Oxford student, C. G. H. Shorting, publicly charged Symonds with having earlier supported Shorting's pursuit of a choirboy and with sharing Shorting's interest in choristers. (Shorting had already been publicly condemned and disgraced for his behavior.) As evidence, Shorting offered extracts from Symonds's private correspondence and privately distributed poems. This was a frightening lesson, no doubt, in the dangers of writing man-love defenses. A month later, at a general meeting of the college, Symonds received a "complete acquittal," though two of his letters to Shorting were "strongly condemned." By writing letters about man-love—at first, just private, confidential letters—Symonds was moving, fearfully and fitfully, toward public statements on the subject.

Graduating from Oxford with honors in the early summer of 1864, Symonds, in London, experienced a "nervous malady" of the brain and eyes and "a terrible disturbance of the reproductive organs," which drove him to seek treatment from several of London's most prominent medical doctors. He paid Dr. William Bowman a guinea a day to drop "deleterious caustic" under his eyelids. He next allowed Dr. William Acton to "cauterize me through the urethra"—a treatment that punished as it supposedly cured. Dr. Spencer Wells successfully treated Symonds's eye problem and advised "a hired mistress, or, what was better, matrimony."[21]

Since hiring a mistress was distasteful to the romantic Symonds, he decided to marry, strongly supported in this decision by his father. In August

1864, Symonds set out in pursuit of Catherine North, whom he had met previously, and three months later, on November 10, the two were wed. Following several nights of unsuccessful intercourse, Symonds finally found that he could attain erection and orgasm with his wife (though he found her body unappealing) and the first of their four daughters was born in October 1865. He also found, after marriage, that his attraction to men increased, though he tried desperately to suppress his desire.[22]

One evening, in the spring of 1865, Symonds, in evening dress, was coming home from his club when, passing a barracks, "a young grenadier came up and spoke" to him. Symonds was "strongly attracted" by the "physical magnetism" of this "strapping fellow in a scarlet uniform," who suddenly "mentioned a house we could go to, and made it quite plain for what purpose." (The existence of such houses is also alluded to in America, and soldiers, like sailors, have a long history in the fantasies and acts of many men-loving men.) Symonds hurried away from the tempting soldier, though "with a passionate mixture of repulsion and fascination"—a "longing . . . after comradeship," and an "animal desire the like of which I had not before experienced."[23]

On another occasion, in the autumn of 1865, Symonds was returning from a solitary walk on a sultry afternoon when he suddenly spied "rude" graffiti scrawled on the street: "Prick to prick, so sweet"—with a "diagram," as he described it, "of phallic meeting, glued together, gushing." The effect of the words and image was "so stimulative," so much "the voice of vice and passion in the proletariat—that it pierced the very marrow of my soul." He experienced the "wolf" of desire for "the thing which I had rejected five months earlier in the alley by the barracks."[24] Symonds's graphically described graffiti documents a rare example of ephemeral, working-class, man-lusting visual art.

Following this incident, Symonds's earlier vague craving "defined itself as a precise hunger after sensual pleasure." But instead of acting on his desire, Symonds wrote about it. He began a series of poems "illustrating the love of man for man in all periods of civilization" (a poetic history of man-loving). It was soon after this, in 1866, that Symonds first discovered Whitman's man-love poems.[25]

∼

Symonds had studied Whitman's poems carefully when, in February 1867, he wrote a "secret letter" to his close friend and confidant, Henry Dakyns, a classicist and professor at Clifton College. If only Symonds had read *Leaves of Grass* earlier, he said, "I should have been a braver better very different man now." *Leaves of Grass* was "not a book," he exclaimed, "it is a man, miraculous in his vigour & love . . . & animalisme & omnivorous humanity."

Whitman, said Symonds, treated man's love for man in a completely new way: "This man has said what I have burned to say; what I should have done if opinion & authority & the contamination of vile lewdness had not ended in sophisticating my moral sense & muddling my brain."[26]

From today's liberal perspective, Symonds's moral sense was still muddled: he still felt that it was bad to act upon his erotic love for men. And yet, he told Dakyns, "even with these bruised wings & faded petals it is good to know that we bear in our breast the Psyche & the Flower of [the] noblest most masculine Democracy."

The poet Alfred Tennyson had spoken "as a prude when he condemned Walt Whitman," said Symonds.[27] For Whitman was "as pure & clean & natural as nakedness." Symonds's excited discovery of Whitman's poems was palpable in his mock command to Dakyns: "Behold! a light has risen which may not be denied. Walk yet by it!"[28]

Two months later, Symonds was embarking on the detective work that would occupy him for a quarter of a century—the documenting, analysis, and publicizing of Whitman's views about man's passionate love for man. Personally, Symonds urgently sought to establish for himself the morality of men's erotic desire and acts with men, and he appealed to Whitman as an older, authorizing guide. It was specifically erotic desire and activity between men that Symonds had trouble reconciling with his Christian training.

In April 1867, Symonds told Dakyns that he was traveling to London to meet the American Unitarian clergyman, Moncure Conway, a Whitman follower and author of an essay on the poet. "I shall not omit to ask him questions about the substance of Calamus . . . with a view to hearing what nidus [nest] for it there is actually in America."[29] The United States, Symonds imagined, was an especially fertile *breeding place* for man's passionate love for man. Whitman's poems and essays certainly fed that idea.

When he met Conway, however, Symonds could not "get him to say anything explicit about Calamus." But even Conway's silence confirmed for Symonds his belief that "Calamus is really very important & that Conway refuses to talk it over with a stranger. He cannot be oblivious of its plainer meanings."[30] If Symonds saw Conway again, he planned to question him more closely.

 ❧

On October 7, 1871, Symonds, in Bristol, England, ventured his first letter to Whitman, prodding the poet about his Calamus theme by way of sending one of his own man-love poems. Man-loving would be the major theme of the letters Symonds wrote to Whitman over the next nineteen years.

In Whitman's poems, Symonds confessed, he had found "pure air and health—the free breath of the world." As simply as he could, Symonds told Whitman "how much I owe to you."

Symonds ended: "I am an Englishman, married, with 3 children, and am aged 30."[31] He was actually thirty-one, but his age was not the only misleading information offered. Symonds's letters to Whitman repeatedly mentioned the Englishman's wife and children, presenting him as a traditional family man. Even though a man-lover, Symonds stressed his having done the right, marital, reproductive thing. A man's marrying and reproducing was thought of then as duty, *not* as demonstrating any exclusive, other-sex erotic interest—heterosexuality had not yet been invented. Whitman may have taken Symonds's repeated references to his marriage and offspring as a taunt about Whitman's own bachelorhood (and, presumably) childless status.

In January 1872, Whitman thanked Symonds for his letter, and said: "I am deeply touched by your poem." He added, seductively, "I should like to know you better."[32] He did have the opportunity, by mail. Whitman repeatedly encouraged Symonds's inquiring letters.

The following month, on February 7, Symonds wrote that he was relieved to hear from Whitman. Symonds worried that he had confused Whitman's "pure feeling with the baser metal of my own nature." Moral judgments about good, pure, asexual feeling and bad, impure, sexual desire tugged in opposite directions in Symonds's conflict-torn conscience.

"For many years," Symonds continued boldly, "I have been attempting to express in verse some of the forms" of what Whitman called "adhesiveness"—the love of men for men. Symonds had himself "traced passionate friendship through Greece, Rome, the medieval & the modern world." "Adhesiveness" and "passionate friendship" alerted Whitman to the focus of Symonds's inquiry.

While engaged on that work, Symonds had first read *Leaves of Grass*. Whitman and his work had taught Symonds "to believe that the Comradeship, which I conceived as on a par with the Sexual feeling for depth & strength & purity & capability of all good, was real—not a delusion of distorted passions, a dream of the Past, a scholar's fancy—but a strong & vital bond of man to man." Associating "sexual feeling" with "comradeship" was a bold, daring move for Symonds in 1872. For the sexual was then cordoned off from comradeship. "Love" was not usually thought then to harbor eros. As a sex radical, Whitman had daringly praised sexual comradeship and erotic love. Early in Symonds's correspondence he made it clear to the American that he understood and approved of Whitman's sexual politics.

Brought up in "English feudalism," Symonds told Whitman, educated at an "aristocratic" school (Harrow), and an "over refined" university (Oxford), he had found it difficult "to winnow from my own emotions and from my conception of the ideal friend, all husks and affectations and aberrations and to be a simple human being." Whitman had helped him in that struggle to feel and be human. Symonds was still struggling to affirm the morality of erotic feelings and acts in the relationships of men friends.

Then Symonds asked a pointed question: "I have pored for continuous hours over the pages of Calamus (as I used to pore over the pages of Plato), longing to hear you speak, *burning* for a revelation of your more developed meaning, panting to ask—is this what you would indicate?" Were American men "really so pure & loving & noble & generous & sincere?" Symonds was afraid to come right out with it, but he was probing to hear directly from Whitman that the manly love evoked in Whitman's poems included erotic desires and acts.

Most of all, Symonds desired "to hear from your own lips—or from your pen—some story of athletic friendship from which to learn the truth." He asked: "Shall I ever be permitted to question you & learn from you?"

Symonds added: "What the love of man for man has been in the Past I think I know. What it is here now, I know also—alas!" Present erotic relationships between men were lacking in love, Symonds suggested, and he wanted to know exactly what future forms Whitman envisioned: "What you say it can & shall be I dimly discern in your Poems. But this hardly satisfies me—so desirous am I of learning what you teach." Some day, Symonds hoped, Whitman would "tell me more about the Love of Friends!"[33]

Here, and in almost every other future letter to Whitman, Symonds asked if the American authorized, specifically, erotic desires and acts in men's love for men. The spiritual love of man for man was already legitimate in Symonds's mind, as it was in his culture. It was only men's erotic man-love with which Symonds struggled to come to terms.

The same day in February 1872 that Symonds wrote to Whitman, a poem of Whitman's was published in an American newspaper, and Whitman sent the Englishman a copy. Whitman's occasional posts encouraged Symonds's continuing pursuit of the poet's views.

In return, Symonds immediately sent Whitman another of his own poems, "a study of Greek friendship," specifically, the intimacy between Callicrates, "the most beautiful man among the Spartans," and the soldier Aristodemus.[34]

The "immediate result" of his study of Walt Whitman, reported Symonds in his *Memoirs,* was his "determination to write the history of paiderastia in Greece."[35] Whitman's poetry directly inspired Symonds's early work on what we now retroactively call "gay history." For nineteenth-century men of the upper classes, the ancient world's "Greek love" between an adult man and a male youth served as the most prominent legitimating ideal.

In 1873, Symonds did actually write "A Problem in Greek Ethics," a history of ancient Greek pederasty. But only ten years later did he dare to publish it, and then only in a limited edition of ten copies, which he distributed privately, warning those who received the pamphlet to keep it to themselves.[36] Researching, writing, and publishing sexual history has long been a dangerous occupation.

In the summer of 1875, Whitman sent Symonds a brief note, and Symonds responded from Switzerland that he was pleased to hear from the American. Symonds had (again) "feared that the last time I wrote to you [three years earlier] I might perhaps have spoken something amiss." He had then "asked questions about 'Calamus.' "[37] Whitman's token encouraged Symonds to believe that the American was *not* offended by those questions.

In January 1877, from Bristol, England, Symonds told Whitman that he hoped for a time when he could, with more authority, publicly bid his countrymen to know the poet's work. For Whitman's "message" was no less valuable for England than for America.[38] Symonds made it crystal clear to the American that he wanted to publicize Whitman's work as prophetic of a new manly love. Whitman found this flattering and frightening, the evidence indicates.

൭

A month later in London, Symonds delivered three lectures on Italian history at the Royal Institution. And, at least partly inspired by Whitman's endorsement of men's sexual intimacy with men, he accompanied a friend "to a male brothel" near the Regents Park Barracks. "There, moved by something stronger than curiosity, I made an assignation with a brawny young soldier for an afternoon to be passed in a private room at the same house. Naturally, I chose a day on which I was not wanted at the Royal Institution."[39]

At this assignation, reported Symonds in his *Memoirs,* "for the first time in my experience I shared a bed with one so different from myself, so ardently desired by me." This was evidently the first time that Symonds fully realized his desire in action. The soldier

> was a very nice fellow, as it turned out: comradely and natural, regarding the affair which had brought us together in that place from a business-like and reasonable point of view. For him at all events it involved nothing unusual, nothing shameful; and his simple attitude, the not displeasing vanity with which he viewed his own physical attractions, and the general sympathy with which he met the passion they aroused, taught me something I had never before conceived about illicit sexual relations. Instead of yielding to any brutal impulse, I thoroughly enjoyed the close vicinity of that splendid naked piece of manhood.[40]

After enjoying that vicinity to its utmost, Symonds had the soldier get dressed, and then "sat and smoked and talked with him, and felt, at the end of the whole transaction, that some at least of the deepest moral problems might be solved by fraternity." Symonds's "fraternity," vaguely echoing the French Revolution and Whitman, named and affirmed erotic intimacy between men.

"Even in that lawless, godless place," added Symonds, "affections, reciprocal toleration, decencies of conduct, asking and yielding, concession and abstention" all "find their natural sphere: perhaps more than in the sexual relations consecrated by middle-class matrimony."[41] This was a radical criticism for its time, an unusually incisive, resistant critique of sex in traditional marriage. In Symonds's mind, the moral value of sex between men was starting to compare favorably to the moral value of sex between men and women, if not going beyond it.

"Meanwhile," Symonds continued, "I was giving my lectures . . . to the Royal Institution." And "very dull lectures they were, for my soul was not in them; my soul throbbed for the soldier." The "man in me," Symonds said, desired escape from that "droning lecture desk into a larger, keener, more dignified, more actual existence. Little did I care what the gentlemen in frock coats and the ladies in bonnets thought of my lectures." The "real arena . . . was not in that theatre of disputations . . . and plausible explications of all kinds of theories." The real world was that "which each penetrates when the voice of the lecturer is no more heard in the theatre."[42]

Thanks, in large part, to Whitman, Symonds's real world for the first time included the full, active expression of erotic desire for another man.

The Swimming Hole (detail), Thomas Eakins, 1885, P1990.19.1. Courtesy Amon Carter Museum, Fort Worth, Texas. ❧

One midnight, in the summer of 1882, on a small farm in the southern United States, an eleven-year-old boy overheard a conversation. His male cousin was talking to the boy's brother about standing on a river bluff and "jumping into the water for a dive."

Suddenly, without warning, the image of the diving body conjured by his cousin's words opened the boy's eyes to his own desire: "The blood rushed to my face, my head throbbed violently, and it seemed that my eyes were bursting from their sockets."

"An erection immediately followed, and I longed to spring from my bed, clasp my cousin in my arms, kiss his lips, and give full expression to this new passion that was simply devouring me."

"I longed to have seen him without his clothing, to have felt his warm flesh with my hand, to have clasped his naked form to my own in one endless embrace."

The boy awoke the next morning to judge himself newly: He was "a miserable victim" of a "strange, unnatural passion." Employing religious terminology, he thought: "The demon of unnatural lust had entered my soul, to blight and ruin all that was noble and good." His lust, he soon discovered, was not confined to his cousin.[1]

This lusting boy later took the pen name "Claude Hartland" and in St. Louis, Missouri, in 1901 published his memoir, a rare document of sexual and affectional relations between men in rural America in the nineteenth century. Given his religious scruples, Hartland's detailed sexual accounts display a suspiciously unrepentant exuberance. But his book was clearly intended to evoke sympathy for the poor victims of "unnatural" appetites. Appealing for sympathy was an early, ambivalent form of resistance. Hartland's memoir is the earliest published account in which an American man-lusting/man-loving man details his public desires and acts.

❦

Born in the early spring of 1871 in a small railway town in a southern state, Hartland moved the next fall with his family to the farm where he grew up. He was a dreamy, sensitive, solitary lad, who liked to sew and play with dolls. Called a "girl-boy" at age nine (1880), he identified closely with his one sister and their mother.[2] "Girl-boy" then named his gender difference but not his budding, off-beat erotic desire.

His mother, he said, "came of an old Virginia family" noted more for "morality than for wealth." Her Christian morality is evident in Hartland's harsh judgment of his own sexual life. His religious values conflicted painfully with his erotic feelings and behavior. Yet, repeatedly in his mem-

oir, Hartland recalled his sexual encounters with obvious gusto, sometimes even humor. His sexual pleasures alternated repeatedly with his feelings of damnation, warring against each other, neither trumping the other.

His mother's father, having been a slave owner until the Civil War, had
never performed hard physical labor, and Hartland's mother often spoke
positively of her father's "skill in ladies' work, such as sewing, knitting,
mending, and even cooking." The skills of the grandfather were visited
upon the grandchild.

Hartland's own father was "descended from a southern family of
greater financial importance" than his wife's, "but with a much less practical sense of life"—seemingly the mother's judgment, repeated by the
son.[3] This southern boy took his white skin for granted, mentioning
nothing about race or black people.

By 1880, the nine-year-old, "serious and gloomy" Hartland was performing mock funerals for his "dead" dolls; he had developed a profound
interest in death and suffering and was "never happier than when allowed
to attend a real funeral and burial." His early, deep, and pleasurable attachment to sorrow is evident throughout his memoir.

෴

After recognizing his erotic desire at age eleven, Hartland tried "self-
abuse" (or "self-pollution") but judged this to be a "far greater sin" than
"intercourse" with men. (By "intercourse" he probably meant acts other
than anal penetration.) Masturbation did not provide the fleshly object
he desired, however, and gave "only temporary relief." So, he said, he did
not pollute himself often enough to damage his health, not "averaging
over three or four times a week."[4] Again, Hartland's judgment is surprising. His fairly large number of pollutions were permitted despite his
judgment that solitary masturbation was a "far greater sin" than intercourse with men.

Though conscious from age eleven of his erotic desire for men, Hartland did not try to act on it until he was between fifteen and seventeen
(1886–88). One night during those years, a young male visitor was assigned to Hartland's bed in his parent's home, and the teenage Hartland
was "delighted" but "scared." Though bed sharing was an unremarkable
custom, this was evidently Hartland's first chance to bed down with so
tempting a visitor.

He undressed, went to bed, and when, "by chance," the young man
touched him under the covers, the shy, inexperienced Hartland trembled
"from head to foot." The young visitor was "not so timid," however, "for

we had not been in bed five minutes, when he turned toward me and boldly placed his hand upon my sexual organ, which was already erected."

"Upon this discovery he placed his strong arms around me and drew me up close to him, at the same time placing his cheek against my own" — the tender display suggesting affection as well as erotic desire.

> I could hear my heart beating and it seemed that the blood would burst from my face. He then unfastened my clothing and his own and brought his organs and body in close contact with mine. I was simply wild with passion. All the pent-up desire of years burst forth at that moment. I threw my arms around him, kissed his lips, face and neck, and would have annihilated him if I could. The intense animal heat and the friction between our organs soon produced a simultaneous ejaculation, which overstepped my wildest dream of sexual pleasure.

But such ejaculations were fairly routine to his bedmate, it seems: "He turned his back on me and was soon fast asleep, while I lay there scared and panting from sheer exhaustion."

The next day, Hartland, feeling extremely guilty, decided "never to repeat the offense." But temptation overrode moral judgment: the young man with whom he had shared the bed made "more frequent visits to our house after this, and we always contrived to sleep together, with the same result."[5]

Hartland's "sexual desires" were now in "a perfect fever" — he flamed "with desire for every handsome man." He next felt "love" for his "handsome" older brother, burned with desire for him, and, one night in bed with him, made an effort to excite him, to no avail.[6]

Between the ages of seventeen and nineteen (1888–90), Hartland found himself "passionately in love" with the principal of his school and longed "to give my feeling sexual expression." When the two finally shared a bed, the principal gently hugged Hartland to his breast and whispered, "God bless this boy." Hartland perceived "no passion" in the principal's voice or embrace, understanding that "He loved me with the sweet, pure love of a brother and that was all."[7]

Impure sexual love and pure brotherly love cleaved Hartland's Christian universe neatly between the spiritual and earthly. Like others of his time, he conceived of pure love and erotic desire as mutually exclusive. So he failed to note that just a few pages earlier he had described his love for his own brother as fully sexual.[8] Hartland's classic distinction between sexual (bad) and spiritual (good) haunted his responses to love; this distinction held strong in the psyches of many nineteenth-century men.[9]

A classmate of Hartland's own age (late teens) was the next object of his love. Visiting at this friend's home, Hartland found him "affectionate and amorous in the extreme." The two became "close friends" and, later, roommates for several years, but soon they tired of each other "in a sexual way, and such relations almost entirely ceased."[10] Hartland began to experience the vagaries of sexual love.

During the same years (1888–90), the teenage Hartland also felt a strong passion for a violinist, whom he described as "very tall, handsome and well-proportioned." Having contrived to become the violinist's bedmate for a night, Hartland "cautiously" placed his hand on his partner's penis, which immediately became erect. The violinist then "unfastened his clothes, rolled over against me, hugged me to his breast," and, said Hartland coyly, "let curtain fall." He situated this scene, in memory, within a romantic, theatrical melodrama.

The violinist's visits to Hartland's home now became "more frequent, and he always insisted upon sleeping with me, stating that he had conceived a great liking for me, and that, as I was always studying, he could not talk to me till I had retired." Hartland and the violinist kept up "our sexual relations for several years" with no one in the family worrying, apparently, that spiritual love might be mating repeatedly with sexual love within the God-fearing Hartland home.[11] As yet, anxiety-provoking assumptions about sexuality were not brought to bear on all relationships, as began to happen just a few years after this time.

In 1890, the nineteen-year-old Hartland began to teach and when one of his young male pupils, a "little boy," smiled at him, Hartland was smitten—but with pure love: "Every lustful feeling and sinful impulse died within me, and I was happy! happy!!" Hartland's belief that sexual love and spiritual love were polar opposites allowed him to view this pedagogical relationship as untouched by eros. When, after eighteen months, the boy finally rejected Hartland's friendship, the adult was inconsolable, and he left his teaching post.[12] His emotions were certainly intense.

Between 1893 and 1895, Hartland, twenty-two to twenty-five, accepted a new teaching job "far back in the barrens among people that were scarcely civilized." His looking down on others was not mitigated by his participation in what his society considered uncivilized sexual activity. He ran this school with a former classmate and bedmate, and reported: "We loved each other dearly, and, as we roomed together, sexual relations soon began."[13]

Quitting this job after three months, Hartland moved home and renewed his former relations with the violinist. But now, "Our passion for each other had grown much stronger after our long separation, and upon two occasions we resorted to more extreme means of gratification"—anal or oral acts are indicated, a progression, it seems, from the earlier rubbing.[14]

When, in 1895, a "handsome" minister preached in his neighborhood, Hartland, now twenty-four, waited after church and expressed his wish "to have him spend the night with me." Breaking a previous engagement, the minister graciously obliged.

"After we had retired," Hartland related,

> and I was convinced by his poor attempt at snoring that he was *not* asleep, I gently placed my arm around his great manly form. This was enough. He turned toward me, placed his arms around my neck, pressed his lips against my own and—forgot to snore. For once I had met my match. We slept but little more, and the next morning when my brother asked him how he had rested, he glanced at me and said: "I never spent a more pleasant night."[15]

Hartland's lighthearted description contrasts with his usual contrition.

Still deeply troubled by his sexual feelings and acts, Hartland, in the mid-1890s, consulted a local physician with a fine reputation, but the doctor "had never heard of a case like mine." The physician gave him "something to remove the weight [of conscience] from my forehead, but it removed the weight from my pocket instead, and I was worse than ever."[16] Hartland's humor at this medical man's expense was a resistant act. For once, Harland refused to revel in his own suffering.

In the spring of 1895, the twenty-five-year-old Hartland met a man several years younger than himself, and the two became the "best of friends." Hartland said, "I loved him very much but there was but little passion in my love," though "I have always had a great desire to kiss him." Passionate love with no kisses was, for Hartland, a new configuration of eros and affection. He reported: "We spent many nights together, but no sexual relations ever existed between us." The first few nights together, however, "I had to relieve myself before I could sleep; but this feeling soon left me, and I thought of him only in a sweet, pure way."[17] Hartland's testimony suggests a residue of sexual desire in his feeling for his friend, desire of which the memorist remains unaware. In his universe, pure (asexual) love cannot coexist consciously with (sexual) passion.

Hartland next encountered a troubled sixteen-year-old male student for whom he felt "sweet, pure, spiritual love." Hartland, formerly the girl-boy, vowed, paradoxically, "to make a man" of this student and was glad to forget, for a while, his own sexual impulses. The young man blossomed under Hartland's tutelage and became "sober, honest and industrious," and "respected and loved by all who know him."[18]

In the fall of 1896, Hartland fell "madly in love" with another of his pupils, "a boy of about fifteen." This was "the strangest affection I have ever felt," reported Hartland, for he could not decide if his feeling was "love or lust." He was completely mystified that his affection seemed to include "a mixture of the two."

Walt Whitman had much earlier pioneered the idea of an intimacy between men that was at once loving and sexual. But for the first time, at century's end, Hartland had a revelation: sexual lust and spiritual love could merge in one attraction. He experienced the new consciousness of a modern American.

This young man's reciprocal response to Hartland worried the teacher so much that he consulted physicians who ran a local insane asylum. Disturbed about his "sinful" desire, he looked to the medical profession, appealing to doctors because his sexual yearning was of the body, and doctors were experts on the flesh. But he probably did not yet comprehend his desire in terms of a medical model, as diseased.

The local doctors did not "understand my case at all, but told me I must give up my school and go away at once." They will "search the records for a similar case," the doctors promised, but he never heard from them.[19] A disease model of sexual nonconformity had not yet reached the hinterlands.

In the winter of 1897, the still-disturbed twenty-six-year-old Hartland again sought "medical treatment," this time in a nearby city that he called "B" (Baltimore perhaps). Here, a "nerve specialist" treated Hartland for some time—but "without the least effect." The doctor then prescribed "sexual intercourse" with a female prostitute. Hartland obligingly consummated what struck him as an odious act. To complete the act he fantasized "a very handsome man, with whom I was madly in love in a passionate way." This, he assured his readers, was his "first and last sexual experience with a woman."[20] His sexual interest was in men exclusively. At the century's end, an erotic interest in one sex rather than another was becoming the basis for a new, modern identity, later called homosexual or heterosexual.

"The city," Hartland found, was "full of handsome men," and in this new urban setting he continually burned with passion.[21] The large populations of towns and cities, he several times suggested, provided many more sexual temptations than the relatively unpopulated countryside.[22] The popular image of the sex-soaked city has a basis in reality.

In this city, in 1897 and 1898, Hartland quickly began to name and think of sexuality in a new way, adopting with a vengeance the new medical concept of diseased pleasures: he soon found "that many others were suffering from a disease similar to my own, and while this knowledge gave me great relief, I was grieved to find the victims so numerous."[23] His earlier idea of his sexuality as "sin" was now overlaid by the new "disease" concept, a development that matched the changing consciousness of the nation.

Up to this time, despite Hartland's having consummated his sexual desire in repeated acts and ongoing relationships with five other men (the young male visitor, his classmate, the violinist, his fellow teacher, and the minister), he still considered his desire for men rare. He perceived that even though his manly partners participated for years in enthusiastically repeated sexual acts with him (including lots of unrestrained kissing), those same men did not think of themselves as any less manly. Nor did they define themselves by their unorthodox sexual activity. Hartland realized that he differed from these men in experiencing his effeminacy and sexual desire for men as defining his sense of self.

Now, in the city, Hartland began to meet and become aware of a large group of men—both effeminate and manly—who desired sex with each other. One night in the street, Hartland was approached by "a very handsome and stylishly dressed man" of about thirty-five who began a conversation. They walked to "a quiet and dark spot" near a river, and the man placed "his arms around my neck and kissed me several times," whispering a suggestion in Hartland's ear. An erotic exchange occurred, though Hartland was here uncharacteristically vague about specifics.[24] Was this his first experience of giving or receiving oral or anal sex? Even this loquacious confessor balked at revealing his exact role in those particular acts. At this time, in any case, Hartland first broadened the range of sexual behaviors in which he participated. City life alerted him to new erotic desires and new sex acts.

Another night, a few months later, Hartland took to the city streets with the conscious aim of gratifying "my maddening passion." Seeing a "handsome" man whose form was "perfect," Hartland asked him directions and soon "he had my hand in his and—we were in love." Feeling was instantaneous and strong in this impetuous, romantic southerner. In a dark street, "He placed his strong arms about me, strained me to his great manly breast and kissed me again and again."

When this manly man asked Hartland to permit or perform a particular act (probably anal or oral intercourse), Hartland, torn between desire and revulsion, finally answered, "No, not if I die," and hurried away. Later, Hartland met this sixty-year-old man again, and this time did "*not* send him away." Recalling in his memoir "those wild sweet moments we spent together," he said his hand trembled and his face burned with passion.[25] Writing his sexual memoirs was itself an erotic act.

Hartland's third urban pickup was a man "as affected [effeminate?] as I am," with whom he spent one night, and then developed a mutual, ongoing, "sweet pure love" that completely subdued their "passion." They continued, however, to embrace all night long, kiss each other "a hundred times," and compare notes on their similar "dark lives." Hartland's "evil passion" for manly men subsided, and his friend wrote to him that his own "passion for men was gone, and he loved no one but me."

Hartland took a new interest in life, enrolled in the university, and during the Christmas holidays his friend, a Christian, sang him "sad religious songs." The two sat for hours with their arms about each other, talking of their love and future life together. Then the friend went away, Hartland never heard from him again, and his "despair" gave way to his old "abnormal passion."[26]

"Abnormal" was a new term in nineteenth-century sex-talk, and a rare one in Hartland's memoir, which most often employed the ubiquitous "unnatural." The normal/abnormal distinction was a late-nineteenth-century way of judging sexuality, a term linked with the medical model of nonreproductive sexuality as "disease."

Hartland returned to his family home in the country, taught school again, suffered again, then left the countryside again and ended up in St. Louis, Missouri, on November 11, 1899. He soon got a job sewing with a ladies' tailor, and one evening, on the corner of Sixth and Olive streets, met another young man as "affected as I am and we knew each other at sight." They spent the night together, had "a most delightful time," and become "fast friends." Immediately, their "sexual relations" ceased and were replaced by "brotherly affection." Though Hartland clearly felt some sexual attraction to other effeminate men, that feeling was not lasting.

Hartland's "gentle, refined and very interesting" friend, he reported, "looks upon his disease as a great misfortune, of course, but has long since learned to bow in submission to the inevitable and now worries but little on its account." This relaxed attitude was "a great source of comfort" to Hartland, who soon met "several men" of like inclination and similarly forgiving dispositions. These unworried friends provided a striking contrast to Hartland's own guilty conscience.

A pickup in the Columbia Theater led nowhere, and a long, drawn out "sweet, pure love" relationship with a grocer finally ended unhappily for Hartland in September 1900, when the grocer lost interest.[27]

Back on the streets of St. Louis, Hartland one night met a kindly policeman who thoroughly understood his "case," was "sorry" for him, and promised not to give him "any trouble." Hartland had apparently cruised a woman-loving cop unfazed by the attention of a man-loving man.

That same busy night Hartland met "a very handsome actor," as "affected as I am," and stayed with him until two in the morning. On his way home, Hartland was robbed and his nose broken. The damage was repaired by a physician who told Hartland to resist his "evil impulses."

In February 1901, having alternately fought and yielded to his sexual desires for almost twenty years, the thirty-year-old Hartland decided to "write the story of my life, place it in the hands of physicians," and do all he could "to arrest the rapid progress of this dreadful disease."[28]

The former girl-boy believed that if doctors and parents kept young boys from becoming sissies, redirecting their gender deviance early enough, they could forestall the later development of diseased sexual desire. Deviant gender behavior led to deviant sexual acts, he thought. Gender deviance and sexual deviance were closely linked. His and others' erotic feelings were acquired, he believed, not inborn.

Hartland composed *The Story of a Life* with the aim of "relieving such sufferers as myself, and preventing the existence of others yet unborn."[29] It was "mainly through physicians," he thought, that information about such sufferers may be disseminated "and the progress of the malady checked."[30] His wish to relieve suffering was a resistant desire, but his harsh judgment about his "malady" collaborated with the puritanical sexual ethic that condemned his impulses.

Hartland wrote with the hope that "science may reach and relieve a certain class of individuals who live, suffer a hundred deaths, and die with their strange secret hidden away in their bosoms." Though he did suffer intensely, his stress on his own and others' pain was partly strategic: he intended to win sympathy for men-lusting men. Real suffering alternated in Hartland's life with repeated moments of erotic bliss, recalled by him with lusty, pleasurable relish.

This memoirist distinguished himself from a "natural man," thought of as financially secure and solidly middle class. This standard was particularly ill-fitted to an economy then daily dislocating numbers of rural workers, many of whom competed with one another for jobs in the newly urban, industrial sector. Hartland explicitly omitted from his memoir his "long and fierce battle with poverty," from age seventeen on—seeing his economic struggle as unrelated to his sexual history, a perception typical of many modern sexual nonconformists.

Hartland described himself as having "the beard and the well-developed sexual organs of a man" and "the delicate, refined tastes of a woman, and what is worse, her sexual desires for men." He spoke as if there was *only one kind of sexual desire,* directed at the *other* sex—a standard nineteenth-century idea. Thinking of himself as an "unnatural man," he compared himself invidiously to a "natural man" or a "true . . . man," who, he assumed, felt sexual desire only for women and displayed a thoroughly "manly" demeanor.[31]

Though by 1901, Hartland was definitely acquainted with the doctors' disease model of sexual difference, he never in his memoir employed such terms as "sexual inversion" or "homosexual." His judgments were founded on an earlier, theological vision: he spoke mostly in religious terms of "sin." He also spoke of "perversion" from the one, true, nature-given sexual desire for the other sex. "Natural" and "unnatural" were his most common, unexamined terms.[32]

He spoke often of romantic and sexual "love," and he used rhetoric derived from his reading of popular, sentimental fiction. He was sometimes aware of how "ridiculous" this "flowery language" sounded—how inadequately it expressed his feelings.[33] That was the same language problem that Walt Whitman had encountered earlier in the century and that had led him to invent a new language of love between men.

Hartland referred repeatedly to love and sexual attraction "for my own sex"—the specific desire prohibited by the one "true . . . love" for the other sex. But he was perfectly clear that *not every* member of his own sex attracted him. As an "effeminate" man, he desired "manly" men, and, even more specifically, only certain "types," with certain physical characteristics.[34] The first type were "either very large" men or those "smaller than the average," but not slender. The second type were lean men with mustaches. ("It is impossible for me to have any sexual desire for a fleshy man without a moustache. . . .")

Though he was aware of and described a large "class" of men erotically attracted to men, he never specifically named this group, nor does he report any name they may have given themselves. Such men constitute, in his memoir, a class without a name.

Hartland's autobiography, with its southern, rural setting and later forays into city life, is unique for the nineteenth-century United States. It is certainly one of the earliest and richest first-person accounts by an American man whose erotic desires focus on men. Out of his moral conflicts and erotic joy he created a rare testament, one that illuminated his own and many other nineteenth-century lives.

18   *I Cannot Get Quite to the Bottom of Calamus*

In the winter of 1884, after a seven-year break in communication with John Addington Symonds, Walt Whitman sent his English admirer a recently published poem. Symonds took this as an invitation to resume his difficult questions about sex between men.

Symonds thanked Whitman from his home in Switzerland, where, he reported, he had his "wife and children around" him, and "the peasants for familiar friends (especially young fellows, drivers, teamsters, post officials, farmers)." The Englishman's intimacies with "familiar friends" *and* a wife and children were reiterated in several letters to the unmarried, apparently childless Whitman.

If Whitman failed to register Symonds's "young fellows," the Englishman, in a postscript, returned to his favorite theme, the American's man-love poems: "I always feel Calamus more deeply than any part of your work." The reason Symonds had not published much literary comment on Whitman's poems "is that I cannot get quite to the bottom of Calamus. I wish I had your light upon it!"[1] He was planning to publish commentary about Whitman and men-loving men, Symonds made it crystal clear, and he wanted the poet's words for international distribution. The publicity-hungry Whitman must have been intrigued and worried.

❧

The Symonds of 1884 was far different from the man with whom Whitman had corresponded seven years earlier. After Symonds's sexual encounter with the soldier in London in the winter of 1877, a "new factor" entered his life. He moved a step closer to accepting his erotic desire for mainly younger, usually working-class men.[2]

In the spring of 1877 while touring Lombardy, Symonds reported in his *Memoirs* "the lesson taught me by the soldier in London found its application." He consorted with men and women whom the world called "the dregs of human nature," but "so strong is custom, so imperious is education, I never condescended to a single act which the most virtuous could call reprehensible." He condescended, however, to enough downward consorting to discover that he could "love and fraternize with the least and last and poorest."[3]

Seeking a climate that would slow the advance of his tuberculosis,

John Addington Symonds, Venice. Courtesy University of Bristol. ❧

Symonds and his family moved in August 1877 to Davos Platz, Switzerland. There, just after his arrival, Symonds saw a handsome young peddlar urinating and a desire for this youth "shot through me with a sudden stab."[4] The Englishman's desire had migrated with him.

Four months after arriving in Switzerland, Symonds met Christian Buol, a nineteen-year-old from a financially strapped, "very ancient noble family." They gradually established what Symonds called a "sensual spiritual" intimacy—a relationship that continued for more than a dozen years after Buol was married. Combining the sensual and spiritual was a major achievement in a society that routinely disparaged the body in favor of the spirit. At the time he met Buol, Symonds reported, his "ruling passion" had "reached a new and better stage," and he felt "free from the sense of sin"[5]—a large achievement for this tortured Englishman.

A few months after meeting Buol, Symonds invited him to dine privately; Buol then asked his new friend to a family party ("like a scene out of one of Whitman's poems," Symonds recalled).

In 1878, Symonds took the young man on a trip to Italy during which, Symonds's *Memoirs* report, "We often slept together in the same bed," and Buol "was not shy of allowing me to view . . . the naked splendor of his perfect body." But no act or word of "lust," said Symonds, clouded their "masculine communion"—another fine romance with no kisses.[6]

Other "young fellows" in Switzerland were ready and eager, however, to concede to Symonds's desires. But with none, he complained, did he share "love for love"—his ideal, democratic equality of desire. None of the Swiss men with whom Symonds had sex, he reported, "shared my own abnormal tastes." Symonds perceived, that is, that none of these Swiss men was ready to define his desire as "abnormal" or to define himself by his sexual acts. Swiss democracy had its limits. But Symonds "frequently" enjoyed with Swiss men "the sweetest fruits of privacy," and a "careless and promiscuous intimacy."[7] Swiss men evidently participated in sex with Symonds without feeling identified forever as sinners or inverts.

In 1881 in Venice, Symonds met a "strikingly handsome" gondolier, Angelo Fusato, for whom he felt "love at first sight." Venetian gondoliers, Symonds learned later, were "so accustomed" to the sexual propositions of travelers "that they think little of gratifying the caprice of ephemeral lovers—within certain limits."[8]

Despite enormous obstacles of class, convention, and erotic desire, Symonds managed slowly to establish with Fusato an intimacy that evolved through several stages and lasted a dozen years—until Symonds's

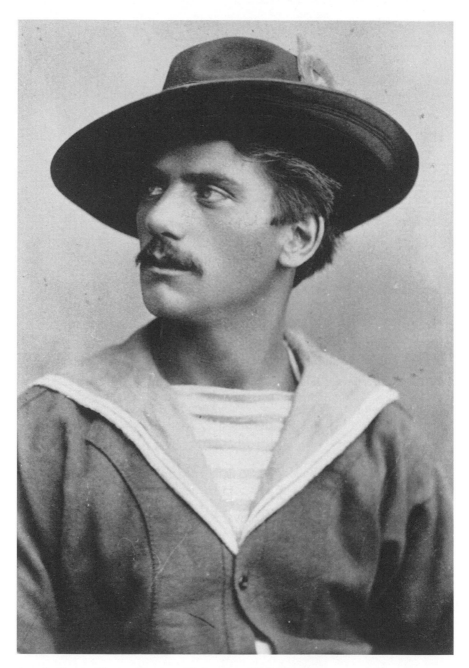

Angelo Fusato, Venice. Courtesy University of Bristol. ‿

death. Their sexual relationship, as Symonds described it, involved his "passion" and Fusato's "indulgence," his "asking" and Fusato's "concession."[9]

Symonds's *Memoirs* also report "Angelo's own theory about liaisons of this sort"—rare documentation of what a nineteenth-century Italian, probably Roman Catholic, working man said privately to his patron about ongoing sexual relationships between men. Fusato believed, said Symonds, that such intimacies "do not signify, if they are monogamous and carefully protected by the prudence of both parties. Then they remain matters for the soul of each in the sight of God." Only the man who went from "love to love—with Jack today and Tom tomorrow—sinks deep into the mire."[10]

How Fusato and his fellow gondoliers reconciled this "monogamous" ethic with their common practice of "gratifying the caprice of ephemeral lovers," Symonds did not say. Perhaps they simply ignored the contradiction.

Fusato's comment that prudent sexual relations between men "do not signify" denied these intimacies any meaning—*as a way, I stress, of affirming them.* Fusato posited a nonsignifying realm where men's sexual intimacies with men existed outside male-female romance, outside reproduction, and outside the rules that constructed meaning. Those intimacies' lack of meaning protected them from moral judgment.

Fusato's monogamous ideal (a bit loosely applied, perhaps) was apparently the same standard by which he and his working-class friends judged sex-love relationships between men and women, married or not.[11] Fusato, Symonds reported, was "living with a girl by whom he had two boys." With Symonds's financial support and moral encouragement, ironically, Fusato married, and Marie Fusato later joined her husband in looking after their employer.[12]

Two years after meeting Fusato, in 1883, Symonds took the daring step of privately publishing a ten-copy edition of his essay on ancient Greek pederasty, *A Problem in Greek Ethics,* written ten years earlier.[13] He distributed it to a select group of friends and acquaintances, asking them to be careful in discussing it and to send him their comments. With this publication, Symonds committed himself to the semipublic intellectual activism on behalf of men loving men that engaged him for the rest of his life.

In 1884, Symonds described *A Problem in Greek Ethics* to an American scholar and educator, Thomas Sergeant Perry, with whom he was corresponding. The essay analyzed the "social conditions" and "philosophical conceptions" out of which "Plato's theory of love . . . emerged."

Symonds's essay, an early, scholarly attempt to write the history of men-loving men, compared the platonic ideal of love with "the medieval ideal of Chivalrous Love."[14] The nobler form of platonic love, as Symonds then understood it, involved a frankly acknowledged, but spiritually trans-figured erotic desire, with no genitally enacted consummation. Chival-rous love, as he understood it, had involved the active expression of erotic desire in men and women's adultery with each other.[15] The phenomenon that interested Symonds, then, was historically changing ideals of "love," and the place within them of erotic desires and acts. His vision was *not* in-formed yet by the medical idea of "sexual inversion" or "homosexuality."

Did Perry really wish to read his essay, Symonds asked uneasily, warn-ing the American that it was "an inquiry into the origin, development, & social relations of that unmentionable custom [Greek love, or pederasty] which perplexed every student of Plato. It is really dangerous in England to allude to such a subject, though every boy who gets a classical educa-tion becomes familiar with it. I shudder to think what the result would be if I were to divulge my treatise to the public."[16] Perry *did* want to read the dangerous essay and later recommended to Symonds a German encyclo-pedia entry on pederasty about which even the well-informed Symonds had not heard. As we will see, Perry's own history included a long, easy-going intimacy with an elite, militant defender of "homosexual love."

෴

On March 28, 1888, the handsome, thirty-year-old Horace Traubel be-gan daily visits with the sixty-nine-year-old Whitman, in the poet's Cam-den, New Jersey, home. After each meeting, Traubel carefully recorded the poet's every word, and his complete diaries now comprise nine, fat, published volumes. Thanks to Traubel, modern readers can eavesdrop on Whitman's response to Symonds's last, dogged attempts to pin down for public dissemination the American's ideas about sex between men.

On April 27, 1888, a month after Traubel first started recording Whit-man's comments, the poet spoke for "an hour or more" about Symonds, and was "very frank, very affectionate." Symonds "is a royal good fel-low. . . . But he has a few doubts yet to be quieted—not doubts of me, doubts rather of himself."

Whitman clearly and consciously understood the source of Symonds's suffering: his difficulty resolving the moral conflict between his conven-tional Christian upbringing and his own pressing interest in erotic rela-tions between men. "One of these doubts is about Calamus," said Whit-man. "What does Calamus mean? What do the poems come to in the round-up? That is worrying him a good deal—their involvement, as he

Horace Traubel. Courtesy Library of Congress. ❧

suspects, is the passional relations of men with men—the thing he reads so much of in the literature of southern Europe and sees something of in his own experience."[17]

Whitman clearly recognized Symonds's *personal* investment in passionate intimacies between men, and the Englishman's pressing need to understand their expression in the American's Calamus poems: "He is always driving at me about that: is that what Calamus means?—because of me or in spite of me, is that what it means? I have said no, but no does not satisfy him."

The poet handed Traubel an old Symonds letter that questioned the American about his Calamus theme explicitly and daringly, linking the "comradeship" of men with "sexual feeling." That letter, said Whitman, "is very shrewd, very cute, in deadliest earnest: it drives me hard—almost compels me—it is urgent, persistent: he sort of stands in the road and says: 'I won't move till you answer my question.'" Symonds "is still asking the question," said Whitman, "he refers to it in one of his latest notes."[18]

Symonds, added Whitman, "is surely a wonderful man—a rare, cleaned-up man—a white-souled, heroic character." Whitman knew that Symonds had long struggled against tuberculosis, as Whitman and others had struggled with bodily infirmities, "but," said Whitman, "Symonds is the noblest of us all." Whitman did not hesitate to identify with Symonds, despite acknowledging the Englishman's erotic interest in men.

"You will be writing something about Calamus someday," Whitman told Traubel, and Symonds's letter "and what I say, may help to clear your ideas. Calamus needs clear ideas: it may be easily, innocently distorted from its natural, its motive, body of doctrine." Thanks to the bold, inquisitive Symonds, Whitman was anticipating increasingly probing questions about his man-love poems. He was deeply concerned about his own and his poems' future reputation, and he was setting Traubel up as the authorized interpreter of his man-love publications. That was one of the earliest and most important tasks that Whitman assigned to this disciple.

Traubel read the letter from Symonds, and Whitman asked: "Well, what do you think of that? Do you think that could be answered?"

Traubel, not yet clued in to the centrality of eros between men in Whitman's work and life, could not understand why the poet was so excited: "I don't see why you call that letter driving you hard . . . it only asks questions."

"I suppose you are right," responded Whitman, " 'drive' is not exactly the right word: yet you know how I hate to be catechised. Symonds is right, no doubt, to ask the questions: I am just as much right if I do not answer them."

Whitman soliloquized: "I often say to myself about Calamus—perhaps it means more or less than what I thought myself—means different: perhaps I don't know what it all means—perhaps never did know. My first instinct about all that Symonds writes is violently reactionary—is strong and brutal for no, no, no. Then the thought intervenes that I maybe do not know all my own meanings."[19]

Considering the erotic acts and feelings that Whitman had written about in his man-love poems, and considering his earlier correspondence with Stoddard, his mystification here seems ingenuous, and strategic. Admitting that he might not know his own meanings, Whitman conceded that Symonds might have a point about their relevance to men-lusting men. But Whitman simultaneously distanced himself from the sexuality to which Symonds pointed—surely an attempt to confuse and mislead Traubel, and, through him, future critics and readers.

Whitman concluded, "Sometime or other I will have to write [Symonds] definitively about Calamus—give him my word for it what I meant or mean it to mean."[20]

Whitman started that day to feed Traubel Symonds's old letters, one by one, testing Traubel's response to the subject of "sexual," "passional relations" between men. Over the next six months (May 24–September 7, 1888) Whitman gave Traubel all seven of Symonds's early letters, discussing each. Whitman's move was carefully, consciously calculated. He was using Traubel's response to work out his own public position on the subject of sexual desire and acts between men. He was also prepping Traubel on how to answer questions about his man-love poems. For the next two years Traubel's notes show that Whitman remained intensely preoccupied with Symonds and with that Englishman's private inquiries and public writing about the ethical place of eros in relations between men.

On May 24, 1888, Whitman gave Traubel another early Symonds letter—Whitman had Symonds on the brain. The poet noted that Symonds "harps on the Calamus poems again—always harping on 'my daughter.' I don't see why it should but his recurrence to that subject irritates me a little."

Whitman's calling his Calamus poems his "daughter" is his own revealing metaphor—Symonds never characterizes these poems as such.[21] Whitman considered his Calamus poems his specifically female or feminine offspring.

By 1888, at least, Whitman conceived of his man-loving poems as expressing a "female" or feminine impulse. This was a historic moment. He, like his society, was beginning to link men's sexual desire for men with gender inversion. He assumed, like others of this time, that the man who experienced sexual attraction to men felt "female" or "feminine" emotions. He would express the same idea later to Symonds as we will see.[22] In this view, sexual desire was sexed, male or female, and focused properly only on the "other," "different," "opposite" sex. In modern terms, there was only one sexual orientation—for the other sex. That was also the only moral sort of erotic desire.

Symonds "is still asking the same question" about his Calamus poems, Whitman complained to Traubel, anticipating Traubel's response: "I suppose you might say—why don't you shut him up by answering him? There is no logical answer to that, I suppose: but I may ask in my turn: 'What right has he to ask questions anyway?'"

Whitman then laughed a bit and said: "Anyway, the question comes back at me almost every time he writes. He is courteous enough about it—that is the reason I do not resent him. I suppose the whole thing will end in an answer, some day. It always makes me a little testy to be catechized about the Leaves—I prefer to have the book answer for itself."[23]

Traubel then read Symonds's old letter,[24] and defiantly told Whitman: "That's a humble letter enough: I don't see anything in that to get excited about. He don't ask you to answer the old question [about the Calamus poems and the "sexual" feelings of men for men]. In fact, he rather apologizes for having asked it."

Traubel's comment got Whitman "fired up," and he asked, defensively, "Who is excited?" Whitman insisted: "As to that question, he does ask it again and again: asks it, asks it, asks it."

Traubel laughed, not fully comprehending Whitman's "vehemence," and answered: "Well, suppose he does. It does no harm. Besides, you've got nothing to hide. I think your silence might lead him to suppose there was a nigger in your wood pile." Traubel, a liberal white man, casually employed a common racist expression to equate two disparaged groups—one racial and one sexual. His phrasing suggested that "a nigger in your woodpile" equaled "a sodomite in your bed." This is one of the earliest known comparisons of African-Americans and sodomites as the morally contagious Other—the alien with whom association proved one's guilt.

"Oh nonsense!" Whitman responded. He then added: "But for thirty years my enemies and friends have been asking me questions about the Leaves: I'm tired of not answering questions."

"It was very funny," Traubel said, "to see his face when he gave a humorous twist to the fling in his last phrase." Then Whitman relaxed and added:

"Anyway, I love Symonds. Who could fail to love a man who could write such a letter? I suppose he will yet have to be answered, damn 'im!"[25]

On September 7, 1888, Whitman handed Traubel yet another old Symonds letter, saying: "A Symonds letter is a red day for my calendar." Praising Symonds's style, Whitman added: "I am always strangely moved by a letter from Symonds; it makes the day, it makes many days, sacred."[26]

❧

In the late nineteenth century Whitman was increasingly concerned about the growing public awareness of the erotic in his poems of intimacy between men. This is indicated by Whitman's comment to Traubel on Christmas 1888 about a recent young English visitor—"a real handsome fellow he was, too—even you would admit that."[27] Traubel laughed and asked, "Why do you say 'even' me?" Whitman answered that after the way Traubel and another friend had responded to his mention of someone the previous day, Whitman "felt I had to be careful what I said."[28]

What was bothering Whitman? This was clarified later that day, when the poet gave Traubel one of his extremely affectionate Civil War letters to Hugo Fritsch (a member of the New York Fred Gray circle). Whitman then told Traubel: "I want you some day . . . to tell what I mean by Calamus: to make no fuss but to speak out of your own knowledge: these letters will help you: they will clear up some things which have been misunderstood: you know what: I don't need to say. The world is topsy turvy, so afraid to love, so afraid to demonstrate, so good, so respectable, so aloof, that when it sees two people or more people who really, greatly, wholly care for each other and say so—when they see such people they wonder and are incredulous or suspicious or defamatory, just as if they had somehow been the victims of an outrage."[29]

Contrary to Whitman's professed desire that Traubel speak out of his own knowledge and understanding, Whitman was actually rehearsing an asexual interpretation of his man-love theme, a defense he wanted Traubel to promulgate. Whitman referred clearly here to a new public awareness of sex in the intimacies of men with men. He specified this in order to deny it: "For instance, any demonstration between men—any: it is always misjudged: people come to conclusions about it: they know nothing, there is nothing to be known; nothing except what might just as well be known: yet they shake their wise heads—they meet, gossip, generate slander: the old women men, the old men women, the guessers, the false-witnesses—the whole caboodle of liars and fools."[30] As in the past, Whitman picked on effeminate men and masculine women as prime misinterpreters of the intimacies he portrayed.

Traubel read Whitman's effusive letter to Fritsch, which led Whitman to recall that Ralph Waldo Emerson had once asked: "Don't you fear now and then that your freedom, your ease, your nonchalance, with men may be misunderstood?" In response, Whitman said he had asked Emerson: "Do you misunderstand it?" To which Emerson replied: "No: I see it for what it is: it is beautiful."[31] Emerson's reassurance was not, however, good enough for Whitman, who now anticipated that his freedom with men would definitely be "misunderstood." Countering that (alleged) misunderstanding was becoming one of Whitman's major preoccupations. (Had Emerson's worry about misinterpreted man-love been expressed in his famous confrontation with Whitman in the Boston Common? Whitman never said so.)[32]

A week later, on January 2, 1889, the interpretation of Whitman's man-love poems was still preying on his mind. On that day, Whitman gave Traubel Charles Warren Stoddard's beseeching, "In the name of CALAMUS" note of nineteen years earlier, calling it "a rather beautiful letter." Stoddard's letter was "startling, too," said Whitman, adding, "not offensively so, however."[33]

The next day, Whitman was extolling women's reproductive capacity ("how gloriously beautiful motherhood is"), which led him to a critique of "our civilization, so called," a civilization that is "afraid to face the body and its issues." He stressed: "We shrink from the realities of our bodily life: when we refer the functions of the man and the woman, their sex, their passion, their normal necessary desires, to something which is to be kept in the dark and lied about instead of being avowed and gloried in."[34]

Surely, Whitman was recalling Stoddard's protest, reread the day before, that, "numbed with the frigid manners of the Christians," he "must get among people who are not afraid of instincts and who scorn hypocrisy."[35]

Whitman continued, excoriating "the woman who has discredited the animal want, the eager physical hunger, the wish of that which[,] though we will not allow it to be freely spoken of[,] is still the basis of all that makes life worthwhile."

Animal want, desire for physical contact between people, made life worth living, thought Whitman, and the subject, carnality, carried him away: "Sex: sex: sex: whether you sing or make a machine, or go to the North Pole, or love your mother, or build a house, or black shoes, or anything—anything at all—it's sex, sex, sex: sex is the root of it all: sex—the coming together of men and women: sex: sex."[36] And the coming together of men and men—though Whitman was afraid here to say it.

Encouraged by Traubel, Whitman continued his lyrical praise of lust: "sex, sex: always immanent: here with us discredited—not suffered: rejected from our art: yet still sex, sex: the root of roots: the life below the life!"

"You grow eloquent on the subject," Traubel told Whitman. The poet answered that he had a "right" to his eloquence, for sex "is the thing in my work which has been most misunderstood—that has excited the roundest opposition, the sharpest venom, the unintermitted slander, of the people who regard themselves as the custodians of the morals of the world."[37] Rereading Stoddard's old letter had motivated Whitman's glorious outburst.

෨

A few weeks later, on January 29, 1889, Symonds thanked Whitman for sending him a few new tokens of remembrance (newspapers with a poem by Whitman as well as a feature story about the poet). Symonds was preparing an article, "Democratic Art," he told the poet, based on Whitman's essay "Democratic Vistas" and *Leaves of Grass*.[38] The reputation-conscious Whitman was reminded once more that Symonds would critically influence the future public reception of his poems.

On March 3, 1889, Symonds confided to his friend, Horatio Brown, that he had recently begun "a new literary work of the utmost importance—my 'Autobiography.'" Later in March, an excited Symonds wrote to another confidant, Graham Daykns, to say that he would let his executors decide what to do with his memoirs, "the most considerable product of my pen." He added: "You see I have 'never spoken out.'" And it is a "great temptation to speak out" when, for two years, he had been researching the biographies of the artists Benvenuto Cellini and Carlo Gozzi, "men who spoke out so magnificently."[39]

That same month, on March 14, Whitman showed Traubel a letter he had received possession of years earlier, charging that "unnatural and criminal practices" and "sodomy" had occurred among the Union soldiers held in Andersonville Prison.[40] Whitman here directly confronted his era's most common ways of naming sexual acts between men, "unnatural practices" and "sodomy." Those were among the major terms Whitman and Symonds were resisting as they strove to create a new language, foster a new political response, and, in Symonds's case, decriminalize sexual activity between men.

By May 1889, Symonds was working on the chapter of his *Memoirs* that recounted his discovery of Whitman's *Leaves of Grass* and how the Calamus poems helped him accept desires that he could not "shake off."

This had brought the Englishman into "close and profitable sympathy with human beings even while I sinned against law and conventional morality."[41] In other words, reading Whitman stimulated Symonds to have sex with men and lessened his guilt about that sex.

Between October 1889 and October 1890, Symonds wrote the brief, detailed history of his sexual life that first appeared anonymously, in German, in 1896 as part of the first edition of his and Havelock Ellis's pioneering book, *Sexual Inversion*. Because it is so detailed in its description of acts, Symonds's history is an extremely rare, valuable account.

By the final stage of his sexual development, Symonds related, writing about himself in the third person,

> his gratification became more frankly sensual. It took every shape: mutual masturbation, intercrural coitus [between the legs], *fellatio* [oral-genital contact], *irrumatio* [rubbing], occasionally *paedicatio* [anal intercourse], always according to the inclination or concession of the beloved male. He himself plays the active masculine part. He never yields himself to the other, and he asserts that he never has the joy of finding himself desired with ardour equal to his own. He does not shrink from passive *paedicatio* but it is never demanded of him. Coitus with males . . . always seems to him healthy and natural; it leaves a deep sense of well-being, and has cemented durable friendships.[42]

Symonds had "suffered extremely throughout life owing to his sense of the difference between himself and normal human beings" (the "normal," he still assumed, was the good and proper model for everyone). He still thought that "his impulse may be morbid," and felt that "in early life his health was ruined, and his moral repose destroyed, owing to the perpetual conflict with his own inborn nature, and that relief and strength came with indulgence. Although he always has before him the terror of discovery, he is convinced that his sexual dealings with men have been thoroughly wholesome to himself, largely increasing his physical, moral, and intellectual energy, and not injurious to others."

Symonds claimed to have "no sense whatever of moral wrong in his actions," failing to see the residue of condemnation that colored his words and feelings. He did say, however, that "he regards the attitude of society towards those in his position as utterly unjust and founded on false principles."

On December 6, 1889, Symonds confided to his twenty-year-old daughter Madge, who was attending art school in London: "I have just completed the painful book I told you I was writing"—his essay on contemporary society's response to sexual relations between men. "If I were to publish it now," said Symonds, "it would create a great sensation. Society would ring with it. But the time is not ripe for the launching of 'A Problem in Modern Ethics' on the world."

Later, Symonds explained to Madge: "I want you to know your father; & so I scribble thus, pretty recklessly." He was "glad," he added, that Madge had "discovered that your family is liberal in Soul beyond most people. I think that we are. Your mother & I form a rare combination. There is nothing middle-class or *bourgeois* here." If Symonds or his family ever came face to face with God "it will be well for us, I fancy, to have been as true, as naked, as incisive, as active, as vital, as devoid of prejudices & conventions, as we can be."[43]

A few days later, on December 9, 1889, Symonds thanked Whitman for sending him a copy of his new, enlarged *Leaves of Grass*.[44] If they ever met, Symonds added, even "beyond the death of this life, I shall ask you about things which have perplexed me here." Symonds threatened to hound Whitman into heaven. When Symonds was to receive the final judgment, he would request that Whitman judge him first, and he hoped that the poet "will not disapprove of my conduct."

Symonds, I believe, was still looking for a father who would authorize his sexual acts with men, and Whitman filled the bill. Politically, Symonds wanted to publicize Whitman's approval—or, at least, tolerance—of sex between men and to promote such tolerance as a liberal alternative to criminalization and condemnation.

But why, asked the inquisitorial Symonds, had Whitman omitted from his Calamus section the poem beginning "Long I thought that knowledge alone would suffice me"—the narrator of which gave up all worldly pursuits to "go with him I love."[45] This was the poem Symonds had first heard read aloud and which "thrilled me like a trumpet-call to you." Symonds still found it deeply moving, and he missed it in Whitman's latest edition of the *Leaves,* from which it had been unaccountably deleted. Whitman cannot have liked this new, pointed inquiry.

Symonds would be writing about Whitman one day, the Englishman warned the American, "if only I have life and time for future working." As it turned out, Symonds did have time left to promote the cause of men-loving men—and to prod Whitman with even more forward questions about sex between men.

19 *Ardent and* Physical *Intimacies*

In December 1889, John Addington Symonds had warned Walt Whitman that he would pursue him to heaven with questions about his Calamus poems. But the American was by no means disturbed by this latest statement of an old theme. The day before Christmas, Whitman showed Symonds's guided missive to Horace Traubel, calling it "a marvelous letter," one that "perhaps surpasses all" that Symonds "has so far said about us." Whitman, then speaking of himself and his disciples as the collective "us," clearly expected Symonds to be saying more, and that in public.

Discussing Symonds's letter with Traubel on Christmas 1889 Whitman called it "more intimate, more personal, more throbbing" than an earlier public tribute by Symonds. Whitman did not remember, he claimed, why he had deleted from *Leaves of Grass* the Calamus poem Symonds had asked about—the poem whose narrator rejected the world's honors to "go with him I love."[1] Whitman then immediately told Traubel to read Symonds's books on ancient Greece—Whitman coupled Greece and the deleted Calamus poem.[2]

Just three months later, Whitman's Calamus poems were again linked with Greece, but this time by a new, hostile question regarding their sexual character.

Traubel was planning to attend a meeting in Philadelphia to discuss the poet's work, he told Whitman on March 24, 1890.[3] Three days later, Traubel reported that Whitman had asked him "about last night's meeting, which sat till after 12—about a dozen men (most of them young) present. A rather unique experience." Whitman's questions were "very scrutinizing," said Traubel.[4]

The next day, March 28, Whitman asked Traubel again about the meeting: "The affair seemingly had a unique interest for him." At the meeting, reported Traubel, the "subject of Calamus had been much discussed—Sulzberger questioning the comradeship there announced as verging upon the licentiousness of the Greek."[5]

Whitman took Sulzberger's criticism "seriously," said Traubel, asking: "He meant the handsome Greek youth—one for the other?—Yes I see!" The poet's vision of handsome youths "one for the other" saw ancient Greece as a land where young men coupled with young men, *not* where older men engaged erotically with younger men. This particular version of ancient Greece did not serve, then, as a model for Whitman's own intimacies with younger men. Nor did the intimacies of males in ancient Greece serve as an explicit model for the democratic, erotic comradeship depicted in Whitman's Calamus poems. Whitman's rare references to ancient Greece in fact distinguished his man-love poems from the classics-influenced verse of upper-class men like Symonds.[6]

Whitman said he could see how the comradeships celebrated in his Calamus poems "might be opened to such an interpretation" (that they verged "upon the licentiousness of the Greek"). "But I can say further, that in the ten thousand who for many years now have stood ready to make any possible charge against me—to seize any pretext or suspicion—none have raised this objection; perhaps all the more reason for having it urged now."[7]

Whitman was almost correct. Before 1890, opposition to the sexuality in *Leaves of Grass* had almost always focused on its explicit evocations of sex between women and men, and, particularly, on its references to female prostitution. Rufus Wilmot Griswold's review of the first edition of *Leaves* was the only published response to warn that these poems promoted, specifically, "the horrible sin not to be named among Christians" (sodomy). John Addington Symonds, Charles Warren Stoddard, and a few other men-loving men had commented *privately,* or semiprivately, on the male-male eros electrifying Whitman's Calamus poems, but they had seen that as a *positive* feature.

Sulzberger's linking Whitman's "comradeship" to ancient Greek "licentiousness" provides telling evidence that, in the late-nineteenth-century United States, a new consciousness of sex, and, specifically, sex between men, was going public. Sulzberger's critique of 1890 signals an increasing awareness of such sex, an increasing concern about it, and an increasing willingness to talk about it, at least among one's peers.

Responding to Sulzberger's charge, Whitman defended his man-love poems: "Calamus, is to me, for my intentions, indispensable . . . not there alone in that one series of poems, but in all. . . . It is one of the United States—it is the quality which makes the states whole—it is the thin thread—but, oh! the significant thread!—by which the nation is held together, a chain of comrades; it could no more be dispensed with than the ship entire."[8]

To the charge that his Calamus poems fostered carnal relationships between men, Whitman stressed that they fostered national unity. Whitman emphasized the socially unifying character of comradeship by way of playing down its sexual character.

Whitman then observed of American laboring men, "I know no country anyhow in which comradeship is so far developed as here—here,

John Addington Symonds, 1880s, dedicated to Whitman. Courtesy Library of Congress. ❧

among the mechanic classes." Whitman pointed often to the abundance of comradeship among American working-class men—the focus of his own erotic interests and experience. But he also pointed to an emotional aspect of class and gender for which there is, as yet, little documentation.

The "same spirit" of comradeship, he added, was amply expressed in Russia, Germany, and "the Oriental countries." Like Symonds, and other men with a special interest in the subject, Whitman had evidently made his own cross-cultural study of comradeship.

Walt Whitman, about 1889 (note photo of Symonds on Whitman's desk). Courtesy Library of Congress. ᒉᕈ

In the United States, Whitman said, this comradeship was found despite a native reserve: "The American is not demonstrative, but I have seen the boys down in the war, in the hospitals, embrace each other, cry, weep." After a quarter-of-a-century, men's emotional intimacies with men during the Civil War lived vividly in Whitman's imagination.

༈

Two months later, another discussion of Whitman's Calamus poems encouraged the developing alliance between John Addington Symonds and a fellow Englishman, Havelock Ellis. This relationship would result, in 1896, in a pioneering, progressive, collaborative book, *Sexual Inversion*.

On May 6, 1890, Symonds wrote to Ellis, thanking him for a copy of the author's recent book, *The New Spirit*. In it, a chapter on Whitman was the first to publicly praise the poet as prophet of a new sex-love. Ellis was also one of the first to question, *publicly, in print,* the relation of Whitman's ideal of "love," "comradeship," and "adhesiveness" to the "intimate and physical love of comrades and lovers."[9] Again, in Ellis's book, Whitman's "manly love" and the "physical love of comrades" were linked, as they had been just a few weeks earlier by Sulzberger. Sex between men was in the late-nineteenth-century air.

But Ellis's comments were too brief for the demanding Symonds, who told Ellis he wished he "had said more about 'Calamus.'" Symonds privately urged Ellis to "tell me what you think" of Whitman's man-love poems.

Symonds told Ellis that Whitman "clearly regards his doctrine of Comradeship as what he might call 'spinal.' Yet he nowhere makes it clear whether he means to advocate anything approaching its Greek form [including sexual intimacies between men and male youths], or whether he regards that as simply monstrous. I have tried but have not succeeded in drawing an explicit utterance upon the subject from him."[10]

Until Symonds better understood Whitman's "prophecy" of comradeship, he told Ellis, "I am unable to judge him in relation to the gravest ethical and social problems." Symonds's specific ethical "problems" concerned the value and justification of men's carnal acts with men—and, more generally, the value of eros in the lives of human beings.

Ellis had suggested that "Whitman *is* hinting at Greek feeling" (including erotic desire). Symonds believed that Whitman's comradeship "includes any passionate form of emotion, leaving its mode of expression to the persons concerned. It is also obvious that he does not anticipate a consequent loss of respect for women."[11]

He could not tell, says Symonds, "what would happen to the world if those instincts of manly love which are certainly prevalent in human nature, and which once at least were idealized in Greece, came to be moralized and raised to a chivalrous intensity." Symonds was seeking Ellis's judgment about sexual activity between men, still looking for a male authority to approve such behavior, salve his conscience, and legitimate his desire and actions. He was also seeking a political collaborator willing to speak out publicly on behalf of men's sexual relations with men, as he himself was not prepared to do.

Did Whitman imagine, Symonds asked, "that there is lurking in manly love the stuff of a new spiritual energy, the liberation of which would prove of benefit to society? And if so, is he willing to accept, condone or ignore the physical aspects of the passion?"[12] Symonds, in his fiftieth year, was still struggling to come to terms, still trying to fully accept his own and other men's sexual acts with men.

Three months later, on August 3, 1890, Symonds wrote Whitman one of the most famous letters in Anglo-American literary history, a document whose exact words and meanings bear close study.[13] During the nineteen years that Symonds and Whitman had sporadically corresponded, the increasing explicitness of the Englishman's questions about the sexual implications of the Calamus poems had paralleled society's increasingly open, public discussion of sexuality in general, and sex between men in particular.[14] Now, Symonds asked Whitman his most explicit questions yet.

"I do not even yet understand the whole drift of 'Calamus,'" and he was not alone in his confusion, Symonds told Whitman. The poet's teaching on the subject of manly love had "puzzled a great many of your disciples and admirers." Symonds cited Havelock Ellis's "perplexity" about Whitman's Calamus poems in *The New Spirit*.

Symonds then popped the question: "In your conception of Comradeship, do you contemplate the possible intrusion of those semi-sexual emotions and actions which no doubt do occur between men? I do not ask, whether you approve of them, or regard them as a necessary part of the relation? But I should much like to know whether *you are prepared to leave them to the inclinations and the conscience of the individuals concerned?*"[15]

Symonds's question about sex "between men" did *not* employ "men" as a universal. He was referring, specifically, to relations between human males. Symonds was *not* asking about a "same-sex" sexuality (the eros of women with women and of men with men)—his understanding of eros was not yet ruled by a same-sex/different-sex distinction.

Asking if Whitman would leave the form of sexual expression to the "individuals concerned," Symonds was indirectly inquiring if the poet opposed the English and American laws penalizing sodomy, buggery, and the crime against nature, and if he advocated their abolition. Symonds also clearly asked Whitman's views *for publication.* He was asking Whitman to come out publicly for sodomy law reform—though the bold Symonds had not dared to publicly link his own name with that controversial cause.

Symonds stated his opinion, to encourage Whitman's overt agreement: the "laws of France and Italy are right upon this topic of morality. They place the personal relations of adults of both sexes upon the same foundation: . . . they protect minors, punish violence, and guard against outrages of public decency." And "they leave individuals to do what they think fit."

Symonds had "not infrequently" heard Whitman's Calamus poems "objected to" among his English friends "as praising and propagating a passionate affection between men which (in the language of the objectors) has 'a very dangerous side,' and might 'bring people into criminality.' "

Just five months earlier Whitman had heard Sulzberger's criticism that his Calamus poems encouraged Greek "licentiousness" between men. Now, he heard that numbers of Englishmen were making the same charge.

Symonds told Whitman that he agreed with the objectors that, "human nature being what it is, and some men having a strong natural bias toward persons of their own sex, the enthusiasm of 'Calamus' is calculated to encourage ardent and *physical* intimacies."[16]

The "*physical*" in men's intimacies with men was central to Symonds's inquiry. Whitman's Calamus poems might encourage men to *act on their desire for men*—as they had encouraged Symonds. Symonds did not agree, he boldly declared, that such sex acts "would be absolutely prejudicial to Social interests."

Because Symonds wanted "to diffuse . . . knowledge" of Whitman's philosophy, it was "of the utmost importance" for him "to know what you really think about all this." Symonds was going public with his pronouncements about Whitman and wanted the poet's clarification so he could "tell the world about your teaching," as Whitman must have nervously noted.

"It is perhaps strange," Symonds said about himself, "that a man within 2 months of completing his 50th year should care at all about this ethical bearing of Calamus." He then disclaimed his caring, adding: "Of course I do not care much" about the ethics of Calamus, "except that ignorance on the subject prevents me from forming a complete view of your life-philosophy."[17]

With that frightened, transparent lie, Symonds asked Whitman for his honest, public opinion about sodomy law reform. Symonds's own fear of public scandal provides a striking measure of the pressure to remain silent about such reform. Symonds's personal failure to accept the morality of sex between men, and his ties to respectability, profoundly affected his politics.

How did Whitman react to Symonds's questions? Luckily for us, and by a most remarkable coincidence, Horace Traubel was actually in Whitman's room on Monday, August 18, 1890, between 5:15 and 6:00 in the evening, when Mrs. Davis, the housekeeper, came in with "a couple of letters." Just a few minutes earlier, as it happened, Traubel says he had been discussing with Whitman the "intellectual integrity" of writers.[18]

Whitman, said Traubel, "seemed pleased with the superscription of one" of the letters, "saying to me after regarding it fixedly—'It is from Symonds'—and after he had opened it—'a long letter too. . . .'" Whitman began to read out to Traubel the first, innocuous paragraphs of Symonds's letter, then laid it down.[19]

If it had not really happened, an unscrupulous historian would be strongly tempted to invent the interruption that then occurred. Just before Whitman got to the sexual questions in Symonds's letter, Mrs. Davis returned to say that a "census taker is downstairs" and that he wanted to question the poet. Having been pursued doggedly for years by the unflagging questions of Symonds, Whitman was now confronted by American society's archetypal asker of questions.

This inquisitive agent of the state was shown up to Whitman's room, where he announced that he had "come to get more specific information" about the writer's paralysis. He was "perfectly willing to tell all," claimed the poet, adding, "I was paralyzed in February, '72." This was no good omen of Whitman's truth-telling abilities. Either Whitman's memory was failing or he was deeply ambivalent about truth telling. He had actually suffered a stroke and become paralyzed on January 23, 1873.[20]

Then Whitman asked the census taker: "How many correct answers out of a hundred do you suppose you got? Would anybody confess the extent to which their house was mortgaged?" The skeptical Whitman doubted the public's proclivity for truth when it came to touchy subjects. He asked: "How large would you say was the proportion of honest answers?" Truth telling and lying were on the poet's mind that day, even before reading Symonds's latest prying questions.

The census taker assured Whitman that fewer then a dozen people out of four hundred lie, and Whitman was surprised: "Do you say that?" He expected more dishonesty. The man with questions thereupon departed.

Then, reported Traubel, Whitman started to read Symonds's letter, "and suddenly his face paled in the strangest way & he laid the letter down & said—'I talked to him [the census taker] too long; it has tired me out.'" Without knowing the content of Symonds's letter, Traubel provided posterity with a snapshot of one of America's most famous poets at the moment he read one of literary history's most famous letters. Traubel stayed with Whitman "till he had recovered himself somewhat . . . then left."[21]

The next day, August 19, 1890, Whitman carefully drafted and sent a reply to Symonds—another famous letter.[22] This, too, bears close examination, for it is, I believe, carefully, consciously, and artfully written to convey, simultaneously, several completely opposed meanings. This letter has also been repeatedly, and sometimes maliciously, misinterpreted.

Whitman began by telling Symonds that he has "just" received his letter and is "glad to hear f'm you as always." Ever the self-publicist, Whitman "may soon send" Symonds some new photographic portraits of himself. Whitman's casual opening misleadingly suggested an uncalculated reply—from its first lines the poet's letter is misleading.

Then Whitman gets to the point: "Ab't the questions on Calamus pieces &c: they quite daze me." Daze, suggesting surprise, was calculated to sound uncalculated. Whitman had, for nineteen years, pondered Symonds's only slightly less explicit versions of the same questions.

Whitman continued: That "the calamus part" of *Leaves of Grass* "has even allowed the possibility of such construction as mention'd is terrible." The "construction" referred to was the possibility that Whitman's man-love poems might, in the words of Symonds's letter, "encourage ardent and *physical* intimacies" (sex acts) between men.

Whitman's calling this possibility "terrible" may be read in several ways. His sentences, I maintain, carefully and purposely construct this ambiguity. As a master poet, long-time journalist, and typesetter, Whitman was an expert word worker, a professional at making words speak precisely or ambiguously.

What exactly was it that Whitman called "terrible"? There are at least three possibilities: (1) that "*physical* intimacies" between men are "terrible," (2) that Whitman's Calamus poems encouraged "*physical* intimacies" between men and that this encouragement was "terrible," (3) that Whitman's Calamus poems might be *understood* to encourage "*physical* intimacies" between men and that this understanding was "terrible."

This last understanding might be "terrible" for at least two different, opposite reasons. That understanding might be "terrible" because it completely *distorted* the meaning of Whitman's Calamus poems. Or this understanding might be "terrible" because it so transparently *revealed the sexual meaning* of Whitman's Calamus poems. The latter revelation might be "terrible" because the poems' author did not want his poems' sexual meaning to be so clearly explicated.

In the last interpretation, Whitman called it "terrible" that his Calamus poems might be understood by the world as encouraging "*physical* intimacies" between men. As we have seen, that particular interpretation of his poems was just beginning to be discussed publicly in 1890, and Whitman knew it.[23] The poet had, in fact, good reason to fear that if mainstream society understood his man-love poems as promoting sex between men, he would no longer be perceived as a "representative man." *Leaves of Grass* would no longer be seen as universal in appeal, and his personal and literary reputation would be in dire jeopardy.[24] In the most generous and politically radical interpretation, Whitman wanted his man-love poems to remain free of sexual taint *so* they could continue to work their subversive way in the world, continuing to encourage men's lust acts with men, as they had encouraged Symonds.

Whitman's ambiguous response to Symonds continued: "I am fain [glad or content] to hope the pages themselves are not to be even mention'd for such gratuitous and quite at the time entirely undream'd & unreck'd possibility of morbid inferences—wh' are disavow'd by me & seem damnable."

Again, Whitman's words convey several opposed meanings. Whitman, who could write poems of crystalline clarity, constructed a sentence commingling and conflating inferences, intentions, mentions, possibilities, disavowals, and damnations, not to mention morbidity and physicality—a sentence that has no unambiguous meaning. His sentence can be read in four (and, possibly more), substantially different ways:

1. Whitman can be understood to deny that his Calamus poems encourage "*physical* intimacies" between men, and as damning such relations as "morbid" (sick or unhealthy). That is how Whitman's comment has usually been read by biographers and critics.

2. Whitman can be read as disavowing and damning the inference that his Calamus poems were *intended* to encourage "*physical*" (and "morbid") intimacies between men. In this case, Whitman's comment referred to his motive, and Whitman may agree or disagree that "*physical* intimacies" between men were "morbid."

3. Whitman can be read as disavowing and damning the inference that his Calamus poems were "morbid," even if they did encourage "*physical*" intimacies between men.

4. In this possible interpretation, the most radical reading, Whitman completely rejected inferences that either his Calamus poems or "*physical* intimacies" between men were "morbid."

In 1890, I argue, Whitman constructed his response to Symonds as a literary time bomb, to explode eventually in meaningless, ambiguous confusion. One-hundred-plus-years later, it has.

Whitman's letter then pointed to "one great difference" between himself and Symonds: *"restraint."* By "temperament & theory" Symonds was always restrained, and, he, Whitman, was not.

In *Leaves of Grass,* said Whitman in his *draft* letter to Symonds, "while I have a horror of ranting & Bawling I at certain moments let the spirit impulse, (?demon) rage its utmost, its wildest, damndest." But in the version of the same letter that Whitman actually sent to Symonds, the poet said: "I at certain moments let the spirit impulse (female) rage its utmost."[25]

That "(female)" is revealing. Whitman here referred to himself as expressing, in some poems, a "female" spirit. Since Whitman's man-love poems were at issue, it is these particular poems that he believed expressed his "female" spirit.

Whitman's thinking was consistent with the idea, common at that time, that sexual attraction was sexed, "female" or "male," like vagina or penis. Sexual attraction to a male was considered a "female" feeling. Sexual attraction to a female was perceived as a "male" feeling. In modern terms, there was only one sexual orientation—toward the other sex. That was also generally considered the only moral sort of erotic desire.

Whitman then told Symonds: "I wholly stand by" *Leaves of Grass* "as it is." Whitman rejected the negative judgments of his work reported by Symonds.

Then the cagy, manipulative Whitman appealed to Symonds for sympathy: "I live here 72 y'rs old & completely paralyzed." *Leaves of Grass* "has been to me the reason-for-being, & life comfort"—a final plea for Symonds to leave him and his poems in peace.

But then the ornery, ambivalent Whitman provocatively added: "My life, young manhood, mid-age, times South, &c: have all been jolly, bodily, and probably open to criticism—" Though he had never married, Whitman claimed "I have had six children"—two children more than the fecund Symonds! Whitman offered Symonds serious rivalry in the fertility department.

Whitman's reproductive proficiency (implicitly and misleadingly including erotic desire for women) was offered to suggest that he had no interest in *"physical* intimacies" with men. An either/or idea of sexual desire was just gaining cultural influence.

Two of Whitman's children "are dead," he continued, mentioning "one living southern grandchild, fine boy, who writes to me occasionally." Whitman did not bother to describe the three other ghost children. Then the poet added: "Circumstances connected with their benefit and fortune have separated me from intimate relations."

Years earlier, Whitman had affectionately called Peter Doyle his "son," as he had also many times addressed Thomas Sawyer, Harry Stafford, and other beloved young men. The idea that he had progeny was by no means new to Whitman. I suggest that Whitman had his six most beloved young men in mind and was speaking poetically, metaphorically, and ironically (even campily) when he told Symonds that he had produced six children. Neither hide nor hair of any of these offspring have ever been found, despite eager investigations by researchers desperate to prove Whitman's agility as reproducer—saving him, they imagined, from the taint of man-loving.[26]

In the last line of his reply to Symonds, Whitman claimed to "have written with haste & too great effusion," then took the time to revise his draft, copy it for Symonds, and stow the draft among his papers. From first to last, Whitman's sentences were either utterly ambiguous, blatantly misleading, or outright lies. This word worker almost cried out to Symonds (and posterity) *not* to take him at his word. The conflicted poet, desperate to deny his sexual love for men, also, typically and desperately, wanted to reveal himself as man-lover.

By "asserting his paternity," concluded Symonds, Whitman was trying "to obviate 'damnable inferences' about himself" (Symonds reported his first response to Whitman's letter in correspondence with a friend).[27] Symonds, the man-loving father of four, must have found Whitman's tactic deeply ironic. Symonds himself was living proof that the ability to experience erection, impregnate a woman, and father multiple children was no evidence whatsoever of erotic preference.

The "Chronology of Whitman's Life and Work," printed in many volumes of the authoritative New York University Press edition of Whitman's correspondence, speaks of his "angry letter . . . denouncing Symonds's interpretation of [his] 'Calamus' poems."[28] This is completely, obtusely false. It is the author of that "Chronology" who is "angry" at Symonds for asking Whitman about sex between men. There is absolutely no evidence whatsoever in Whitman's letter, or in any of his numerous later comments on Symonds, that he is angry at the Englishman, though he clearly understood Symonds's inquiry into his man-love poems and Symonds's personal interest in the subject.

Five days after replying to Symonds, on August 25, 1890, Whitman wrote to his Canadian psychiatrist friend and disciple, Richard Maurice Bucke, who had earlier harshly criticized Symonds's prose (not his morals). Whitman told Bucke, "you are a little more severe on Symonds than I sh'd be." Whitman then mentioned his recent "singular letter" from Symonds, adding in parentheses "(sometimes I wonder whether J A S don't come under St Paul's famous category)."[29]

Whitman referred to Saint Paul's condemnation of men, who "leaving the natural use of the woman, burned in their lust one toward another; men with men working that which is unseemly, and receiving in themselves that recompense of their error which was meet"—that is, death.[30] Whitman knew Paul's condemnation as one of the major, influential, death-dealing Christian commentaries on men's lust for men. But Whitman rejected the deathly moralism of Paul's category, employing it casually, in a nonjudgmental, descriptive way. Categorizing Symonds as man lusting did not prevent Whitman's many later, friendly comments on the Englishman.[31]

Symonds replied to Whitman's misleading letter on September 5, 1890, answering on an equally deceptive note (deception now completely ruled their interchange): "It is a great relief to me to know so clearly and precisely what you feel about the question I raised."[32] Whitman's denying " 'morbid inferences' " set the matter "as straight as can be." Symonds now understood, he claimed, that "the 'adhesiveness' of comradeship" had "no interblending with the 'amativeness' of sexual love."

The obsessive Symonds could not, however, resist prodding Whitman one last time about his man-love poems, pointing out that the "emotional language of Calamus" had not before "been used in the modern world about the relation between friends." Whitman's fervent speech was analogous to that used about ancient Greek comradeship—"And you know what singular anomalies were connected with this lofty sentiment." Ancient Greek sentiment led to ancient Greek sex acts. Whitman "cannot be ignorant," said Symonds, "that a certain percentage . . . of male beings are always born into the world, whose sexual instincts are what the Germans call 'inverted.' "

This is a historic moment, the first time in Symonds's correspondence that he used one of the new psychiatric terms to describe the "sexual instincts" of men for men.[33] This was also probably the first time that Whitman had heard the new psychiatric jargon—the scientific lingo that would deeply influence the negative response to "homosexuality" in the twentieth century.

Symonds, the sophisticated European, then explained the new "inverted" instincts to the provincial American: "During the last 25 years [since 1870] much attention, in France, Germany, Austria and Italy, has been directed to the psychology and pathology of these abnormal persons." In 1889 the Penal Code of Italy had erased these persons' "eccentricities from the list of crimes."

Speaking as a "modern man" (and from a traditional condemnatory position), Symonds referred to the "moral abominations" of ancient Greek comradeship (the Greeks not only desired it, they did it). Symonds's moralism was tactical, it seems. He was trying, for the last time, to provoke Whitman to defend inverts. Given those "abominations," Symonds continued, it was essential that interpreters of Whitman's "prophecy . . . be able to speak authoritatively" about the "emotional and moral quality of the comradeship he announces."

Having Whitman's last letter, "which you give me liberty to use," Symonds pointedly declared that he could now speak publicly without fear that "the enemy should blaspheme." That is, should Whitman be attacked for defending sex between men, Symonds could quote Whitman to deny the accusation.

Now that Symonds understood Whitman's comradeship as a *spiritual, not a carnal* relationship, the Englishman saw how it could constitute "a salutary human bond." He could repudiate "those 'morbid inferences' authoritatively—should they ever be . . . stated openly, either by your detractors or by the partizans of some vicious crankiness." Casting aspersions on "partizans of some vicious crankiness," Symonds adopted the language of his own detractors, disparaging himself. Despite Symonds's fear of challenging convention, his behind-the-scenes activism made him, for his time, one of his century's boldest, crankiest "partizans" of sodomy law reform.

Symonds was "still doubtful," he stressed, "whether (human nature being what it is), we can expect wholly to eliminate some sensual alloy from any emotions which are raised to a very high pitch of passionate intensity. But the moralizing of the emotions must be left to social feeling and . . . the individual conscience"—not to the law, he implied, not to the state.

Two years after this last cat-and-mouse exchange between Symonds and Whitman, the Englishman told his fellow man-lover and sex reformer, Edward Carpenter, about Whitman's "very singular letter." Symonds felt sure the poet would not have written it in 1860, "when he first published Calamus." As Symonds suggested, Whitman had grown more circumspect about the implications of his Calamus poems toward the end of the nineteenth century, as sex between men came more frequently to the surface of consciousness and was more openly discussed.

Symonds concluded that Whitman "was afraid of being used to lend his influence to 'Sods.' Did not quite trust me perhaps."[34] Lending his influence to sodomites (understood then as men who engaged, specifically, in anal intercourse) was exactly what Symonds had asked of Whitman and exactly what Whitman had, at least apparently, declined.

On February 7, 1891, Whitman asked Traubel if he had written yet to Symonds and encouraged him to do so. That same day Whitman discussed an American who had been sent to jail twice for his public, militant activism on behalf of sexual reform. Whitman referred to the most recent imprisonment of Ezra Heywood for publishing and distributing "obscene" material through the United States mail.[35]

Two weeks after the sixty-two-year-old Heywood's indictment he had been tried for obscenity, found guilty, and sentenced to two years at hard labor with no appeal. Heywood was still in jail and sick when Whitman discussed him with Traubel.[36] Heywood, Whitman told Traubel, "has cast himself into the sex vortex—has given his all for that." Whitman was *not* willing to give his all for sex reform, not willing to cast himself and his poems into the "sex vortex." And yet his erotic poems are among the most explicit, affirmative, and lyrical in the English language, inspiring Symonds and many other activists since to give their all for sex reform—even to cast themselves into the sex vortex.

❧

In 1891, an increasingly emboldened Symonds printed fifty anonymous copies of *A Problem in Modern Ethics,* one of the earliest essays in English to defend "sexual inversion."[37] He addressed it to "medical psychologists and jurists" and distributed it among persons likely to support his plea for the decriminalization of sex between men.

A section in Symonds's essay was one of the earliest to analyze the sexual implications of Whitman's man-love poems. Symonds quoted Whitman's negative response to his own inquiry, accepting it, unfortunately, at face value. Symonds did stress the intensity, even physicality, of the "comradeship" that Whitman's poems evoked, but denied that this intensity had any "interblending with . . . sexual love."[38] This is simply counterfactual, as a close reading of Whitman's poems demonstrates.

Certainly, Whitman had refused to be classified as a supporter of "sods." In that refusal, I suggest, Whitman was attempting to preserve the ability of his man-love poems (and all his poems) to work their way in the world, subtly influencing readers—a resistance tactic, though less directly political, perhaps, than Symonds's pamphleteering.

❧

Before Whitman died on March 26, 1892, from his deathbed he sent Symonds one of fifty hastily bound copies of the final edition of *Leaves of Grass.*[39]

By that time Symonds himself was manifesting a new audacity in his defense of sex between men. He was corresponding privately with friends and acquaintances, trying to foment interest in sodomy law reform. He initiated, encouraged, and contributed to the relatively liberal medical book that was published as Ellis's *Sexual Inversion*.

In 1893, Symonds's *Walt Whitman: A Study* was published after the author's death, incorporating comments from his earlier, privately published *A Problem in Modern Ethics*. In his book on Whitman, Symonds finally spoke publicly about sex between men in the American's work.

"It is obvious," says Symonds, "that those unenviable mortals who are the inheritors of sexual anomalies will recognize their own emotion in Whitman's 'superb friendship, exalté, previously unknown.' . . ." Had Whitman not "repudiated any such deductions from his 'Calamus,' I admit that I should have regarded them as justified."[40] Symonds denied in his written work that Whitman's "Love of Comrades" had any *intended* sexual component.

But even Symonds's denial caused consternation in the land of the chaste and home of the pure. On February 26, 1894, Whitman disciple Charles Eldridge asked Whitman's friend John Burroughs if he had seen Symonds's book, adding, "part of it is abominable—and contains the very worst things ever said about Walt—It seems that 'Calamus' suggests *Sodomy* to him, and from some remarks he makes I judge he was suspicious about Walt's relations with Peter Doyle." Eldridge continued: "Truly I think much learning, or too much study of Greek manner and customs hath made this Englishman *mad*. Was ever such folly or madness shown before by a profound friend?"[41]

"We here in America," wrote another Whitman disciple, William Sloan Kennedy, in 1896, "were astounded" that Symonds found it necessary "to relieve the Calamus poems of the vilest of all possible interpretations. It was a sad revelation to us of the state of European morals, that even the ethical perfume of these noblest utterances on friendship could not save them from such a fate."[42]

Despite such protests, Whitman's man-love poems continued to work their trouble-making way in the world. In that world, men-lusting men were, increasingly, a public presence.

At midnight in the Slide. *New York Herald,* January 5, 1892. ❧

In the last decade of the nineteenth century, men-lusting men were
exposed to public view as a new form of urban entertainment. A
profitable sexual freak show, the activities of these men were ripe, also, for
political exploitation. In the spring of 1890, a Republican Party newspaper, the *New York Press,* publicized the whorehouses and gambling
dens, robbers, thugs, and burglars to which the city's on-the-take Tammany Party politicians and paid-off police were turning a blind eye.[1]

On May 11 of that year, the *Press* printed a sensational story about a
bar named the Slide, which it headlined as "The Wickedest Place in New
York." The "lowest and most disgusting place" on Bleecker Street, said
the paper, "is Frank Stevenson's dive," at 157th (just west of Sullivan
Street). The basement floor is "filled nightly with from one hundred to
three hundred people most of whom are males but are not worthy the

name of man. They are effeminate, degraded and addicted to vices which are inhuman and unnatural."

With whom the effeminates' vices were enacted the paper never said — the men with whom the effeminates committed unnatural vices were invisible. Those men were, implicity, just regular guys, though not the most moral.

The *Press* explained that "Stevenson caters to these people" who, earlier, "had no place in which they could gather." They "were like lepers, and were rejected by keepers of the lowest dives. Stevenson saw an opportunity to make money out of a business in which he could have a monopoly, because none other cared to enter into competition with him" — a concise explication of the capitalist economy of sexuality.

"He employed several of these people as singers and waiters," the *Press* continued, and "it was given out that in this dive . . . the outcasts from even the lowest order of society could find a resort." These "low" fellows, "who had heretofore kept in hiding and were ashamed to appear in their true light," found in Stevenson's Slide "a place where they could publicly announce themselves, and there they flock in droves each night to practice their loathsome habits."

The reporter quoted Stevenson: "I want this house known from Maine to California as the worst dive in New York. There is money in such a reputation. Nearly every prominent man who comes to New York and who wants to see the town by gaslight must see 'The Slide,' for there is not another place like it in the world. These sightseers always leave plenty of money behind them."

"Stevenson's ambition is fairly well-satisfied," concluded the paper, "for his place has the reputation of being the worst dive in the city." Though Stevenson was then "having trouble . . . getting a renewal of his license," and the Slide was closed temporarily, he had assured its patrons that he would reopen shortly. A businessman's search for profit and big city politics brought the denizens of the night into the light of day.

Two years later, on January 5, 1892, another anti-Tammany newspaper, the *New York Herald,* urged the city's district attorney to prosecute and close the Slide. This appeal was part of a larger Republican crusade to expose Tammany corruption, to embarrass Tammany politicians and police, and to defeat Tammany at the polls.[2]

"Witness the Scenes in 'the Slide' as the *Herald* Describes Them to You," the paper urged its readers and the district attorney. It warned, alluringly, of "Depravity of a Depth Unknown in the Lowest Slums of London or Paris," and of "Orgies Beyond Description." The paper retailed its readers a safe, voyeuristic glimpse of sexual sin, which they could enjoy without leaving their armchairs.

The Slide, and "the unspeakable nature of the orgies practiced there are a matter of common talk among men who are bent on taking in the town," reported the *Herald,* echoing the earlier *Press* account. When the *Herald*'s reporter had visited the Slide the previous evening, the steps leading down from the sidewalk had suggested the "proverbial easy descent to hell." For this "haunt has been a dragon of vice in whose maw souls as well as dollars have been lost forever."

When the reporter had arrived, at ten, the bar was "running at full blast," populated by a number of "bloated, dissipated looking men, some young and some old, who were bandying unspeakable jests with other fastidiously dressed young fellows, whose cheeks were rouged and whose manner suggested the infamy to which they had fallen."

As the reporter ordered a drink, "one of the gaudily bedecked young men minced up to me and lisped—'Aren't you going to buy me something?'" As early as 1842 Sally Binns, the New York City male prostitute, had been described as "mincing," but this, to my knowledge, is the earliest reported lisp.

The reporter left, then returned to the Slide at midnight, when it was even busier. Men and women sat at tables at the foot of a raised platform on which perched "half a score of the rouged and powdered men and youths who usually amuse the company with their songs and simpering requests for drinks." There was no music that night, however, for the Slide's operator, Frank Stevenson, had announced that the place would remain quiet until "the 'd——n newspapers' dropped their crusade against dives."

The day after the *Herald* attacked the Slide, the district attorney's response was printed in the paper: "Stevenson's Vile Den Must Be Closed."[3] And, on January 17, 1892, the *Herald* reported the start of Stevenson's trial the day before.

Thanks to the district attorney's prosecution of Thomas Frank Stevenson, the Slide's operator, "for keeping a disorderly house," a place used for "prostitution or assignation," a 140-page, typed, stenographer's transcript of the testimony of eighteen witnesses provides a full picture of the goings-on at this bar—the earliest-known sexually detailed description of such an American tavern.[4]

The bar's name, "the Slide," derived from prostitutes' generic name for a place where they solicited customers—the Slide was a slide.[5] Though such establishments were already an urban institution, the Slide may have been the first to welcome, specifically, male prostitutes.

At nine o'clock on Saturday night, January 2, 1892, testified reporter William A. Gramer, he made his first visit to the Slide, walking down a flight of stairs from the street, and entering a barroom about twenty feet wide and eighteen feet deep.[6] At its far end a swinging door in a partition topped with stained glass opened into a second big room where most customers gathered, a man played the piano, and another man, called "the Fairy," sometimes sang.

This is the earliest-known use of "fairy" for a sexual nonconformist.[7] But here it is a capitalized proper name for one particular individual—the mother of all fairies? The term derived, perhaps, from the late-nineteenth-century fascination with fairies and other flighty, unworldly creatures.

At the end of the Slide's second room, a few steps led up to a large floor extended over a yard, where effeminate men sometimes waltzed (whether with each other or with their male customers was not specified). Along with whiskey, wine, and beer, the Slide sold cigars and cigarettes, and the smokey air was filled with ribald jests and loud laughter.

About midnight, Gramer recalled, "the place began to fill up with men and women"—some female prostitutes apparently made the Slide a base of operation. This reporter and other witnesses listed the self-appointed names of the Slide's effeminate males: Fanny Davenport, Madam Fisher, Maggie Vickers, Princess Ida, Princess Toto, and Sarah Bernhardt. One went by several names: Phoebe, Miss Phoebe, Princess Phoebe, Phoebe Pinafore, Hebe, and Queen of the Slide. "Those are the names they called themselves," stressed one witness.[8] Adopting the names of memorable female characters from the English theater, and of famous female performers, the Slide's effeminate men memorialized invented or real women.[9]

As Gramer sat at a table with a beer he was "approached by a person . . . designated as the 'Fairy,'" who also called himself Maud Granger (or Greenoway). Maud had "a partner," called Lois Fuller (a name adapted from that of a famous dancer), and asked the reporter to invite them both for drinks. "I had no objection," Gramer testified.[10]

After some preliminary talk, Gramer was "asked whether I would not like to go and see a circus." Inquiring what that was, Gramer was told he could pick out one of the girls he saw in the room. She would then go with "one or two" of the effeminate men to another place where a "performance" would take place.

On the witness stand Gramer hesitated, embarrassed to continue. But the prosecuting attorney urged him on. "It is very vulgar," Gramer warned. The prosecutor said he understood Gramer's "delicacy," but insisted that he testify.

Gramer continued: "He said that if I wished to go to a house which he named . . . that on the payment of ten dollars [about $180 today] they would go through a certain vile performance." Gramer added, "To use his language . . . they would suck a girl's cunt."[11]

Oral-genital sex is spoken of in this trial record, and in other late-nineteenth-century documents, as something new under the sexual sun. It appeared here as an act pioneered by effeminate men and cooperative women prostitutes.

Without referring to oral sex, another witness recalled that "one or two" of the men at the Slide "had a slight moustache."[12] These moustaches were referred to by an independent source, Charles Nesbitt, a young doctor who visited the Slide about 1890 and recorded his impressions in the 1930s. When Nesbitt asked the Slide's Princess Toto the meaning of that "little tuft moustache," Toto explained that the tufted males "belonged to a fraternity of perverts who provided sexual gratification to both men and women."[13]

Toto identified the moustachioed men by their participation in an oral-genital act, not by their sex and the sex of their partners. The same-sex/different-sex division had not yet conquered eros.

The women, Dr. Nesbitt assured his readers, used the tufted males "as the active participants in that form of perversion which is scientifically known as cunnilingus." The "little tuft of moustache was really important in producing satisfactory results," claimed Toto, either putting on the researcher, repeating a bit of sexual folklore, or describing a belief that provided a self-fulfilling prophecy of pleasure. This moustache, Toto said, had long been "a visible advertisement of the profession of the wearer." The popular folklore of oral sex is difficult to disentangle here from the practice.

Upon visiting the Slide, a police officer, Michael J. Cooney, testified that he saw men "subject to unnatural practices, commonly known as 'tasters.' "[14] That interesting term also defined persons by their oral acts, *not* the configuration of their genitals or those of their partners.

When police officer George T. Leeson testified at the Stevenson trial, he refused to utter another vulgar word describing the "unnatural habits" of the Slide's effeminate men. He would only "write it down." Written carefully, in a clear, neat hand, on a blank space on the typed trial transcript (the judge's copy), is the term "cock suckers."[15]

In contrast to the embarrassed policeman, Gustus Bendix, a cigar dealer and another witness at the trial, was not ashamed to say that term

Detective Cooney testifies. *New York Herald,* February 13, 1892. ❧

out loud. He confirmed that the "feminine inclined" men at the Slide were "people commonly known as 'cock suckers.' " He added, "that is the English of it."[16]

The term "cocksucker," first documented in the United States a year earlier, in 1891, defined persons by their interactions with a male organ and packed a triple whammy, the accusation of procreative, erotic, and gender heresy.[17] The act of sucking on a penis in order to pleasure the organ's owner contravened the penis-in-vagina-intercourse-for-reproduction that still constituted the single acceptable sex act (but only within marriage and not to "excess"). The act of penis sucking also represented matrimonial and gender heresy because a proper wife did not perform oral-genital acts. The man who was willing to provide oral gratification functioned, it was thought, as a "loose woman" in an erotic relation with a "man."

When the reporter, Gramer, declined to see the circus, Maud and Lois left his table. He remained there and watched "the 'wall flowers,' " a term, he explained, for the effeminate men who "sat at one side of the room."[18]

The reporter observed "these men go to different persons who entered and have drinks with them. I saw some of them leave with strangers and heard them use vile language." For example, they would "refer to each other as 'she' and 'her,' " and "would call each other 'bitch.' " They also "spoke of each other as being 'kept.' "[19]

Another witness, Officer Thomas Dolan, remembered: "They called each other 'dear' and 'pet' and told each other about what nice times they had the night previous." Officer Leeson heard one say to the other: "I wish you would let my husband alone."[20] Marriage, once again, provided a model for some men-lusting men.

The effeminate males of the Slide wore men's shoes, remembered Officer Dolan—"they generally have nice feet those class of people, small." Officer Leeson agreed: "They had very tidy feet; some of them had patent leather shoes on."[21] The idea that effeminate men had small feet was mentioned as early as 1849, in Herman Melville's *Redburn*.[22]

Leeson recalled the effeminate men of the Slide wearing "odd looking straw hats, very wide rims and generally blue ribbons." One "had a fan in his hand fanning himself," Officer Dolan recalled, and he would "put the fan to his face like a lady does and speak to the other one." Some of the men "wore their shirts very low here," testified Leeson (apparently indicating his chest).[23]

A printer, Henry Woelpper, described the effeminate men of the Slide as "very natty in their appearance"—a surprisingly positive comment given the context. Asked if he had seen such men elsewhere, he answered "Well, yes." One might go through the streets and "meet them daily"; he specified Sixth Avenue.[24]

Officer Leeson had seen one of the effeminate men "play with a powder box and puff." They "had a kind of red flush on their cheeks," Officer Dolan recalled, as though "they had painted." Some of the men "appeared to have very fine complexions" recalled witness James Bavier. That the effeminate men actually wore makeup was not a matter of direct knowledge to these witnesses, so their testimony kept to what they saw. When the effeminates "would smile they tried to smile as a woman would smile," recalled Bavier.[25]

The effeminate who called himself Sarah Bernhardt "had his hair bleached in tissue red" reporter Gramer recalled (Bernhardt, in later years, was known for her red hair). This fellow "carried the illusion as far as he could imitating her, wearing bangles and bangs and dance shoes. I was told he wore corsets and chemise."[26]

This hearsay raised an objection, and Judge Randolph B. Martine ordered Gramer to "leave out the corsets." The reporter then testified that Sarah Bernhardt "wore long stockings; he requested me to put something in his stocking for luck; he raised his trousers leg and showed women's stockings and diamond garters; they appeared to me to be diamonds." The effeminate named Maud informed the reporter that " 'Sarah' wasn't hustling, she was being 'kept . . . in a house on 32nd Street.' "

When a new customer appeared at the Slide, Gramer heard Fanny Davenport and the other "effeminate creatures" called up "in sibilant

Miss Lillian Cheever. *New York Herald,* February 16, 1892. ⌁

tones by a waiter." The waiter "would motion to the one he wanted to introduce."[27]

The reporter saw the effeminate men put their hands near visitors' "private parts," and "lean over and whisper in a very affectionate manner."[28] Officer Leeson saw effeminate men leaving the Slide: "They would hold men's arms going up Fifth Avenue as if they were ladies."[29]

In this testimony, the effeminates partnered "men," and there was not the slightest hint that the manliness of the men, or the character of their sexual desire, was compromised by going off with such partners. The masculine men retained their normative gender status. Only the effeminates were called "unnatural" and thought of as "depraved."

The effeminates of the Slide were repeatedly described as "men given to unnatural practices," "men with unnatural desires and depraved tastes," and "men of unnatural habits." The "natural" procreative intercourse of men with women—the dominant reproductive ideal—defined the "unnatural" as any kind of nonprocreative act with either sex.

Another witness, Lillian Cheever, said she had last visited the Slide on Christmas Eve.[30] On that holy night she saw some of the "fellows" at the Slide "put their hand in an improper place" on men. With the "girls," she said, referring to the women habitués of the Slide, "I saw them simply fool around . . . skylarking, nothing wrong." Cheever's testimony for the prosecution suggests an affectionate, playful camaraderie between the effeminate men and women prostitutes of the Slide.

Witness John McTiernan, who took bets on races, testified that "one

of the [effeminate] men came over to me. . . . I asked him over to drink—
we were a party for a little jollification; he came over, and he put his hand
on my person." The effeminate then said of McTiernan: "I would like to
have that 'neat' " (that time's slang for "young bull"). McTiernan laughed
out loud in court as he related this joke about his penile endowment. He
was immediately rebuked by the judge: "This is not funny."[31]

The prosecuting attorney presented the effeminacy of the Slide's men
as visual evidence of their unlawful soliciting of sex with men. If the district attorney could prove such unlawful sexual commerce, he would have
then proved that Thomas Stevenson's bar was a "bawdy house," the
charge that was before the court.

But Judge Martine did not believe there was any necessary link between deviant masculinity and criminal erotic acts. When witness James
Bavier testified that he had seen one of the Slide men dressed as a woman
at "a masquerade ball," the judge objected to the implication of wrong-
doing. He told the jury that cross-dressing was not "improper." There
could be many reasons for cross-dressing, he suggested, it could even be
"a pretty general scheme of his [the cross-dresser's] to like women."[32]
Dressing as a woman could mean that a man liked and was even attracted
to women—it did not necessarily mean that he desired to have sex with
men.[33]

The jury, however, found the effeminacy of the Slide's male patrons,
along with other evidence, to have proven their soliciting and thus the
bar's criminal character. The jury linked gender deviance with erotic deviance, a historic moment in the construction of a new infraction of gender and sexuality soon known as "homosexuality." They therefore found
Thomas Frank Stevenson guilty of running a "house of ill-fame." Judge
Martine sentenced him to one year in prison and a $500 fine.[34] Though
the Slide was closed for good in 1892, the lure of profit insured that, by
1895, New York City was hosting half-a-dozen new resorts catering to
fairies and the men who loved them.[35]

Today, more than a hundred years after the closing of the Slide, 157
Bleecker Street still houses a bar. There, on a quiet afternoon, students of
sexual history—and of economics, politics, and the press—may sit for a
moment with a beer and commune with the ghosts of tasters past.

21   *To Unite for Defense*

"**D**uring the last decade of the nineteenth century, the headquarters for avocational female impersonators of the upper and middle classes was 'Paresis Hall,'" in New York City, on Fourth Avenue, south of Fourteenth Street.

So wrote a self-styled "female impersonator," a man who published two memoirs and called himself "Earl Lind," as well as "Ralph Werther" and "Jennie June."[1] The name "Werther" was probably derived from the title character of Goethe's storm and stress novel, and "Jennie June" from the pen name of a famous American journalist, Jane Cunningham Croly, one of the first women to hold a regular salaried position at a major American newspaper and a political and community activist.

Lind's use of "female impersonators" for effeminate, cross-dressing, men-lusting men was specific to him. The term usually named professional imitators of women who performed on the stage. Class distinctions between effeminate men were important to the cultured, educated Lind, and class is prominent in his two memoirs. He speaks disparagingly of "the lowest class of bisexuals who had never known anything better than slum life."[2]

Lind's "bisexuals" referred not to persons attracted to both sexes, but to *two-sexed persons,* a condition he thought of as characterizing effeminate, cross-dressing men like himself. Men combining the traits of both sexes described for Lind a distinct, double identity. His idea of two-sexed persons made no distinction between physical characteristics and what are now usually thought of as differences in masculine and feminine deportment—gender distinctions. For him, as for most others of his time, there were only sex distinctions.

His "bisexuals," I stress, were *not* persons sexually attracted to both men and women. They were *not* a third group between homosexuals and heterosexuals. He did, sometimes, use "heterosexual" to name those men and women he more often called the "sexually full-fledged"—implying that he and other bisexuals were somehow sexually incomplete.

For Lind, the group of men and women in which he counted himself was defined by its deviations from the day's standard masculinity and femininity, its sexual acts, and by its class and "culture."

Paresis Hall, continued Lind, "bore almost the worst reputation of any resort of New York's Underworld. Preachers in New York pulpits would

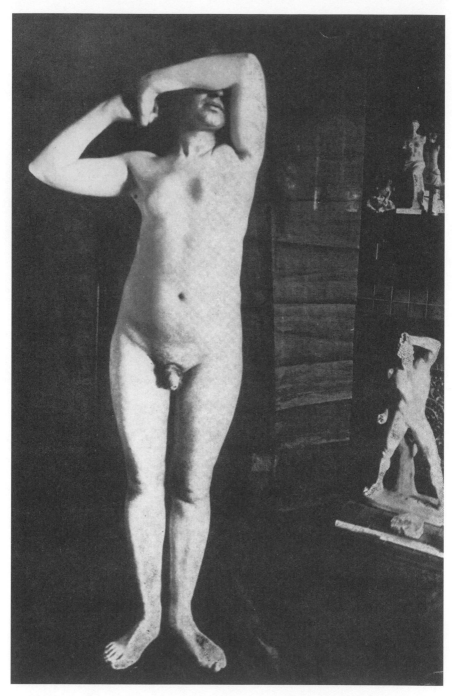

Earl Lind, front view of author at thirty-three. Lind, *Female* (1922). Courtesy Mayo Foundation History of Medicine Library. ❧

thunder Philippics against the 'Hall,' referring to it in bated breath as 'Sodom!' "[3]

Lind's memoir employs "the resort's popular name," Paresis Hall, but, he reports that its "androgyne habitués always abhorred that nickname," calling it, simply, "The Hall."[4] (Columbia Hall was its official name.) The word "androgyne" ("andro" = "man" and "gyne" = "woman"), used by Lind as a major term for effeminate men, was uncommon and may also have been his own creation. Like many other men, he felt the need to invent new, nonpejorative words for sexual and gender nonconformists.

The popular name Paresis Hall "arose in part," he explained, "because the numerous full-fledged male visitors . . . thought the bisexuals who were its main feature, must be insane in stooping to female-impersonation"—"paresis," he added, named a form of insanity associated with syphilis.[5] Rejecting the name Paresis Hall, androgynes rejected the implicit link between themselves and disease.

But the linking of ailment and androgyne provided an enticing urban spectacle for tourists, drawing them to Paresis Hall: "It was one of the 'sights' for out-of-towners who hired a guide to take them through New York's Underworld."[6] Diseased sexuality was an exotic attraction for travelers to Sin City and their paid guides. Stevenson, the operator of the Slide, and New York City newspapers cashed in on the public's desire to see or read about those they considered perverts. For some, this watching and reading was one of the few acceptable forms of nonprocreative, pleasurable sex.

Public gossip about Paresis Hall also alerted effeminate men to its existence as a place to meet others like themselves: "On one of my earliest visits to Paresis Hall," in around January 1895, recalled Lind, "I seated myself alone at one of the tables. I had only recently learned that it was the androgyne headquarters—or 'fairie' as it was called at the time."[7] "Fairy," first mentioned in 1892 as the name of a Slide performer, quickly became a popular, generic name for effeminate males interested in sex with men.[8]

"Since Nature had consigned me" to the class of androgynes, explained Lind, "I was anxious to meet as many examples as possible."[9] He had no doubt that other androgynes existed, no thought that he was unique.

Invoking "nature" as the inborn cause of his fairydom, Lind resisted any link with the unnatural. Like Walt Whitman, Lind adapted the terms "natural" and "unnatural" to his own defense, creating a reverse discourse: Lind reversed the curse of the unnatural, arguing that his two-sexed character was inborn, therefore *natural,* therefore something he could not help and something for which he should not be jailed or punished. Lind failed, however, to take one final affirmative step, that of feeling, then asserting, his and other androgynes' absolute equality with those he called the sexually full-fledged. He never completely stopped thinking of himself as sexually lacking and accursed. Like Symonds, Lind struggled long and hard to affirm the carnal in his relations with men.

In January 1895, Lind had sat for just a few minutes in the Paresis Hall beer garden when, his memoir recalls, "three short, smooth-faced young men approached and introduced themselves as Roland Reeves, Manon Lescaut, and Prince Pansy—aliases, because few refined androgynes would be so rash as to betray their legal name in the Underworld."[10]

The alias "Manon Lescaut" documents another early association of effeminate men and opera, a link noted in Melville's *Redburn*. "Prince Pansy" suggests a male-female combination, and the association of "pansies" with effeminate men and, specifically, "fairies" dated to this time.[11] From these men's names, adds Lind, "their loud apparel, the timbre of their voices, their frail physique, and their feminesque mannerisms, I discerned they were androgynes."

As Lind reconstructed the "essence" of the discussion that followed (almost twenty-five years after its occurrence), he was identified as a fellow effeminate by Roland Reeves, who acted as chief speaker. Reeves told him some extraordinary news: "A score of us have formed a little club, the CERCLE HERMAPHRODITOS. For we need to unite for defense against the world's bitter persecution of bisexuals." (Would Reeves have said "bisexuals"? Not likely, that was Lind's own term.)

Reeves continued: "We care to admit only extreme types—such as like to doll themselves up in feminine finery. We sympathize with, but do not care to be intimate with, the mild types, some of whom you see here tonight even wearing a disgusting beard! Of course they do not wear it out of liking. They merely consider it a lesser evil than the horrible razor or excruciating wax-mask."[12]

The most effeminate men, Reeves (and Lind) suggested, carefully assessed degrees of deviation from the masculine to distinguish "types" of androgynes. Their rejection of intimacy with their more masculine fellows, and their refusal to have the masculines in their CERCLE, indicates that gender differences among androgynes already divided this group.

But the same strong sense of difference among these men united the most effeminate *with each other* in the remarkable CERCLE HERMAPHRODITOS. That is the earliest American reference I have found to an organization of sexual and gender nonconformists, established to resist their oppression. Though the CERCLE could be the fictitious product of Lind's imagination, it would not be surprising if the most "extreme" effeminate men had formed such a daring, pioneering group. Three-quarters of a century later, in June 1969, it was effeminate, cross-dressing men who played a prominent role in the Stonewall Rebellion, the spark that inspired the contemporary gay liberation movement. The most obvious nonconformists are often the most persecuted, and, sometimes, the most determined resisters.

The CERCLE's name adapted the popular term "hermaphrodite," used broadly in the nineteenth century for persons who combined the bodily and/or psychological and behavioral characteristics of men and women (again, no distinction was made between biological sex and masculine or feminine mannerisms or acts). "Hermaphrodite" had earlier been used for centuries to mean an effeminate man or virile woman, though, not necessarily, one who desired erotic contact with their own sex.[13]

Given the idea, prevalent in nineteenth-century America, that sexual desire for a man was a "female" feeling, sexual desire for a woman a "male" feeling, a person who felt the "wrong" desire for their sex was hermaphroditic. The late-nineteenth-century medical category "psychosexual hermaphroditism" is built on the same sexual folklore.[14] In 1908, an American, Edward Stevenson, contested this common notion, the "rooted vulgar idea that the Uranian and Uraniad *must* be hermaphroditic. This antiquated notion is strong in America and England."[15] As Xavier Mayne, Stevenson was a pioneering defender of "the intersexes" and "similisexualism" (later, more commonly called homosexuals and homosexuality).

The group's name also referred to the ancient Greek and Roman figure of the hermaphrodite, statues of which Lind made his model when posing for photographs.[16] HERMAPHRODITOS was also consistent with Lind's employment of "androgyne" and "bisexual" for persons thought of as combining the male and female within themselves.

"We ourselves are in the detested trousers," Reeves explained that January evening, because they had just arrived at the hall from work: "We keep our feminine wardrobe in lockers upstairs so that our every-day circles can not suspect us of female-impersonation. For they have such an irrational horror of it!"[17]

Lind then reconstructed "a typical hour's conversation" among ten of the "ultra-androgynes," leaving out their "prattle," he said, to focus on what he considered most important in their talk.[18]

About eight in the evening, in April 1895, as Lind recreated the scene, in the upper room in Paresis Hall on which they held a long-term rental, some members of the group were still in male apparel, some were changing into women's evening gowns, some were "busy with padding and the powderpuff," and some were "ready to descend to the beer-garden below to await a young-blood friend."[19] Though Lind did not mention Oscar Wilde, it is no coincidence that Lind dated this scene to April 1895. For this was the month that news of Wilde's legal troubles were first reported in the American press.[20]

As Lind constructed the scene, an androgyne who called himself Angelo-Phyllis referred to the murder of a young heiress, a "gynander," Lind's term for a two-sexed woman-man (a mannish woman).[21] "Gynander" did *not* signify the same person as our present "lesbian," a term which makes no necessary reference to masculine or feminine traits. "Lesbian" generally refers now only to women's erotic desire for or acts with women. The gynander and lesbian represent substantially different historical ways of naming, conceiving, and, ultimately, constructing sexuality, gender, and kinds of persons.

The heiress's murder, Lind interjected, was "only one of a number of similar occurrences in New York." He added: "Gynanders, as well as androgynes, are doomed to suffer murder at the hands of hare-brained prudes because of the false teaching of the leaders of thought."[22]

Lind's identification of androgynes and gynanders encouraged him to protest the social fate of *both* groups. He moved beyond the defense of androgynes alone—he was not concerned, as was Walt Whitman, solely with the fate of male comrades. Lind began to formulate the idea of a class of persons—men and women—defined by their sexual and gender nonconformity.

Lind protested that a "continuous string of both men-women and women-men are being struck down in New York for no other reason than loathing for those born bisexual." Publicity about the "facts of bisexuality," Lind wrote in his 1922 memoir, would "put an end to these mysterious murders of innocents."[23] Knowledge will set free the oppressed, he optimistically suggested, ignoring the need for collective action (paradoxically, since the scene he recollected involved members of the CERCLE HERMAPHRODITOS).

As Lind recreated the scene, a twenty-three-year-old effeminate called "Plum" then joined the others in their rented room, sobbing that he had been fired from his job: "Some bigot denounced me to the boss," who "called me into his private office."[24]

Plum then described the scene for his fellow androgynes. Confronted by his boss, Plum said: "I confess to being a woman-man, and throw myself upon your mercy."

Effeminate man (top right): one of the urban types included in *Pictures of Life and Character in New York*, 1878. Courtesy David Kahn. ❧

The boss answered: "That confession . . . proves you an undesirable person to have around."

Plum appealed for sympathy: "It will be hard to find a new job, since I have been with you for five years and must depend on your recommendation."

The boss retorted: "Knowing your nature, Plum, I could not recommend you *even to shovel coal into a furnace*!"

"But you have steadily advanced me for five years!" Plum responded, "Why should to-day's discovery make any difference in your opinion of my business ability?"

The boss answered: "An invert ought to leave brain work for others! [A male "invert" was like a woman, he implied, unequipped for serious thinking.] He ought to exhaust himself on a farm from sunrise to sunset. . . . He should pass his life in the backwoods; not in a city. He has no right in the front ranks of civilization where his abnormality is so out of place!"

"You mean that he should commit intellectual and social suicide," asked Plum, "in obedience to the aesthetic sense of Pharisees?"

"Certainly!" the boss responded, "The innate feelings and the conscience, as well as the Bible teach that the invert has no rights! I myself have only deep-rooted contempt for him! . . . He is the lowest of the low!" Lind implicitly suggested the reverse, that inverts do and should have "rights"—a radical idea for its time.

The boss then asked if Plum, "at the bottom of your heart," was not "thoroughly ashamed of the confession" he had made about being a "woman-man."

"By no means," Plum answered. "I have learned to look upon bisexuality as a scientist and a philosopher. But you have just shown yourself to be still groping in the Dark Ages."

Plum appealed to religion: He was not "ashamed of the handiwork of God," he said, adding, "a bisexual has no more reason than a full-fledged man or woman to be ashamed of his God-given sexuality."

"You appear . . . unable to get my point of view," Plum told his boss. "All in my anatomy and psyche that you gloat in calling depraved and contemptible I have been used to since my early teens. If your views have any justification in science or ethics, I am unable to see it. Although it almost breaks my heart to be made an outcast and penniless by yourself," Plum preferred that lot to being in the wrong, like his employer.

Plum then cited a list of famous and accomplished men-lusting men: if the boss excluded "Socrates, Plato, Michael Angelo, and Raphael, then you exclude me also." Citing the creative accomplishments of famous men-lusting men became a common defense of homosexuals in general.

But Plum's sexuality "works against the multiplication of the human race," objected the boss.

To this "race suicide" argument, Plum responded, "Hasn't the human race survived the best decades of classic Greece?" Those Greeks, he claimed, "gave to the women-men who happened to be born among them . . . an honorable place." Ancient Greece, he continued, was "acknowledged by all modern historians to have attained the highest development of mind and body ever known."

The boss insisted: "Nature . . . instilled in all but the scum of mankind this utter disgust for the invert." So the invert "must always be condemned to a life of unsatisfied longing." For this reason "he should be imprisoned for life," said the boss, "not for only ten or twenty years as the statutes now provide!"

The boss conflated sexual inversion and disease: "We strictly segregate diphtheria and scarlet fever, Plum. Why should we not similarly quarantine against inversion?"

Plum answered that the freedom of "bisexuals" caused no harm "to any individual, nor to the race as a whole." Moreover, "the segregation of bisexuals would affect for a lifetime tens of thousands of our most useful members of society. It would occasion, among those already accursed by Nature, additional intense mental suffering, despair, and suicide."

Bisexuals, "accursed by Nature," should not also be cursed at by their fellow human beings, Plum argued. To modern, liberal ears, Plum's naturally "accursed" people conceded too much to bigotry.

Inversion "lowers humanity down to the lowest levels of animal life!" the boss exclaimed.

To which Plum nicely retorted: "So does eating!"

The boss argued from emotion: "I detest it! My disgust is innermost and deep-seated! To begin now to show any mercy to the invert after having for two thousand years confined him in dungeons, burned him at the stake, and buried him alive, would be a backward step in the evolution of the race!" The "invert was not fit to live with the rest of mankind!" the boss repeated. "He should be shunned as the lepers of biblical times! If generously allowed outside prison walls, the law should at least ordain that the word 'Unclean' be branded in his forehead, and should compel him to cry: 'Unclean! Unclean!' as he walks the streets, lest his very brushing against decent people contaminate them!"

"All that is only bigotry and bias!" Plum declared.

The boss admitted: "it is bias!" But "bias is justifiable in matters of sex!"

The employer questioned Plum's argument that "medical writers have declared inverts *irresponsible!*" Plum argued that inverts, because born

"The Bowery Queen," professional female impersonator. Stereopticon cards courtesy Herbert Mitchell; photographs by Dwight Primiano. ☙

with their desire, were not guilty of moral lapses or crime. The boss responded that inverts *were* responsible for their desire and therefore should be punished: "You say inverts are assaulted and blackmailed! Thy deserve to be! It would be wrong for any one at all to show any leniency! Their existence ought to be made so intolerable as to drive them to lead their sexual life along the lines followed by other men!"

The boss could not rest "knowing you were around the office!" he finally told Plum.

As Plum's story ended, Roland Reeves concluded, ironically, that whatever mankind was "not personally inclined to is always horribly immoral!"

In this brief scene, Lind's memoir reviewed and answered almost every argument used against men-lusting men and women-lusting women, then and since. His memoir constitutes a militant American manifesto in defense of sexual and gender nonconformists. Another such manifesto was produced by a different sort of author, in Cambridge, Massachusetts, at a world-famous university.

James Mills Peirce, born May 1, 1834, in Cambridge, Massachusetts, was the son of Benjamin Peirce, a Harvard University professor and the most famous American mathematician of his day. James Mills was also grandson of a Harvard librarian and the historian of the university. His younger brother was Charles Sanders Peirce, the noted mathematician and pragmatist philosopher.[1]

In 1853, during his senior year at Harvard, Peirce appeared in female roles in several theatrical productions of the Hasty Pudding Club. He was also a walk-on in Boston opera productions, an early expression of his lifelong delight in opera and plays. After graduating from Harvard, Peirce attended the university's law school in 1854, tutored mathematics, and then, in 1857, entered the university's divinity school. Graduating in 1859, he preached for two years in Unitarian churches in New Bedford, Massachusetts, and in Charleston, South Carolina. Giving up the ministry, he returned to Harvard to teach mathematics, attaining the rank of professor in 1869. He lived in Harvard Yard among his students until 1880, when he was forty-six.

In 1863, eighteen-year-old Thomas Sargent Perry was a student in the math class of the twenty-nine-year-old Peirce. Meeting in this pedagogical setting, the two became lifelong, devoted friends. On Peirce's part, at least, the feeling was more than friendly. Seven years after their meeting, on February 14, 1870, Peirce sent Perry a note addressed "To my dear Valentine."[2] Whatever Perry's feelings for Peirce, he apparently took the older man's attraction in his stride and developed an intellectual interest, at least, in the history of sex and affection between men.

On May 17, 1873, Peirce responded to Perry's announcement that he had recently shed tears of joy: Lilla Cabot had accepted his marriage proposal. "I am so glad you are so happy," Peirce said. "It makes life seem less cruel to me, even if it has no mercy for me, that you have found its only joy."[3]

The message was mixed, as it often was when one of two men friends felt threatened by the other's marriage. But marriage as life's "only joy" was a clichéd response to such an announcement; Peirce certainly experienced continuing joy in his intimacy with Perry following his friend's marriage. "Our friendship is among the things I value most in life," Peirce told Perry. He liked to think "that now its pleasure is to be heightened for all coming time." He was anticipating the new friendship of Perry's wife.

James Mills Peirce. Courtesy Harvard University Archives. ❧

Peirce did admit, "I am apt to dread my friends' friends, for you know how few people there are who can like or understand me. But here I feel that I have already a strength which you have given me." Perry's strong affection for Peirce had evidently bolstered the older man's self-confidence. Peirce signed himself, "Your affectionate J." Peirce and Perry remained close after Perry's marriage, and, in the summer, Peirce often visited Perry and his wife, a painter, in an artists' colony in France.

In 1884 Perry, who had become an editor, literary historian, and professor of German and English at Harvard, corresponded with John Addington Symonds. The English scholar sent Perry his essay on ancient Greek pederasty, *A Problem in Greek Ethics.* He warned Perry that it discussed an "unmentionable," "dangerous" subject, and to be "discreet" in showing it around. Perry, undoubtedly, showed it discretely to Peirce, as we shall see. Perry responded enthusiastically to the essay, and informed Symonds of a German scholarly article on ancient Greek pederasty. Perry had researched the subject himself.[4]

In 1889, James Mills Peirce traveled to Europe with "a bright young physicist," a "Mr. Clifford," probably Harry Ellsworth Clifford, who had graduated from the Massachusetts Institute of Technology in 1886 and who later joined the Harvard faculty.[5] Peirce had evidently found a new companion.

In February 1891, John Addington Symonds sent Perry his newest essay, *A Problem in Modern Ethics,* which discussed the contemporary implications of sexual relations between men.[6] Perry undoubtedly also shared this with Peirce, who then composed a defense of "homosexual love" and sent it to Symonds.

On May 20, 1891, Symonds informed his confidant, Henry Dakyns, that he had "received a great abundance of interesting and valuable communications in consequence of sending out a few copies of that 'Problem in Modern Ethics.' People have handed it about." One of the "oddest" responses had come from America, "in the shape of sharply-defined acute partizanship for Urningthum" (a play on Ulrichs's Urning, that German's invented term for men-loving men).[7]

A month later, on June 22, Symonds told his friend, the writer Edmund Gosse, of finding "a fierce & Quixotic ally, who goes far beyond my expectations in hopes of regenerating opinion on these topics," a Professor Pierce, of Cambridge, Massachusetts, a mathematician.[8] Symonds clearly was referring to James Mills Peirce and his "acute partizanship for Urningthum."

The following month, Peirce and Clifford again traveled to Europe. Peirce wrote to Perry that he had received a letter from Symonds, who had asked him to visit. Peirce hoped to do so.[9]

⌒

The Harvard dean's militant defense of "Urningthum" is contained in a letter to Symonds, composed by May 1891, when Peirce was fifty-seven. This manifesto was published anonymously, in 1897, in the first English edition of Havelock Ellis and Symonds's book, *Sexual Inversion*.[10]

Peirce had "inquired into this question for many years." He wrote, "It has long been my settled conviction that no breach of morality is involved in homosexual love."[11] Peirce's bold statement mobilized the new term "homosexual" to defend a kind of "love" and "passion," emotions that were, at once, spiritual and sexual—a radical idea.

Peirce's central, explicit concern was the same pressing issue that bothered Symonds and many other nineteenth-century men: the basis for establishing the moral worth of men's sexual desire for men. Men's erotic attraction for men was often experienced then as, first and foremost, a moral problem. In contrast, by the middle of the twentieth century, homosexual desire would be typically experienced as a medical/psychological issue.

Like "every other passion," Peirce added, the homosexual passion also "tends when duly understood and controlled by spiritual feeling, to the physical and moral health of the individual and the race." Did Peirce imply that a spiritually controlled sexual passion allowed, morally, for the active erotic expression of the homosexual passion? He did not say so directly, but his argument suggested that homosexual passion, at least when accompanied by spiritual love, was as legitimately enacted as the spiritual-sexual love of men and women for each other.

Only "brutal perversions" of homosexual passion "are immoral," he argued, referring, no doubt, to forcible acts and to acts with youths under a reasonable age of consent. But that qualification would apply, logically and equally, to sexual relations between men and women, though he did not make that point.

"I have known many persons more or less the subjects of this [homosexual] passion," Peirce declared, "and I have found them a particularly high-minded, upright, refined, and (I must add) pure-minded class of men."

The many "more or less" homosexual persons he knew were, I stress, only and specifically men. Peirce did not apparently know any women who loved women in the same spiritual-sexual way, and he did not consider such women's existence. His universe, like Harvard's, did not include women not attached to a man, as wife, blood relation, or servant. Peirce's world of spiritual-sexual love was sex segregated. Peirce's world differed from that of Earl Lind, whose universe included androgynes and gynanders (effeminate, men-lusting men, and masculine, women-lusting women).

Peirce's term "homosexual" may have logically referred to "same-sex" love, but he extended it, in practice, only to men. His homosexual passion was opposed to what he called the "intersexual passion"—between men and women—the excesses of which he criticized: "In view of what everybody knows of the vile influence on society of the intersexual passion as it actually exists in the world . . . it seems a travesty of morality" to invest that desire "with divine attributes and denounce the other as infamous and unnatural." Comparing society's unequal response to these two sexualities was already a powerful weapon in the arsenal of men-lusting, men-loving men.

The intersexual passion, Peirce maintained, made "men and women sensual, low-minded, false, every way unprincipled and grossly selfish, and this especially in those nations which self-righteously reject homosexual love." Peirce's essay included an embryonic critique of men and women's sexual relations.[12]

Peirce argued specifically against one of his time's dominant assumptions about love: "There is an error in the view that feminine love is that which is directed to a man, and masculine love that which is directed to a woman." That "doctrine," he declared, "involves a begging of the whole question." That view assumed what ought to be questioned: Was there really a love proper to a sex, a love that was sexed, male or female? That idea, said Peirce, "is a fatal concession to vulgar prejudice." This was a rare, major, innovative insight into his age's conception of sex, sexuality, and love.

Peirce also rejected another basic assumption of his day, that the sexual passion of men and women was always, innately, naturally, and properly focused on what was called the "other," "opposite" biological sex.

"Passion is in itself a blind thing," he asserted. By way of example, he cited ancient Greek custom as portrayed in the writings of John Addington Symonds. He also noted "the natural evolution of our race," which he presumed was moving away from any fixed, innate, animalistic desire for the "other sex."

Passion, he argued, "is a furious pushing out, not with calculation or comprehension of its object, but to anything which strikes the imagination as fitted to its need. It is not characterized or differentiated by the nature of its object, but by its own nature. Its instinct is to a certain form of action or submission."

Here, Peirce anticipated Sigmund Freud's theory of an originally roaming libido that, only gradually, through a child's interactions with the world, became focused on a particular object or specific sex. How that originally blind instinct became focused "is largely accidental," Peirce argued. "Sexual passion is drawn by certain qualities which appeal to it." It may see those qualities "in a man or a woman." Those "two directions," sexual attraction to a man or to a woman, "are equally natural to unperverted man," Peirce declared.

Peirce then developed his theory of an originally blind libido into a new sexual ethic: The "*abnormal* form of love," he judged, "is that which has lost the power of excitability in either the one or the other of these directions. It is *unisexual* love (a love for one sexuality) which is a perversion. The normal men love both." Peirce deployed the old nineteenth-century idea of a nonexclusive spiritual love to uphold a new, nonexclusive spiritual-sexual love.

Peirce's new sexual ethic combined the old notion of "natural" and "unnatural" desires, "perverted" and "unperverted" yearnings, with the new, modern, medical notion of "normal" and "abnormal" sexualities. But Peirce reversed the charge of "abnormality" leveled at homosexual love. He redirected that accusation at love focused on only one sex. His moral system approved the passion aroused by both sexes (though, presumably, not at exactly the same moment).

Peirce's normal sexuality was *not*, I note, the bisexuality of the twentieth century. For, in its dominant twentieth-century version, bisexuality was thought of as opposing a "normal" heterosexuality and an "abnormal" homosexuality. In contrast, Peirce advocated a normal spiritual-sexual love that men could feel for both men and for women. He criticized what he felt was an abnormal spiritual-sexual love—the love and desire of men only for women.

Peirce also answered the traditional argument that sexual desire must be socially controlled for the sake of civilization: "It is true . . . that in primitive society all passion must have been wholly or mainly animal, and spiritual progress must have been conditioned on subduing it. But there is no reason why this subjugation should have consisted in extirpation, or trying to extirpate, one of the two main forms of sexual passion [homosexual], and cultivating the other [intersexual]."

There were two reasons for subduing sexual desire, said Peirce. The first was "to reserve all sexual energy for the increase of the race." The second was "to get the utmost merely fleshly pleasure out of the exercise of passion." He doubted whether "either of these reasons adds to the spiritual elevation of love," his primary value. "Fleshly pleasure" had no inherent value in his eyes apart from spiritual love. As militant as he was, he maintained the nineteenth-century, American denigration of fleshly pleasure at the expense of spiritual love.

The aim of getting the most "fleshly pleasure" out of passion, he claimed, was "now the moving influence" in the world. A pleasure ethic, he believed, already ruled modern life, and he rejected this unqualified valuing of pleasure and passion. He argued, "All passion needs to be unceasingly watched, because the worst evils for mankind lie hidden in its undisciplined indulgence. But this is quite as true of intersexual as of homosexual love."

Homosexual and intersexual love are of equal moral worth, he boldly argued. Later, in the mid-twentieth century, that argument would once more be asserted by homosexual activists who made powerful claims to equal social, civil, and legal responses to "heterosexuals" and "homosexuals."

Peirce argued that "our civilization suffers from want of the pure and noble sentiment" which the ancient Greeks "thought so useful to the state." Greek morality, he claimed, "was far higher than ours, and truer to the spiritual nature of man." His stress on the "spiritual" did not exclude the sexual, but valued its controlled expression. Exactly how controlled Peirce did not say.

In conclusion, Peirce argued forcefully against four of the theories then in use to explain homosexual passion. First, we should not "think and speak of homosexual love . . . as 'inverted' or 'abnormal' "—the condemnatory medical theory. Second, homosexual love was not "a sort of color-blindness of the genital sense"—the most liberal medical theory. Third, homosexual love was not "a lamentable mark of inferior development"—the theory of evolutionary degeneracy, one version of which appeared in Freud's analysis of homosexuality as a "fixation" of sexual development. And, fourth, homosexual love was not "an unhappy fault, a 'masculine body with a feminine soul' "—Karl Heinrich Ulrichs's theory of Urnings.

Instead, Peirce put forth his own idea. We ought to think of homosexual passion, he declared, as "being itself a natural, pure and sound passion, as worthy of the reverence of all fine natures as the honourable devotion of husband and wife, or the ardour of bride and groom." With that defense, Peirce ended his manifesto.

᭡

When Peirce and Thomas Sargent Perry returned to the United States from Europe in the early 1890s, Peirce persuaded Perry to join the St. Botolph Club, in Boston. From there Perry wrote with comic exaggeration to a male friend on February 1, 1892: "I have nothing more to do with my own happy home, it is deserted; the fire is never lit in my library; I scarcely know my children by sight. I spend all my time here wildly reveling." He stressed, "we are a wild set." James Mills Peirce and he sat up to midnight and, "as it were, personally lead the danse."[13] Whatever dance, and whatever wildness, Peirce and Perry remained friends for more than forty years.

When Havelock Ellis in 1897 published Peirce's defense of homosexual love, he presented it, anonymously, as the work of "Professor X," an "American of eminence, who holds a scientific professorship in one of the first universities of the world."[14]

Ellis added that the unnamed professor "has carried to the furthest extent the theory of the sexual indifference of the genital impulse, and the consequently normal nature of homosexuality." Ellis judged Professor X's statement "as representing the furthest point to which the defense of sexual inversion has gone, or, indeed, could go, unless anyone were bold enough to assert that homosexuality is the only normal impulse, and heterosexual love a perversion."

Peirce's statement was too bold for the less militant Ellis. After 1901, he deleted it from subsequent editions of *Sexual Inversion* published in the United States.

When James Mills Peirce died in 1906, at the age of seventy-two, he was recalled in the *Harvard Graduates' Magazine* by Thomas Sargent Perry as having had "many friends old and young."[15]

> His old friends he kept, and to do that is an art; he made new ones and young ones. He had a great fondness for the young who are really young, as he was himself till the day of his death. He was a fiery soul and he understood and sympathized with their enthusiasm, and hopes and eagerness, because he too was enthusiastic, hopeful and eager. His fervour, his intensity made him a marked figure in a world where there are more counters than coins. He sympathized intensely with good and honourable things and hated what was odious with equal intensity. He was no friend of compromise. A vivid figure is gone from Cambridge.

A Harvard colleague, W. E. Byerly, remembered Peirce as "deeply interested in the young men around him," and for "his quick indignation at any suggestion of injustice, and his scorn of everything narrow or crooked or mean. . . . His ready interest in everything human, and his keen enjoyment of life made him the most charming of companions."[16]

When Peirce's library was sold after his death it included the 1860 edition of Walt Whitman's *Leaves of Grass* (the first to contain his Calamus poems) and a rare first edition of Havelock Ellis's *Sexual Inversion,* with Peirce's anonymous essay on homosexual love as a "natural, pure and sound passion."[17]

A late-nineteenth-century diary records a fluidity of libido similar to that found earlier in the diary of Albert Dodd. But this later diary documents a desire troubled, consciously and significantly, by the possibility of "abnormal passion" (a medical judgment). This is the erotic journal of the aspiring writer and exuberant women-lover, Frederick Shelley Ryman, born in 1858 in Pennsylvania, the son of a farmer.[1]

A revealing entry of November 1885 provides some perspective on Ryman's later statements. Here, Ryman reports the comments of O. L. Fuller, a fellow resident of Catskill-on-Hudson, New York, a man unashamed to discuss and affirm his sexual behavior: "He told me in so many words one day that he is a 'C——sucker' & that he loves & enjoys that d——d custom so revolting to every right minded person."[2] Here, Ryman strongly condemned the mouth-penis contacts of men that were brought to his attention by his unabashed fellow townsman.

Ryman was unmarried and sexually active with women, but that flouting of social convention in his sexual behavior with women did *not* make him less judgmental about men's oral sex with other men. In fact, Ryman's active rejection of the traditional rules governing men and women's relations seems to have made him *especially moralistic* about his neighbor's preference. The condemnation of sodomites in the sporting press earlier in the century is another example of this need to condemn someone more unconventional than oneself.

The following year, on May 3, 1886, while Ryman was hiking in the country, the twenty-eight-year-old man spied "one of the prettiest boys I ever saw in my life," and his powerful response surprised him: "It is next to never that beauty in my own sex attracts me but he was beautiful." Calling the boy, thirteen, his "pet," Ryman looked forward to the lad's physical maturity: "I would like to see that boy when he is about 19. I'll bet he will be a veritable Apollo."[3]

Ryman struggled to understand why he was "so attracted" by this youth. His attraction seems to have bothered him a little, but he still did not see it as sexual in origin. Stressing the unusualness of his response, Ryman added that the boy and a friend, Fred Squires, "are about the only male beings now living whose beauty I ever gave a second thought." So Ryman had given an earlier first thought to male beauty. The "Apollo Belvedere," he added, "is the only statue of a male figure that ever impressed me in the least & that did thrill me through & through."[4] Thrilled   317 by at least three earlier examples of male beauty, Ryman fended off some allegation not yet explicit in his mind or in his era's consciousness.

Three months later, in August 1886, Ryman reported that his friend, Robert M. Luke, then twenty-one years old, "came over to stay with me last night. I have slept with him many a night at the American Hotel [where Luke worked as a clerk] but last night was his first night with me." This inaugural bed sharing had special meaning for Ryman.[5] Each of these men had easy access to his own bed, so sleeping together was a contact both had voluntarily sought.

"Rob & I had a good time talking together concerning our lives loves etc.," reported Ryman, adding: "I confess I like the oriental custom of men embracing & kissing each other if they are indeed dear friends." Here, a supposed "oriental" custom justified uncustomary physical acts of affection between European-American men. A popular orientalism legitimated a newly suspect form of bodily contact between white men.[6]

Ryman added: "When we went to bed Rob put his arms around me & lay his head down by my right shoulder in the most loving way & then I put my arms around his neck & thus clasped in each others arms we talked for a long time till we were ready to go to sleep & then we separated as I cannot sleep good with anyone near me."

In the morning Luke got up and, before starting off to work, "came to the bed & threw his arms around my neck & we kissed each other good bye though I expect to see him again to-day."

Then Ryman, for the first time, defended himself against his own accusation: "Now in all this I am certain there was no sexual sentiment on the part of either of us. We both have our mistresses whom we see with reasonable regularity & I am certain that the thought of the least demonstration of unmanly & abnormal passion would have been as revolting to him as it is & ever has been to me, & yet I do love him & loved to hug & kiss him because of the goodness & genius I find in his mind." Ryman's consciousness of eros in the air was beginning to pollute his loving relation with another man. Before our eyes, we see Ryman becoming a modern man.

Ryman justified his contacts with Luke as normal, nonsexual, and nonviolative of manly norms, even constructing a biblical defense: "Christ kissed & embraced those whom he loved I believe & why shall I fear to do the same?"[7] Why, indeed? Only because by 1886 some American men were confronting a new, uneasy awareness of men's sexual passion for men—including, sometimes, their own.

The following month, on September 30, Ryman reaffirmed: Rob Luke "is one G——d——d good fellow"—his refusal to spell "God" and "damned" hinted at earlier religious training or a class-based rejection of swearing, and an aspiration to the finer sensibilities of his age. The swearing also masculinized Ryman and, perhaps, defeminized his beloved Luke.

"I truly love him," he said about Luke: "He gave me his picture tonight & as I left him he took my right hand in his & quick as thought put it up to his lips & kissed it before I knew it hardly. I am truly proud to be so loved by any one & especially by one whom I can love & respect in return as I certainly do him."[8]

A week later, on October 7, Luke's twenty-second birthday, he came to Ryman's room, and Ryman read a Byron poem aloud to him.[9] Ryman was "sorry" that Luke "could not stay all night but he could not so I had to part with him."[10]

A month later, "about midnight Rob Luke came over to the house." Ryman "was in bed asleep but he called & I got up & went down & let him in. He threw his arms around my neck & kissed me as soon as I opened the door."[11]

In November 1886, Ryman wrote in his diary: "By God I do love Rob no use of talking. He bunked with me & says he is doing well in Rochester. I am so glad. He is grand." Ryman planned to introduce Rob Luke and Fred Squires to each other by letter, commenting: "How dear they both are to me. I truly love them not as ideals or instructors for I am much older than either of them [Ryman was twenty-eight, Rob Luke twenty-two] but as true noble boys worthy of the love of the best men & women."[12]

Love still usually held no conscious, necessary erotic connotation for Ryman. As Martin Duberman has already pointed out, Ryman (and, evidently, Luke) did not perceive these passionate embraces and loving declarations as sexual, though to modern eyes their relation seems drenched in eros. The same "gestures," said Duberman, "can decisively shift their symbolic meaning in the course of one hundred years, can 'signify' different emotions during different eras."[13]

I will venture further. It was not just the subjective meaning of Ryman's and Luke's loving embraces that shifted between 1886 and today. The meaning of their acts was embedded within a particular, shifting historical arrangement of affection and sexuality. That social structuring of emotion was radically transformed, along with its meaning. The rise to prominence of an institutionalized, idealized heterosexuality and a decried, ostracized homosexuality made it impossible for the Rymans and Lukes of this world to maintain that their kisses, embraces, and love contained no hint of sexuality.

In the 1880s, Ryman found it difficult to hold to the idea that his love for Luke was spiritual, his love for his mistress, sexual. That old compartmentalizing of flesh and spirit was becoming increasingly untenable: society was ceasing to relegate eros to a separate sphere and was selling a new pleasure-in-consumption ethic. That enjoyment ethic would soon openly and enthusiastically celebrate heterosexuality.

Ryman's disclaiming of any link between his loving contacts with Luke and an abhorred "abnormal passion" alerts us to a new, end-of-the-century suspicion of sexuality in the intimate relations of men. Today, a century later, many men still suffer that same suspicion.

In June 1923, Gavin Arthur, born Chester Alan Arthur III and the grandson of the twenty-first president of the United States, walked expectantly up a lane in Guilford, England, to a large rose-covered cottage. It was the lair of Edward Carpenter, the writer-defender of the "intermediate sex," sandalmaker, and activist-supporter of women's emancipation, socialism,the labor movement, nature, animals, and mysticism. He was also one of the most famous early, public proponents of sexual reform and defenders of those he called the "intermediate sex." Carpenter was born in 1844, four years after John Addington Symonds, into an upper-middle-class family. Ordained an Anglican deacon in 1869 and a curate in 1870, Carpenter gave up the church to teach, write, and work for the English socialist labor movement, and as a pioneering sex reformer. By 1906 Carpenter was daring enough to defend, publicly, the intermediate sex (persons later called homosexuals).[1]

"Welcome, my boy!" exclaimed the seventy-eight-year-old Carpenter, hugging his visitor and kissing the handsome, twenty-two-year-old Arthur on both cheeks. Arthur recalled that Carpenter's eyes were a "vivid sky-blue," his face "copper," and his "hair shining silver." The angelic, bearded Carpenter smelled "like leaves in an autumn forest," Arthur remembered, "A sort of seminal smell."[2]

Taking Arthur by the hand, Carpenter lead him into a cozy living room, where he introduced him to two working men, his "comrades," George Merrill, about sixty, and Edward "Ted" Inigan, about forty. The working-class Merrill had been Carpenter's companion and lover since 1898. Inigan had more recently joined them to form a commune of three.[3]

Over tea, Carpenter read the letter of introduction Arthur brought from a woman friend with whom Carpenter had marched for woman suffrage. As Carpenter read, he growled "a little in his throat the way a loving dog does when you pet him too much or too little." The Englishman remarked that Arthur's grandfather was president during Carpenter's 1884 trip to the United States.[4]

When Inigan suggested a sunset walk, Arthur accompanied him. Inigan was delighted, he said, that Arthur had "come to liven things up for the 'Old Man.'" Arthur responded, "You can't imagine how I've loved him, just through his books."[5]

Carpenter had published many articles and books, including poetry   321

Chester "Gavin" Arthur III. Courtesy Library of Congress. ❧

Edward Carpenter and George Merrill. Courtesy Sheffield Archives, Carpenter Collection Box 8/48. ❧

imitative of Whitman's, several accounts of his visits with the American poet, and numerous pioneering prose works on the intermediate sex and on sexuality and affection between men and women. His books included a sexually self-revealing autobiography, *My Days and Dreams* (1916).[6]

In Arthur's first version of his encounter with Carpenter, published in 1966, Inigan suggested that Arthur "sleep with the Old Man" that night: "A young man's electricity is so good for recharging the batteries of the old." Arthur answered that he would consider it a privilege.[7]

A second, more sexually explicit account of this encounter, unpublished during Arthur's lifetime, is dated 1967. In it, Arthur remembers, "Carpenter asked me if I would do him a favor and sleep with him. 'George and Ted need a rest,' he grinned."[8]

In Arthur's first account, Ted Inigan looks lovingly at Carpenter and says: "Chester wants to sleep with you tonight, Eddie. Ain't you the lucky old dog?" Carpenter then puts his hand on Arthur's shoulder and leads him to his bedroom. The Old Man undresses and uses the chamber pot, and Arthur does the same. He then gets into bed beside Carpenter, who is "trembling slightly." Arthur puts his arms around Carpenter.

This time the "seminal smell of autumn leaves" causes a strong, tender feeling in Arthur, the opposite of his experience as a youth, at home: "My father had been one of those conventional New York clubmen who thought it disgraceful to show tenderness to any male, even one's son." For Arthur senior, upper-class manhood at century's end required the suppression of tender feelings between men, even between fathers and sons. Physically expressed affection between men was becoming suspect.

Arthur's first version of this bed-sharing scene speaks of "diffused ecstasy." He says, "There was no orgasm in the sense of spilling seed."[9]

But Arthur's second, private account tells a different story.[10] In it, George Merrill and Ted Inigan go off to bed together, and Arthur, sitting alone with Carpenter before the fire, asks the Englishman if he "had ever been to bed with a woman." Carpenter answers no, "that he liked and admired women but that he had never felt any need to copulate with them. 'But that wasn't true of Walt, was it?' I asked." Carpenter idolized Whitman and had twice visited him during his trips to the United States, the first time staying with Whitman for a week.[11]

Carpenter told Arthur that Whitman's sexual "contact with women was far less than his contact with men."[12] Arthur then asked, nervously: "I suppose you slept with him?" Carpenter answered: "Oh, yes—once in a while—he regarded it as the best way to get together with another man.

He thought that people should 'know' each other on the physical and emotional plane as well as the mental. And that the best part of comrade love was that there was no limit to the number of comrades one could have—whereas the very fact of engendering children made the man-woman relationship more singular."[13]

Whitman, who carried on simultaneous intimacies with Harry Stafford and Edward Cattell, may well have believed in monogamy for man-woman relationships and open, extended relationships for men with men.

Arthur then asks whether Whitman had any interest in the "husband-father relationship," and Carpenter says no, that Whitman considered that "all the young men of American were his spiritual sons and all the young women his spiritual daughters." This tallies with Whitman's repeated metaphorical adoptions of children, especially sons.

Arthur, anxious about his personal queries, then dares to ask how Whitman made love. "I will show you," Carpenter smiles, "Let us go up to bed."

"It was a warm night," recalled Arthur, and under a light cover he and Carpenter lay naked "side by side on our backs holding hands."

Then Carpenter was holding Arthur's head in his hands, "making little growly noises, staring at me in the moonlight." Arthur thought: "This is the laying on of hands." First Whitman. Then Carpenter. "Then me."

Carpenter "snuggled up to me and kissed my ear," Arthur recalled. "His beard tickled my neck."

Arthur, who had once shipped out as a sailor, suddenly thought of a song his mates had sung: "If you can't get a woman, get a clean old man!" He also thought of "Walt's indignant denial to Symonds' inquiry was he a pederast." Arthur had clearly studied Whitman's life; now he was wondering what kind of sex Carpenter wanted with him.

"The old man at my side was stroking my body with the most expert touch," recalled Arthur, who "just lay there in the moonlight that poured in at the window and gave myself up to the loving old man's marvelous petting."

Arthur remembered: "Every now and then he would bury his face in the hair of my chest, agitate a nipple with the end of his tongue, or breathe in deeply from my armpit. I had of course a throbbing erection but he ignored it for a long time. Very gradually, however, he got nearer and nearer, first with his hand and later with his tongue which was now flickering all over me like summer lightning. I stroked whatever part of him came within reach of my hand but felt instinctively that this was a one-sided affair, he being so old and I so young, and that he enjoyed petting me as much as I delighted in being petted. There are many possible relationships, and one misses so much if one limits oneself to one sex or color or age."

"At last his hand was moving between my legs and his tongue was in my bellybutton. And then when he was tickling my fundament just behind the balls and I could not hold it longer, his mouth closed just over the head of my penis and I could feel my young vitality flowing into his old age."

Carpenter "did not suck me at all," Arthur stresses, "It was really *karezza,* which I knew he recommended in his books." *Karezza* referred to a sexual act in which men practiced muscular control to contain their ejaculation during orgasm.[14] But Arthur had not learned that control, and Carpenter "did not want to waste that life-giving fluid." Later, he lectured Arthur: "It isn't the chemical ingredients which are so full of vitality—it's the electrical content, like you get in milk if you get it direct from the cow—so different from cold milk!"

Arthur emphasized that Carpenter "was in no sense a succubus like so many old men, draining the young men of all the vitality they can get, like a vampire." The myth of the older, energy-consuming predator lived on in twentieth-century sexual folklore.

Carpenter was "caressing and loving," stressed Arthur. "I fell asleep like a child safe in father-mother arms, the arms of God. And dreamed of autumn woods with their seminal smell."

"The following morning," said Arthur, "Carpenter made love to me again, this time gazing at my body rapturously between kisses and growling ecstatically. And the same thing happened at the end. I had the distinct feeling that he felt my coming as if he were coming himself—that in that moment he *was* me.

Afterward Carpenter said: "When I was a clergyman I thought at Communion I was at one with God. But I realize now that this is a much more intimate communion—for is not Man made in the image of God?"[15]

⁂

Arthur's second, more sexually detailed account of sleeping with Carpenter was written in 1967, at the request of the poet Allen Ginsberg. In giving it to him, Arthur told Ginsberg that he was sorry the account had to remain private. He worried that his "work for humanity" would be ruined if this version of his encounter with Carpenter was publicized—though the earlier, no-emission version, daring for its time, had been published by Arthur himself. Between 1940 and 1941 Arthur had been the secretary of the Democratic State Central Committee of California, and between 1949 and 1951 he had taught a course in comparative religion at San Quentin Prison. (There, one of Arthur's students was Neal Cassady, the future beat writer, inspiration for Jack Kerouac's Dean Moriarty in *On the Road,* and sometime lover of Allen Ginsberg.)[16] Such humanitarian work might have become closed to Arthur if his name became associated with a sexually explicit memoir.

In 1962, Arthur had published the first edition of his book, *Circle of Sex.* His second edition (1966) had included the tamer account of his sleeping with Carpenter. Arthur was an astrologer; he believed in reincarnation, experimented with mind-transforming drugs, and was an avid student of sex studies, who corresponded with Havelock Ellis and Alfred Kinsey, and, who, throughout the 1960s, was considered a San Francisco "character." He was already married to his first wife when he visited Carpenter, and he married twice more, the last time in 1962 when he was sixty-one.

As noted, Gavin Arthur's second, sexually explicit account of sex with Carpenter was written at the request of Ginsberg, an outspoken, out-to-shock, openly gay poet. It was given to him, seemingly, as a keepsake. Is it, perhaps, wholly invented or grossly exaggerated, a kind of classy piece of literary-spiritual pornography? Could the whole meeting between Arthur and Carpenter be a figment of the American's admittedly fertile imagination?

Two letters from Arthur to Carpenter indicate that the American did indeed visit the Englishman in 1923.[17] Three months after his June visit, on September 8, 1923, Arthur wrote from Dublin and apologized for not being in touch since bidding Carpenter good-bye. He stressed "the joy, the comfort, the awe with which meeting such a great and sweet avatar filled me." As Arthur had told Carpenter in person, "I have nothing whatever in common with my father," and reading Carpenter's books had inspired "the first really heart to heart talks I have ever had with anyone."

The young, audacious Arthur, who had "a large preponderance of Irish blood," told Carpenter of his "daring dream." He aspired to be "to Ireland what Walt Whitman was to America and what you are to England!" Arthur imagined that Carpenter, having known Whitman, must have "gained much from him to which you added the fire of your own heart." Arthur fantasized of likewise "lighting my torch from yours, and carrying it over here, to light the way for these fearless dreamers who fight the mightiest empire of our day," a reference to the Irish Republicans battling British rule.[18]

Before visiting Carpenter, Arthur reports, he had "fearlessly yielded to temptation" (that is, to sex with men). Arthur had thought then that "I had lost the power to love—that I could not love a woman because she was not a man, nor a man because of the thought . . . that I was drifting away from the power to have a son. But I think perhaps the hell I went through opened my eyes to visions I had never dreamed of—and once again my dream possessed me, and I went over to see you."

"I have only seen you once," Arthur told Carpenter, "and yet I love you as a knight of old must have loved some human saintly confessor, as some eager pupil in Athens must have loved old Socrates, with a pure love and veneration more calming and deeply satisfying than any love I have ever felt before."

A year after his visit, on May 14, 1924, Arthur wrote again to Carpenter: "To the end of my days I shall have the most beautiful memories of you and your comrades."

Of "all the umpteen questions I asked you," Arthur recalled, "you only asked me one," about "comrade love in Ireland." On that subject, Arthur thought that "a handful of young Irishmen could not have stood up against the British empire if they had not been formed by the same spiritual love which formed the Theban Band. While I have never seen this love to be actually physical, it may be in many instances. But certainly nowhere in the world have I seen such real devotion between men, such communism of spirit, as I have in the ranks, and especially among the leaders of the Irish Republican Army. It was that which first interested me [in] their cause, and I am quite confident that that will win their cause in the end."

"I shall keep your photograph always with me to remind me of the dear old man who was so very gentle in my unhappiness, and whose songs are my inspiration and my comfort," said Arthur. He sent his love to George Merrill and "Teddy" Inigan. "How I envy them being always near you!"

Further, telling, support of Arthur's recollection of sex with Carpenter exists in the correspondence between Carpenter and John Addington Symonds. In these letters, Symonds responded to Carpenter's earlier speculations about the transfer of one man's vitality to another through the ingestion of semen.

On December 29, 1892, Symonds responded to a question Carpenter had raised about the "physiological grounds" for "passionate comradeship" and "homosexual love." Symonds had "no doubt" that "the absorption of semen implies a real modification of the physique of the person who absorbs it, & that, in these homosexual relations, this constitutes an important basis for subsequent conditions—both spiritual & corporeal."[19]

On January 29, 1892, Symonds addressed Carpenter, asking: "When you wrote to me upon the subject of assimilated semen, were you thinking about a book," published that year by an Italian, Silvio Venturi, about "psycho-sexual degeneration" and its effect on the individual and society?[20]

As early as 1892, then, Carpenter had been involved in discussions about the "spiritual" and "corporeal" benefits of "assimilated semen"— precisely the sexual act and views that Arthur attributed to Carpenter in 1922. Could Arthur have known of Carpenter's ideas about semen from Carpenter's published writings, or Symonds's interchange with Carpenter on the subject? It is possible, but doubtful.

The health benefits of ingested semen were also, as we have seen, the subject of American sexual folklore publicly contested by Dr. Mary Walker, in 1878. In addition, the narrow cultural construction of "sodomy" as anal intercourse, and the identification of sodomy as the single most terrible sex act, probably left oral-genital sexual activity relatively free of taint.

Gavin Arthur died in 1972 at the age of seventy. In 1978, thanks to Allen Ginsberg, the explicit version of Arthur's encounter with Carpenter appeared under Arthur's name in *Gay Sunshine,* the San Francisco liberation newspaper edited by Winston Leyland. Interviewed in that paper, Ginsberg stressed the link constituted by Walt Whitman's sexual connection with Edward Carpenter, Carpenter's with Gavin Arthur, Arthur's with the writer Neal Cassady, and Cassady's with Ginsberg himself. This is a "line of transmission," Ginsberg thought, that is now "part of the mythology"—a fabulous, historical daisy chain.[21]

Sex and Affection between Men—Then and Now

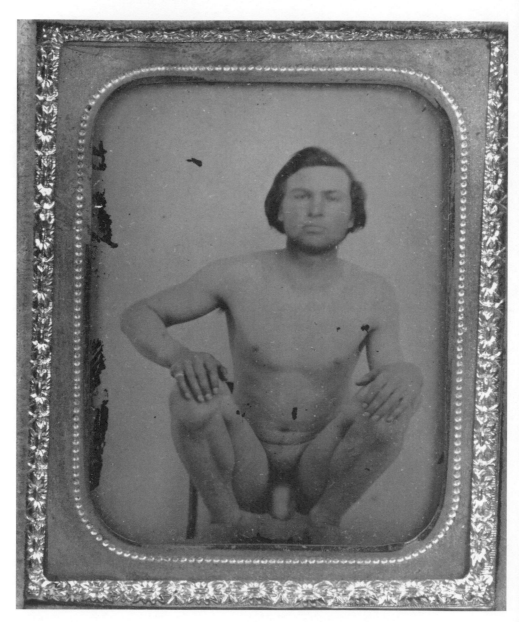

Nude man in velvet case. Ambrotype courtesy Herbert Mitchell; photograph by Dwight Primiano. ঔ

For twenty-five years now, historians of sexuality have struggled against the earlier, dominant idea of an ahistorical, unchanging eroticism. We have demonstrated how many aspects of sexuality have changed substantially over time. We have asked what, if anything, about sexuality might *not* have changed—what might be essential, universal, uninfluenced by history. We have questioned whether there is an essence of sexuality—or homosexuality, heterosexuality, or bisexuality—that takes different historical forms.

Since the birth of the modern feminist movement and the militant gay and lesbian liberation movement of the 1970s, the British historian Jeffrey Weeks and others have stressed that *responses* to homosexuality, *concepts* of homosexuality, the *words* used about homosexuality, and *identities* associated with homosexuality have changed radically over time. Taking up Weeks's challenge to historicize, we have come a long way since Weeks himself distinguished "between homosexual behavior, which is universal, and a homosexual identity, which is historically specific."[1]

Since then, historians of sexuality have emphasized the substantial difference between behaviors in the twentieth century called "homosexual" and those earlier called "sodomy."[2] The twentieth-century idea of sexual acts between people of the "same sex" points to a fundamentally different phenomenon than sodomy, understood, in the nineteenth-century United States, for example, as anal intercourse between men and men, men and women, men and children, *and,* as the penis-vagina intercourse of humans and animals of different sexes. Now, we have begun to historicize sexual behavior. Or, more accurately, we have begun to demonstrate the extent to which time, history, and changing social arrangements have substantially altered the place of erotic desire and acts in human lives.

In this book, I have tried to further that historical specifying of sexuality. I have struggled against a stubborn, residual essentialism that still creeps into the analyses of historians and their readers, causing a time-stopping effect on our understanding of eros.[3] I have explored here the extent to which everything about sexuality is historical and changing: sex acts, sexual desires, sexual relationships, and sexual regimes, and, of course, sexual identities, society's response to sexuality, ideas and judgments about sexuality, and the language of lust.

In particular, the nineteenth-century American evidence of sodomy and love provides insight into fundamental changes over time in the social organization of sexual desire and its expression in acts. As we have seen, "love" was one of the words that men used often in the nineteenth century to name, characterize, and affirm the value of what were sometimes their sexual relationships with men. When the twenty-two-year-old, unlettered, New Jersey farmhand Edward Cattell wrote in 1877 to his "loving . . . friend," Walt Whitman, Cattell stressed, "i love you Walt and all ways will."

Cattell's "love" was no casual characterization. His words asserted his basic feeling for Whitman; he made, in effect, a claim about the fundamental nature of his emotion—a statement about its essential character. If we want to understand the ordering of affection and sexuality in Cattell's time, we must take his love seriously.

Men of Cattell's century, it turns out, fought word wars, idea conflicts, interpretation battles, and knowledge contests. All of these were fundamental struggles over the basic character of their sexual desire for men, their sexual acts with them, and society's response to that sex. The importance of that strife only becomes clear when we stop assuming the universal existence of homosexual desires and same-sex acts and start paying close attention to men's own, old, native ways of feeling, acting, and naming. We must take into account men's particular historical ways of identifying and structuring their sexualities. What was at stake for them, I stress, were not just words or ideas, but the basic character of their relationships.

Many men affirmed the lust in their relations with men by creatively adapting their society's existing terms and concepts: for example, Albert Dodd's "love" and "friendship"; Walt Whitman's "adhesiveness" and "amativeness," his "Calamus" desire and his "live-oak" symbol. Alternatively, we can see men inventing completely new words and symbols: the "Urning" and "Dioning" of the German Karl Heinrich Ulrichs, and the "homosexual," "heterosexual," and "normal sexual" of the Hungarian-German Karl Maria (Kertbeny) Benkert. Some men's urge to speak was strong.

All of these men struggled for words to use against the dominant, condemnatory sexual terms of nineteenth-century society. As we read above, these included "sodomy," "buggery," the "crime against nature," "mutual onanism" (or "masturbation")—language that carried dire connotations of sin and damnation, marginalization, and, sometimes, prison. These stories reveal some men taking active steps against such fire and brimstone words as they struggled to create new, approving ways of naming and reconceiving sexual relations between men. Studying their words reveals a sexual world in the making.[4]

Edward Cattell took his term "love" from the everyday vernacular. Perhaps, since he was probably not a reader, he drew from a popular oral tradition that transmitted the language of romance. That vocabulary reflected the historical, institutional development of romantic love—a kind of love associated with the end of feudalism, the rise of capitalism, the dominance of the middle class, and the romantic movement. Marriage for love instead of marriage to increase the family's land was once a new, controversial idea. Cattell's love emerged from a tradition entirely different from the medicalized vocabulary that named and defined sexual relations between men according to a scientific framework: inversion or homosexuality.

Cattell's love constituted a popular, affirmative way of characterizing his feeling for Whitman. As such, his love is much more revealing of his world than the later medical terminology, applied retrospectively.

Using the vocabulary of the present to describe the past is not always or necessarily a mistake. Looking backward, we can often find good evidence of what we now call homosexual, bisexual, and even heterosexual relationships. But from a historical viewpoint, that retrolabeling is not informative. It begs too many questions about the sexual desires and acts of people from the past *in their original context.*

Cattell's love was an intensely personal experience and at the same time, a politically loaded, affirmative ideology with a particular historical resonance. Within the genteel language of his day, this farmhand could be understood to express a spiritual, nonsexual, disembodied "true love." The true love of Cattell and Whitman's day distinguished emphatically between good, pure emotion and bad, sensual feeling. When John Lankton felt love for the boy Charles in Whitman's story, "The Child's Champion" of 1841, this man and boy met in what Whitman called a Pure Country, a nonsexual nation separate and distinct from an impure Lust Land. Nineteenth-century ideologists of eros imagined a crack in the world, with love on one side, lust on the other.

It would take Sigmund Freud's rutting around in the late-nineteenth-century unconscious to demonstrate lust's common cohabitation with love. It would take Freud and a host of twentieth-century experts to revise radically the nineteenth-century idea that lust and love never met and mated. Freud and company pointed out how often lust and love did conjoin. And, in an important moment in the history of eros and affection, they actively encouraged some forms of that copulation; they formulated a positive new ideal of "sex-love" and promoted a new sort of male-female relationship called, yes, "heterosexual."[5] Those new terms then helped the dominant-culture builders create a substantially new organization of sexuality and affection. That placed good heterosexuality at one pole, bad homosexuality at the other, consigning bisexuality to a not-so-good place between.

In contrast, the arbiters of nineteenth-century culture put spirit at one pole, flesh at the other. That century's Christian division of love from lust, soul from body, enabled Walt Whitman, Charles Warren Stoddard, and many others to speak quite freely of their passionate love for other males. That love was not then perceived as including sexual desire.

In such cases, our present interest in the sexual does not *mis*lead when it leads us to see that eros was indeed a component of past relationships whose participants were sometimes unconscious of such hot spots. Homing in on the historically specific character of nineteenth-century men's love of men and friendship with them requires us to take their language, ideas, and social arrangements seriously. But it *does not* require us to take those words, concepts, and institutions exactly as they were understood in the past. Looking back it is possible for us to see sexuality in relationships that may not have been perceived then as erotic.

Some nineteenth-century authors were aware of the lust inhabiting their love, but they wrote with confidence that their readers would not understand that lust as lust. Some men of the nineteenth century were perfectly conscious of and even at ease with the lust inhabiting their love. Farmhand Edward Cattell seems to have been among them. A note from Cattell to Whitman and the poet's diary both suggest that they shared more than one private, moonlight intimacy, and that this farm lad's love had found active, sexual reciprocation: "it seems an age Since i last met With you down at the pond and a lovely time We had of it to[o] old man. i would like to Com up Som Saterday afternoon and Stay all night With you"—his clearest expression of desire. He added: "i love you Walt and Know that my love is returned." When Cattell used the word *love* to describe those lovely evenings, and when he expressed his desire for a sleepover, it seems highly likely that he referred to feelings and acts that were at once loving *and* sexual. Cattell and Whitman, I believe, consciously used their time's language of spiritual true love to speak safely and freely of a relationship that was actively affectionate and erotic.

Because Cattell and Whitman's intimacy apparently included a sexual exchange between two men, we can view it, retroactively, as involving members of the same sex, and therefore as homosexual. But, I stress, those are our ways of naming desire and behavior—words and concepts that express sexual systems of our time. They are not Cattell's, or Whitman's, or their time's ways of naming or understanding.

Certainly, it mattered greatly to Cattell and Whitman that both of them were men. Their mutuality of sex, in fact, informed their intimacy. Precisely because they were men they felt free to recognize their sexual desires and to act on them, meeting alone at that pond, or in Camden, New Jersey, and making multiple lovely nights of it.

But for Cattell's love to have become for him a same-sex love, a conceptual move would have been required for which his letters offer no documentation. No evidence suggests that Cattell made a link between his particular love for Whitman and a more general desire of men for men. Nothing suggests that Cattell perceived his love for Whitman as an even more general same-sex sexual-love defined in opposition to a different-sex sexual-love. Nothing suggests that Cattell thought of his love for Whitman as one expression of an emotion that included the lust of women for women. Neither is there evidence that this farmhand was thinking of himself as a member of a class of men-loving men. There is no evidence that Cattell made any link between his love for and acts with Whitman and those persons called sodomites or that act called sodomy, buggery, or the crime against nature. If we want to understand Cattell in his time, we in the present must be careful how we name and conceptualize Cattell's love. We are faced not only with evidence problems but also with fundamental problems of interpretation.

Because nineteenth-century love did not necessarily imply sex, there was no need for it to be exclusive and no need to limit it to different, "opposite" sexes: men or women could love men or women. While that century's love was broadly defined, for most of the nineteenth century sodomy, buggery, and the crime against nature were narrowly defined. In the world of U.S. legal case appeals, oral-genital contacts were not thought of as sodomy and not criminalized until century's end. Only in 1879 were oral-genital connections first criminalized by Pennsylvania legislators, the first such American law.[6] Soon, other legislators began to name and pass new "gross indecency" laws, and other statutes outlawing a new "unnatural and lascivious act with another person." They promoted the late-nineteenth-century surveillance and criminalizing of oral-genital contacts, and other, more vaguely defined, acts. Only during the last decade of the century did oral-genital copulation emerge in U.S. legal appeals cases as a subject of debate, judicial decision, and state regulation.

The world of sodomy, depicted in nineteenth-century American legal appeals reports, a few newspapers, and an occasional sensational novel, was loveless. It made no reference to romantic, spiritual love, which was that society's dominant, genteel ideal. And the world of pure, true love of course included no reference to sodomy or sodomites. Romantic lovers and sodomites inhabited different spheres, leaving a great unmapped space between them. It was in that space that a few men began a daring struggle to construct a new language of erotic love between men. I refer to Walt Whitman in America, John Addington Symonds in England, and Karl Heinrich Ulrichs and Karl Maria (Benkert) Kertbeny in Germany. But their resistance, I think, extended beyond language and ideas. They helped to create a fundamentally new, twentieth-century, social structuring of sexual desires and acts—a modernization of sexuality. This brought lust and love together in new legitimate and illegitimate combinations. Following the initiatives of Whitman and other men, lust changed its position in the social universe of love, moving from margin to center. Co-opted by psychiatrists, then by other master builders of the new sexual order, that twentieth-century world promoted hetero-sex-love and denigrated homo-sex-love.

In contrast to the modern homo/hetero polarity, the nineteenth-century sexual order distinguished between procreative acts and nonprocreative or improperly procreative acts. Though proper reproduction was authorized by true love and legal marriage, true love was not thought of as sexual in itself. True love and marriage functioned then to redeem even proper reproduction from its sensual, animalistic associations. The procreative-sexual potential of relationships between men and women even subjected their intimacies to greater surveillance than those between men and men and women and women. For the sexual was defined narrowly then as the intercourse of penis and vagina, so true love, however passionate and physical, could flourish between men and between women without raising suspicions of illicit intercourse.

❧

The old (that is, twentieth-century) view of a timeless, ahistorical homosexuality suggested that people in the past did not know their own minds. Whatever past desires and acts between human males were called in their own time, if the sexual was in evidence, then those relationships were really homosexual. In that view, the words used in the past—sodomy, contrary sexual feeling, sexual inversion, love, and friendship—might be quaint, but they were only superstructural, a thin, superficial skin covering the real homosexual body.

Only when we stop assuming that nineteenth-century men experienced same-sex or homosexual desire and performed same-sex or homosexual acts does that old world open newly before our eyes. Only then does it become clear how hard some men struggled for a language, a conceptual system, a morality, and institutions that affirmed their sexual relationships with men. I stress that loving, friendly, intimate, affectionate relationships between men were already accepted. So it was specifically erotic desires and acts with which men fought, literally and metaphorically, to come to terms. The struggles of Walt Whitman, John Addington Symonds, and other men for an affirmative language of lust between men were among the major projects of their lives—probably the major insight of this study.

If we reject the ahistorical assumption of a timeless same-sex sexual behavior, we start our research without knowing the basic character of men's past acts with men. We are faced with the problem of how to understand those acts. And we are faced with the problem of a major conflict between the nineteenth-century ideology of true love (excluding the sexual) and the age's practice of love and friendship between men (which sometimes included the sexual).

If we stop assuming a universal same-sex sexual desire and behavior, we are provoked to ask new questions about men's past relationships with men. *First,* what words did they use back then about those relationships and what sort of relationships did those words help to create? *Second,* how did they think about those past relationships, and how did those ideas function in that past social world? *Third,* how were those relationships evaluated? And, *fourth,* how were those relationships socially structured? How were they integrated with other socially and historically specific relationships?

The last question points us to a link between nineteenth-century men's sexual desires for and acts with men and the age's historically specific political economies of pleasure, procreation, and production.

At the nineteenth century's end, as I see it, human beings made substantial changes in their desires and activities, constructing a new, modern "sex/gender system" (in Gayle Rubin's phrase), a new "heterosexual dictatorship" (in Christopher Isherwood's naming), a new relationship between the social-historical "mode of engendering," the "mode of procreation," and the "mode of pleasure" (in my adaptation of Marx).[7]

Two major social shifts begin to explain the changes of that time in sexual desire and activity.[8] A fundamental change in the procreative practices of the urban, American middle class questioned the old, assumed reproductive character of sexual relations. More and more commonly, middle-class women and men employed some means to limit offspring. More and more often, I think, the middle class desired sexual activity as relationship enhancer and pleasure producer. The old moral distinction between good, natural procreative acts and bad, unnatural nonprocreative acts began to give way to a new moral distinction naming normal and abnormal pleasures.

At the same historical moment, the profit motive produced a general, societywide sexualization of commerce and commercialization of sexuality. Numbers of nineteenth-century businessmen began to cash in on the spectacle of sexual freaks and the fulfilment of the public's commodified pleasures. These included publishers of novels, film and play producers, and restaurant, bar, and bath owners. They included entrepreneurs who sold newspaper exposés of the Slide while denouncing its evils. Cashing in on sex, entrepreneurs of desire brought the blushing face of Eros into the light of day. The expansion of capitalism into the formerly private realm of sexual relations tore the old mask of mystery off the sexual body. And so sexual desire moved from the mind's margin to the center of consciousness, and sexual activity moved from society's edge to the culture's center.

If we stop assuming a universal same-sex desire we are forced to ask just what kind of yearning it is that we confront in the pre-twentieth-century documents. We are encouraged to ask, Was this a desire for a particular sex, or for a particular configuration of gender? Was it a desire to possess some aspect of the "masculine" or "feminine"? Was this the yearning of younger for older, older for younger? Was this a desire for class-crossing or "race" crossing? A desire for a particular act, a desire for a specific physical characteristic, a desire for domesticity and reliability, or a desire for erotic adventure? Our questions must be creative and varied.

If we stop assuming a universal same-sex sex act, we are forced to ask exactly what it was people did in bed (as far as the evidence shows), how those acts were understood in their time, how named, how judged, by whom, and with what consequences. We are encouraged to confront how a specific act or desire fit or did not fit with an age's larger arrangement of gender, procreation, production, and power.

The sort of historical work I am trying to encourage will help all of us locate sexual desire and activity more firmly in time. The full, historical specifying of the sexual is, I think, about time. In time, we might even come to see our own desire as historical, and we might find it surprising.

I posit no ideal, romanticized past. Nineteenth-century society was, I stress, substantially, qualitatively different from our own, neither better nor worse. That difference points us to multiple, historically changing ways of making love. We inhabit different social arrangements of human reproduction and gender, construct different ways of producing affection and pleasure. The social ordering of sex and affection can be made, un-made, and remade.

In 1895, the effeminate males of Paresis Hall were just realizing their need to organize against "the world's bitter persecution." We can still take a cue from them. Earthly pains and pleasures are manufactured, not fated.

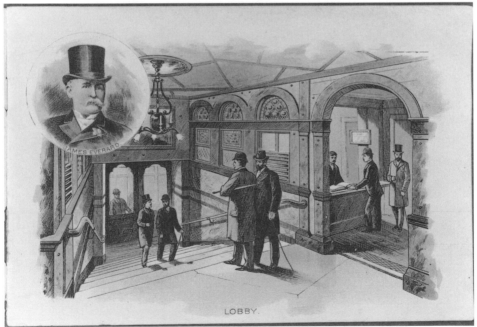

Everard Baths: cover of brochure (top) and lobby, 1892. Courtesy Herbert Mitchell; photographs by Dwight Primiano. ❧

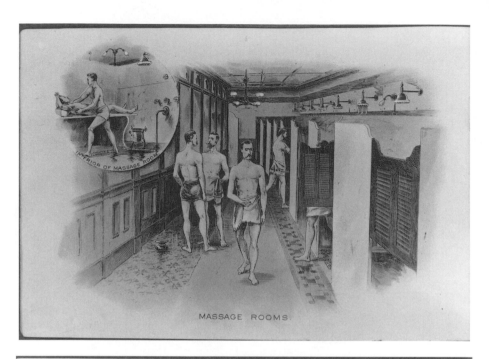

MASSAGE ROOMS.

LARGE PLUNGE & FIRST HOT ROOM.

Everard Baths: massage rooms and first hot room. Courtesy Herbert Mitchell; photographs by Dwight Primiano. ❧

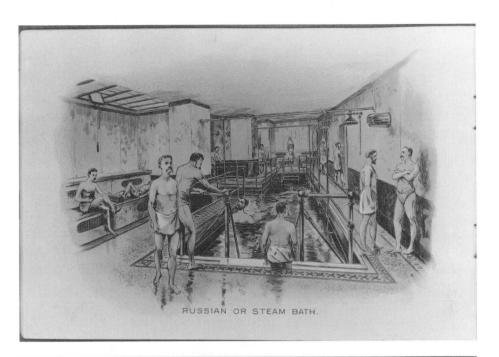

RUSSIAN OR STEAM BATH.

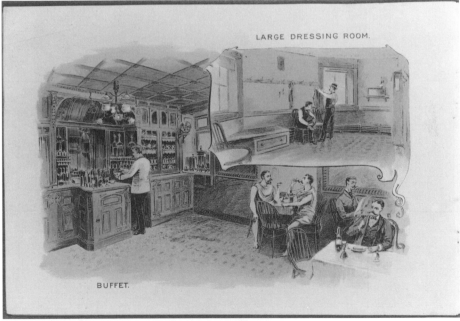

LARGE DRESSING ROOM.

BUFFET.

Everard Baths: Russian or steam bath and large dressing room and buffet. Courtesy Herbert Mitchell; photographs by Dwight Primiano.

They are not merely private and personal but matters of public debate and political organizing. The eros and love of the future will be shaped by all of us together.

ॐ

On December 17, 1955, the *New York Times* reported that Roman Catholics of the Camden, New Jersey, diocese had launched a campaign "to prevent the naming of a new Delaware River bridge after Walt Whitman."⁹

When asked why Whitman was "objectionable," the Reverend Edward B. Lucitt, diocesan director of the Holy Name Society, cited a recent biography of the poet by Gay Wilson Allen, professor of American literature at New York University. Reverend Lucitt "noted that Dr. Allen had called the poet a 'homo-erotic.'"

> But Dr. Allen said last night . . . that he had no intention of implying that Whitman was a homosexual.
>
> "I used the term 'homo-erotic' rather than 'homosexual' because the latter suggests sex perversion," Dr. Allen declared. "There is absolutely no evidence that Whitman engaged in any perverted practice."
>
> Dr. Allen said that Whitman's writings showed "a strong affection for man," hence were "homo-erotic."
>
> That affection, he said, has dominated much religious writing. "Many saints show the same feeling," he added.

"Children of fifty-eight parochial schools in the diocese," the newpaper reported, "are being asked to submit essays on 'great men of New Jersey,'" in the hope "of inspiring another name for the bridge."

Almost half a century after the Walt Whitman Bridge protest, the Walt Whitman Bridge still serenely spans the Delaware. But the existence of sex in the relations of men with men still provokes ludicrous responses, still promotes heated debates, still motivates anxious denials, still causes profound discomfort, and still, too often, incites murder. Whitman's dream city, safe for *all* comrades and lovers, is still to be constructed.

ॐ

But a poet often says it best, even when the poet is speaking prose. When leaders of a massive antiwar protest in Chicago, in 1968, outside the Democratic Party Convention, were tried for a conspiracy to cause a public riot, the poet Allen Ginsberg testified for the protestors. He was then asked by the prosecutor whether he had written a book titled *Reality Sandwiches,* and whether he would read to the jury one of its pieces, "Love

Poem on Theme by Whitman." The prosecutor evidently believed that the poem would outrage the jury and thus injure the defense.

Ginsberg explained that the poem began with a quotation of a line by Walt Whitman: "I'll go into the bedroom silently and lie down between the bridegroom and the bride."

"Would you explain the religious significance of that poem?" the prosecutor asked (his words no doubt dripping sarcasm).

Ginsberg replied: "As part of our nature, as part of our human nature, we have many loves, many of which are denied, many of which we deny ourselves. [Whitman] said that the reclaiming of those loves and the becoming aware of those loves was the only way that this nation could save itself and become a democratic and spiritual republic."

> He said that unless there was an infusion of feeling, of tenderness, of fearlessness, of spirituality, of natural sexuality, of natural delight in each other's bodies, into the hardened, materialistic, cynical, life-denying, clearly competitive, afraid, scared, armored bodies, there would be no chance for spiritual democracy to take place in America. And he defined that tenderness between the citizens as, in his words, adhesiveness, a natural tenderness flowing between all citizens, not only men and women but also a tenderness between men and men as part of our democratic heritage, part of the adhesiveness which would make the democracy function: that men could work together not as competitive beasts but as tender lovers and fellows.

Ginsberg concluded: "Walt Whitman is one of my spiritual teachers and I am following him in this poem, taking off from a line of his own and projecting my own actual unconscious feelings, of which I don't have shame, sir; which I feel are basically charming, actually."

The judge, notoriously hard-of-hearing, declared: "I didn't hear that last word."

To which Ginsberg replied: "Charming."[10]

Two working-class friends, 1875–90. Tintype courtesy Herbert Mitchell; photograph by Dwight Primiano. ❧

Acknowledgments

I am deeply thankful for the research efforts, information, and original documents discovered and contributed by Joel Honig and Martin G. Murray, both of whom provided critical readings of the whole manuscript. My thanks to them for their large generosity.

This book first saw life as *Comrades and Lovers,* a theater piece about Walt Whitman and John Addington Symonds. I thank the directors of several public performances and readings, among them Nicholas Deutsch, Nick Mangano, and Laurence Senelick.

My writers' group—Allan Bérubé, Jeffrey Escoffier, Amber Hollibaugh, and Judith Levine—gave support through the ups and downs of publishing. Carole S. Vance provided ongoing support, friendship, and her critical intelligence. Bert Hansen provided a critical reading of the Millet chapter, and numerous enlightening discussions. My aunt, Cecily Brownstone, lent a sympathetic ear and wise advice at all stages of this project.

I thank Thomas Waugh for putting me in touch with Herbert Mitchell, who generously allowed me to reproduce many old photographs from his marvelous collection, and for recommending Dwight Primiano to photograph them. Russell Bush also advised me about old photographs, as did Allen Ellensweig, James Gardiner, Gerard Koskovitch, and Carl Morse. David Kahn provided an illustration.

John D'Emilio and Leila Rupp provided detailed and most constructive critiques of the whole manuscript, and John and his partner Jim Oleson hosted and provided friendly support over many years.

I thank the Center for Lesbian and Gay Studies in New York for a Ken Dawson Award that supported my early research on men's intimacies with men in the nineteenth century. The fruit of that labor was published in *The Queer World,* edited by Martin Duberman, who has provided support of many kinds over many years. I am also grateful to the Monette/Horwitz Trust for a grant that helped to enrich this book. Detailed sage advice about book contracts was twice provided by Philip Mattera of the National Writers Union, of which I was a founding member and which I urge all writers to join.

I am extremely grateful for many others' generous contributions:

William A. Cohen provided his personal notes and photocopies on the trial of Boulton, Park, and Fiske.

John W. Crowley sent me the original manuscript of Roger Austen's "Genteel Pagan: The Double Life of Charles Warren Stoddard," which differs in detail from the published book. He also directed me to Austen's photo collection and provided leads to additional materials about Stoddard.

William Eskridge gave important advice about the legal chapter. Ed Folsom provided research advice and access to a Whitman photograph. Timothy Gilfoyle informed me of the trial record of the Slide's manager, Thomas Frank Stevenson, and gave me many other wonderful leads.

Manfred Herzer found and sent me many German documents. James E. Hough sent the results of many large legal searches, as did Robert H. Murphy. Hubert Kennedy kindly translated German material for me.

Michael S. Montgomery generously provided extensive research assistance. Wilhelm von Rosen provided information about Danish gay history and lovely accommodations in Denmark.

James Steakley advised me about German history and documents, translated several, and has long provided steadfast support.

Catharine R. Stimpson has supported my work over many years and helped me obtain visiting scholar status at New York University, a position which greatly facilitated my research.

The following individuals generously provided documents or assistance of other kinds:

Dan Bacalzo
Drew Bartley
Gail Bederman
Thomas B. Brumbaugh
Mark Brustman
Richard Burg
James Van Buskirk
David Carter
Michael Chesson
Thomas Cook
Louie Crew
John P. De Cecco
Lisa Duggan
Peter Engstrom
Stephen W. Foster
Frank Free
Alvin Fritz
Louis Godbout
David F. Greenberg
Douglas M. Haller

Janet E. Halley
John W. M. Hallock
Paul Halsall
Gert Hekma
Paul Hennefeld
Stephen Hunt
Nan Hunter
Eric Jarosinski
Erik Jensen
Susan Lee Johnson
Arnie Kantrowitz
Barbara Kerr
J. Bradley King
Marie Kuda
Thomas P. Lowry
Deacon Mccubbin
Robert K. Martin
Jeffrey Merrick
Alan Miller
Dick R. Miller

J. Bradford Millet
Michael J. Murphy
Marilyn Neimark
Rictor Norton
Connell O'Donovan
Winifred Okamitsu
David M. Perkins
Tim Retzloff
Mihaly Riszovannij
Gillian Rodger
John Sailant
James Saslow
Robert Schanke

Nayan Shaw
Charley Shively
Michael F. Sibalis
Clarence Ray Slavens
Barbara Smith
Regina Smith
Emery Snyder
Amhad Tabari
Joyce Thompson
Scott Thompson
Coll-Peter Thrush
Evan Wolfson
Marilyn B. Young

At the following archives and libraries I am much indebted to the following people:

Abraham Lincoln Museum: Leanne Garland

Alabama Department of Archives and History: Norwood A. Kerr

American Antiquarian Society: Georgia B. Barnhill, Dennis R. Laurie, Jenna Loosemore, Russell L. Martin III, Joyce Ann Tracy

Amon Carter Museum: Courtney DeAngelis

Arizona State Archives: Melanie I. Sturgeon

Atwater Kent Museum: Jeffrey R. Ray

Auraria Library: Frank Tapp

Baltimore County Public Library: Kenna Forsyth

Bloomington [Ill.] Public Library: Mrs. Donald D. Wood

British Library: Mark Widdop

Calaveras County Archives: Lorrayne Kennedy

California Historical Society: Bo Mompho, Scott A. Shields

Colorado Historical Society, Stephen H. Hart Library: Barbara Dey, David N. Wetzel

Duke University Library: Gary R. Boye, Janie C. Morris

George Eastman House: Janice Madhu

Essex Record Office: Jennifer Butler

Filson Club: Becky Rice

Gay and Lesbian Historical Society of Northern California: Walker

Georgetown University Library: Lynn Conway

Gerber/Hart Library: Russell Kracke, Karen C. Sendziak

Harvard University Archives: Brian A. Sullivan

Historic Homes Foundation: Jennifer C. Siegenthaler

Historical Society of Pennsylvania: Pamela Webster

Hobart College Archives, Warren Hunting Smith Library: Charlotte Hegyi

Houston Public Library: Blaine Davis

Huntington Library: Gayle M. Barkley, Kate McGinn

Indiana University, Kinsey Institute for Research in Sex, Gender, and Reproduction: Paul Burk

Library of Congress, Manuscript Division: Alice Birney, Jeffrey M. Flannery

Los Angeles County Museum of Art: Cheryle T. Robertson

Massachusetts Historical Society: Brenda M. Lawson, Alyson Reichgott, Jennifer Tolpa

Mayo History of Medicine Library: Andy Lucas

McLean County Historical Society: Patricia A. Hamilton

National Archives, Reference Branch: Kenneth Heger

New Brunswick Museum: Janet Bishop

New Jersey State Library: Robert Lupp

New York City, Department of Records, Municipal Archives: Kenneth R. Cobb

New-York Historical Society: Nicole Wells

New York Public Library, Rare Books and Manuscript Division: Mary B. Bowling

Notre Dame University Archives: Kevin Cawley

Ohio Wesleyan University, Beeghly Library: Hilda M. Wick

Panhandle-Plains Historical Museum Research Center: M. Lloyd

Philadelphia City Archives, Department of Records: Ward J. Childs

Pratt Institute Library: Margot Karp

Princeton Historical Society: Maureen Smyth

Provincial Archives of New Brunswick: Robert Fellows

Rhode Island State Historical Society: Rick Stattler

San Antonio Public Library: J. Myler

Schomberg Center for Research in Black Culture: Genette McLaurin

Sheffield Libraries Archives: William Bell, Rachel Moffat

Speed Art Museum: Lisa Parrott Rolfe

Stanford University, Cantor Center for Visual Arts: Alicja T. Egbert

Stanford University Medical Center, Lane Medical Library: Dick R. Miller

Syracuse University Library: Terrance Keenan

Texas State Library: John Anderson

Trinity College Archives: Peter Knapp

University of Bristol: Hannah Lowery

University of California, Bancroft Library: Mary W. Elings, Susan Snyder

University of Louisville: Susan Knoer

University of Manchester, John Rylands Library: Peter McNiven

University of Michigan, Warren L. Clements Library: Don Wilcox

University of Texas, Harry Ransom Humanities Research Center: Cathy Henderson, Barbara L. Smith-LaBorde

University of Texas, Tarlton Law Library: Mike Widener

University of Virginia: Edward Gaynor, Gregory A. Johnson, Regina Rush

University of Washington: Gary Lundell

U.S. Army Military History Institute: David A. Keough

Victoria University Archives: Marcia L. Childs

Virginia State Law Library: Gail Warren

Walt Whitman House: Margaret O'Neil

Yale University Library: Tim Hyry, Diane E. Kaplan, William R. Massa, Christine Weideman

Yale University, Beinecke Rare Book and Manuscript Library: Lynn Braunsdorf, Kevin L. Glick

I am grateful to several institutions whose archives I quoted from: the Head of Leisure Services, Sheffield City Council and to Sheffield Archives, for portions of two letters from Chester "Gavin" Arthur III to Edward Carpenter; Syracuse University Library, for portions of letters from Francis Davis Millet to Charles Warren Stoddard; and Yale University Library, for portions of Albert Dodd's diary.

Finally, I am grateful for the unfailing enthusiasm of Douglas Mitchell of the University of Chicago Press, and for the dedication of the Press's team: Robert P. Devens, editorial associate; Mark Heineke, promotions manager; Leslie Keros, production editor; Robert Williams, designer; Susan Allan, copy editor; and Margie Towery, indexer.

Notes

Chapter 1. No Two Men Were Ever More Intimate

1. On Speed's having heard Lincoln speak, but not having met him, see Donald, *Lincoln,* 66. I first read about the intimacy between Lincoln and Speed in a popular article in the gay liberation press; see Doty, "Lincoln's," 42–51, which cites Lorant, *Lincoln.* The Lincoln-Speed intimacy is most fully and subtly discussed in Wilson, *Honor's,* and Strozier, *Lincoln's.* Other authors who explore this intimacy (some of whom touch, sometimes gingerly, sometimes heavy-handedly, on the possibility of eros) include, in chronological order: Kinkaid, *Joshua;* Williams, *James;* and "Psychosexual"; Katz, "Abe"; Shively, "Big Buck and Big Lick" in *Drum;* Rotundo, *American;* Dunlap, "In Search," citing Thompson's "Was Abe"; Kalk, "Lincoln."

2. Wilson and Davis, *Herndon's,* 589–90. I have modernized the erratic spelling and capitalization in quotes from this source and from Lincoln's letters. Wilson and Davis say that Speed's statement "seems to have been sent" to William Herndon, Lincoln researcher and his former law partner, by Speed sometime before his death in 1882 (588).

3. Wilson and Davis, *Herndon's,* 590.

4. This biographical information about Speed is found in Donald, *Lincoln,* 69.

5. Wilson, *Honor's,* 172–73, citing interview with Butler, quoted in Burlingame, *An Oral,* 23. H. W. Thornton also testified that Lincoln boarded at the Butlers' (see Wilson, *Honor's,* 235, 356 n. 9).

6. Williams, "Psychosexual," 13 n. 1, citing Speed to Holland, June 22, 1865.

7. Wilson and Davis, *Herndon's,* 430.

8. Wilson, *Honor's,* 245, 358 n. 44.

9. Donald, *Lincoln,* 67–70.

10. Sensual romantic friendships between men are documented and discussed in Abzug, *Passionate,* 186, 233; Bray, *Homosexuality;* Gay, *Tender,* 207–10; Richards, "'Passing'"; Yacovone, "Abolitionists," 234–40; Rotundo, *American,* 75–91, 278, 321 n. 29, 361 n. 93; Lynch, "'Here Is'"; Haggerty, *Men;* Martin, *Hero; Homosexual;* and "Knights-Errant"; Seidman, *Romantic;* Sedgwick, *Between;* Duberman, "Intimacy"; Hansen, "'Our.'" Rupp, *Desired,* discusses "same-sex" friendships.

For sensual romantic friendships between women, see Smith-Rosenberg, "Female"; Cott, *Bonds;* Faderman, *Surpassing;* Vicinus, "Distance"; Donoghue, *Passions,* esp. 109–50; Hansen "'No Kisses'"; Rupp, "'Imagine.'" Some historians of women have argued that the nineteenth-century ideological distinction between spiritual love and sexual passion was contradicted in the actual practice of marital relationships between women and men; see, e.g., Lystra, *Searching.* How spiritual vs. sexual ideology played out in nineteenth-century men's relationships with men needs to be more thoroughly studied.

11. Melville, *Moby-Dick,* 52.

12. Strozier, *Lincoln's,* 42.

13. Herndon and Weik, *Herndon's,* 150.

14. Ibid., 151.

15. Ibid.

16. James Matheny's testimony, Wilson and Davis, *Herndon's,* 470. A cleaned up version of the same poem appears in Herndon and Weik, *Herndon's,* 151: "No woman ever went astray / Without a man to help her."

17. Wilson and Davis, *Herndon's,* 171.

18. Ibid., 171. Ellis's class bias was showing; Ellis was a businessman and the son of a businessman; the Hanks's were poor, backwoods relations of Lincoln's mother; Ellis's testimony quoted here is from Wilson and Davis, *Herndon's*, 747–48, 752.

19. Wilson and Davis, *Herndon's*, 443–44.

20. Ibid., 644, 617.

21. Elizabeth Crawford to Herndon, January 4, 1866, Wilson and Davis, *Herndon's*, 152; for the members of the Grigsby family and their wives, see the index of Wilson and Davis.

22. Ibid., 130.

23. Whitman, *Leaves* (1856), 157. Also see Whitman, *Leaves* (1860), 140.

24. See Katz, *Invention*.

25. In a classic, pioneering statement of this idea Jeffrey Weeks distinguished "between homosexual behavior, which is universal, and a homosexual identity, which is historically specific"; see Weeks, *Coming Out,* 3. Appreciating and engaging Weeks's work have been among my most rewarding exercises for a quarter of a century. Another inspiration has been Michel Foucault, who is now often mistakenly credited with initiating the recent historicizing of sex, an honor I believe should go to the modern feminist and gay and lesbian liberation movements of the 1960s and 1970s.

26. Katz, "Was There?"

27. Wilson and Davis, *Herndon's*, 774.

28. Lincoln to Mary S. Owens, December 13, 1836, 54–55; May 7, 1837, 78–79; August 16, 1837, 94–95; in Lincoln, *Collected*, vol. 1.

29. Lincoln to Mrs. Orville H. Browning, April 1, 1838; Lincoln, *Collected*, 1:117–19.

30. Mentor Graham describes Owens as "a very intellectual woman—well educated—and well raised—free and social—beautiful and even teeth"; Wilson and Davis, *Herndon's*, 243. L. M. Green recalls: "She was tall and portly—weighed in 1836 about 180 lbs. [——] at this time she was 29 or 30 years of age—had large blue eyes with the finest trimmings I ever saw. . . . None of the Poets or Romance writers have ever given to us a picture of a heroine so beautiful as a good description of Miss Owens in 1836"; ibid., 250. Caleb Carman recalls: "Miss Owens was a handsome woman—fine looking woman—was Sharp—Shrewd and intellectual"; ibid., 374. Esther Summers Bale recalls Owens as "blue Eyed—dark hair—handsome—not pretty—is rather large & tall—is handsome—truly handsome—matron looking—over ordinary size in height & weight of a standard woman"; ibid., 527.

31. Wilson and Davis, *Herndon's*, 256.

32. The Lincoln-Rutledge relationship is summarized in Wilson, *Honor's*, 114–16.

33. Lincoln's lack of romantic interest in women is discussed in Wilson, *Honor's*, 109–10, 115, 131, 180,

34. Wilson and Davis, *Herndon's*, with Dennis Hanks quoted on 91.

35. Wilson and Davis, *Herndon's*, 105.

36. Ibid., 455.

37. Ibid., 108.

38. Ibid., 131.

39. Ibid., 170.

40. Ibid., 518.

41. Ibid., 541.

42. Wilson and Davis, *Herndon's*, 350. Herndon agreed with Davis's comment; see Wilson, *Honor's*, 128, and 180, 182.

43. Wilson, *Honor's*, 182.

44. The story of Lincoln's use of Speed's "girl" is found in Wilson and Davis, *Herndon's*, 719.

45. Wilson and Davis, *Herndon's*, 443.

46. Ibid.

47. Ibid., 623.

48. Some historians of nineteenth-century women's and men's relationships have questioned whether the middle-class ideology of separate male and female spheres was realized in practice; see Lystra, *Searching*, 122–56. I believe that a separate spheres analysis clarifies Lincoln's relationship with men and women.

49. Turner and Turner, *Mary*, 16.

50. Ibid., 17.

51. Ibid., 18.

52. Ibid.

53. Ibid., 20.

54. Ibid.

55. Lincoln's and Speed's interest in Matilda Edwards is discussed in Wilson, *Honor's*, 221–22, 225–26, 228–31, 237, 242, 245–47, 319. See also Wilson and Davis, *Herndon's*, 133, 251, 443, 444, 475, 771; and Wilson, "Abraham," 127–29.

56. Turner and Turner, *Mary*, 21.

57. Ibid.

58. Ibid., 22.

59. Lighter, *Random*, 2:522.

60. Wilson and Davis, *Herndon's*, 342; Wilson, *Honor's*, 356 n. 5, citing Strozier, *Lincoln's*, 242n.

61. James C. Conkling wrote on January 24, 1841 that Speed was "about to leave" Springfield; Speed returned to Kentucky in the late spring of 1841; Wilson, *Honor's*, 238 and 245.

62. Wilson, *Honor's*, 246–47, 358 n. 52, citing Speed to Eliza J. Speed, March 12, 1841.

63. The most careful, scholarly consideration of the January first episode is Wilson, "Abraham": "The only thing that happened on January 1, 1841 . . . for which there is hard evidence is Speed's liquidation of his interest" in the general store (125). Also see Wilson, *Honor's*, 233, which stresses that "uncertainties abound" about Lincoln and Todd's engagement, and that Mary Todd may not even have been in Springfield on January 1.

64. Lincoln's loss of Speed on January 1, 1841, has been consistently underrated by Lincoln scholars. Even the unusually insightful Wilson says that "there is no evidence of anything unusual in Lincoln's life on January 1" (*Honor's*, 233).

65. Lincoln, *Collected*, 1:228–29.

66. Ibid.

67. Turner and Turner, *Mary*, 25.

68. Wilson and Davis, *Herndon's*, 430.

69. Lincoln, *Collected*, 1:265–66. Wilson, one of the most sensitive, subtle readers of Lincoln's letters to Speed, fails to make much of Lincoln's expressed foreboding.

70. Lincoln, *Collected*, 1:267–68.

71. Ibid., 1:269–70. The date of Speed's marriage is cited 170, n.2.

72. Lincoln, *Collected*, 1:280–81.

73. Rosenberg, "Sexuality," 140; see also 144–46; Williams, "Psychosexual," 7. Wilson, *Honor's*, 255, says that Speed "endured the dreaded culmination of his ordeal—married union," but fails to explain why intercourse with a new wife should be so traumatic for a man with a mistress.

74. Wilson, *Honor's*, 256.

75. Lincoln, *Collected*, 1:280–81.

76. Ibid., 1:281.

77. Ibid., 1:281.

78. Ibid., 1:282–83.

79. Ibid., 1:288–90.

80. Ibid., 1:302–3.

81. Sandburg, *Abraham* (1926), 1:264–69. In the 1929 abridged edition of Sandburg's volumes (reprinted in 1954), Speed becomes the deviant and Lincoln is untainted. Sandburg's repeated references to "lavender" are reduced to "Joshua Speed, deep-chested, broad between the ears, had spots soft as May violets. And he and Abraham Lincoln told each other their secrets about women" (70). For the association of "Flower Words" with homosexuals, see Dynes, *Homolexis*, "Pansy," 107; for the linking of "violets" and homosexuality (specifically, lesbianism), see Curtin, *We Can*, 43–67 (chap. 2, "They Said It with Violets in 1926"). For the association of "lavender" and effeminate men and homosexual males, see Lighter, *Random*, 2:402, which quotes an 1874 source on city life: "You may talk about your . . . exquisitely dressed creatures, with their lavender kids [gloves], and their la-de-das." Another line (from the film *Broadway Melody*, 1929) is delivered to an effeminate costume designer: "Your hats would look better in lavender."

Chapter 2. Dear Beloved Trio

1. Albert Dodd's diary, other papers, three letters to his family between 1841 and 1843, and an obituary from the *Hartford Daily Times*, June 1844, are in Yale University Library. Quotations from Dodd are from photocopies provided to me by Diane E. Kaplan, Yale University archivist, except where indicated. Dodd's diary was first discussed by Peter Gay in *Tender*, 212. Brief biographies of Dodd are in *Biographical Record* (1879), 53 (this says he was born "about 1818"); Dexter, *Biographical Notices*, 288 (this says he died at the age of 27, in 1844, which means that he was born in 1817). Information about Dodd, Anthony Halsey, and John Francis Heath was also provided by Peter J. Knapp of the Trinity College archives. Dodd is also discussed in Rotundo, *American*, 81–82, 84, 88–89.

2. Dodd diary, February 2, 1837.

3. Dodd diary, February 7, 1837.

4. This, by no means unusual, physical mutilation of a sexual document tellingly exemplifies a strong, active, persistent desire to cut sex out of American history; see Katz, "Alexander," 29.

5. Dodd diary, February 14, 1837.

6. Dodd diary, March 27, 1837.

7. This entry from Dodd's diary and the subsequent entries concerning Elizabeth and "Old Webb's daughter" are quoted in Gay, *Tender*, 209.

8. Dodd refers only to the first name "Jabez." Jabez Sidney Smith was the only student with that first name among the entering freshmen listed in the Yale catalog for 1837/38; Diane E. Kaplan, archivist, Manuscripts and Archives, Yale University Library to Katz, June 10, 1999.

9. Ganymede has a particularly important, iconic place in the history of men's erotic and affectionate relationships with men; see, e.g., Fone, ed., *Columbia*, 15, 16, 69, 107; Boswell, *Christianity*, 217, 236–37, 401; Saslow, *Ganymede*.

10. A document in the Dodd papers shows that he copied a poem from the *Greek Anthology*, for which see Fone, *Columbia*, 40–45. The obituary of Dodd from the *Hartford Daily Times*, June 1844, calls Dodd "a finished classical scholar": "It was one of his favorite recreations to translate from the Greek poets; and his success exhibited his scholarship, and poetic talent."

11. For a fairly detailed biography of Fell, including his birthdate (November 10, 1808), see *Historical Encyclopedia*, 2:1027–31. It does not mention Dodd. For information about Fell and Dodd, see Duis (*Good Old Times*, 43, 44, 45, 187, 298–99,

330–34), who says that, before being admitted to the bar in the early months of 1841, Fell had "formed a partnership with Albert Dodd, a promising young lawyer from Connecticut" (333). I assume this means a law partnership. On Fell, also see Donald, *Lincoln,* 237, 248; Wilson and Davis, *Herndon's,* 578–80, 635, 650, 748. Much additional information on Fell is available at the Bloomington [Ill.] Public Library; Mrs. Donald D. Wood, local historian, to Katz, June 30, 1990; the McClean County Historical Society, Bloomington, holds many photos of Fell; Patricia A. Hamilton to Katz, July 12, 1999.

12. *Biographical Record,* 53; Dexter, *Biographical Notices,* 288.

13. Historians suggest that in the early-nineteenth-century United States, most men married by age twenty-five or thirty. See Rotundo, *American,* 115, citing Rothman, *Hearts,* 22–23.

Chapter 3. A Gentle Angel Entered

1. The *New World* is described in Hudson, *Journalism,* 587. "The Child's Champion" is reprinted under its later title, "The Child and the Profligate," in Whitman, *Early,* 68–79.

2. For "he-festivals" and "bull-dances," see Whitman, *Leaves* (1855), 58. For "bull-dance," see also Lighter, *Random,* 1:300.

3. For a source dating this use of "one-eyed" to 1775, see Lighter, *Random,* 2:720.

4. For impairment symbolizing sexual irregularity, see Martin, "Billy." For sailors in the literature on men-loving men, see Martin, *Hero;* Creech, *Closet.* I will explore Whitman's associations of beards, hairiness, and sexiness below; see "Rub to me with your chalfing beard," Whitman, *Leaves* (1855), 127, l.68; "The beauty of wood-boys and wood-men, with their clear untrimmed faces," Whitman, *Leaves* (1980), 1:178, l.37. See also "Here are the roughs, beards, friendliness, combativeness, the soul loves," Whitman, *Leaves* (1856), 1:194, l.64.

5. See Moon's "Rendering the Text and the Body Fluid: The Case of 'The Child's Champion,'" chap. 1, in *Disseminating,* 26.

6. Definition is from Lighter, *Random,* 1:137.

7. See Folsom, "'This,'" 7, photos 1 and 2.

8. Whitman, *Early,* 74 n. 23.

9. Ibid., 76 n. 40.

10. Ibid., 77.

11. Ibid., 76.

12. Ibid., 76 n. 38.

13. Ibid., 78 n. 43.

14. Ibid., 79 n. 46.

15. Quoted from a manuscript by Calder, "Personal Recollections," cited by Allen, *Solitary,* 37, 549 n. 113. Allen says that Calder's published version of this article (*Atlantic Monthly,* June 1907) omits this story. See also Reynolds, *Walt,* 72, 598n.

16. Mollinoff, *"Walt"*; Reynolds, *Walt,* 70–74.

17. For "sex-love," see, Katz, *Gay/Lesbian,* 141–42, 250–51, 254.

18. For "make love to," see Katz, *Gay/Lesbian,* 291.

19. For an exception, see "sleep with" used in a sexual sense, in 1866, in Wilson and Davis, *Herndon's,* 527.

Chapter 4. Already Do the Beastly Sodomites of Gotham Quake

1. Krieg, *Whitman Chronology,* 11–13.

2. "The Sodomites," *Whip,* January 29, 1842, 2. *The Whip*'s exposés continue with "Our ARROW Has Hit the Mark!" February 5, 1842, 2; "The Sodomites and Their Practices, No. 3," February 12, 1842, 2; "Sodomites," February 26, 1842, 3; "Sod-

omites and Their Practices, No. 6" (probably No. 5), March 5, 1842, 2. Another *Whip* story refers to "sodomy": "Morbid Appetite" (white female prostitutes with black men—"worse . . . than sodomy!"), March 12, 1842, 2.

3. *Whip,* February 12, 1842, 2.

4. For attacks on sodomites in London, see Bray, *Homosexuality,* 81–114; Trumbach, "Gender," and "Sex, Gender." See also Norton, *Mother,* and the review by Trumbach. For attacks on sodomites in Paris, see Rey, "Parisian," and "Police." See also Merrick and Ragan, *Homosexuality.* For attacks on sodomites in the Netherlands, see van der Meer, "Persecutions," and "Sodomy."

5. Eight sodomites are cited by name in various stories published in *The Whip:* Johnson, Adly (not otherwise named or described), Captain Collins, Johnny L'Epine, John Emmanuel, Jem Barnes, Sally Binns, and Andrews (Andrew Isaacs). The first six are *not* mentioned for any special deviation from masculinity.

6. *Whip,* February 12, 1842, 3.

7. *Whip,* February 5, 1842, 2. Concert Rooms identified in Gilfoyle, *City,* 129. Johnson named in *The Whip,* February 12, 1842, 2, and, in passing, January 29, 1842, 2.

8. *Whip,* February 5, 1842, 2.

9. *Whip,* February 12, 1842, 2.

10. *Whip,* January 29, 1842, 2.

11. *Whip,* February 5, 1842, 2.

12. *Whip,* February 12, 1842, 2.

13. *Whip,* February 12, 1842, 2.

14. Odell, *Annals,* 4:594. Odell also refers to Ferdinand Palmo as, at different times, a famous "restaurateur," the coproducer of a marionette show, the proprietor of another saloon opened in 1842 on Chambers Street, and an Italian opera house on Chambers Street, opened on 3 February 1844 (258, 590, 685, 695). By 1849, as Melville indicates, Palmo had evidently opened the opera house on or near Broadway; see Melville, *Redburn;* Katz, "Melville's."

15. For Lord Lovely as Harry Bolton's "old chum," see Melville, *Redburn,* 222; Katz, "Melville's." For "chum" also see Martin, "Chums: The Search for a Friend," in his *Hero,* 40–66. For "chummying" (in Melville's *White-Jacket*), see Martin, 40; for "chummy" (in Melville's *Pierre*), see Martin, 62. Charles Warren Stoddard called a student his "chum" (see Austen, *Genteel,* 110).

16. See Trumbach, *Sex;* Bray, *Homosexuality.*

17. *Whip,* January 29, 1842, 2. "Lechrous" [lecherous] is used consistently in the *Whip. The Whip*'s comments on Captain Collins, Johnny L'Epine, and John Emmanuel will be discussed below.

18. On Horatio Alger, see Katz, *Gay American History,* 12, 33–34; Scharnhorst with Bales, *Lost Life,* esp. 66–87; Westgard, "Following"; Scharnhorst, "Brewster Incident"; Moon, " 'The Gentle Boy.' "

19. *Whip,* January 29, 1842, 2.

20. U.S. Census (1840), New York County, Sixth Ward, 94. None of the other sodomites named in *Whip* or *Rake* has been identified in the census or in the residential or business directories of New York City.

21. *Whip,* February 12, 1842, 2.

22. *Whip,* January 29, 1842, 2.

23. *Whip,* February 12, 1842, 2.

24. *Whip,* February 26, 1842, 3.

25. *Whip,* January 29, 1842, 2.

26. *Whip,* February 26, 1842, 3.

27. Reynolds, *Walt Whitman's,* 53–54.

28. *Whip,* February 26, 1842, 3.

29. For "mincing" in 1933, see a reference to a "street corner 'fairy' of Times Square" who was "rouged, lisping, and mincing," in Chauncey, *Gay New York*, 67.

30. See the story of Peter Sewally in chap. 6 below.

31. For "morbid," see, e.g., "Morbid Appetite," *Whip*, 12 March 1842, 2; Whitman to Symonds, denying "morbid" inferences of his Calamus poems, in Whitman, *Correspondence*, 5:72–73; John Addington Symonds to Havelock Ellis, in Symonds, *Letters*, 3:693–94, 709–10, 787–90; Symonds to Edmund Gosse, 3:804–5.

32. See Senelick, "Mollies?"

33. *Whip*, February 26, 1842, 3.

34. See Rosenberg, "Disease."

35. "Sodomites and Their Practices, No. 6," *Whip*, March 5, 1842, 4.

36. Ibid.

37. Ibid.

38. As of 1847, the maximum penalty for sodomy in New York state was ten years; see Dalloz, *Jurisprudence*, 5:403.

39. For Emmanuel, *Whip*, March 5, 1842, 4; for L'Epine, *Whip*, February 26, 1842, 3.

40. *Whip*, February 12, 1842, 2.

41. Among the now-voluminous historical literature on masturbation, see Barker-Benfield, *Horrors;* on the "spermatic economy," 118, 179–88, 198; on "masturbation, male," 136–37, 163–78, 273–74; and the articles in Bennett and Rosario, *Solitary*, especially the essay by Roy Porter, and all the bibliographies.

42. "Awful Depravity! Sodomy!" *Rake*, July 30, 1842, 2.

43. *Whip*, March 5, 1842, 2.

44. *Whip*, January 29, 1842, 2.

45. *Whip*, January 29, 1842, 2.

46. Katz, *Gay/Lesbian*, 48–51.

47. *Whip*, January 29, 1842, 2.

48. For "diabolic enticements," see *Whip*, January 29, 1842, 2; for Andrews and Thebault, see *Whip*, March 5, 1842, 2.

49. *Whip*, March 5, 1842, 2.

50. *Whip*, January 29, 1842, 2.

51. Melville, *Redburn*, 239; Katz, "Melville's."

52. *Whip*, January 29, 1842, 2.

53. *Whip*, January 29, 1842, 2; City Hall Park is mentioned as a sodomite meeting place in Thompson's novel, *City Crimes* (1849). The City Hall area is also mentioned as a meeting place in a *New York Herald* report of June 29, 1846; see Katz, *Gay American History*, 574 n. 40. The four-shilling, east side of Broadway is mentioned as Sally Binn's site, as we have seen.

54. *Whip*, January 29, 1842, 2; on the Palais Royal as a center of homosexual prostitution in the 1790s, see Sibelis, "Regulation," 87; personal correspondence, Sibelis to Katz, February 22–23, 1997; personal correspondence, Merrick to Katz, February 21, 1997.

55. *Whip*, January 29, 1842, 2.

56. "Robbers Cave," *The Subterranean*, December 26, 1846, (photocopy from Timothy J. Gilfoyle).

57. "Leprous male prostitutes" are denounced in *The Whip*, February 11, 1843, but the referent is not clear; this source is cited in Reynolds, *Walt Whitman's*, 395, 625.

58. *Whip*, February 5, 1842, 2.

59. *Whip*, February 12, 1842, 2.

60. George B. Wooldridge is identified in each issue of *The Whip* as "ALONE *responsible for every article that appears in it*," so he was probably the man behind its anti-

sodomite crusade. For Wooldridge, see the U.S. Census (1850), New York County, Eighth Ward, First District, p. 142; the census spelled his named Wooldredge, as did the New York City directory for 1850–51. Wooldredge was 33 in August 1850, at the census taking, so he was 24 or 25 when he attacked sodomites; he was married in 1850, and his wife's name was Mary; they had five children; he owned, or ran, and lived above an "alehouse" at 6 Mercer Street, one block north of Canal Street; he was born in New York. I thank Joel Honig for this research. The "proprietors" of *The Whip* are listed as "Colburn, Renshaw, & Co."; *Whip,* March 12, 1842, 2. Wooldridge is also mentioned in Gilfoyle, *City,* 133–34, 368 n. 29, 369 n. 32.

61. Gilfoyle, *City,* 99.

62. Ibid., 98.

63. Ibid., 135–36. Gilfoyle was the first to discuss the sodomite mongering of New York's sporting press.

64. *Whip,* March 12, 1842, 2.

65. For the different responses to sex between whites and blacks, see Hodes, *White.*

66. Thompson, *City Crimes,* discussed in Gilfoyle, *City,* 136, 138, 144; the scenes from the book that follow are quoted from Woods, *History,* 151–54.

67. Quotes from the tale of Josephine and the Spanish ambassador are in Woods, *History,* 151–52.

68. Quotes from the tale of the boy on the steamboat are in Woods, *History,* 154.

69. Ibid., 153.

70. Ibid.

71. "A Sodomite Nabbed," *Rake,* October 1, 1842, 2.

72. For the historical vicissitudes of the Sodom story, see, e.g., Boswell, *Christianity;* Hallam, *Book;* Jordan, *Invention.*

Chapter 5. Abominable and Detestable Crimes

1. *Davis v. State* (1810); see the complete citation for this and other appeals cases in the bibliography. The full names of Davis and of Carpenter appear in the original records of this case. The existence of these original records, in this earliest of appeals cases, suggests that other such documents can be found and analyzed, as does the discovery of the original records in the cases of William Davis and Warren Campbell: see the records listed under Davis and under Campbell in the general bibliography.

2. For the historian, all 105 published appeals cases mentioning sodomy, buggery, or the crime against nature are important documents to analyze. But not all of these cases involve charges of completed or attempted sodomy, and there are major differences among these cases, as my discussion will make clear. Numbers of these published reports, e.g., do not specify what they mean by sodomy, buggery, or the crime against nature. I have provided a brief description of each case in the legal section of the bibliography.

The 105 cases were found by searching the LEXIS database on June 11, 1998, for published U.S. appeals court decisions dated January 1, 1800 through December 31, 1899. The keywords "bestiality," "bugger," "buggery," "crime against nature," "sodomy," "sodomite," and "sodomitical" were used. The same search was made of the Westlaw database on July 7, 1998.

These appeals were also found by searching for American "sodomy" and "buggery" cases in the following printed sources: *American and English Encyclopedia of Law* (1893, 1903); *Century Edition of the American Digest* (1903); *American Digest System 1906 Decennial Edition* (1910).

Cases were also found by noting case citations in the published appeals court decisions. I suspect that a few more relevant appeals cases will turn up as more old cases are added to computerized databases, but I doubt that these cases will substantially alter our understanding of the presently known cases: the compilers of the published state appeals cases, and the indexes to these cases, appear to have included the most substantive, influential decisions.

Cases *not* listed among the 105 in my sample include several in which a man is called a "bugger" with no apparent sexual connotation; several in which "bestiality" is used without reference to human-animal contacts, or to anal intercourse between men and women, boys, or girls; and one in which "crime against nature" is used with no sexual connotation.

The twenty-five states, districts, or territories in which these appeals cases were heard include Alabama, Georgia, California, Colorado, Connecticut, Florida, Hawaii, Iowa, Illinois, Indiana, Louisiana, Maine, Massachusetts, Maryland, Michigan, Missouri, Montana, New Jersey, New York, Ohio, Pennsylvania, Texas, Virginia, Vermont, and Washington.

The 105 cases are a particular sample of all the cases referring to sodomy, buggery, and the crime against nature. Because they represent only those cases that were appealed, they are thus limited to those in which someone believed he had legal grounds for appeal, as well as the financial and psychological wherewithal to pursue redress.

These appeals cases are touched on by Katz, *Gay American* and *Gay/Lesbian;* Murphy, "Defining"; Goldstein, "History"; Eskridge, "Law" and *Gaylaw.*

3. *Hallinger v. Davis* and *Bergemann v. Backer.*

4. "Quest for union" is borrowed from Strozier, *Lincoln's.*

5. *Mascolo v. Monesanto.*

6. Katz, *Gay/Lesbian,* 666–67 n. 30.

7. Crompton, "Homosexuals"; Katz, *Gay/Lesbian,* 663–64 n. 8.

8. Crompton, "Homosexuals," 287, is the source of all the following information on the abolition of the death penalty and the imposition of new punishments.

9. Katz, *Gay/Lesbian,* 23–65, 662–64 n. 8.

10. *State v. Frank; People v. Wilson; Medis v. Hill; Lewis v. State; State v. Grusso.*

11. In one negligence case included in my sample, reference is made to the "outrage" of girls under seven as "crimes aginst nature"; see *Hughes v. Detroit* (1887).

12. *State v. Williams.*

13. *Cleveland v. Detweiler.* Detweiler's alleged act of bestiality is referred to as "sodomy" in this case report, but it is not clear whether this is the language of the case reporter or the language of the Iowa high court judges.

14. The eighteen cases referring to human-beast contacts are *Commonwealth v. Thomas; Goodrich v. Woolcott; Edgar v. McCutchen; Haywood v. Foster; Harper v. Delp; Ausman v. Veal; McKean v. Folden; Cleveland v. Detweiler; State v. Campbell; Davis v. Brown; Collins v. State; Cross v. State; State v. Frank; Strange v. State; Bradford v. State; Meigs County Court v. Anonymous; People v. Frey; Commonwealth v. J.*

The word "bestiality" is mentioned in three cases not referring specifically to human-beast contacts, so I have not included them on the above list of bestiality cases. These cases are: *Wood v. Wood* (MA; 1886, May 7; 141 MA 495; 6 N.E. 541; "masturbation" of a husband in front of wife called "bestiality"; the appeals court refuses to find it grounds for divorce); *Thibault v. Sessions and Phipps* (teacher's "indecent liberties" and "sodomy" with boy and girl pupils called "bestiality"; included among human with human sodomy cases); *Bunfill v. People* (IL; 1895, January 14; 154 IL 640; 39 N.E. 565; incest of a stepfather with two stepdaughters, and some "more hideous bestiality," unspecified). Wood and Bunfil are not listed in the bibliography.

15. The eight slander cases are *Goodrich v. Woolcott; Edgar v. McCutchen; Haywood v. Foster; Harper v. Delp; Ausman v. Veal; McKean v. Folden; Cleveland v. Detweiler; Davis v. Brown.*

16. *Strange v. State* and *People v. Frey.*

17. *Edgar v. McCutchen.* The terms "carnal knowledge" and "fuck," used in this case as general terms for sexual intercourse, apply equally to human-beast acts and the acts of human males with each other.

18. *Davis v. State.*

19. *Goodrich v. Woolcott.*

20. *People v. Williams.*

21. In *Ausman v. Veal,* the court excludes human-beast contacts from the category of "sodomy"; it defines sodomy as a "connection between two human beings of the same sex—the male—named from the prevalence of the sin in Sodom" and cites biblical passages. In *Cleveland v. Detweiler,* the court uses sodomy to include human-beast contacts. The term "crime against nature," the same Indiana court says, is less commonly used for human-beast contacts, "more generally used in reference to sodomy."

22. For example, *Commonwealth v. Thomas* ("penetration of a beast, by a man . . . without emission" constitutes "buggery"); *State v. Gray* ("penetration and emission have been, generally, deemed necessary" to constitute "buggery"); *Foster et al. v. State* ("carnal knowledge or sexual intercourse . . . complete upon proof of penetration only"); *People v. Hodgkin* ("carnal knowledge . . . complete upon proof of penetration only").

23. *Davis v. State* ("Sodomy," man with "youth," called a "most horrid and detestable crime, [among christians not to be named]") *Coburn v. Harwood* ("crime against nature," unspecified, called "a crime not fit to be named among Christians"); *Honselman v. People* ("crime against nature," man with man, fourteen and a half years old, called "not fit to be named among Christians").

24. *Ausman v. Veal.*

25. *Bunfill v. People.* See note 14 above.

26. *Harper v. Delp.* The marital, reproductive norm also surfaced in an 1869 decision of the California Supreme Court equating "laws against rape, the crime against nature, and . . . prostitution and abortion." And the reproductive norm was completely explicit in a Pennsylvania decision that attempted abortion "violates the mysteries of nature, in that process by which the human race is propagated. . . . It is a crime against nature." *Ex parte Smith and Keating.* See also *Lamb v. State* (citing decision in *Mills v. Commonwealth,* 13 PA St. 631, 633, that abortion or the attempt is a "crime against nature"). The same decision is quoted in *Wells v. New England Mutual.*

A Texas bestiality case made explicit another norm that usually operated silently in these appeal reports. In Karnes County, "Warren Campbell, a freedman of color," was indicted on October 14, 1866 for a "crime against nature" with "a certain mare of color commonly called a bay." (The Texas high court decided this case in 1867.)

The published summary of the case refers to the crime of "Warren Campbell, a freedman of color" with "a certain mare of color." See *State V. Campbell.* The original indictment form, obtained from the Texas State Archives, Austin, refers to Campbell's crime "with a certain mare of a color commonly called a bay"; see Campbell, *Warren.*

The redundant reference to an ex-slave "of color" (there were no "white" ex-slaves) underscores the absence of class or race identifiers in the other appeals case reports, implicitly constructing their participants as free and white. White here represented an absence of color and the universal norm from which this man and horse deviated. But the foreign-sounding names of the parties in several other appeals cases—Mascolo, Montesanto, Chandonette, McCutchen, Mahaffey, and Jose Grusso—may also have signaled national origins considered dubious, and may have, in practice, deprived those charged of the unmarked, privileged status of white people.

The indictment's equation of a brown-skinned man and reddish-brown horse recalled the time, just four years earlier (before Lincoln's Emancipation Proclamation of January 1, 1863), when Jones and the red-brown horse were both held as property.

The indictment's specification of a man "of color" charged with bestiality also pointed to white men's long-term concern with black men's bodies, body parts, and bodily urges. This male marked by hue and accused of bestiality may well hint at other *male-female* sexual acts linked to men of color. I refer specifically to the intercourse of black men with white women so sharply condemned in New York City's sporting press, and, later, a standard rant of reactionary Reconstruction rhetoric.

Given the emotionally charged, politically loaded character of Campbell's case, it is remarkable that both the district court and Texas appeals court quashed the indictment against him. The act charged, they found, was not described clearly enough to permit him a defense.

27. *Goodrich v. Woolcott* and *Woolcott v. Goodrich.*

28. "Against the order of nature" appears in *Davis v. State; Lambertson v. People; State v. Smith; State v. Romans.* The phrase "against nature" appears in forty-two of the appeals case records.

29. The "unnatural" is mentioned in eight of these appeals case reports; *Goodrich v. Woolcott; U.S. v. Gallagher; Enos v. Sowle; Viera v. Sowle; Commonwealth v. Dill; Meigs v. Anon.; People v. Boyle; Honselman v. People.*

30. *Davis v. State.*

31. Earlier, I ignored these bestiality cases because they seemed irrelevant to the subject of gay and lesbian history; I first looked at these cases and began to think about them in the early 1970s. The late Lawrence Murphy also ignored these bestiality cases; see Murphy, "Defining."

32. *Prindle v. State.*

33. *Hodges v. State.*

34. Man with "boy" or "youth": *Davis v. State; Enos v. Sowle; Commonwealth v. Snow; Territory v. Mahaffey; People v. Miller; People v. O'Brien; State v. Smith; People v. Boyle; People v. Wilson.*

35. "Assault" is mentioned or described in *Lambertson v. People; People v. Williams; Foster et al. v. State; State v. Place; People v. O'Brien; People v. Hickey; People v. Boyle; People v. Wilson; Darling v. State; State v. Romans.*

36. *Davis v. State.*

37. *State v. Romans.*

38. *People v. Hickey.*

39. *State v. Romans* quotes an indictment charging "an assault" resulting in the "crime against nature of buggery," but it is by no means clear if this refers to a metaphorical or actual attack. *People v. Boyle* refers to an attempted "crime against nature" as a "carnal assault" without indicating what may have actually happened in this case. In *People v. Wilson* it seems quite clear that the alleged "assault" that sends James Wilson to Folsom Prison for five years for an attempted "crime against nature" was actually a mild solicitation. In *McCray v. State,* a conviction for a "simple assault" is buttressed by the defendant's admission that he had earlier "been sent to the reformatory for . . . sodomy" (assault and sodomy are linked). In *Darling v. State* the appeals court rules: "In a prosecution for sodomy, the court need not, in defining an assault as an element of that crime, charge the penalty for assault and battery." *Commonwealth v. J.* refers to an earlier law that links "assault . . . with the intent to commit sodomy or buggery" with a solicitation, incitement, and "endeavor to persuade another" to participate in sodomy or buggery.

40. "Force" is cited in eight cases of sex between males: *Davis v. Maryland; Enos v. Sowle; Vieira v. Sowle; Lambertson v. People; Foster v. State; Mascolo v. Montesanto; People v. O'Brien; People v. Wilson.*

41. *Enos v. Sowle* and *Vieira v. Sowle.*

42. *Lambertson v. People.*

43. *Foster et al. v. State.*

44. *State v. Smith.*

45. *People v. Wilson.*

46. *Mascolo v. Montesanto.*

47. Rape/sodomy analogy: *Davis v. State* (1810); *Commonwealth v. Thomas; United States v. Gallagher; Ex parte Smith and Keating; People v. Murat; Cross v. State; Wood et al. v. State; Patterson v. State; Louisiana v. Deschamps; Hallinger v. Davis; People v. Hodgkin; Bergemann v. Backer; Roesel v. New Jersey; Brown v. New Jersey.*

48. *Foster et al. v. State.*

49. *Commonwealth v. Snow.*

50. *Territory v. Mahaffey.*

51. *State v. LaForrest.*

52. *Dial v. Holter* and *McKean v. Folden.*

53. *Meigs County Court v. Anonymous.*

54. *Honselman v. People.*

55. Eskridge, *Gaylaw,* 24–25, 37–38, 62, and esp. 158–61; Goldstein, "History," 1085–86 and nn. 71, 74.

56. *Prindle v. State.*

57. *Commonwealth v. Dill.*

58. Katz, *Gay/Lesbian,* 31–60; Foucault, *History.*

59. Eskridge, "Law," 1027–28. See also Cohen, "Legislating."

60. *Lewis v. State.*

61. *People v. Boyle.*

62. *Honselman v. People.* Referred to as "a man," Kessler was fourteen and a half at the time of the crime; his age was listed in the published report, though it was not a legal issue.

63. Eskridge, "Law," 1025–33.

64. Whitman, *Leaves* (1980), 1:226.

Chapter 6. The Man Monster

1. These letters were first discussed by Duberman, " 'Writhing.' "

2. Van Buskirk's diary was first discussed by Burg, *American.* How much sexual life aboard nineteenth-century ships differed from sexual life ashore, and what insights sex at sea provides into sex on land, is a rich subject for future historical study.

3. Burg, *American,* 78.

4. Ibid., 75.

5. Ibid., 79.

6. Ibid., 24.

7. Ibid.

8. Ibid., 77.

9. Ibid., 74. On another occasion, between 1849 and 1851, in New Orleans, a Spaniard offered the teen-age Van Buskirk lodging, and "had a fancy to handle my person indelicately—more plainly to play with my pene—which I had to submit to; in the morning he gave me a half-dime or a dime to buy something to eat" (ibid.). Van Buskirk's rather matter-of-fact report of the Spaniard's behavior suggests that he thought of his own passivity as saving him from being a party to onanism, which he considered a grave sin.

10. Ibid., 40.

11. This evidence does not document the "confusion" of masturbation and same-sex sex acts or "homosexuality"; see Katz, *Gay/Lesbian Almanac,* 2–3. It's just that today's "homosexuality" is confronted here by a radically different, but equally valid, sexual system.

12. Burg, *American,* 114.

13. Ibid., 74.

14. Ibid., 113.

15. In the 1850s, Van Buskirk characterized his ship's storeroom as a "sodomy den," the name he also gave to a dormitory at the U.S. Naval Academy in Annapolis in 1869; Burg, *American,* 79, 154.

16. Burg, *American,* 114. This contrasts with the American colonial era in which acts of sodomy did *not* constitute a sodomite, a person defined by the practice of sodomy; Katz, *Gay/Lesbian Almanac.*

17. Burg, *American,* xi.

18. *New York Herald,* June 17, 1836. All the quotations in the following section come from this source, unless otherwise noted.

19. The word "conversation," as in the legal phrase "criminal conversation" (illicit sexual intercourse), may be a suggestive pun.

20. *New York Sun,* June 17, 1836.

21. Bowyer, says the paper, "also discovered that the prisoner, to sustain his pretension, and impose upon men as sexus femineus, fabrefactus fuerat pertio bovillis, (cara bubulu) terebratus et apertus similis matrix muliebris, circumligio cum cingulum!!!"

22. *People v. Sewally,* June 16, 1836.

23. The *Sun,* June 17, 1836, says that the court sentenced Sewally to the state prison for three years. But the *Herald* of June 20, 1836, says he was sentenced to five years.

24. For these newspaper references of 1845 and 1846, I am indebted to George Thompson, of New York University's Bobst Libarary, who shared his original research with me.

25. Whether Sewally also fulfilled his emotional needs in this manner we can only guess.

26. Fiedler, *Love.*

27. Katz, "Melville's," 11–12.

28. Melville's other "mythological oil paintings" were literally just that—mythological—Melville's little joke, intended to excite readers' prurient curiosity. The nonexistence of those paintings was no failure of "realism" on Melville's part, as Gilman stuffily suggested. Those paintings were Melville's means of inciting pedants like Gilman to explore the history of what, in 1951, was still called "unnatural" sex.

29. Katz, *Gay American,* 246.

30. The anonymous German's account is in Casper, *Handbuch* (1889), 1:169–74, and all of the quotes from him are from that publication. James D. Steakley pointed out this passage to me, and Regina Smith provided the translation. Part of the passage is quoted in Symonds, *Problem* (1896), see esp. 116n.

31. John Addington Symonds translated the tamest part of this German's history and included it in his pioneering, proselytizing defense of same-sex sexuality, *A Problem in Modern Ethics,* written in 1889. Symonds did not, however, translate or mention any of this individual's more decried practices, wishing, no doubt, not to contribute further to the poor reputation of sex between men. For the same reason, eighty-seven years later, in 1976, I failed to include the German's account in a first book on gay American history. That I feel able to include his full account here suggests that we may sometimes, at least, speak of progress.

32. Quoted in Katz, *Gay American,* 312.

33. Ibid., 41.

34. *Dracula,* quoted from Christopher Craft, "Just," 92.

35. Ibid., 85.

36. For Whitman's blood/semen analogy, see *Leaves of Grass* (1855), 49; for "udder," see 53. For Stoker's relationship with Whitman as well as his other erotic attachments to men, see Belford, *Bram.*

37. Craft, "Just," 85.

38. Ibid., 75.

Chapter 7. Voices of Sexes and Lusts

1. Whitman, *Daybooks,* 3:740–41.

2. Ibid., 3:745.

3. Whitman, *Leaves* (1855), 84–85.

4. Ibid., 48.

5. Ibid., 52, 45.

6. The author of the first *Leaves of Grass* is identified as "Walt Whitman" only on the book's copyright page.

7. Whitman, *Leaves* (1855), 34.

8. Ibid., 127.

9. Ibid., 107. Bed sharing is eroticized throughout *Leaves of Grass.*

10. Whitman, *Leaves* (1855), 129.

11. Ibid., 28–29.

12. Ibid., 130.

13. Ibid., 28.

14. Ibid., 49.

15. Ibid., 19.

16. Ibid., 17.

17. Ibid., 53.

18. Ibid., 49.

19. Ibid., 56.

20. Ibid., 30.

21. Ibid., 48–49.

22. Ibid., 37.

23. Ibid., 36.

24. Ibid., 27.

25. Ibid., 116.

26. Ibid., 73.

27. *Criterion* 1 (November 10, 1855), 25; rpt. in Price, *Walt Whitman,* 26–27. This review is credited to Rufus Wilmot Griswold in a handwritten note in William Douglas O'Connor's copy of *Leaves of Grass Imprints* (1856, 1860), an advertising supplement in which Whitman and his publisher attempted to cash in on the book's notoriety by republishing even critical reviews; see Perry, *Walt Whitman,* 100 nn. 1 and 2.

28. See the account of Griswold in the *Dictionary of American Biography.*

29. Hudson, *Journalism,* 587–89.

30. As noted in chap. 3 above, Whitman began working at the *New World* office in May 1841; "The Child's Champion" was published therein on November 20 of that year; see Krieg, *Whitman Chronology,* 10. A copy of the 1855 *Leaves of Grass,* inscribed "R. W. Griswold," "from the author," is held by the Alderman Library, University of Virginia.

31. See Griswold, "Statement"; and Cuyler, "Remarks," which indicates that Griswold had applied for a divorce as early as March 1852.

32. Whitman, *Leaves* (1856), 309–12.

33. Ibid., 311.

34. Ibid., 142, 183.

35. Ibid., 208.

36. Ibid., 157.

37. Blood/semen analogies appear elsewhere in Whitman's poems, bolstering this interpretation; see "blood . . . milky stream" in *Leaves* (1855), 49.

38. Whitman, *Leaves* (1856), 217.

39. Ibid., 229.

40. Ibid., 230.

41. Whitman, *Leaves* (1856), 355–56. In *Leaves of Grass: The Comprehensive Readers Edition,* 731, editors Blodget and Bradley call this the poet's "best statement" of his demand for the free development of sexuality. This edition is referenced in text as *Leaves* (1965).

42. Whitman, *Leaves* (1965), 737.

43. Later, in the 1860 *Leaves of Grass,* Whitman would compare "amativeness"— meaning the sexual love of men and women for each other—to "adhesiveness"—the sexual love of men for men.

44. Thoreau to H. G. O. Blake, December 7, 1856; Thoreau, *Correspondence,* 444.

45. Thoreau, *Correspondence,* 444–45.

46. Alcott, *Journals,* 290–91.

47. Whitman, *Leaves* (1860).

48. Whitman, *Notebooks,* 1:413. The phrenologists' word "adhesiveness" appears in the 1860 *Leaves of Grass* as another of Whitman's appropriations signifying men's love for men. "O adhesiveness! O pulse of my life!" concludes one narrator. It is enough that his suppressed feeling for men shows itself "in these songs" (1860, 352). Writing about adhesiveness was, itself, sufficient sexual expression, Whitman claims. But other of his Calamus poems picture adhesive desire expressed in adhesive acts.

49. For "Spontaneous Me," see *Leaves* (1860), 304–7.

50. Emory Holloway was the first to report that the original love interest of Whitman's male narrator was a man; see Holloway, "Walt Whitman's," 477.

51. Whitman, *Leaves* (1860), 311.

52. Ibid., 310–11.

53. Ibid., 311.

54. Ibid., 10–11.

55. Ibid., 348

56. Whitman's friend/pursuer, Fred Vaughan, suggested that both already know a network of "Sincere Friends," the particular, self-chosen identity tag that Vaughan applied to this group; see chap. 8 below for more detail.

57. For "sweet-flag," see Whitman, *Leaves* (1860), 56 (the poem titled "Walt Whitman") and (1855), 49.

58. Whitman, *Leaves* (1860), 341.

59. For "manly love," see Whitman, *Leaves* (1860), 365; for "robust American love," 371; for "robust love," 373. The Calamus poems, as a whole, provide a typology of love.

60. Whitman, *Leaves* (1860), 348.

61. Ibid., 360.

62. Ibid., 363.

63. Ibid., 368.

64. Ibid., 371.

65. Ibid., 368.

66. Ibid.

67. Ibid., 351.

68. Ibid., 345.

69. Ibid., 372–73.

70. Ibid., 350.

71. Ibid., 363–64.

72. Ibid., 357.

73. Ibid., 371.

74. Ibid., 350.

75. Ibid., 375.

76. Ibid., 347.

77. Ibid., 351.

78. Ibid., 357.

79. Ibid., 369.

80. Ibid., 366; for men sleeping together also 206, 219, 262.

81. Ibid., 366.

82. Ibid., 346.

83. Ibid., 359.

84. Ibid., 364–65.

85. In yet another Calamus poem a twig from a live oak and a bit of moss from Florida are among the tokens the narrator gives "only to them that love, as I myself am capable of loving"; see ibid., 348.

86. Ibid.

87. Ibid., 377.

88. Ibid., 368.

89. Ibid., 357–58.

90. Ibid., 371.

91. Ibid., 353.

92. Ibid., 120.

93. Ibid., 361.

94. Ibid., 374.

95. Ibid., 377.

96. Ibid., 364.

97. Ibid., 368.

98. Millett, *Sexual;* see also Katz, *Invention,* 121, 134, 145, 147, 160, 162, 165, 202 n. 16, 240 n. 100.

99. Whitman, *Leaves* (1860), 371.

100. Ibid., 373.

101. Ibid.

102. Ibid., 374.

103. Whitman, *Leaves* (1965), 113 n. 15. Whitman, *Notebooks,* 1:406 n. 20, gives an early version of "In Paths Untrodden" and mentions other manuscript versions.

104. A manuscript version of this poem sets it two years earlier, in 1857, its likely composition date and when Whitman was thirty-eight years old; Whitman, *Leaves* (1965), 136.

105. Whitman, *Leaves* (1860), 368.

106. For Ulrichs and Benkert, see Blasius and Phelan, *We Are,* 61–66 and 67–79, respectively.

107. Ibid., 63.

Chapter 8. Sincere Friends

1. Vaughan's importance in Whitman's life was first discussed and his letters quoted by Shively, *Calamus,* 36–50. Vaughan's letters are in the Library of Congress, from which I obtained photocopies. Martin G. Murray reports that the 1880 population census lists Frederick Vaughan, of Brooklyn, New York, forty-three years old, so I calculate his birth date as 1837, and he was thus twenty-three years old in 1860; see Murray, " 'Pete,' " 48 n. 55. The census lists Vaughan as an engineer, birthplace Canada, living with his wife Frank (presumably, for "Frances") and their children: Frederick B., 17; Frank C., 15; Harry C., 11, a student; and Mabel L., 1 year. The ages of the three boys correspond approximately to the ages given by Vaughan for three of his sons in a November 1874 letter to Whitman (Shively, *Calamus,* 50).

2. Whitman, *Leaves* (1860), 344–45.

3. Ibid., 345.

4. Ibid., 345–46.

5. Ibid., 358–59.

6. These twelve Whitman poems are reprinted in their manuscript versions in Baym et al., *Norton,* 1:2097–2101. These poems are authoritatively discussed in Parker, "The Real," a critique of Helms's "Whitman's."

7. It was Martin Murray who suggested to me that Whitman could have been the original pursuer, that Vaughan could have earlier rejected Whitman, and that Vaughan, in 1860 and forever afterward, could have regretted that rejection and become Whitman's pursuer.

8. Quoted from Vaughan's letter of March 27, 1860.

9. Whitman's account of his meeting with Emerson on Boston Common in 1860 was first published in December 3, 1881; see Whitman, *Prose,* 1:281–82.

10. Emerson's lecture "Manners" was given at the New York Christian Union, on March 23, 1860; Pollak, *Erotic,* 221 n. 25.

11. For more on the Emerson/Gay relationship, see Katz, *Gay American,* 456–60.

12. Vaughan spells it *Freinds,* but the mistake seems unrevealing so I have corrected it.

13. Whitman, *Notebooks,* 2:889–90, and 890 n. 7.

14. Piers are presented as sites of sexual activity and opportunity in Herman Melville's novel *Redburn* (see Katz, "Melville's," 10) and in Stoddard, "In a Transport."

15. See Whitman, *Daybooks,* for Vaughan's visits with Whitman in 1876 (1:28) and his visit in May 1890 (2:554).

Chapter 9. A Major Fell in Love with a Boy

1. For his pioneering research and for several letters I am indebted to Thomas P. Lowry, author of *The Story the Soldiers Wouldn't Tell: Sex in the Civil War,* which alerted me to much of the material quoted in this chapter. I have obtained and quote from photocopies of almost all the cases cited by Lowry. For the navy cases, see Lowry, *Story,* 109–10, 187 n. 2, and U.S. Navy, Record. I am grateful to Martin G. Murray for photocopies.

2. See Bérubé, *Coming Out,* the classic historical work on gays in the military.

3. King, *Three,* 94–96; James Foshee directed me to this reference.

4. Letter of Willey to wife, March 20, 1864; a photocopy of a typed copy was supplied from the Norman Daniels Collection, Harrisburg Civil War Round Table Collection, by David A. Keough, chief, manuscript archives, U.S. Army Military History Institute, Carlisle, Penn. This letter is discussed in Mitchell, *Vacant,* 71–72 n. 1, 179; and Lowry, *Story,* 113 nn. 19 and 20, 188.

5. For "gash" and "hatchet," see Lighter, *Random,* 1:867 and 2:43, respectively.

6. Lighter, *Random,* 1:257, 898.

7. Cram to Ellen, April 3, 1864; photocopy supplied by David A. Keough. See also Mitchell, *Vacant,* 71–72, 179 n. 1.

8. "You shall not lie with a male as with a woman. It *is* an abomination"; Leviticus 18:22, King James Version. To "sleep with" used to mean sexual intercourse; see a U.S. legal case appeal: *Stewart v. Major,* 17 WA 238; 49 P. 503 (1897, June 25). For "to sleep with" meaning sexual intimacy or cohabitation, see the *Oxford English Dictionary,* 2d ed., s.v. "sleep."

9. Quoted from photocopy of the *Richmond Daily Dispatch,* May 13, 1862, p. 2, col. 3, supplied by Joel Honig; also quoted in Wiley, *Life,* 54; Lowry, *Story,* 71, 110, 183 n. 26.

10. Gilfoyle, *City,* 106, 361 n. 26. Gilfoyle quotes John Vose's *Diary* (New York

1852), which refers to "fancy men" who pursue "careers of male prostitution" through the seduction and extortion of married women.

11. Quoted in Lowry, *Story,* 112; from a diary in the possession of Roger Long, Port Clinton, Ohio, 1988. Brig. Gen. J. J. Archer is listed among the "Prisoners of War at Johnson's Island," 239. See biography of James Jay Archer in *Encyclopedia of the Confederacy,* 1:50–51. I thank Joel Honig for the research. Contrary to a note in *The Private Mary Chestnut,* 142 n. 2, the "Sally Archer" named by Chestnut was not James Jay Archer but a "pretty" unmarried "Tom Archer"; see Chestnut, *Diary,* 476, also 120–21, 428–29. I thank Dan Bacalzo for research on Archer.

12. Lowry, *Story,* 112, citing "Letter in files of Manassas National Park." Neither Lowry nor the Manassas National Battlefield Park can supply more information about this letter; correspondence from Edmund Raus, park ranger, September 30, 1997. Raus confirms that the Lowery mentioned in this letter was William Martin Lowery, that Bryan was Thomas Andrew Bryan, and that a history of the unit, with rosters, can be found in Scott, *Lowry's.* I thank Joel Honig for research indicating that William M. Lowery belonged to the Virginia Wise Legion Artillery Battalion, Company C.

13. McElroy, *Andersonville.*

14. For "chum" as a sailor term with sexual connotations, see Katz, "Melville's" (esp. my comment on Harry Bolton and his "old chum," Lord Lovely). Also see Martin, "Chums," in *Hero,* 40–66. For "chummying" (used in Melville's *White Jacket*) and "chummy"(used in Melville's *Pierre*) see Martin, *Hero,* 40 and 62, respectively.

15. McElroy, *Andersonville,* 50. In March 1863, an all-male burlesque show in which one of the principals completely undressed is reported among a contingent of Confederate soldiers; manuscript, March 16, 1863, private collection; quoted and described in Wiley, *Life,* 52.

16. Burg, *American,* 79.

17. McElroy, *Andersonville,* 361–62.

18. Ibid., 290–91.

19. Ibid., 203–4.

20. Ibid., 62–63. Another romantic friendship between men during the Civil War years was that of the Confederate General Patrick Ronayne Cleburne with his adjutant, Captain Irving Ashby Buck. Cleburne's "attachment" to Buck "was a very strong one," says Cleburne's biographer, and Buck "for nearly two years of the war, shared Cleburne's labors during the day and his blankets at night." Buck's own memoir calls his intimacy with Cleburne "close and confidential. I habitually messed [ate] with him and shared his tent and often his blankets." See Shilts, *Conduct,* 14–15, citing Buck and Hay, *Cleburne.*

21. Loring's *Two College Friends* was first published in a periodical, *Old and New* (April and July 1871), then, by Boston's A. K. Loring, the version from which I quote. Also see Shand-Tucci, "Gay," which alerted me to this document. For a biography of Loring, see Stearns, *Real and Ideal,* 88–107. Loring dedicated his novel to his Harvard friend, William Wigglesworth Chamberlin; the text and external evidence suggests that Ned is modeled loosely on Loring, Tom on Chamberlin. Chamberlin was born July 25, 1850; Loring was born December 12, 1848; in the novel (54), Tom is "not quite two years younger" than Ned. Biographical folders on Loring and Chamberlin are in the Harvard University Archives.

22. Loring, *Two,* 10–11.

23. Ibid., 12.

24. Ibid., 47.

25. Ibid., 36.

26. Ibid., 18.

27. Ibid., 19.

28. Ibid., 92.
29. Ibid., 84.
30. Ibid., 111.
31. Ibid., 118–19.
32. Ibid., 120.
33. Ibid., 154–61.

Chapter 10. I Got the Boys

1. Whitman, *Notebooks,* 1:438.
2. Allen, *Solitary,* 272.
3. Whitman, *Correspondence,* 1:186–88: Whitman had "enough" of New York "amusements, suppers, drinking, & what is called *pleasure.*"
4. Allen, *Solitary,* 279. In his recent biography of Whitman, Jerome Loving claims to have identified "Eyre" as an actress, Jane McElheny; see Loving, *Walt,* 259–61.
5. Whitman, *Notebooks,* 2:488.
6. Ibid., 2:487.
7. Ibid., 2:496.
8. Ibid., 1:11, 20, 22, 23, 416 and 416 headnote.
9. Katz, "Melville's."
10. Whitman, *Notebooks,* 2:497.
11. Whitman, *Notebooks,* 2:486 (Ward), 487 (Miller), 487–88 (Cohn), 492–93 (Carr), 493 (English and Sloan).
12. Loving, *Walt,* 13, says George Whitman was injured at Fredericksburg; Whitman, *Correspondence,* 1:58 n. 1, says the second battle of Bull Run.
13. Whitman, *Notebooks,* 2:504–5.
14. Letter to Bloom and Gray; Whitman, *Correspondence,* 1:81.
15. Ibid., 1:81 and n. 56.
16. Ibid., 1:81.
17. Ibid., 1:82.
18. Whitman, *Notebooks,* 2:8 n. 22; Whitman, *Correspondence,* 1:90–91 n. 86.
19. Whitman, *Notebooks,* 2:530 n. 11; Whitman, *Correspondence,* 1:119 n. 7.
20. Whitman, *Correspondence,* 1:91–92.
21. Whitman, *Leaves* (1860), 11.
22. Whitman, *Correspondence,* 1:93.
23. Ibid., 1:93.
24. Shively, *Drum,* 74–75.
25. Whitman, *Correspondence,* 1:93.
26. Referring to the rejected gifts, Sawyer casually asked Brown to tell Whitman: "I came away so soon that it slip[p]ed my mind." Quoted in Shively, *Calamus,* 72–73; see also Whitman, *Correspondence,* 1:90 n. 86.
Much of Whitman's revealing correspondence with Civil War soldiers was first published, and its sexual implications discussed in detail, by the pioneering Shively in *Calamus* and *Drum.* I obtained and closely examined photocopies of all these letters, but I provide references to Shively for readers' convenience; my transcriptions sometimes differ from Shively's. Most of the letters are in the Library of Congress; see Shively for exact locations.
27. Whitman, *Correspondence,* 1:94.
28. Ibid., 1:107.
29. See Calamus 9, "Hours continuing long"; Whitman, *Leaves* (1860), 355–56.
30. Whitman, *Correspondence,* 1:119–21.
31. Shively, *Calamus,* 76–77.
32. Whitman, *Correspondence,* 1:139.
33. Ibid., 1:132–34.

34. Ibid., 1:142.

35. These letters are collected in Shively, *Drum*.

36. Whitman, *Correspondence*, 1:145.

37. Whitman, *Notebooks*, 2:537.

38. Shively, *Drum*, 143.

39. Whitman, *Correspondence*, 1:181.

40. Ibid., 1:175–82.

41. Akin to sister [name unknown], August 10, 1863; from Murray, "Traveling," 70–71. Murray quotes from Stearns, *Lady*, 56–57.

42. Shively, *Calamus*, 79.

43. Ibid., 80.

44. Whitman, *Correspondence*, 1:187.

45. Ibid., 1:186–88.

46. Shively, *Calamus*, 84.

47. Bush's letter to Whitman of December 22, 1863, is reprinted in Shively, *Calamus*, 81–82; Bush's letter of February 11, 1864, in Shively, *Drum*, 128–29.

48. For the nineteenth-century use of "gay," see Lighter, *Random*, 1:871.

49. Lighter, *Random*, 1:872; Lighter is wrong in reporting that a 1903 use of "gay boy" refers to a homosexual; for this information I thank Joel Honig. See also Katz, "Up."

50. Shively, *Calamus*, 23, 69, 81. Shively cites no sources showing that "buck" was nineteenth-century slang for penis, and my attempt to document this has failed. Shively also suggests that "BK" may refer to "Big Kock." The use of "cock" for "penis" goes back to the fourteenth century, at least. Reference to a "big cock" appears in an English pornographic novel in 1866 (Lighter, *Random*, 1:444). For what it is worth, the abbreviation "BJ" is used for "blow job" in 1949 (Lighter, *Random*, 1:174), so the possibility of the initials "BK" standing for sexual words is not entirely implausible. There is no nineteenth-century evidence showing that "to go down on" was used to refer to oral-genital contacts.

51. Whitman, *Notebooks*, 2:669.

52. Whitman, *Correspondence*, 1:119 n. 70.

53. Murray, "Traveling," 68; McGill, "Memorandum re: Lewis Kirk Brown"; photocopy from Alice L. Birney, Manuscript Division, Library of Congress, October 9, 1997.

54. Whitman to Hiram Sholes, May 30, 1867; Whitman, *Correspondence*, 1:331. Martin G. Murray reports that, according to Sawyer's Civil War pension record (National Archives Record Group 94), Sawyer was born on October 3, 1841, and had grey eyes and dark hair. He moved to Cincinnati after the war, where he worked as a traveling salesman. He married Annie Bell Chapin in Cincinnati on December 8, 1865, and eventually moved to Covington, Kentucky (1865–80). He and his wife had eight children. He lived in Indiana from 1886 to his death on January 14, 1928; Murray to Katz, July 23, 2000.

55. Shively, *Calamus*, 97, first printed Palmer's letter and Whitman's comment written on the envelope. Both are in the Library of Congress, which provided a photocopy.

56. Palmer's "I will *blow* on no one" is not a reference to oral-genital contact. The earliest known use of "to blow" meaning "to perform oral sex on" dates to about 1930; see Lighter, *Random*, 1:198.

57. Shively, *Calamus*, 24. Note that the supposedly authoritative Whitman, *Correspondence*, 1:376, lists this revealing letter with no description and no reference to Whitman's important note on the envelope!

58. For example, see Traubel, *With*, 1:27.

59. Ibid., 4:345–47.

60. George Whitman was imprisoned in Libby Prison (Richmond, Va.), before he was transferred to Salisbury Prison (Salisbury, N. C.), and then to Danville Prison (Danville, Va.); see Whitman, *Notebooks,* 743 headnote, 747, 762, and George Whitman, *Civil,* edited by Loving, who refers to the "infamous" Libby Prison, 281.

61. This letter of August 1865 dates, incidentally, to about one or two months after Palmer's seductive note to Whitman.

62. Traubel, *With,* 4:345–46.

63. Ibid., 2:370–71. Traubel is reading Whitman's letter of April 15, 1870, to the former soldier Benton Wilson.

64. Traubel, *With,* 3:581–82.

Chapter 11. Yes, I Will Talk of Walt

1. Murray, " 'Pete.' " Murray's detailed, carefully researched biography of Doyle is an amazing study of a nineteenth-century working man's life.

2. Whitman, *Calamus,* 5.

3. Quinn, *Same-Sex,* 314–15, 338 n. 4.

4. Whitman, *Calamus,* 4. The original manuscript of the interview with Doyle exists as Traubel wrote it, and it differs, sometimes substantially, from the version published in Whitman, *Calamus;* see Murray, " 'Pete,' " 46 n. 30.

5. Whitman, *Correspondence,* 2:45–47, n. 33; Doyle to Whitman, September 18, 1868, in Shively, *Calamus,* 104–6.

6. Ibid.

7. Shively, *Calamus,* 106.

8. Ibid., *Calamus,* 107.

9. Doyle to Whitman, September 23, 1868; Shively, *Calamus,* 109.

10. See, for example, Whitman to Doyle, Whitman, *Correspondence,* 1:4, 110, 124, 125.

11. Whitman to Doyle, September 25, 1868; Whitman, *Correspondence,* 2:47.

12. Whitman, *Correspondence,* 2:51. Doyle to Whitman, September 27, 1868; Shively, *Calamus,* 106.

13. Whitman, *Correspondence,* 2:59.

14. Whitman, *Calamus,* 10.

15. Whitman to Doyle, October 17, 1868; Whitman, *Correspondence,* 2:60, 61.

16. Whitman to Doyle, October 18, 1868; Whitman, *Correspondence,* 2:62–63.

17. Whitman, *Calamus,* 7–8.

18. Ibid., 5, 7, 8–9.

19. Whitman to Doyle, August 3–5, 1870; Whitman, *Correspondence,* 2:103–4.

20. Whitman to Doyle, August 21, 1870; Whitman, *Correspondence,* 2:83–85.

21. At my request, the Library of Congress subjected this diary entry to scientific tests designed to expose blocked out words, but no words were visible; Alice Birney, literature historian, manuscript division, Library of Congress, to Katz, February 23, 1998; Whitman, *Notebooks,* 2:888–89.

22. Whitman, *Correspondence,* 2:89; Whitman, *Notebooks,* 2:885–90.

23. Whitman, *Correspondence,* 2:101.

24. Whitman, *Leaves* (1855), 122. Although Whitman first used "son" in an October 18, 1868, letter to Doyle (Whitman, *Correspondence,* 2:62), he started to use "son" on a regular basis only after their third parting; see Whitman to Doyle, August 3–4, August 7, and August 12, 1870, in Whitman, *Correspondence,* 2:103–4, 104–6, and 106, respectively. Whitman called himself Doyle's "father" in letters of September 6, 1870, and June 30 and July 7, 1871. See Whitman, *Correspondence,* 2:109–10, 124–25.

25. Whitman to Doyle, September 2, 1870, *Correspondence,* 2:108–9, and 109

n. 53. It would be interesting to know more about Whitman's rich, single friend Charles H. Russell and all the members of the Fred Gray association.

26. On the Irish working class, blacks, and whiteness, see Roediger, *Wages;* Saxton, *Rise;* and Ignatiev, *How.* Allan Bérubé and David Gibson helped me interpret this difficult, painful passage.

27. Whitman, *Prose,* 2:414–15.

28. Whitman, *Correspondence,* 2:85; see also Shively, *Calamus,* 110.

29. The Metropolitan Rooms are identified as a theater of a "low order," and Canterbury Hall as one of Washington's variety halls; Whitman, *Notebooks,* 2:532 n. 29.

30. Lighter, *Random,* 1:494, and *Webster's New International Dictionary,* 2d ed. (Springfield, Mass.: Merriam Company, 1942), 613.

31. Stewart to Whitman, February 25, 1870; Shively, *Calamus,* 110–12. Stewart says the salute with which he signed his letter is one used by the character Weller in Charles Dickens's *Pickwick Papers.*

32. Whitman, *Calamus,* 11, 15–16.

Chapter 12. In the Name of CALAMUS Listen to Me!

1. Whitman, *Correspondence,* 2:81 n. 21.

2. The poem is Whitman's "To You," in the Messenger Leaves section of *Leaves* (1965), 403.

3. Stoddard to Whitman, March 2, 1869; reprinted in Traubel, *With,* 4:267–69.

4. "When I Heard at the Close of the Day," in Whitman, *Leaves* (1965), 122.

5. Whitman, *Correspondence,* 2:81–81.

6. Stoddard, "A South-Sea Idyl," *Overland Monthly,* September 1869, 257–64, from which I quote. Reprinted as "Chumming with a Savage: Kánána," 31–45 in Stoddard, *Cruising.*

7. Stoddard, "Idyl," 258.

8. Ibid., 258.

9. Ibid.

10. Ibid.

11. Ibid., 259.

12. Ibid.

13. Ibid.

14. Ibid., 260.

15. Ibid.

16. Ibid., 261, 262, 263

17. Ibid., 264.

18. Quoted in Traubel, *With,* 3:444–46.

19. Whitman, *Correspondence,* 2:97.

20. Ibid.

21. Stoddard's "In a Transport," published in his essay collection *South Sea Idyls* (1873; 2d ed. 1892). Reprinted in Stoddard, *Cruising,* 141–53, the version from which I quote. The text of the first edition of "In a Transport" is identical to the second edition.

22. Stoddard, "In a Transport," 142.

23. Ibid., 144.

24. Ibid., 141.

25. Ibid., 145.

26. Ibid., 147.

27. Ibid.

28. Ibid., 149.

29. Ibid., 152.

30. Stoddard's trip to Tahiti and his stay there are discussed in Austen, *Genteel,* 48–52.

Chapter 13. A Heart Full of Love and Longing

1. Mullin to Seward, August 26, 1867; this is only one of the letters sent by local politicians to Seward in support of Fiske. The same file in the National Archives contains a letter from Fiske to Seward, August 28, 1867, soliciting the consul position; see [Fiske], Application. Kenneth Heger, archivist, wrote to me October 6, 1997, informing me of these documents; he also sent me photocopies.

2. Fiske's journalism remains to be investigated; see Wall, *Cumulative,* 145; and Cushing, *Nineteenth,* 938.

3. [Fiske], *Second Report,* 58; and see letters, in [Fiske], Application.

4. Fiske to Ernest Boulton, April 18, 1870; quoted from Roughead, "Pretty," 166.

5. Park to Lord Arthur Clinton, November 1868, quoted by Upchurch, "Forgetting," 1, from the trial transcripts of the 1871 *Case of the Queen vs. Boulton and Others,* Department of Public Records, PRO, London, DPP4/6, 1:36 –37; also quoted by Cohen, *Sex,* 116 n. 36; Cohen quotes from the London *Times,* May 30, 1870. Cohen also notes that when this letter was read into the Boulton and Park trial record, the court transcriber misread "campish" as "crawfish." For "camp" also see Lighter, *Random,* 1:351, which lists 1909 as the earliest homosexual use of the term. William Cohen generously allowed me to photocopy his files on Boulton and Park and gave me all of his typed transcriptions relating to Fiske from the original trial record.

6. For Whitman to Bloom and Gray in 1863, see Whitman, *Correspondence,* 1:80–85, 135, 141–43; for Alonzo Bush to Whitman in 1863, see Shively, *Calamus,* 23, 69–70; letter printed 81 –82; and Shively, *Drum,* letters printed 128 –29; for Edward C. ("Ned") Stewart to Whitman (in 1870), see Shively, *Calamus,* 110 –12; and for my comment on Stoddard's travel writing (starting in the late 1860s), see chap. 12 above.

7. Fiske to Boulton, March 20, 1870, quoted from Roughead, "Pretty," 167; Cohen, *Sex,* 112, prints the same letter. For "drag," see Cohen, *Sex,* 116 n. 36; and Lighter, *Random,* 1:650.

8. Lais is referred to by the prosecutor, during the trial of Boulton and Park, as "one of the most famous prostitutes in antiquity." The prosecutor also says that, "if Antinous [the beloved of the Roman emperor Hadrian] is not wronged," he was "a male prostitute"; Cohen, *Sex,* 112–13.

9. "Outraging public decency" is how Cohen, *Sex,* 76, names the charges first lodged against Boulton and Park.

10. Roughead, "Pretty," 155.

11. Cohen, *Sex,* 77.

12. The legal documents produced by the prosecution of Boulton and Park now reside in the Public Record Office, Chancery Lane, London. Cohen, *Sex,* 74, lists these legal documents, as well as the London newspapers that carried reports of the prosecution: *The Times, Pall Mall Gazette, Daily News, Daily Telegraph, Standard, Illustrated Police News,* and *Globe and Traveller.*

Reports also appeared in a pamphlet by Clark, *Lives,* reprinted with additions as *Men in Petticoats;* and *Annual Register,* 220–24. For modern accounts see, in addition to Roughead and Cohen, Hyde, *Love,* 94–98; Ackroyd, *Dressing,* 83–85; Weeks, "Inverts"; and Upchurch, "Forgetting." Twenty-nine photographs of Boulton and Park are now held in the Essex Record Office; Jennifer Butler, principal archivist (User Services), to Katz, February 9, 1999. James Gardiner helped in tracking down the photos, two of which are printed in his wonderful book, *Who's a Pretty Boy Then,* 14.

13. Roughead, "Pretty," 153.

14. Ibid.

15. Ibid., 154.

16. Cohen, *Sex,* 79.

17. Roughead, "Pretty," 154, 165.

18. Fiske's resignation letter of June 24, 1870, is in the National Archives, Microfilm Publication T396; Kenneth Heger, archivist, to Katz, October 15, 1997.

19. Cohen, *Sex,* 83.

20. Roughead, "Pretty," 173.

21. Ibid.

22. Ibid., 177–78.

23. Matthews comments are quoted from typed notes made by William Cohen from the trial records; Cohen to Katz, November 7, 1997.

24. Roughead, "Pretty," 182.

25. Ibid.

26. Ibid.

27. [Fiske], *Triennial,* 58; [Fiske}, *History* (1889), 60–61, and *History* (1905), 86–87, including photos of Fiske, one as a youth, and two as an old man (one in a class picture). Thomas Hyry, archivist, Manuscripts and Archives, Yale University Library supplied copies; Hyry to Katz, October 8, 1997.

28. [Fiske], *History* (1889), 61.

29. See "John Safford Fiske," a detailed memorial by a friend and Hobart professor, J. H. McDaniels. The unsigned memorial is attributed to McDaniels on p. 3 of the same volume. The Warren Hunting Smith Library of the Hobart and William Smith Colleges also holds a letter from Fiske, probably to McDaniels, dated June 4, 1899, and other brief printed materials referring to the collection of books about art, architecture, and French and Italian literature that Fiske willed to Hobart.

30. [Fiske], *History* (1905), 86–87.

31. Charlotte Hegyi, archivist, Warren Hunting Smith Library, Hobart and William Smith Colleges, to Katz, January 8, 1998.

32. McDaniels, "John," 10. Freeman's book was either *The History of Sicily from Earliest Times,* 4 vols. (Oxford: Clarendon Press, 1891–94) or *Sicily Phoenician, Greek and Roman* (London: T. Fisher Unwin, 1892). Schuyler was the U.S. charge d'affairs to Romania, 1880, and later the U.S. minister to Romania, Serbia, and Greece. He also wrote several books.

33. McDaniels, "John," 12, 14.

34. Ibid., 15.

35. Ibid., 18, 20.

Chapter 14. Empty Chair, Empty Bed, Empty House

1. Stoddard, "Modern," 463–64. See also Austen, *Genteel,* 72–79. For help with this research I am deeply indebted to John Crowley and Martin Murray; Bert Hansen also provided insightful comment on an earlier version of this chapter.

2. Gale, "Francis Davis Millet"; see also *Dictionary of American Biography* (1933), 4:644–46.

3. Stoddard, "Modern," 464.

4. Millet's letters to Stoddard are in the Syracuse University Library, Department of Special Collections. Terrence Keenan, special collections librarian, provided photocopies and research assistance. Parts of Millet's letters to Stoddard are quoted in Austen, *Genteel.*

5. Stoddard, "Modern," 464.

6. Ibid., 465.

7. Ibid., 466.

8. Stoddard, "Afloat," *San Francisco Chronicle,* January 10, 1875, 1.

9. Austen, *Genteel,* 73–74.

10. Quoted by Austen in the manuscript version of his biography of Stoddard (published as *Genteel Pagan*), 154. Austen must quote from a revised version of Stoddard's original *San Francisco Chronicle* article on Padua (March 28, 1875, sec. 1, p. 1), for this scene is not in the original. Stoddard revised these Italian travel articles around 1887, for republication in *Ave Maria;* see Austen, *Genteel.* Austen's original manuscript was sent to me by John W. Crowley, whose generosity is much appreciated.

11. Austen, *Genteel*, 74, citing "Florence," *Ave Maria*, 24 (January 15, 1887), 418. This later version of the incident differs in wording from the original in the *San Francisco Chronicle*, April 4, 1875, sec. 1, p. 1, which leaves out "he bellowed lustily" and "doubtless each in his turn had been similarly affected," as well as the explanation that men kissing men is a custom in Italy.

12. Quoted from Whitman, "What Think You I Take My Pen in Hand?" *Leaves* (1965) 133.

13. Stoddard also mentions a bronze "David," a "slender boy . . . full of youthful bravery," another traditional icon of men-loving men. He also mentions a "Hermaphrodite" sculpture and nude Apollos; "Royal Galleries," *San Francisco Chronicle,* April 11, 1875, 1.

14. "Genoa, The Superb," *San Francisco Chronicle,* June 13, 1875, 1.

15. Austen, *Genteel*, 74, 182 n. 31. See Whitman's poem, "When I Heard at the Close of the Day," *Leaves* (1965), 122–23.

16. In Pisa, Stoddard reports, his companion insisted on showing him the leaning tower from a vantage point highlighting its deviance from erect perpendicularity ("It *does* lean!"). Stoddard thus adds one of the world's famous phallic symbols to the other sexual allusions in his travelogues; "The Leaning Tower," *San Francisco Chronicle,* May 30, 1875, sec. 1, p. 1.

17. Stoddard, "Modern," 464.

18. Ibid., 467.

19. Ibid., 466.

20. Ibid., 468.

21. For "The Orient" and the *Arabian Nights,* see Woods, *History,* 53–67.

22. Austen, *Genteel*, 67, 75, 76. Austen gives no source for the letters of Robert William Jones, and I have not discovered one.

23. For "spoon," see Stoddard's "Afloat," "The Venetian Islands," and "Fair Florence."

24. Millet's friend, Charles Francis Adams, had no daughter named Charlotte (nicknamed "Donny"), and I have not traced which Adams family is referred to here.

25. For the era's ideas about animal magnetism, see Reynolds, *Walt,* 259–61, 267, 273.

26. Katz, *Gay American,* 246.

27. For Julia Fletcher, see Austen, *Genteel,* 22, 71, 100, 120, 147.

28. Millet to Stoddard, June 10, 1875. For "How high is that?" see "How's that for high?" in Lighter, *Random,* 2:91.

29. Millet to Stoddard, August 15, 1875, 5.

30. Lightner, 1:335, reports that the verb to "butterfly" in 1945 meant "to be sexually unfaithful" to a partner. A "butterfly ring" is "a coterie of effeminate homosexuals," according to Rodgers, *Queens',* 39.

31. Millet refers to the weather being oppressively hot and sultry, and this context suggests that the word "yawn" is a correct transcription of the unclear original. Terence Keenan, special collections librarian, Syracuse University Library, assisted with this clarification.

32. For Fred Stoddard, see Austen, *Genteel,* 4, 87, 102–3, 155, 165.

33. Millet to Stoddard, September 6, 1875, 5.

34. Ibid., 7.

35. Millet to Stoddard, November 15, 1875, 2.

36. For "grind," see Lightner, 1:969. Lightner does not include "organ grinder."

37. Austen, *Manuscript*, 165; Stoddard to Ambrose Bierce, September 13, 1875; Stoddard, "A Sea Siren."

38. Millet to Stoddard, September 27, 1875, 1.

39. Richard B. Morris, ed., *Encyclopedia of American History* (NY: Harper & Row, 1970), 251.

40. Lighter, *Random*, 1:562, indicates that in 1970 "D.B." was working-class slang for "deadbeat."

41. Millet to Stoddard, December 2, 1875, 1.

42. Ibid., 4.

43. Stoddard, "Gay Paris," *San Francisco Chronicle*, April 9, 1876.

44. Here, "bedfellow" may not imply a sexual partner, though Millet may have intended the ambiguity to provoke Stoddard's interest. "William," Millet's bedfellow, may have been William Bradford Merrill, brother of Millet's future wife.

45. Sharpey-Schafer, *Soldier*, 54–55.

46. For Millet in Broadway, England, see James, "Our Artists." See also Millet's translation of Tolstoi's *Sebastopol*; Millet's, *A Capillary Crime; The Danube;* and *The Expedition*. For Whitman's praise of Millet's translation of *Sebastopol* see Traubel, *With*, 7:116.

47. Millet to "Dear Strong", dated "Monday," no year; in Millet's letters in Syracuse University Library. Strong is probably Joe Strong, an artist friend, mentioned in Austen, *Genteel*.

48. Sharpey-Schafer, *Soldier*, 130–31.

49. "Millet was last seen encouraging the Italian women and children to go into the lifeboats": *Dictionary of American Biography*, 6:645.

Chapter 15. I Wish You Would Put the Ring on My Finger Again

1. Stafford's letters to Whitman, and Whitman's to Stafford, are discussed and quoted in Shively, *Calamus*, 136–71. I have checked most of Shively's transcriptions against photocopies of the originals. For Stafford's birth date, March 23, 1858, see Whitman, *Notebooks*, 3:960. For a discussion of the Stafford-Whitman intimacy also, see Edwin Haviland Miller's introduction to Whitman, *Correspondence*, 3:2–9. Shively quotes thirty letters from Stafford to Whitman, all that are mentioned in Whitman, *Correspondence*, 4. For two additional Stafford letters to Whitman, see Golden, "Recovered," and Folsom, "Another."

2. Whitman, *Notebooks*, 2:818; Allen, *Solitary*, 468.

3. Shively, *Calamus*, 150.

4. Whitman, *Correspondence*, 3:6–7; see also Whitman, *Daybooks*, 1:44 n. 111 (entry of September 26, 1876).

5. Folsom, "Unknown"; Shively, *Calamus*, 145.

6. Whitman, *Daybooks*, 1:48, 49 (entry of November 25–28, [1876]).

7. Whitman, *Daybooks*, 1:51 (entry of December 19, [1876]).

8. Whitman, *Correspondence*, 3:67–68.

9. Ibid., 3:68.

10. Ibid.

11. John H. Johnston's long friendship with Whitman is mentioned throughout Allen, *Solitary*.

12. Whitman, *Correspondence*, 3:70 and n. 20.

13. Ibid., 3:76–77 n. 10, citing *Diary Notes* (no page), in the Feinberg Collection. No reference to these diary entries appears in Whitman, *Notebooks*.

14. Whitman, *Correspondence,* 3:77.

15. Ibid.,77 n. 10, citing the misnamed Commonplace-Book; see Whitman, *Notebooks,* 3:960.

16. Whitman, *Correspondence,* 3:76–77 n. 10, citing *Diary Notes,* October 29.

17. The triangular Stafford-Cattell-Whitman relationship mirrors the earlier triangular intimacy that Whitman attempted to initiate with the soldiers Lewis Brown and Thomas Sawyer.

18. Shively, *Calamus,* 151.

19. The original of this letter is undated; the date of May 1, 1877, was suggested to Edwin Haviland Miller by internal references; see Whitman, *Correspondence,* 3:2–9; Shively, *Calamus,* 151.

20. See chap. 25 below for the intimacy of Carpenter and Chester Arthur III.

21. Shively, *Calamus,* 152.

22. Edward Carpenter to Walt Whitman, May 13, 1878, mentions having had a letter from Harry Stafford, and Carpenter asks for Stafford's photo; Traubel, *With,* 4:391–92.

23. Whitman, *Correspondence,* 3:86; Shively, *Calamus,* 152.

24. Stafford to Whitman, July 21, 1877; ibid., 153.

25. Stafford to Whitman, August 6, 1877; ibid., 154.

26. Shively, *Calamus,* 154. My transcription from this letter corrects Shively's.

27. Stafford to Whitman, October 4, 1877; Shively, *Calamus,* 155.

28. In addition to the Muybridge photo included in this chapter, there is a detail from an Eakins painting in chap. 16 below.

29. Carpenter to "Harry," June 18 [no year], from 1929 North Twenty-second Street, Philadelphia; Library of Congress, Manuscript Division. Martin G. Murray gave me information about this note.

30. Stafford to Whitman, October 17, 1877; Shively, *Calamus ,* 155.

31. Stafford to Whitman, October 24, 1877; ibid., 156.

32. Shively also interprets two other letters from working-class men to Whitman as referring to oral-genital contacts, but this is even more speculative (see discussion of Alonzo Bush and of Nicholas Palmer, chap. 10 above). The anonymous German tourist's memoir, referring to the years 1872–73, suggests that oral-genital contacts between men *were* common by this time in America (see chap. 6 above). Legal documents also indicate that oral-genital contacts became a topic of shocked, explicit discussion in the United States in the late 1870s (see chap. 5 above). But until more evidence is uncovered, my interpretation of Cattell's letter must remain inconclusive.

33. Cattell to Whitman, October 21, 1877; Shively, *Calamus,* 156.

34. Stafford to Whitman, November 26, 1877; ibid., 160.

35. Stafford to Whitman, November 17, 1877; ibid.

36. Stafford to Whitman, January 18, 1878; ibid., 162.

37. Stafford to Whitman, January 24, 1878; ibid., 163.

38. Stafford to Whitman, March 26, 1878; ibid., 164.

39. Stafford to Whitman, July 27, 1878; ibid., 165. The transcription of this water-stained letter is somewhat uncertain.

40. Whitman to Stafford, May 28, 1879; Whitman, *Correspondence,* 3:155.

41. Whitman to Stafford, February 11, 1881; ibid., 3:211.

42. Whitman to Stafford, February 28, 1881; ibid., 3:214–16.

43. Ibid., 3:215

44. Stafford to Whitman, April 4, 1881; Shively, *Calamus,* 169.

45. Whitman, *Correspondence,* 3:9.

46. Reynolds, *Walt,* 526.

47. Whitman to Stafford, January 25, 1882; Whitman, *Correspondence,* 3:264; Shively, *Calamus,* 169–70.

48. Stafford to Whitman, December 17, 1883; Shively, *Calamus,* 171.

Chapter 16. He Cannot Be Oblivious of Its Plainer Meanings

1. Whitman, Calamus 8, *Leaves* (1860), 354–55. Although this appears in *Leaves* (1965), the poet cut this poem from all of his subsequent editions of *Leaves of Grass.*

2. Symonds, *Memoirs,* 189.

3. For Symonds's writing of his *Memoirs,* see Symonds, *Letters,* 3:356; for his sexual case history, see Symonds, *Memoirs,* 21, 284–88.

4. Ellis and Symonds, *Sexual Inversion,* 58.

5. See, e.g., Martin, *Hero.*

6. Ellis and Symonds, *Sexual Inversion,* 58.

7. Ibid., 59.

8. Ibid.

9. Ibid., 59–60.

10. Ibid., 60.

11. Symonds, *Memoirs,* 97.

12. Ibid., 60–61.

13. Ellis and Symonds, *Sexual Inversion,* 61.

14. Ibid.

15. Symonds, *Memoirs,* 191–92. *Memoirs* transcribes "anderastes" from Symonds's original manuscript, but neither *The Oxford English Dictionary,* 2d ed., nor *The American Heritage Dictionary,* 4th ed., lists "ander." He probably meant "andro," Greek for "male."

16. Symonds, *Letters,* 1:370 n.1.

17. Symonds, *Memoirs,* 191–92.

18. Ibid., 109.

19. Ibid., 110–15, 118–19n, 131–32.

20. Ibid., 122, 124–28.

21. Ibid., 151.

22. Ibid., 156–58.

23. Ibid., 186–87.

24. Ibid., 187–88.

25. Ibid.

26. Symonds, *Letters,* 1:696–97.

27. Ibid., 1:388 n. 2. Dakyns had tutored Tennyson's sons.

28. Symonds, *Letters,* 1:696–97.

29. Ibid., 1:706.

30. Ibid., 1:707.

31. Ibid., 2:166–67.

32. Whitman, *Correspondence,* 2:158–59.

33. Symonds, *Letters,* 2:201–3.

34. Ibid., *Letters,* 2:205.

35. Symonds, *Memoirs,* 189.

36. Grosskurth, *Woeful,* 272.

37. Symonds, *Letters,* 2:374–75.

38. Ibid., 2:446–47.

39. Symonds, *Memoirs,* 253.

40. Ibid., 254.

41. Ibid.

42. Ibid., 253–55.

Chapter 17. Wild with Passion

1. Hartland, *Story*, 18. For the contemporary reader's convenience, I use this reprint for quotations. In this later edition, the type is reset and a dozen minor typographical errors are silently corrected. A few missing words are supplied in brackets.

2. Ibid., 11.

3. Ibid., 3.

4. Ibid., 19, 24, 41.

5. Ibid., 34–35.

6. Ibid., 35–36.

7. Ibid., 39.

8. Ibid., 39–40.

9. Ibid., 33.

10. Ibid., 40.

11. Ibid., 41.

12. Ibid., 43–49.

13. Ibid., 53.

14. Ibid., 54.

15. Ibid., 55.

16. Ibid., 57.

17. Ibid., 58–59.

18. Ibid., 59–64.

19. Ibid., 63–64.

20. Ibid., 66–67.

21. Ibid., 68.

22. Ibid., 28, 50.

23. Ibid., 68.

24. Ibid.

25. Ibid., 67–68.

26. Ibid., 68–72.

27. Ibid., 77–85.

28. Ibid., 88.

29. Ibid., 8–9.

30. Ibid., 8.

31. Ibid., 5, 59.

32. He first learns "vulgar" and "profane" words—the vernacular vocabulary of sex—from his classmates when he starts school; ibid., 17.

33. Ibid., 34, 44–45, 49, 81.

34. Ibid., 94.

Chapter 18. I Cannot Get Quite to the Bottom of Calamus

1. Symonds, *Letters*, 2:972–74.

2. In March 1877 a public attack in the *Contemporary Review* by the Reverend Richard St. John Tyrwhitt accused Symonds of defending the sensuality of ancient Greek sculpture and the example, in Whitman's works, of "Hellenism," which the writer associated with the "total denial of any moral restraint"; Symonds, *Letters*, 2:462 n. 2. Tyrwhitt's public attack on Symonds's morals led Symonds to withdraw his candidacy for a prestigious teaching post at Oxford University that would have meant his entrance into an academic career.

3. Symonds, *Memoirs*, 257.

4. Ibid., 261.

5. Ibid., 263.

6. Ibid., 265–66.

7. Ibid., 267–68.

8. Ibid., 276.

9. Ibid., 276.

10. Ibid., 277.

11. Ibid., 276.

12. Ibid., 275.

13. Symonds, *Letters,* 2:881.

14. Ibid., 2:896.

15. Ibid., 2:923, and 3:345–47, 365, 458, 664, 755.

16. Ibid., 2:934.

17. Traubel, *With,* 1:73.

18. Ibid.; Whitman refers to Symonds to Whitman, November 28, 1884; Symonds, *Letters,* 2:972–74.

19. Traubel, *With,* 1:76–77.

20. Ibid., 1:77.

21. The letter referred to is the one Symonds wrote to Whitman on June 13, 1875; Symonds, *Letters,* 2:374–75. Nowhere in this letter did Symonds refer to Whitman's or to his own "daughter." And nowhere in any of Symonds's letters did he refer to the Calamus poems as Whitman's "daughter." Symonds's three daughters were mentioned in his first letter to Whitman, and his most recent letter cited his "wife and children," along with the "young fellows" with whom he was "familiar."

22. On another occasion, Whitman responded to a Symonds inquiry about his man-love poems by saying that he sometimes let "the spirit impulse (female) rage"; Symonds to Edward Carpenter, February 13, 1893; Symonds, *Letters,* 3:818–19. Symonds is quoting Whitman's response to him on August 19, 1890, the draft version of which appears in Whitman, *Correspondence,* 4:72–73. See my discussion of this in chap. 19.

23. Traubel, *With,* 1:203.

24. Symonds to Whitman, June 13, 1875; Symonds, *Letters,* 2:374–75.

25. Traubel, *With,* 1:201–5.

26. Ibid., 2:276–77.

27. Ibid., 3:378–79.

28. Ibid., 3:378. Whitman said that the handsome young man was an Englishman named Rathbone, the son of a man who had "spoken about the nude in art." Rathbone had visited with a man named Corning. That same busy Christmas Day, Whitman praised Frank Millet's translation of a Tolstoy novel, *Sebastopol.*

29. Traubel, *With,* 3:385–86.

30. Ibid., 3:386.

31. Ibid., 3:388.

32. See chap. 8 above, on Whitman and Fred Vaughan, for more about Emerson and Whitman on Boston Common.

33. Traubel, *With,* 3:444.

34. Ibid., 3:452.

35. Ibid., 3:444–45. Whitman referred to Stoddard's letter of April 2, 1870, opening: "In the name of CALAMUS listen to me!" That letter was quoted in chap. 12.

36. Traubel, *With,* 3:452–53.

37. Ibid., 3:452–53.

38. Symonds to Whitman, January 29, 1889; Symonds, *Letters,* 3:343–44. This is Symonds's eighth letter to Whitman.

39. Symonds, *Letters,* 3:363–64.

40. Traubel, *With,* 4:345–47, describing their meeting of March 14, 1889.

41. Symonds, *Memoirs,* 189, 191.

42. [Symonds], "Case XVIII" in Ellis and Symonds, *Sexual,* 62; a later revision of Symonds's anonymous case history appears in Symonds, *Memoirs,* as app. 1, 284–88.

43. Symonds, *Letters,* 3:419–20.

44. Ibid., 3:424–25.

45. Calamus, no. 8; in Whitman, *Leaves* (1860), 354–55.

Chapter 19. Ardent and *Physical* Intimacies

1. The poem is "Long I thought that knowledge alone would suffice me," which appeared as the eighth Calamus poem in the 1860 edition of *Leaves of Grass,* but was deleted by Whitman from all later editions.

2. Traubel, *With,* 6:210–12, 213–14.

3. Ibid., 6:337. A few days earlier, Traubel had received an invitation to attend a meeting of The Club, a discussion group that was to meet at the Philadelphia home of the lawyer John Stoker Adams. Traubel may have been invited to the meeting earlier by a "Mr. Morris" before receiving his written invitation. See Adams to Traubel, March 25, 1890, Papers of Horace L. Traubel and Anne Montgomery Traubel, Container 47, Library of Congress. I am grateful to Martin G. Murray for this information.

4. Traubel, *With,* 6:341.

5. Ibid., 6:342. Research by Martin G. Murray in Gopsill's Philadelphia City Directory for 1890 suggests that, of the Sulzbergers listed, Mayer S., a lawyer, is the one most likely to have attended this meeting; Murray to Katz, May 12, 1997. By the turn of the century Mayer S. Sulzberger is said to have become "one of the foremost leaders and one of the most outstanding personalities of American Jewry"; Marx, *Essays.* Considering the comments by "Sulzberger" on Whitman's Calamus poems, it is interesting to note that Mayer S. Sulzberger was "too occupied with his legal career and communal endeavors to find time to marry and raise a family"; see Dicker, *Mayer,* introduction, first page. More research is needed to identify the Sulberger who commented on Whitman. I thank Martin Murray for the suggestion that it is possible that this discussion of Whitman's Calamus poems had been inspired by Havelock Ellis's *New Spirit,* first published in March 1890; see Grosskurth, *Havelock,* 125.

6. Whitman's notebooks refer to his reading the first volume of Bohn's six-volume edition of Plato (translated by Henry Cary, 1858). Whitman commented, significantly, on Socrates' discourse on love: "By love he evidently means the passion inspired in one man by another man, more particularly, a beautiful youth. The talk seems to hinge on the question whether such a youth should bestow his 'favors' more profitably on a declared lover or one not specially so." Whitman added that Socrates' "whole treatment assumes the illustration of Love, by the attachment a man has for another man, (a beautiful youth . . . more especially) — (it is astounding to modern ideas)"; Whitman, *Notebooks,* 5:1881–82; I have edited the punctuation for clarity. See also Martin, *Homosexual,* 85. Whitman's knowledge of and response to ancient Greek love is the subject for a major study.

7. Traubel, *With,* 6:342.

8. Ibid., 6:342–43.

9. "With a sound insight," says Ellis, Whitman "finds the roots of the most universal love in the intimacy and physical love of comrades and lovers"; Ellis, *New,* 117. Elsewhere, in the same book, however, Ellis criticizes Whitman's "defective scientific perception" rather than "any failure of moral insight" for "the vigourous manner in which an element of 'manly love' flourishes in 'Calamus' and elsewhere. Whitman is hardy enough to assert that he expects it will to a large extent take the place of love between the sexes. 'Manly love,' even in its extreme form [expressed, that is, in sexual acts between men], is certainly Greek, as is the degradation of women with which it is always correlated" (104 n. 1).

10. Symonds, *Letters,* 3:458.

11. Ibid., 3:459; and see Ellis, *New,* 104 n. 1.

12. Symonds, *Letters,* 3:459.

13. Ibid., 3:481–84.

14. Symonds's first letter to Whitman was written on October 7, 1871; Symonds, *Letters,* 2:166–67.

15. Symonds, *Letters,* 3:482.

16. Ibid., 3:483.

17. Ibid., 3:483–84.

18. Traubel, *With,* 7:64.

19. Ibid., 7:65–66.

20. Allen, *Solitary,* 447.

21. Whitman, *Correspondence,* 5:66–67.

22. Ibid., 5:72–73.

23. That exposure has continued into the 1990s, so that Whitman's Calamus poems are now generally recognized as (among other things) celebrating, and therefore encouraging, "*physical* intimacies" between men.

24. At the beginning of the twenty-first century, Whitman's poems can be understood both as affirming men's sexual acts with men *and* as universal in their humanity and appeal.

25. Symonds to Edward Carpenter, February 13, 1893; Symonds, *Letters,* 3:818.

26. See, e.g., Holloway, *Free,* and Loving, "Emory."

27. Symonds to Carpenter, February 13, 1893; Symonds, *Letters,* 3:819.

28. See, e.g., Whitman, *Correspondence,* 1:382, and Kaplan's statement that "anger prevailed" in Whitman's response to Symonds; Kaplan, *Walt,* 46.

29. Whitman, *Correspondence,* 5:75.

30. See Rom 1:26–27, King James Version. Whitman, focusing on men, seemed to forget about the first part of St. Paul's condemnation: "For this cause God save them up unto vile affections; for even their women did change the natural use into that which is against nature."

31. On August 28, 1890, for example, Traubel reported that Whitman was reading Symonds's collected essays and praised his "calm," "judicial" style. Though Symonds was not a "first-rater" as a writer, the Englishman was "a great critic" (ironic, in light of Symonds's critical insight into Whitman's man-love poems). Whitman added, "I have great charity for Symonds," and urged Traubel to read him; Traubel, *With,* 7:85–86. In the weeks and months after the historic interchange between Symonds and Whitman, the poet continued to read Symonds's writing, to praise his character, and to value his support. In conversations with Traubel, Whitman referred to Symonds in a friendly manner about a dozen times between September 26, 1890, and February 9, 1891, and many times afterward. In December 1890, for example, Whitman placed Symonds among those "literary men of a high type," who "yet in a sense belong to us, too"; Traubel, *With,* 7:379. On February 9, 1891, Whitman said: "I consider the friendship of men like Symonds . . . a great plume in our cap—great. Symonds is the quintessence of culture: he's the culture of culture—the essence of an essence"; Traubel, *With,* 7:457. From his deathbed, Whitman sent Symonds one of fifty hastily bound copies of the final edition of *Leaves of Grass;* Symonds, *Letters,* 3:649–50, and n. 3.

32. Symonds to Whitman; Symonds, *Letters,* 3:492–94.

33. That this is the first use of "inverted" to appear in Symonds's correspondence I conclude from my own survey of those texts and from the index to Symonds, *Letters,* which lists references to "Inverted Sexuality" and to "Sexual Inversion" (the topic), and *Sexual Inversion* (the title).

34. Symonds to Carpenter, January 21, 1893; in Symonds, *Letters,* 3:808.

35. Traubel, *With,* 7:453–54.
36. On Heywood, see Sears, *Sex.*
37. *A Problem in Modern Ethics. Being an Enquiry into the Phenomenon of Sexual Inversion. Addressed especially to Medical Psychologists and Jurists* (no author, place, publisher, or date of publication). This original edition is dated and discussed in Babington, *Bibliography,* 75–76. It is available in an edition dated 1896 and reprinted in 1971.
38. Quoted from Symonds, "Literature — Idealistic," chap. 7 in Symonds, *Problem,* esp. 116–120, 122–23.
39. Symonds, *Letters,* 3:649–50, and n. 3.
40. Symonds, *Walt,* 75–76.
41. Eldridge to Burroughs, February 16, 1894; Berg Collection, New York Public Library.
42. Kennedy, *Reminiscences,* vi.

Chapter 20. Men Given to Unnatural Practices

1. "The Slide. The Wickedest Place in New York," *New York Press,* May 11, 1890. I am grateful to Joel Honig for generously sharing this original research discovery. On the political warfare that caused the Slide's exposure, see "The Reverend Parkhurst Samples Vice," in Ellis, *Epic,* 423–39. For more about the Slide, see Katz, *Gay/Lesbian,* 219 n. 233, 582; and Chauncey, *Gay,* 68, 155, 243.
2. "Here, Mr. Nicoll, Is A Place To Prosecute," *New York Herald,* January 5, 1892, 8:1, 2.
3. "Freeze Out 'The Slide': District Attorney Nicoll Says That Stevenson's Vile Den Must Be Closed," *New York Herald,* January 6, 1892, 5:3.
4. *People v. Thomas Frank Stevenson,* Supreme Court, General Sessions, Indictments, January 1892, Box 10039, sh 106170, New York City Municipal Archives. For informing me of this document, I am deeply indebted to Timothy Gilfoyle.
5. Chauncey, *Gay,* 68.
6. *People v. Stevenson,* 106–16.
7. For "fairy," see many references in Katz, *Gay America* and *Gay/Lesbian,* and see Lighter, *Random,* 1:718.
8. Dolan's testimony, *People v. Stevenson,* 43.
9. Several of these names were either creatively adapted by the Slide's denizens, or misheard, or incorrectly transcribed by the court stenographer. Fanny Davenport was named after an actress, Fanny Lily Gypsy Davenport (1850–98); see the *Dictionary of American Biography,* and Odell, *Annals,* 14:529. Madam Fisher was named, probably, after a famous actress, Alice Fischer (1869–1947); see her papers in the New York Public Library, Rare Books and Manuscripts Collection. Maggie Vickers was named after actress Mattie Vickers; see Odell, *Annals,* 10:653. Princess Ida was named after the title character of Gilbert and Sullivan's 1884 opera. Phoebe, Miss Phoebe, Princess Phoebe, Phoebe Pinafore, and Hebe probably derived from Gilbert and Sullivan's *HMS Pinafore or The Lass That Loved a Sailor.* Princess Toto was named after the title character of a comic opera for which Frederic Clay wrote the music and W. S. Gilbert the words, performed in London in 1870 and in New York nine years later. I am grateful to Joel Honig for most of this research.
10. Maud Granger was named after an actress, Maude Granger (1851–1928); obituary, *New York Times,* August 18, 1928; Odell, *Annals,* 11:41. No actress named Greenoway has been discovered. Lois Fuller is either adapted from, or a transcriber's mishearing of, the name of the dancer Loie Fuller (1862–1928); *Dictionary of American Biography.* I thank Joel Honig for this research.
11. "Circus" is used in the United States, as early as 1878, as slang for a sexual exhibition by prostitutes; Lighter, *Random,* 1:424; for more detail, see Katz, *Gay/Lesbian,* 298n, 299, 574.

12. Doland's testimony, *People v. Stevenson*, 46.

13. Katz, *Gay/Lesbian*, 218–22.

14. Cooney's testimony, *People v. Stevenson*, 27. Other witnesses at the trial refer to "tasters"; see Dolan's testimony, 43, 48, and Meakim's testimony, 116, 118.

15. *People v. Stevenson*, 95.

16. Ibid., 86. For "cocksuckers," also see trial testimony of Leeson, 95, and Franke, 98.

17. For "cocksucker," see Lighter, *Random*, 1:447.

18. *People v. Stevenson*, 110.

19. Ibid., 111.

20. Dolan's testimony, *People v. Stevenson*, 46; Leeson's testimony, 57.

21. Dolan's testimony, *People v. Stevenson*, 45; Leeson's testimony, 57.

22. See the description of Lord Lovely's "small feet like a doll's," quoted from Melville's *Redburn* in Katz, "Melville's," 11.

23. *People v. Stevenson*, 56.

24. Ibid., 65–66.

25. Leeson's testimony, *People v. Stevenson*, 57; Dolan's testimony, 46; Bavier's testimony, 69, 71.

26. *People v. Stevenson*, 111.

27. Ibid., 112.

28. Ibid., 115.

29. Ibid., 59.

30. Ibid., 88–91.

31. Ibid., 77. McTiernan first testified that his name was "John Turner."

32. *People v. Stevenson*, 72–73.

33. The same distinction between gender deviance and sexual misconduct had been made in 1872 by the British judge in the trial of Boulton, Park, and Fiske; see chap. 13 above. In that case the jury agreed with the judge that gender infractions were no evidence of sexual crime.

34. The verdict and sentencing are reported in the *New York Herald*, February 17, 1892, 4:3; February 20, 1892, 5:5.

35. Katz, *Gay American*, 297–99.

Chapter 21. To Unite for Defense

1. Lind, *Autobiography*, 1918. His second volume of memoirs is *The Female-Impersonators*, 1922. The quoted sections are from the latter, 146. See references to Lind in Katz, *Gay American*, 336, 366–71, 575 n. 57, 592 nn. 17 and 26; Katz, *Gay/Lesbian*, 158, 394–95, 403–4; Chauncey, *Gay*, 42, 44, 51, 52, 54, 55, 59, 60, 77, 79, 110, 118, 187, 190, 291–92.

2. Lind, *Female-Impersonators*, 147.

3. Ibid., 146.

4. Ibid., 148.

5. Ibid.

6. Ibid.

7. Ibid., 150.

8. See my reference to "fairy" in chap. 20.

9. Lind, *Female-Impersonators*, 150.

10. Ibid., 151.

11. See "pansy" in Dynes, *Homolexis*, 107.

12. Lind, *Female-Impersonators*, 151–52.

13. For "hermaphrodite," see the *Oxford English Dictionary*. For "mental hermaphrodites" used as an antifeminist epithet, see Katz, *Gay/Lesbian*, 140.

14. In May 1892, Dr. James G. Kiernan spoke of "heterosexuals" as people with a

mental condition, "psychical hermaphroditism," because of their "inclinations to both sexes"; see Katz, *Gay/Lesbian*, 147, 231. In November 1892, Dr. Irving C. Rosse spoke of men engaging in oral-genital contact with men as "moral hermaphrodites"; see Katz, *Gay American*, 42. In April 1894, Havelock Ellis referred to Dr. Albert Moll's use of the term "psycho-sexual hermaphroditism and homosexuality"; Katz, *Gay/Lesbian*, 248. In December 1895, Ellis used "psychosexual hermaphrodites" for people now called "bisexual"; Katz, *Gay/Lesbian*, 288 For "hermaphrodite" as a name for cross-dressing Native Americans, see Katz, *Gay American*, 285, 286, 289, 299, 318, 611–12 n. 7, 615 n. 36, 616 n. 38, 617 n. 40. The folk variant, "morphodite," is documented in 1941 as a name for persons not of ambiguous sex, but those whose erotic interests focus on their own sex; see G. Legman, "Language of Homosexuality," 1171; and Dynes, *Homolexis*, 64–65.

15. Mayne, *Intersexes*, 415.
16. Lind, *Female-Impersonators*, see photos opposite title page, and on 26 and 83.
17. Lind, *Female-Impersonators*, 152.
18. Ibid., 152.
19. Ibid.
20. Quinn, *Same-Sex*, 423.
21. Lind, *Female-Impersonators*, 154–56.
22. Ibid., 154 n. 1.
23. Ibid., 157.
24. For Plum's story, see Lind, *Female-Impersonators*, 159–63.

Chapter 22. A Natural, Pure, and Sound Passion

1. Peirce's story was first told by Kennedy in "The Case" and " 'fierce.' " See also Katz, *Gay American*, 629 n. 42. For basic details of Peirce's life, also see *American National Biography*, 17:255–56, and the *Dictionary of American Biography*, 405–6.
2. Kennedy, "Case," 182.
3. Kennedy, " 'fierce,' " 62.
4. The first extant letter from Symonds to Perry is dated July 15, 1883; see Symonds, *Letters*, 2:832–33. On February 2, 1884, Symonds first mentioned to Perry that he was working on an essay on "some aspects of Greek social life" (*A Problem in Greek Ethics*); *Letters*, 2:888–82. On March 22, 1884, Symonds explained to Perry the sexual content of his essay on Greek ethics; *Letters*, 2:895–96. On July 30, 1884, Symonds asked Perry if he really wanted to see the Greek essay; *Letters*, 2:934. On March 27, 1888, Symonds responded to an encouraging letter from Perry, who had read the Greek essay and had suggested a source not known to the knowledgeable Symonds; *Letters*, 3:301–303.
5. Kennedy, " 'fierce,' " 63.
6. Symonds's sending Perry *A Problem in Modern Ethics* is mentioned in Symonds to Edmund Gosse, February 23, 1891; *Letters*, 3:554.
7. Symonds to Dakyns, May 20, 1891; *Letters*, 3:579.
8. Symonds to Gosse, June 22, 1891; *Letters*, 3:586.
9. Peirce to Perry, July 13, 1891, quoted in Kennedy, " 'fierce,' " 63.
10. "Letter from Professor X," in Ellis and Symonds, *Sexual Inversion*, App. D, 273–75.
11. Ibid., 273.
12. For discussion of the twentieth-century critique of heterosexuality as institution, see Katz, "Questioning the Heterosexual Mystique," in *Invention*, 113–38.
13. Kennedy, " 'fierce,' " 62.
14. Ellis and Symonds, *Sexual Inversion*, 273.
15. Perry's sketch is printed in a footnote to a memorial tribute to Peirce published after his death; see Byerly, "James Mills Peirce."

16. Ibid., 576, 577.

17. Kennedy, " 'fierce,' " 64; "Case," citing *Auction Sale. May 25th and 26th. Catalogue of the valuable private library of the late Prof. James Mills Peirce* (Boston: C. F. Libbie, 1909). For information that this catalog also lists Whitman's *Leaves of Grass* (1860), I thank Bert Hansen.

Chapter 23. Abnormal Passion

1. Ryman's diary, held by the Massachusetts Historical Society, Boston, was first discussed and quoted by Martin Duberman in *The New York Native*. I quote from that source.

2. Duberman, "Intimacy," 62.

3. Ibid.

4. Ibid.

5. Ibid., 63.

6. Theodore Tilton also reportedly said he "liked the Oriental style of kissing; he liked to see gentlemen kiss"; Fox, *Trials,* 118. Tilton was a good friend of the Rev. Henry Ward Beecher, who was himself accused of adultery with Tilton's wife.

7. Duberman, "Intimacy," 63.

8. Ibid.

9. Ryman refers to this as Byron's "Dream"; I cannot identify what Byron piece this is.

10. Duberman, "Intimacy," 63–64.

11. Ibid., 64.

12. Ibid.

13. Ibid., 65.

Chapter 24. A Much More Intimate Communion

1. For copies of documents and information on the life of Chester (later, Gavin) Arthur, I am deeply indebted to Martin G. Murray, who graciously shared his original, unpublished research. Those documents and that information are cited in many of the following notes. Brief comments on Arthur's life are found in his book *The Circle of Sex,* first published in 1962, and in an article by Edwina Bowe (*San Francisco Examiner,* January 19, 1964). In a brief chapter "About Edward Carpenter," the 1966 edition of Arthur's *Circle* provides a no-emission version of the encounter described here. A manuscript copy of that section, identical to the published version, is in Arthur's papers, Library of Congress (see below and n. 8).

Unpublished information on Arthur is contained in an unsigned "Biographical Note" and a "Scope and Content Note" in Arthur Family Papers, Manuscript Division, Library of Congress (the notes were written by the donor of the papers, the historian Thomas C. Reeves). These indicate that Chester Alan Arthur III was born on March 21, 1901, in Colorado Springs, Colorado, and died on April 28, 1972, in San Francisco. For further information on Carpenter, see Tsuzuki, *Edward*.

2. Arthur, *Circle* (1966), 131.

3. Ibid.; Tsuzuki, 188.

4. Arthur, *Circle* (1966), 131.

5. Ibid., 132.

6. Carpenter, *My*. For more information on Carpenter, see Katz, *Gay American*, 358–65, esp. 364 for a list of his publications on sexuality and affection.

7. Arthur, *Circle* (1966), 132–33.

8. A typescript of Gavin Arthur's second version of his encounter with Carpenter (beginning "You asked me to tell you") was given in 1967 to Allen Ginsberg; note by Ginsberg, dated July 1, 1972. Photocopies of Arthur's typescript and Ginsberg's note are now archived with a letter from Winston Leyland to Allen Ginsberg, August 28,

1990,(M733), in the Ginsberg Papers, Special Collections, Stanford University Libraries. This emission version of Arthur's going to bed with Carpenter was first published in *Gay Sunshine* 35 (1978), ed. Winston Leyland. It was reprinted in Leyland, *Gay Sunshine Interviews,* vol. 1:126–28. This latter is the text I quote below. The published version is cited as Arthur (1978). The photocopy of Arthur's manuscript and the published version are substantially the same, according to the research of Martin G. Murray. Arthur's papers contain no other emission-explicit account of his encounter with Carpenter (Murray to Katz, February 20, 1998). Murray mentions the documentation of Arthur's encounter with Carpenter in a review of Gary Schmidgal's *Walt Whitman: A Gay Life,* published in the *Walt Whitman Quarterly Review,* 131.

As early as October 30, 1964, Arthur wrote to Alan Watts, [John Bryan] "is going to publish in the next issue of 'Notes from Underground' my account of what Edward Carpenter liked in bed, which was also what W. W. [Walt Whitman] likes—*carezza*. This has taken courage on my part, but I think with Walt that 'we have had ducking and deprecating about enough' [a Whitman paraphrase]. Isherwood in his last letter doubted if I could ever get it published" (Arthur Family Papers, Manuscript Division, Library of Congress). Arthur apparently refers here to one of his two accounts of his sexual encounter with Carpenter. In the same letter, Watts is referred to as writing a piece for *Playboy* about Arthur's sexual theories.

In a letter of October 5, 1966, Arthur wrote to Ginsberg that the second edition of his *Circle of Sex* "has the account of my sleeping with Edward Carpenter" (Ginsberg Papers, Special Collections, Stanford University Libraries). Arthur's encounter with Carpenter had evidently been much discussed with Ginsberg.

Two letters from Christopher Isherwood to Arthur also mention an account of Carpenter by Arthur (September 23 and December [1964?]; Arthur Family Papers, Manuscript Division, Library of Congress).

9. Arthur, *Circle* (1978), 135.

10. Ibid.

11. Tsuzuki, 34, citing Carpenter to Charles George Oats, August 22, 1877, MSS 351.24, Carpenter Collection, Sheffield City Library.

12. In Arthur, *Circle* (1967), 127, Carpenter also tells the American that Whitman "did engender several children and his greatest female contact was that Creole in New Orleans. I don't think he loved any of them as much as he loved Peter Doyle." Either this is what Arthur actually remembered Carpenter telling him about Whitman, or Arthur had been reading the large biographical literature on the American poet.

13. In Arthur, *Circle* (1966), 136–37, the young Arthur also asks Carpenter "You did sleep with him?" (Whitman) and Carpenter answers affirmatively. Arthur then asks: "Do you think he liked women too—I mean in bed?" To which Carpenter answers: "Yes, especially when he was young and bursting with potency. I believe he was not lying when he said he had several children. But after he got that infection during his hospital work in your Civil War, and he knew he might not be potent enough to satisfy women, I think he was more at ease, in bed at least, with his men friends." Arthur's Carpenter adds, of Whitman, "essentially he was bisexual—or better ambigenic."

14. It would be interesting to know exactly what Carpenter may have written about carezza or karezza. Sears, *Sex,* 209–10, says that penis-vagina intercourse without male emission was first discussed by John Humphrey Noyes, *The Bible Argument* (1848), and later in George Noyes Miller's *Karezza* (1895), Alice B. Stockham's *Karezza: Ethics of Marriage* (1896), and in Marie Stopes's *Married Love* (1918) and *Contraception* (1926).

15. Arthur, *Circle* (1966), includes a chapter "In Defense of Mouth-Genital Contacts," in which he speaks of Alfred Kinsey's idea that the experience of worship associated with oral-genital acts was "the origin of Holy Communion" (121). This

chapter is immediately followed by a chapter on Walt Whitman, then one on Carpenter.

16. Intimate letters between Cassady and Ginsberg are reprinted in Norton, *My,* 253–57.

17. For photocopies of the two Gavin Arthur letters that follow I am again grateful to the generosity of Martin Murray. He discovered them, misidentified, during a search of the Carpenter Collection in the Sheffield City Archives, Sheffield, England. The letter of September 8, 1923, is manuscript 271/187; the letter of May 14, 1924, is manuscript 396/397.

18. From 1922 to 1924 Arthur lived in Ireland with his wife, and had served in 1922 as the secretary to the Irish Republican delegation in Lausanne, Switzerland. See "Biographical Note," Arthur Family Papers, Library of Congress.

19. Symonds, *Letters,* 3:798.

20. Symonds, *Letters,* 3:810–11. A footnote to this letter lists the book as by Silvio Venturi (1850–1900), and titled *Le Degenerazioni psico-sessuali nella vita degli individui e nella storia delle società* (Psychosexual degeneration in the life of individuals and in the history of society), 1892; I thank David F. Greenberg for the translation. It would be interesting to know what this book says about ingested semen.

21. Arthur (1978).

Sex and Affection between Men—Then and Now

1. Weeks, *Coming Out,* 3.

2. An early example of this sodomy history can be seen in Gerard and Hekma, "Pursuit."

3. I explored that residual essentialism in a public talk; Katz, "Was There?"

4. For a survey of the range of nineteenth-century American terms, see Katz, "Conceptualizing."

5. Only at the end of the century was the term "sex-love" coined to signify a new ideal of erotic love; see Katz, *Gay/Lesbian,* 141–42, 250–51, 254; see also my discussion of the early-nineteenth-century separation of lust and love and Sigmund Freud's rejoining of libido and love; Katz, *Invention,* 40–55.

6. Eskridge, "Law," 1027–28.

7. Rubin's and Isherwood's terms are discussed in Katz, *Invention.*

8. For a good overview of the change from a procreative regime to a specifically sexual order, see D'Emilio and Freedman, "Toward."

9. "Catholics Decry Whitman Bridge," *New York Times,* December 17, 1955, 16. A full and hilarious account of the protest against the naming of the Walt Whitman Bridge can be found in Stein, *City,* 138–54.

10. Quoted in Richmond and Noguera, *Gay,* 200–202.

Bibliography

The general section of this bibliography includes all of the books, periodicals, and other literature abbreviated in the notes. For reasons of space it excludes many texts that profoundly influenced my thought about the history of sexuality and affection. In the legal section, I provide an annotated list of published appeals case reports (see chap. 5). Other legal sources are listed in the general section.

General

Abzug, Robert. *Passionate Liberator: Theodore Dwight Weld and the Dilemma of Reform.* New York: Oxford University Press, 1980.

Ackroyd, Peter. *Dressing Up: Transvestism and Drag, the History of an Obsession.* New York: Simon & Schuster, 1979.

Alcott, Bronson. *The Journals of Bronson Alcott.* Edited by Odell Shepard. Boston: Little, Brown, 1938.

Altman, Dennis, et al. *Homosexuality, Which Homosexuality?* London: GMP Publishers, 1989.

Allen, Gay Wilson. *Solitary Singer: A Critical Biography of Walt Whitman.* New York: New York University Press, 1967.

American and English Encyclopedia of Law. Edited by Charles F. Williams. Northport, New York: Edward Thompson, 1893.

American and English Encyclopedia of Law, 2d ed. Edited by James Cockcroft. Northport, New York: Edward Thompson, 1903.

Annual Register: Review of Public Events at Home and Abroad. London: Rivington, 1872.

Anthony, Carl Sferrazza. "Was James 'Aunt Fancy' Buchanan Our Gay President?" *The Advocate,* no. 571 (February 26, 1991): 50–53.

Arthur, Gavin. *The Circle of Sex.* San Francisco: Panagraphic Press, 1962.

———. *The Circle of Sex,* 2d ed. New Hyde Park, N.Y.: University Books, 1966.

———. Encounter with Edward Carpenter, written 1967. *Gay Sunshine,* no. 17, 1978; reprinted in *Gay Sunshine Interviews,* vol. 1. Edited by Winston Leyland, 126–28. San Francisco: Gay Sunshine Press, 1978.

———. Two letters to Edward Carpenter. September 8, 1923, manuscript 271/187; May 14, 1924, manuscript 396/397. Carpenter Collection, Sheffield City Archives, Sheffield, England.

———. Encounter with Edward Carpenter. Includes note by Ginsberg, dated July 1, 1972; photocopy of Arthur's typescript and Ginsberg's note enclosed with a letter from Winston Leyland to Allen Ginsberg, August 28, 1990. Ginsberg Papers, M733, Stanford University Libraries.

Austen, Roger. *Genteel Pagan: The Double Life of Charles Warren Stoddard.* Edited by John Crowley. Amherst: University of Massachusetts Press, 1991.

———. "Genteel Pagan." Manuscript. Katz Collection. New York, n.d.

———. *Playing the Game: The Homosexual Novel in America.* Indianapolis: Bobbs-Merrill, 1977.

Babington, Percy L. *Bibliography of the Writings of John Addington Symonds.* London: 1925; reprint, New York: Burt Franklin, 1968.

Barker-Benfield, G. J. *The Horrors of the Half-Known Life: Male Attitudes toward Women and Sexuality in Nineteenth-Century America.* New York: Harper & Row, 1976.

Baym, Nina, et al., eds. *Norton Anthology of American Literature,* 4th ed. 2 vols. New York: W. W. Norton, 1994.

Belford, Barbara. *Bram Stoker: A Biography of the Author of* Dracula. New York: Alfred A. Knopf, 1996.

Bennett, Paula, and Vernon A. Rosario, eds. *Solitary Pleasures: The Historical, Literary, and Artistic Discourses of Autoeroticism.* New York: Routledge, 1995.

Bérubé, Allan. *Coming Out under Fire: The History of Gay Men and Women in World War Two.* New York: Free Press, 1990.

Blasius, Mark, and Shane Phelan, eds. *We Are Everywhere: A Historical Sourcebook of Gay and Lesbian Politics.* New York: Routledge, 1997.

Boswell, John. *Christianity, Social Tolerance, and Homosexuality.* Chicago: University of Chicago Press, 1980.

Bray, Alan. *Homosexuality in Renaissance England.* New York: Columbia University Press, 1982.

[Brown, Lewis Kirke.] "Memorandum of Miss McGill re Lewis Kirk Brown Letters." Manuscript Division, Library of Congress.

Buck, Irving A., and Thomas Robson Hay, eds. *Cleburne and His Command.* Jackson, Tenn.: McCowat-Mercert Press, 1959.

Burg, B. R. *An American Seafarer in the Age of Sail: The Erotic Diaries of Philip C. Van Buskirk, 1851–1870.* New Haven, Conn.: Yale University Press, 1994.

Burlingame, Michael. *An Oral History of Abraham Lincoln: John G. Nicolay's Interviews and Essays.* Carbondale: Southern Illinois University Press, 1996.

Byerly, W. E. "James Mills Peirce." *Harvard Graduates' Magazine* 14, no. 56 (June 1906): 573–77.

Calder, Ellen O'Connor. "Personal Recollections of Walt Whitman." Copy of Calder's original manuscript by C. J. Furness, location of original unknown. Published with revisions. *Atlantic Monthly,* June 1907.

Campbell, Warren. *Warren Campbell . . . v. The State of Texas,* October 19, 1866. Filed November 27, 1866. Texas State Archives, Austin.

Carnes, Mark C., and Clyde Griffen, eds. *Meanings for Manhood: Constructions of Masculinity in Victorian America.* Chicago: University of Chicago Press, 1990.

Carpenter, Edward. Letter to Harry Stafford. June 18, no year. Feinberg Collection, Library of Congress.

———. *My Days and Dreams: Being Autobiographical Notes.* London: George Allen & Unwin, 1916.

[Casper, Johann Ludwig.] Anonymous German's report of sex with men in America. In *Handbuch der gerichtlichen Medicin.* Revised and edited by Carl Liman. Berlin: Hirschwald, 1889.

Century Edition of the American Digest: A Complete Digest of All Reported American Cases from the Earliest Times to 1896, vol. 44. St. Paul, Minn.: West Publishing, 1903.

Chamberlin, William W. Biographical folder. Harvard University Archives.

Chauncey, George. *Gay New York: Gender, Urban Culture, and the Making of the Gay Male World, 1890–1940.* New York: Basic Books, 1994.

Chestnut, Boykin Mary. *A Diary from Dixie.* Edited by Ben Ames Williams. Cambridge, Mass.: Harvard University Press, 1980.

———. *The Private Mary Chestnut: The Unpublished Civil War Diaries.* Edited by C. Vann Woodward and Elizabeth Muhlenfeld. New York: Oxford University Press, 1984.

Clark, George. *The Lives of Boulton and Park: Extraordinary Revelations,* 1870;

reprinted, with new text, as *Men in Petticoats: The Trial of Boulton and Park, with Hurt and Fiske. A Complete and Accurate Report of the Proceedings.* Manchester: John Heywood, 1871.

Cohen, Ed. "Legislating the Norm: From Sodomy to Gross Indecency." *South Atlantic Quarterly* 88, no. 1 (1989): 181–217.

Cohen, William A. *Sex Scandal: The Private Parts of Victorian Fiction.* Durham, N.C.: Duke University Press, 1996.

———. Typed notes. Boulton, Park, Fiske trial records. Cohen to Katz, November 7, 1997.

Cott, Nancy F. *The Bonds of Womanhood: "Woman's Sphere" in New England, 1780–1835.* New Haven, Conn.: Yale University Press.

Crompton, Louis. "Homosexuals and the Death Penalty in Colonial America." *Journal of Homosexuality* 1, no. 3 (1976): 277–93.

Craft, Christopher. "Just Another Kiss: Inversion and Paranoia in Bram Stoker's Dracula." In *Another Kind of Love: Male Homosexual Desire in English Discourse, 1850–1920.* Berkeley: University of California Press, 1994.

Cram, Oscar. Letter to Ellen. April 3, 1864. Civil War Miscellany. U.S. Army Military History Institute. Carlisle, Penn.

Creech, James. *Closet Writing/Gay Reading: The Case of Melville's* Pierre. Chicago: University of Chicago Press, 1993.

Crompton, Louis. "Homosexuals and the Death Penalty in Colonial America." *Journal of Homosexuality* 1, no. 3 (1976): 277–94.

Curtin, Kaier. *"We Can Always Call Them Bulgarians": The Emergence of Lesbians and Gay Men on the American Stage.* Boston: Alyson, 1987.

Cushing, Helen Grant, and Adah V. Morris, eds. *Nineteenth Century Readers' Guide to Periodical Literature, 1890–1899.* 2 vols. New York: H. W. Wilson, 1944.

Cuyler, Theodore. *Remarks upon a recent opinion of the Honorable Osward Thompson . . . in a part of the divorce case of Griswold v. Griswold.* Philadelphia: King & Baird, 1857.

D'Emilio, John. "Capitalism and Gay Identity." In *Powers of Desire: The Politics of Sexuality.* Edited by Ann Snitow, Christine Stansell, and Sharon Thompson. New York: Monthly Review Press, 1983; reprinted in *Making Trouble: Essays on Gay History, Politics, and the University.* Edited by John D'Emilio. New York: Routledge, 1992.

D'Emilio, John, and Estelle B. Freedman. *Intimate Matters: A History of Sexuality in America.* New York: Harper & Row, 1988.

———. "Toward a New Sexual Order, 1880–1930." In *Intimate Matters: A History of Sexuality in America.* Edited by John D'Emilio and Estelle B. Freedman. New York: Harper & Row, 1988.

Dalloz, Victor A. D. *Jurisprudence Générale: Répertoire méthodique et alphabétique de législation . . .* Paris: Bureau de la Jurisprudence Générale 1845.

Davis, William S. Court of Appeals (Judgments, Western Shore). *William S. Davis v. State of Maryland,* 1806–1810, nos. 267 and 268, MdHR 683–122, 1-62-8-32 (19 pp.). Maryland State Archives, Annapolis.

———. MSA no. C183, Baltimore County, Court of Oyer and Terminer and Gaol Delivery (Docket and Minutes), William S. Davis, September 22, October 3, October 9, 1810, Minutes, MdIIR 16654, 3-29-14-6 (4 pp.).

Dexter, Franklin B. *Biographical Notices of Graduates of Yale College.* New Haven, Conn., 1913.

Dicker, Herman, ed. *The Mayer Sulzberger [and] Alexander Mark Correspondence, 1904–1923.* New York: Sepher-Hermon Press, 1990.

[Dodd, Albert.] *Biographical Notes of Graduates of Yale College*. . . . Edited by Franklin B. Dexter. New Haven, 1913.

[————.] *Biographical Record of the Class of 1838 in Yale College*. New Haven, Conn.: Tuttle, Morehouse & Taylor, 1879.

————. Diary, letters, papers. Archives, Yale University Library.

[————.] Obituary. *Hartford Daily Times,* June 1844. Archives, Yale University Library.

Donald, David Herbert. *Lincoln*. New York: Simon & Schuster, 1995.

Donoghue, Emma. *Passions between Women: British Lesbian Culture, 1668–1801*. New York: HarperCollins, 1993.

Doty, Dennis. "Lincoln's Other Love." *Chicago Gay Crusader,* Issue 26 (April 1976): 6.

Duberman, Martin. *About Time: Exploring the Gay Past,* rev. ed. New York: Meridian/Penguin, 1991.

————. "Intimacy without Orgasm." *New York Native,* 1982; reprinted in *About Time: Exploring the Gay Past,* rev. ed. New York: Meridian/Penguin, 1991.

————. " 'Writhing Bedfellows' in Antebellum South Carolina: Historical Interpretation and the Politics of Evidence." *Journal of Homosexuality* 6 (Fall–Winter 1980–81): 79–84; reprinted in Duberman, *About Time;* Duberman et al., *Hidden from History;* and Howard, *Carrying On in the Lesbian and Gay South.*

Duberman, Martin, Martha Vicinus, George Chauncey, Jr., eds. *Hidden from History: Reclaiming the Gay Past*. New York: New American Library, 1989.

Duis, E. *The Good Old Times in McLean County, Illinois*. Bloomington: Leader Publishing and Printing House, 1874.

Dunlap, David W. "In Search of History: When Today's Agenda Is a Prism for the Past." *New York Times,* October 1, 1995.

Dynes, Wayne. *Homolexis: A Historical and Cultural Lexicon of Homosexuality*. Gai Saber Monograph, no. 4. New York: Scholarship Committee, Gay Academic Union, 1986.

Ellis, Edward Robb. *The Epic of New York City*. New York: Kondansha International, 1997.

Ellis, Havelock. *The New Spirit,* 3d ed. London: W. Scott, 1892.

Ellis, Havelock, and John Addington Symonds. *Sexual Inversion*. London: Wilson & Macmillan, 1897; reprint, New York: Arno Press, 1975.

Eskridge, William N., Jr. *Gaylaw: Challenging the Apartheid of the Closet*. Cambridge, Mass.: Harvard University Press, 1999.

————. "Law and the Construction of the Closet: American Regulation of Same-Sex Intimacy, 1880–1946." *Iowa Law Review* 82, no. 4 (May 1997): 1009–1136.

Encyclopedia of the Confederacy. Edited by Richard N. Current. New York: Simon & Schuster, 1993.

Faderman, Lillian. *Surpassing the Love of Men: Romantic Friendship and Love between Women from the Renaissance to the Present*. New York: Morrow, 1981.

Fiedler, Leslie A. *Love and Death in the American Novel*. New York: Criterion, 1960; rev. ed., New York: Dell, 1966.

————. *The New Fiedler Reader*. New York: Prometheus Books, 1999.

[Fiske, John Safford.] *History of the Class of 1863 Yale College*. . . . New York: 1889.

[————.] *History of the Class of 1863 Yale College*. . . . New Haven, Conn.: Tuttle, Morehouse & Taylor, 1905.

————. Letter and printed materials. Archives, Warren Hunting Smith Library of the Hobart and William Smith Colleges.

[————.] Application and Recommendation File—John S. Fiske, 1867. Andrew Johnson Administration, National Archives.

————. Letter of Resignation, June 24, 1870. National Archives, Microfilm Publication T396.

————. Letter to William H. Seward, August 28, 1867. Application and Recommendation File—John S. Fiske, 1867. Andrew Johnson Administration, National Archives.

[————.] *Second Report of the Class of Sixty-Three, in Yale College.* New York: Evening Post Steam Presses, 1878.

[————.] *Triennial Meeting and Biographical Record of the Class of Sixty-Three, in Yale College.* New Haven, Conn.: Tuttle, Morehouse & Taylor, 1869.

Folsom, Ed. "Another Harry Stafford Letter." *Walt Whitman Quarterly Review* 5, no. 4 (Spring 1988): 43–44.

————. "An Unknown Photograph of Whitman and Harry Stafford." *Walt Whitman Quarterly Review* 4, no. 1 (Summer 1986): 51–52, back cover.

————, ed. " 'This Heart's Geography's Map': The Photographs of Walt Whitman." Special double issue of *Walt Whitman Quarterly Review* 4, nos. 2–3 (Fall/Winter 1986–87): 1–36.

Fone, Byrne S., ed. *The Columbia Anthology of Gay Literature: Readings from Western Antiquity until the Present Day.* New York: Columbia University Press, 1998.

Foucault, Michel. *The History of Sexuality.* Vol. 1: *An Introduction.* Trans. Robert Hurley. New York: Pantheon, 1978.

Fox, Richard Wightman. *Trials of Intimacy: Love and Loss in the Beecher-Tilton Scandal.* Chicago: University of Chicago Press, 1999.

Gale, Robert L. *Charles Warren Stoddard.* Boise, Idaho: Boise State University, 1977.

————. "Francis Davis Millet." *American National Biography* 15 (1999): 525–27.

Gardiner, James. *Who's a Pretty Boy Then: One Hundred and Fifty Years of Gay Life in Pictures.* London: Serpent's Tail, 1997.

Gay, Peter. *The Bourgeois Experience; Victoria to Freud.* Vol. 2: *The Tender Passion.* New York: Oxford University Press, 1986.

Gerard, Kent, and Gert Hekma, eds. "The Pursuit of Sodomy: Male Homosexuality in Renaissance and Enlightenment Europe." Special issue of *Journal of Homosexuality* 16, nos. 1–2 (1988).

Gifford, James. *Dayneford's Library: American Homosexual Writing, 1900–1913.* Amherst: University of Massachusetts Press, 1995.

Gilfoyle, Timothy J. *City of Eros: New York City, Prostitution, and the Commercialization of Sex, 1790–1920.* New York: W. W. Norton, 1992.

Golden, Arthur. "A Recovered Harry Stafford Letter to Walt Whitman." *Walt Whitman Quarterly Review* 5 no. 4 (Spring 1988): 40–41.

Goldstein, Anne B. "History, Homosexuality, and Political Values: Searching for the Hidden Determinants of *Bowers v. Hardwick.*" *Yale Law Journal* 97, no. 6 (May 1988): 1073–1103.

Grosskurth, Phyllis. *The Woeful Victorian: A Biography of John Addington Symonds.* New York: Holt, Rinehart & Winston, 1964.

————. *Havelock Ellis: A Biography.* New York: Alfred Knopf, 1980.

Griswold, Rufus W. "Statement of the relations of Rufus W. Griswold with Charlotte Myers . . ." Philadelphia: H. B. Ashmead, 1856.

Haggerty, George E. *Men in Love: Masculinity and Sexuality in the Eighteenth Century.* New York: Columbia University Press, 1999.

Hallam, Paul. *The Book of Sodom*. New York: Verso, 1993.

Hansen, Karen V. " 'No Kisses Is Like Youres': An Erotic Friendship between Two African-American Women during the Mid-Nineteenth Century." *Gender and History* 7, no. 2 (August 1995): 153–82.

———. " 'Our Eyes Behold Each Other': Masculinity and Intimate Friendship in Antebellum New England." In *Men's Friendships*. Edited by Peter M. Nardi. Newbury Park, Calif.: Sage, 1993.

Hartland, Claude [pseud.]. *The Story of a Life: For the Consideration of the Medical Fraternity*. St. Louis: 1901; reprinted, with a foreword by C. A. Trip. San Francisco: Grey Fox Press, 1985.

Helms, Alan. "Whitman's 'Live Oak with Moss.' " In *The Continuing Presence of Walt Whitman: The Life after the Life*. Edited by Robert K. Martin. Iowa City: University of Iowa Press, 1992.

Herndon, William H., and Jesse W. Weik. *Herndon's Lincoln*. Cleveland: World Publishing, 1965.

Historical Encyclopedia of Illinois and History of McLean County. Edited by Newton Bateman et al. Chicago: Munsell Publishing, 1908.

Hodes, Martha. *White Women, Black Men: Illicit Sex in the Nineteenth-Century South*. New Haven, Conn.: Yale University Press, 1997.

Holloway, Emory. *Free and Lonesome Heart: The Secret of Walt Whitman*. New York: Vantage Press, 1960.

———. "Walt Whitman's Love Affairs." *Dial*, November 1920, 473–83.

Hudson, Frederic. *Journalism in the United States, from 1690 to 1872*. New York: Harper & Row, 1968.

Hyde, H. Montgomery. *The Love That Dared Not Speak Its Name: A Candid History of Homosexuality in Britain*. Boston: Little, Brown, 1970.

Ignatiev, Noel. *How the Irish Became White*. New York: Routledge, 1995.

Jordan, Mark D. *The Invention of Sodomy in Christian Theology*. Chicago: University of Chicago Press, 1997.

Kalk, Sarah. "Lincoln Was Gay, Activist [Larry Kramer] Contends." *Madison [Wisconsin] Capital Times,* February 23, 1999.

Kaplan, Justin. *Walt Whitman: A Life*. New York: Simon & Schuster, 1980.

Katz, Jonathan Ned. "Abe and Josh and Mary and Mercy." *The Advocate* (September 13, 1988): 47.

———. "Alexander Hamilton's Nose." *The Advocate* 10 (October 1998): 29.

———. "Coming to Terms: Conceptualizing Men's Erotic and Affectional Relations with Men in the United States, 1820–1892." In *A Queer World: The Center for Lesbian and Gay Studies Reader*. Edited by Martin Duberman. New York: New York University Press, 1997.

———. *Comrades and Lovers*. Unpublished theater piece on Whitman and Symonds. Katz Collection. New York.

———. *Gay American History: Lesbians and Gay Men in the U.S.A*. New York: T. Y. Crowell, 1976; reprinted, with a new preface and bibliography, New York: Meridian, 1992.

———. *Gay/Lesbian Almanac*. New York: Harper & Row, 1983; reprint, New York: Carrol & Graf, 1994.

———. " 'Homosexual' and 'Heterosexual': Questioning the Terms." In *A Queer World: The Center for Lesbian and Gay Studies Reader*. Edited by Martin Duberman. New York: New York University Press, 1997.

———. *The Invention of Heterosexuality*. New York: Dutton, 1995.

———. "Melville's Secret Sex Text." *Village Voice Literary Supplement,* April 1982, 10–12.

———. "Up from Underground: Tracking the History of the Word *Gay.*" *The Advocate* (May 23, 1989): 40.

———. "Was There Heterosexuality (or Homosexuality) before 1892? Problems in Sexual History." Paper presented at "Do Ask, Do Tell: Conference on Outing Pacific Northwest History." October 24, 1998. Washington State History Museum, Tacoma.

Kennedy, Hubert. "The Case for James Mills Peirce." *Journal of Homosexuality* 4, no. 2 (Winter 1978): 179–84.

———. ". . . fierce & Quixotically." *Harvard Magazine* 85, no. 2 (November–December 1982): 62–64.

———. *Sex & Math in the Harvard Yard: The Memoirs of James Mills Peirce; A Fictional Biography.* . . . San Francisco: Peremptory Publications, 2000.

———. "The 'Third Sex' Theory of Karl Heinrich Ulrichs." *Journal of Homosexuality* 6, nos. 1–2 (Fall–Winter 1980–81): 103–12.

———. *Ulrichs: The Life and Works of Karl Heinrich Ulrichs, Pioneer of the Modern Gay Movement.* Boston: Alyson Publications, 1988.

Kennedy, William Sloan. *Reminiscences of Walt Whitman.* . . . 1897; facsimile, New York: Haskell House Publishers, 1973.

King, John. *Three Hundred Days in a Yankee Prison: Reminiscences of War Life, Captivity, Imprisonment at Camp Chase, Ohio.* Atlanta: Jas. P. Davis, 1904.

Kinkaid, Robert L. *Joshua Fry Speed: Lincoln's Most Intimate Friend.* Harrogate, Tenn.: Department of Lincolniana, Lincoln Memorial University, 1943.

Krieg, Joann P. *A Whitman Chronology.* Iowa City: University of Iowa Press, 1998.

Legman, G. "The Language of Homosexuality: An American Glossary." In *Sex Variants: A Study of Homosexual Patterns,* by George Henry. New York: Hoeber, 1941.

Licata, Salvatore J., and Robert P. Petersen, eds. "Historical Perspectives on Homosexuality." *Journal of Homosexuality* 6, nos. 1–2 (Fall–Winter 1980–81).

Lighter, J. E., ed. *Random House Historical Dictionary of American Slang.* 2 vols. New York: Random House, 1994, 1997.

Lincoln, Abraham. *The Collected Works of Abraham Lincoln.* Edited by Roy P. Basler. New Brunswick, N.J.: Rutgers University Press, 1953.

Lind, Earl. *Autobiography of an Androgyne.* Edited and with an introduction by Alfred W. Herzog. New York: Medico-Legal Journal, 1918; reprint, New York: Arno Press, 1975.

———. *The Female-Impersonators.* Edited with an introduction by Alfred W. Herzog. New York: Medico-Legal Journal, 1922; reprint, Arno Press, 1975.

Lorant, Stefan. *Lincoln: A Picture Story of His Life.* New York: Harper & Brothers, 1952; rev. ed., 1957.

Loring, Frederick W. Biographical folder. Harvard University Archives.

———. *Two College Friends: Old and New.* Boston: A. K. Loring, 1871.

Loving, Jerome. *Walt Whitman: The Song of Himself.* Berkeley: University of California Press, 1999.

———. "Emory Holloway and the Quest for Whitman's Manhood." *Walt Whitman Quarterly Review* 11 (Summer 1993): 1–17.

Lowry, Thomas P. *The Story the Soldiers Wouldn't Tell: Sex in the Civil War.* Mechanicsburg, Penn.: Stackpole Press, 1994.

Lynch, Michael. " 'Here is Adhesiveness': From Friendship to Homosexuality." *Victorian Studies* 29, no. 1 (Autumn 1995): 67–96.

Lystra, Karen. *Searching the Heart: Women, Men, and Romantic Love in Nineteenth-Century America.* New York: Oxford University Press, 1989.

Martin, Robert K. "Billy Budd's Stutter." *The Nation,* February 14, 1976, 184–86.

———. *Hero, Captain, and Stranger: Male Friendship, Social Critique, and Literary Form in the Sea Novels of Herman Melville.* Chapel Hill: University of North Carolina Press, 1986.

———. *The Homosexual Tradition in American Poetry.* Austin: University of Texas Press, 1979.

———. "Knights-Errant and Gothic Seducers: The Representation of Male Friendship in Mid-Nineteenth-Century America." In *Hidden from History: Reclaiming the Gay Past,* edited by Martin Duberman, Martha Vicinus, and George Chauncey, Jr. New York: New American Library, 1989.

Marx, Alexander. *Essays in Jewish Biography.* Lanham, Md.: University Press of America, 1986.

Mayne, Xavier [pseud.]. *The Intersexes: A History of Similisexualism as a Problem in Social Life.* Privately printed, 1908; facsimile, New York: Arno Press, 1975.

McDaniels, J. H. "John Safford Fiske." *Hobart College Bulletins* 6 (1907–8): 7–22.

McElroy, John. *Andersonville: A Story of Rebel Military Prisons . . . a private soldier's experience in Richmond, Andersonville, Savannah, Millen, Blackshear and Florence.* Toledo, Ohio: D. R. Locke, 1879.

Melville, Herman. *Moby-Dick, or The Whale.* Evanston and Chicago: Northwestern University Press and the Newberry Library, 1988.

———. *Redburn: His First Voyage.* Evanston and Chicago: Northwestern University Press and the Newberry Library, 1969.

Merrick, Jeffrey, and Bryant T. Ragan, eds. *Homosexuality in Modern France.* New York: Oxford University Press, 1996.

Millet, Francis Davis. *A Capillary Crime and Other Stories.* New York: Harper, 1892.

———. *The Danube from the Black Forest to the Black Sea.* New York: Harper, 1893.

[———.] *Dictionary of American Biography.* 6:644–46.

———. *The Expedition to the Philippines.* New York: Harper, 1899.

———. Letters to Charles Warren Stoddard. Department of Special Collections, Syracuse University Library.

———, trans. Lev Nikolaevich Tolstoi, *Sebastopol.* London: Greening, 1887.

Millett, Kate. *Sexual Politics.* Garden City, N.Y.: Doubleday, 1970.

Mitchell, Reid. *The Vacant Chair: The Northern Soldier Leaves Home.* New York: Oxford University Press, 1993.

Mollinoff, Katherine. *Walt Whitman at Southold.* Stony Brook: State University of New York Press, 1966.

Moon, Michael. *Disseminating Whitman: Revision and Corporeality in* Leaves of Grass. Cambridge, Mass.: Harvard University Press, 1991.

———. " 'The Gentle Boy from the Dangerous Classes': Pederasty, Domesticity, and Capitalism in Horatio Alger." *Representations* 19 (Summer 1986): 87–110.

Morris, Roy, Jr. *The Better Angel: Walt Whitman in the Civil War.* New York: Oxford University Press, 2000.

Mullin, J. Letter to William H. Seward, August 26, 1867. Application and Recommendation File—John S. Fiske, 1867. Andrew Johnson Administration, National Archives.

Murphy, Lawrence R. "Defining the Crime against Nature: Sodomy in the United States Appeals Courts, 1810–1940." *Journal of Homosexuality* 19, no. 1 (1990): 49–66.

Murray, Martin G. " 'Pete the Great': A Biography of Peter Doyle." *Walt Whitman Quarterly Review* 12, no. 1 (Summer 1994): 1–51.

———. Review of *Walt Whitman: A Gay Life*, by Gary Schmidgal. *Walt Whitman Quarterly Review* 15, nos. 2–3 (Fall–Winter 1997–98): 130–32.

———. "Traveling with the Wounded: Walt Whitman and Washington's Civil War Hospitals." *Washington History* 8, no. 2 (Fall–Winter 1966–67): 59–73, 92–93.

New York City. *People v. Sewally.* June 16, 1836. District Attorney Indictment Papers, Court of General Sessions. New York City Municipal Archives and Records Center.

1906 Decennial Edition of the American Digest: A Complete Digest of All Reported Cases from 1897 to 1906. St. Paul, Minn.: West Publishing, 1908.

Norton, Rictor. *Mother Clap's Molly House: The Gay Subculture in England, 1700–1830.* London: GMP Publishers, 1992.

———. *My Dear Boy: Gay Love Letters through the Centuries.* San Francisco: Leyland Publications, 1998.

Odell, George. *Annals of the New York Stage.* 15 vols. New York: Columbia University Press, 1927–49.

Parker, Hershel. "The Real 'Live Oak, with Moss': Straight Talk about Whitman's 'Gay Manifesto.' " *Nineteenth-Century Literature* 51, no. 2 (1996): 145–60.

[Peirce, James Mills.] "Letter from Professor X." Appendix D in *Sexual Inversion.* Edited by Havelock Ellis and John Addington Symonds. London: Wilson & Macmillan, 1897; reprint, New York: Arno Press, 1975.

Peiss, Kathy, and Christina Simmons, with Robert A. Padgug, eds. *Passion and Power: Sexuality in History.* Philadelpia: Temple University Press, 1989.

People v. Thomas Frank Stevenson. Supreme Court, General Sessions, Indictments, January 1892. Box 10039 sh 106170. New York City Municipal Archives.

Perry, Bliss. *Walt Whitman: His Life and Work.* Boston: Houghton, Mifflin, 1906.

Price, Kenneth M., ed. *Walt Whitman: The Contemporary Reviews.* New York: Cambridge University Press, 1996.

Pollak, Vivian R. *The Erotic Whitman.* Berkeley: University of California Press, 2000.

"Prisoners of War at Johnson's Island. . . ." *Miscellaneous Papers, 1672–1865.* Collections of the Virginia Historical Society. New ser., vol. 6. Richmond: Virginia Historical Society, 1937.

Quinn, D. Michael. *Same-Sex Dynamics among Nineteenth-Century Americans: A Morman Example.* Urbana: University of Illinois Press, 1996.

Rey, Michel. "Parisian Homosexuals Create a Lifestyle, 1700–1750: The Police Archives." *Eighteenth-Century Life* 9 (1985): 179–91.

———. "Police and Sodomy in Eighteenth-Century Paris: From Sin to Disorder." In *The Pursuit of Sodomy: Male Homosexuality in Renaissance and Enlightenment Europe.* Edited by Kent Gerard and Gert Hekma. New York: Haworth, 1989.

Reynolds, David S. *Walt Whitman's America: A Cultural Biography.* New York: Alfred A. Knopf, 1995.

Richards, Jeffrey. " 'Passing the Love of Women': Manly Love and Victorian Society." In *Manliness and Morality.* Edited by J. A. Mangan and James Walvin. New York: St. Martin's Press, 1987.

Richmond, Len, and Gary Noguera, eds. *The Gay Liberation Book.* San Francisco: Ramparts Press, 1973.

Rodgers, Bruce. *The Queens' Vernacular: A Gay Lexicon*. San Francisco: Straight Arrow Books, 1972.

Roediger, David R. *The Wages of Whiteness: Race and the Making of the American Working Class*. New York: Verso, 1991.

Rosenberg, Charles E. "Disease and Social Order—Perceptions and Expectations." In *AIDS: The Burdens of History*. Edited by Elizabeth Fee and Danial M. Fox. Berkeley: University of California Press, 1988.

———. "Sexuality, Class and Role in 19th-Century America." *American Quarterly* 25 (May 1973): 131–53.

Rothman, Ellen K. *Hands and Hearts: A History of Courtship in America*. New York: Basic Books, 1984.

Rotundo, E. Anthony. *American Manhood: Transformations in Masculinity from the Revolution to the Modern Era*. New York: Basic Books, 1993.

———. "Romantic Friendship: Male Intimacy and Middle-Class Youth in the Northern United States, 1800–1900." *Journal of Social History* 23 (1989): 1–25.

Roughead, William. "Pretty Fanny's Way . . ." In *Bad Companions*. Edinburgh: W. Green, 1930.

Rupp, Leila J. *A Desired Past: A Short History of Same-Sex Love in America*. Chicago: University of Chicago Press, 1999.

———. " 'Imagine My Surprise': Women's Relationships in Mid-Twentieth-Century America." In *Hidden from History: Reclaiming the Gay Past*, edited by Martin Duberman, Martha Vicinus, and George Chauncey, Jr. New York: New American Library, 1989.

Sandburg, Carl. *Abraham Lincoln: The Prairie Years*. New York: Harcourt, Brace, 1926. Abridged edition, same publisher, 1929.

Saslow, James. *Ganymede in the Renaissance: Homosexuality in Art and Society*. New Haven, Conn.: Yale University Press, 1986.

Saxton, Alexander. *The Rise and Fall of the White Republic: Class Politics and Mass Culture in Nineteenth-Century America*. New York: Verso, 1990.

Scharnhorst, Gary. "The Brewster Incident: Additional Evidence." *Newsboy*, no. 19 (December 1980): 8–13.

Scharnhorst, Gary, with Jack Bales. *The Lost Life of Horatio Alger, Jr.* Bloomington: Indiana University Press, 1985.

Scott, Colin. "Sex and Art." *American Journal of Psychology* 7, no. 2 (January 1896).

Scott, J. L. *Lowry's, Bryan's, and Chapman's Batteries of Virginia Artilery*. Lynchburg, Va.: H. E. Howard, 1988.

Sears, Hal D. *The Sex Radicals: Free Love in High Victorian America*. Lawrence: Regents Press of Kansas, 1977.

Sedgwick, Eve Kosofsky. *Between Men: English Literature and Male Homosexual Desire*. New York: Columbia University Press, 1985.

Seidman, Steven. *Romantic Longings: Love in America, 1830–1980*. New York: Routledge, 1991.

Senelick, Laurence. "Mollies or Men of Mode? Sodomy and the Eighteenth-Century Stage." *Journal of the History of Sexuality* 1, no. 1 (1990): 33–67.

Shand-Tucci, Douglass. "A Gay Civil War Novel Surfaces." *Harvard Gay and Lesbian Review* 3, no. 2 (Spring 1996): 9–12.

Sharpey-Schafer, Joyce A. *Soldier of Fortune: F. D. Millet 1846–1912*. Utica, N.Y., 1984.

Shilts, Randy. *Conduct Unbecoming: Gays and Lesbians in the U.S. Military: Vietnam to the Persian Gulf*. New York: St. Martin's Press, 1993.

Shively, Charley. *Calamus Lovers: Walt Whitman's Working-Class Camerados*. San Francisco: Gay Sunshine Press, 1987.

———. *Drum Beats: Walt Whitman's Civil War Boy Lovers.* San Francisco: Gay Sunshine Press, 1989.

Smith-Rosenberg, Carroll. "The Female World of Love and Ritual: Relations between Women in Nineteenth-Century America." *Signs* 1 (1975): 1–29; reprinted in *Disorderly Conduct: Visions of Gender in Victorian America.* Edited by Carroll Smith-Rosenberg. New York: Oxford University Press, 1986.

Somerville, Siobhan. "Scientific Racism and the Invention of the Homosexual Body." *Journal of the History of Sexuality* 5, no. 2 (October 1994): 243–66; reprinted in *Queer Studies: A Lesbian, Gay, Bisexual, and Transgender Anthology.* Edited by Brett Beemyn and Mickey Eliason. New York: New York University Press, 1996.

Speed, Joshua. Letter to Eliza J. Speed. March 12, 1841. Speed Papers, Illinois State Historical Library.

———. Letter to Josiah G. Holland, June 22, 1865. Abraham Lincoln Papers, Josiah Holland Folder, New York Public Library.

Stearns, Amanda Akin. *The Lady Nurse of Ward E.* New York: Baker & Taylor, 1909.

Stearns, Frank Preston. *The Real and Ideal in Literature.* Boston: J. G. Cupples, 1892.

Stein, Marc. *City of Sisterly & Brotherly Love: Lesbian and Gay Philadelphia, 1945–1972.* Chicago: University of Chicago Press, 2000.

Stoddard, Charles Warren. "Afloat in Venice." *San Francisco Chronicle,* January 10, 1875, 1.

———. *Cruising the South Seas: Stories by Charles Warren Stoddard.* Edited by Winston Leyland. San Francisco: Gay Sunshine Press, 1987.

———. "Fair Florence." *San Francisco Chronicle,* April 4, 1875, 1.

———. "A Farewell to Venice." *San Francisco Chronicle,* March 28, 1875, 1.

———. "Florence." *San Francisco Chronicle,* April 4, 1875, 1; revised and reprinted in *Ave Maria* 24 (January 15, 1887): 418.

———. "Genoa, The Superb." *San Francisco Chronicle,* June 13, 1875, 1.

———. "In a Transport." *South Sea Idyls,* 1873; 2d ed.,1892; reprinted in *Cruising in the South Seas: Stories by Charles Warren Stoddard.* Edited by Winston Leyland. San Francisco: Gay Sunshine Press, 1987.

———. "The Leaning Tower." *San Francisco Chronicle,* May 30, 1875, 1.

———. Letter to Ambrose Bierce, September 13, 1875. Yale University Library.

———. "A Modern Monte Cristo." *National Magazine* 24 (August 1906): 463–69.

———. "Royal Galleries." *San Francisco Chronicle,* April 11, 1875, 1.

———. "A Sea Siren." *San Francisco Chronicle,* December 12, 1875, 1.

———. "A South-Sea Idyl." *Overland Monthly,* September 1869, 257–64; reprinted as "Chumming with a Savage: Kánána" in *Cruising the South Seas: Stories by Charles Warren Stoddard.* Edited by Winston Leyland. San Francisco: Gay Sunshine Press, 1987.

———. "The Venetian Islands." *San Francisco Chronicle,* February 21, 1875, 1.

Stroven, Carl. *A Life of Charles Warren Stoddard.* Ph.D. thesis. Duke University, 1939.

Strozier, Charles B. *Lincoln's Quest for Union: Public and Private Meanings.* Urbana: University of Illinois Press, 1982.

Summers, Claude J., ed. *The Gay and Lesbian Literary Heritage: A Reader's Companion to Writers and Their Works.* New York: Henry Holt, 1995.

Symonds, John Addington. *Letters.* 3 vols. Edited by Herbert M. Schueller and Robert L. Peters. Detroit: Wayne State University Press, 1967–69.

———. *The Memoirs of John Addington Symonds.* Edited by Phyllis Groskurth. New York: Random House, 1984.

———. *A Problem in Modern Ethics. Being an Enquiry into the Phenomenon of Sexual Inversion. Addressed especially to Medical Psychologists and Jurists.* London: 1896; reprint, New York: B. Blom, 1971.

———. *Walt Whitman: A Study.* London: John C. Nimmo, 1893.

Thompson, W. Scott. "Was Abe Lincoln Gay, Too? A Divided Man to Heal a Divided Age." Unpublished paper.

Thompson, George [Greenhorn, pseud.]. *City Crimes; Or, Life in New York and Boston: A Volume for Everybody: Being a Mirror of Fashion; A Picture of Poverty, and A Startling Revelation of the Secret Crimes of Great Cities.* Boston: William Berry, 1849.

Thoreau, Henry David. *Correspondence of Henry David Thoreau.* Edited by Walter Harding and Carl Bode. New York: Washington Square Press, 1958.

Thornton, H. W. Interview. Ida Tarbell Papers, Allegheny College Library, n.d.

Traubel, Horace. *With Walt Whitman in Camden.* 9 vols. Boston: Small, Maynard, 1905–96.

Trumbach, Randolph. "Gender and the Homosexual Role in Modern Western Culture: The 18th and 19th Centuries Compared." In *Homosexuality, Which Homosexuality?* Edited by Dennis Altman et al. London: GMP Publishers, 1989.

———. Review of Norton, *Mother. Journal of the History of Sexuality* 5 (1995): 637–40.

———. "Sex, Gender, and Sexual Identity in Modern Culture: Male Sodomy and Female Prostitution in Englightenment England. In *Forbidden History: The State, Society, and the Regulation of Sexuality in Modern Europe.* Edited by John C. Foud. Chicago: University of Chicago Press, 1992.

Tsuzuki, Chushichi. *Edward Carpenter, 1844–1929: Prophet of Human Fellowship.* New York: Cambridge University Press, 1980.

Turner, Justin, and Linda Turner. *Mary Todd Lincoln: Her Life and Letters.* New York: Fromm International Publishing Corp., 1972.

Upchurch, Charles. "Forgetting the Unthinkable: Cross-Dressers and British Society in the Case of the Queen vs. Boulton and Others." Unpublished paper, 33 pp.

U.S. Navy. Record Group 45, Office of Naval Records: Library Series 464, Subject File, U.S. Navy, 1875–1910. Box no. 284, 1855–1870—NJ—Discipline Minor Delinquencies. National Archives.

van der Meer, Theo. "The Persecutions of Sodomites in Eighteenth-Century Amsterdam: Changing Perceptions of Sodomy." In *The Pursuit of Sodomy: Male Homosexuality in Renaissance and Enlightenment Europe.* Edited by Kent Gerard and Gert Hekma. New York: Haworth, 1989.

———. "Sodomy and the Pursuit of a Third Sex in the Early Modern Period." In *Third Sex, Third Gender: Beyond Sexual Dimorphism in Culture and History.* Edited by Gilbert Herdt. New York: Zone Books, 1994.

Vicinus, Martha. "Distance and Desire: English Boarding-School Friendships" *Signs* 9 (Summer 1984): 600–22; reprinted in *Hidden from History: Reclaiming the Gay Past.* Edited by Martin Duberman, Martha Vicinus, and George Chauncey, Jr. New York: New American Library, 1989.

Wall, C. Edward, ed. *Cumulative Author Index for Poole's Index to Periodical Literature 1802–1906.* Ann Arbor, Mich.: Pierian Press, 1971.

Weeks, Jeffrey. "Capitalism and Sexuality." In *Homosexuality, Power, and Politics.* Edited by the Gay Left Collective. London: Allison & Busby, 1980.

———. *Coming Out: Homosexual Politics in Britain from the Nineteenth Century to the Present.* London: Quartet Books, 1977.

————. "Inverts, Perverts, and Mary-Annes: Male Prostitution and the Regulation of Homosexuality in England in the Nineteenth and Early Twentieth Centuries." *Journal of Homosexuality* 6, nos. 1–2 (Fall–Winter 1980–81): 113–34; reprinted in *Hidden from History: Reclaiming the Gay Past*. Edited by Martin Duberman, Martha Vicinus, and George Chauncey, Jr. New York: New American Library, 1989.

Westgard, Gilbert K. "Following the Trail of Horatio Alger, Jr." *Newsboy*, no. 18 (December 1979): 5–7.

Whitman, Walt. *Calamus: A Series of Letters Written during the Years 1868–1880 by Walt Whitman to a Young Friend (Peter Doyle)*. Edited by Richard Maurice Bucke. Boston: Small, Maynard, 1897; reprinted in *The Complete Writings of Walt Whitman*, vol. 8. New York: G. P. Putnam's Sons, 1902.

————. *The Correspondence*. 6 vols. Edited by Edwin Haviland Miller. New York: New York University Press, 1961–1977.

————. *Daybooks and Notebooks*. 3 vols. Edited by William White. New York: New York University Press, 1978.

————. *The Early Poems and the Fiction*. 3 vols. Edited by Thomas L. Brasher. New York: New York University Press, 1963.

————. *Leaves of Grass: Comprehensive Readers Edition*. Edited by Harold W. Blodgett and Scully Bradley. New York: New York University Press, 1965.

————. *Leaves of Grass: Facsimile Edition of the 1856 Edition, with an Introduction by Gay Wilson Allen*. Norwood, Pa.: Norwood Editions, 1976.

————. Leaves of Grass; *Facsimile Edition of the 1860 Text, with an Introduction by Roy Harvey Peace*. Ithaca, N.Y.: Cornell University Press, 1961.

————. *Leaves of Grass, The First (1855) Edition*. Edited by Malcolm Cowley. New York: Viking Press, 1959.

————. *Leaves of Grass: A Textual Variorum of the Printed Poems*. 3 vols. Edited by Sculley Bradley et al. New York: New York University Press, 1980.

————. *Notebooks and Unpublished Prose Manuscripts*. 6 vols. Edited by Edward F. Grier. New York: New York University Press, 1984.

————. *Prose Works 1892*. Vol. 1: *Specimen Days*. Vol. 2: *Collect, and Other Prose*. Edited by Floyd Stoval. New York: New York University Press, 1963–64.

Wiley, Bell I. *The Life of Johnny Reb*. Baton Rouge: Louisiana State University Pressres, 1971.

Willey, John S. Letter to his wife, March 20, 1864. Norman Daniels Collection, Harrisburg Civil War Round Table Collection. U.S. Army Miliary History Institute.

Williams, Gary Lee. *James and Joshua Speed: Lincoln's Kentucky Friends*. Ph.D. thesis. Duke University, 1971

————. "The Psychosexual Fears of Joshua Speed and Abraham Lincoln." Paper prepared for delivery at the Annual Meeting of the Organization of American Historians, 1980.

Wilson, Douglas L. "Abraham Lincoln and 'That Fatal First of January.'" *Civil War History* 38, no. 2 (June 1992): 101–30.

————. *Honor's Voice: The Transformation of Abraham Lincoln*. New York: Alfred A. Knopf, 1998.

Wilson, Douglas L., and Rodney O. Davis, eds. *Herndon's Informants: Letters, Interviews, and Statements about Abraham Lincoln*. Urbana: University of Illinois Press, 1998.

Woods, Gregory. *A History of Gay Literature: The Male Tradition*. New Haven, Conn.: Yale University Press, 1998.

Yacovone, Donald. "Abolitionists and the Language of Fraternal Love." In *Meanings for Manhood: Constructions of Masculinity in Victorian America*. Edited by Mark C. Carnes and Clyde Griffen. Chicago: University of Chicago Press, 1990.

Legal: Published Appeals Case Reports

Ausman v. Veal, 10 IN 355; 71 Am. Dec. 331 (1858, Jun 2) (slander; charging "bestiality," "crime against nature," woman with dog, sex unspecified).

Benedict v. People, 23 CO 126; 46 P. 637 (1896, Sep 21 [WESTLAW]; Sep [LEXIS]) ("crime against nature," unspecified).

Bergemann v. Backer; 157 U.S. 655; 15 S. Ct. 727 (U.S. Supreme Court; 1895, Apr 1) (murder; cites section of New Jersey Crimes Act that murder "committed in perpetrating, or attempting to perpetrate, any arson, rape, sodomy, robbery or burglary, shall be deemed murder of the first degree").

Bishop v. Florida, 41 FL 522; 26 So. 703 (1899, Jun 15) (cites FL law: "Persons . . . convicted in any court in this State of murder, perjury, piracy, forgery, larceny, robbery, arson, sodomy or buggery shall not be competent witnesses").

Bradford v. State, 104 AL 68; 53 Am. St. Rep. 24 (Aug 9, 1894) ("crime against nature," man with cow).

Bresnan v. State, 43 S.W. 111 (TX; 1897, Dec 1) ("sodomy" unspecified, man with man).

Brown v. New Jersey, 62 N.J.L. 666; 42 A. 811 1899, Mar 6 [WESTLAW]; May 6 [LEXIS]) (murder; cites NJ law "that every person indicted for treason, murder or other crimes punishable with death, or for misprision of treason, manslaughter, sodomy, rape, arson, burglary, robbery, or forgery," was allowed to challenge peremptorily twenty jurors).

Cleveland v. Detweiler, 18 IA 299 (1865, Apr 10) (slander, charging "sodomy," woman with dog, sex unspecified).

Coburn v. Harwood, 12 Am. Dec. 37; Minor 93 (AL; 1822, Dec) (slander; words charging crime against nature, unspecified).

Collins v. State, 73 GA 76 (1884) ("bestiality," unspecified).

Commonwealth v. Dill, 160 MA 536, 36 N.E. 472 (Sup. Jd. Ct. 1894) (1894, Feb 28) ("sodomy," "crime against nature," "unnatural and lascivious act," unspecified; man with "another person," sex unspecified).

Commonwealth v. J., 21 PA Co. Ct. 625 (1899, Jan 16) (attempted "buggery" with young cow).

Commonwealth v. Randolph, 146 PA 83; 23 A. 388 (1892, Jan 4) (murder case referring to English decision "that to solicit or make overtures to another to commit sodomy was a crime; but to threaten to accuse another of having made such overtures, was not a threat to charge him with having committed the crime of sodomy").

Commonwealth v. Snow, 111 MA 411 (1873, Jan) ("sodomy," man with boy [implicitly], age unspecified).

Commonwealth v. Thomas, 1 VA Cases 307 (Gen. Ct.)(1812, Jun 16) ("buggery," man with mare).

Cross v. State, 17 TX App. 476 (1885, Jan 31) ("sodomy," "crime against nature," "carnal connection," man with mare).

Darling v. State, 47 S.W. 1005 (TX; 1898, Nov 30) ("sodomy," unspecified).

Davis v. Brown, 27 OH St. 326 (1875, Dec) (slander, charging "crime against nature," "sodomy," man with unspecified beast).

Davis v. State, 3 Har. & J. 154; 3 MD Rep 154 (1810) (attempted "sodomy," "buggery," man with male "youth," 19).

Davis v. State, 37 TX Crim. Rep. 47 (1897, Jan 21) (robbery by threatening illegal act; notes: "In England, and perhaps in this country, in the absence of statute, a threatening charge of sodomy [unspecified] is the only threat of prosecution for a crime from which can be inferred the fear necessary to constitute the crime of robbery").

Dial v. Holter, 6 OH St. 228 (1856, Dec) (slander, libel; reference to "sodomy," unspecified, as charge involving "great moral turpitude").

Edgar v. McCutcheon, 9 MO 768 (1846, Jan)(slander, charging man's "carnal knowledge" of mare, using word "fuck").

Enos v. Sowle, 2 HA 332 (1860, Dec 11) ("sodomy"; man with "boy" "youth," age unspecified).

Estes v. Carter, 10 IA 400 (Sup. Ct.) (1860 Apr 18) (slander; words charging "sodomy," unspecified).

Ex parte Bergen, 19 TX App. 52 (1883, Apr 13) (sodomy," "crime against nature," unspecified).

Ex parte Smith and Keating, 38 CA 702 (1869, Oct) (reference to laws against "rape," "crime against nature," "prostitution," "abortion").

Fennel v. State, 32 TX 378 (Sup. Ct.) (1869) ("crime against nature," "sodomy," unspecified).

Foster et al. v. State, 1 OH C.D.; 1 OH Cir. Ct. R. 467 (1886, Apr) ("sodomy," "carnal copulation against nature," three men with man).

Frazier v. State, 39 TX (Sup. Ct. 1873) (1873) ("crime 'against nature,'" unspecified, "sodomy," unspecified).

Goodrich v. Woolcott, 3 Cow. 231 (NY; 1824, Aug) (slander; words charging "person of unnatural passions" with "crime against nature," man with sow) (see *Woolcott v. Goodrich*).

Green v. State, 29 S.W. 1072 (TX; 1895, Mar 9) ("sodomy," unspecified).

Green v. Superior Court of San Francisco, 78 CA 556; 21 P. 307 (1889, Apr 16) (extortion case referring to persons convicted of "a capital offense, a crime against nature, or . . . forgery, perjury," etc.; on appeal, a dissenting CA Supreme Court judge mentions that "At common law, persons convicted of petty larceny and whipped were held incompetent witnesses because infamous, but no matter how infamous the punishment, unless it was inflicted for, or some other species of crimen falsi, infamy did not attach").

Hall v. State, 34 S.W. 124 (TX; 1896, Feb 12) ("sodomy," unspecified).

Hallinger v. Davis, 146 U.S. 314; 113 S. Ct. 105 (1892, Nov 7) (murder case appealed to U.S. Supreme Court; quotes article of NJ constitution which says that murder "committed in perpetrating or in attempting to perpetrate arson, rape, sodomy, robbery, or burglary, shall be deemed murder in the first degree").

Harper v. Delp, 3 IN 225 (1851, Nov) (slander, charging "bestiality" and "buggery," man with cow).

Haywood v. Foster, 6 OH 88 (Westlaw; LEXIS 6 OH 98) (1847, Dec) (slander, charging "unchastity and bestiality [unspecified]").

Hawaii v. Edwards, 11 HA 571 (1898, Nov 4) (conviction for attempted "sodomy," man with Hawaiian, "Kui" [no sex specified]).

Hawaii v. Edwards, 2 HA 55 (1899, May 31) ("sodomy," unspecified; argues that 5th and 6th amendments of U.S. Constitution extended to Hawaii at time of Edwards's conviction, August 16, 1898, four days after transfer of Hawaiian sovereignty to U.S.).

Hawaii v. Luning, 11 HA 390 (1898, Apr 20) (attempted "sodomy," unspecified).

Hawaii v. Parsons, 10 HA 601 (1896, Jan 27) ("sexual intercourse," man with female under age fourteen; cites law referring to "Polygamy," "Adultery," "Fornication," "Incest," "Sodomy," unspecified). "C. G. Parsons argues that the statute under which the charge is made is unconstitutional, for technical reason, and that even if it did set forth the full title of the alleged amended act, namely, 'Chapter XIII. it would still be insufficient (for technical reasons).' "

Haynes v. Ritchey, 30 IA 76; 6 Am. Rep. 642 (1870, Oct 24) (slander, charging "sodomy," "beastility" [sic]).

Hodges v. State, 94 Ga. 593; 19 S.E. 758 (1894, Jun 4) ("sodomy," anal intercourse, "boy," under 14, with "child").

Honselman v. People, 168 IL 173, 48 N.W. 304 (1897, Nov 1) ("crime against nature," penis of accuser, fourteen and a half years old, in man's mouth).

Houston v. Commonwealth, 87 VA 257; 12 S.E. 385 (1890, Dec 16) (robbery case referring to threat of "sodomy").

Hughes v. Detroit . . . Railway Company, 65 MI 10; 31 N.W. 603 (1887, Feb 10) (negligence case, referring to outrage of girls under age seven and to "such crimes against nature").

Jones v. State, 38 TX Crim. 364; 43 S.W. 78 (1897, Nov 24) (libel; Irish men, employed as conductors by street car company, who discriminated against "colored ladies," were called "the descendants of Oscar Wilde [meaning that they commit the crime of sodomy]"; bracketed quote in original).

Lamb v. State, 10 A. 298 (MD; 1887, Jun 23) ("abortion" referred to as a "crime against nature").

Lambertson v. People, (Sup. Ct. Gen. T.) 5 Park. Crim. (N.Y.) 200 (1861, May) ("crime against nature," "buggery," "carnal knowledge," man with man).

Lefler v. State, 23 N.E. 154 (1889, Dec 20) ("sodomy," man with man).

Lewis v. State, 36 TX Cr. R. 37; 35 S.W. 372; 61 Am. St. Rep. 831 (1896, Apr 29) ("sodomy," anal intercourse, man with woman; accusation of "copulating in the mouth" with same woman).

Little v. State, 35 S.W. 659 (TX; 1896, May 13) ("sodomy," unspecified).

Louisiana v. Deschamps, 7 So. 703 (1890, May) (reference to "homicide" committed while engaged in a felony "such as rape or sodomy").

Mascolo v. Montesanto, 61 CT 50; 23 Atl. 714; 29 Am. St. Rep. 170 (1891, Jun 19) (civil suit, completed "buggery"; Mascolo, twelve, by Montesanto, fifteen).

McCray v. State, 8 TX Crim. 609; 44 S.W. 170 (1898, Feb 9) (assault; reference to earlier "sodomy," unspecified, of accused).

McKean v. Folden, 2 OH Dec. 248 (1859)(slander; words charging "bestiality," "buggery," unspecified).

Medis v. Hill, 27 TX App. 194; 11 S.W. 112; 11 Am. St. Rep. 192 (1889, Feb 9) ("sodomy," two men with man).

Meigs County Court v. Anonymous, 3 OH Dec. 450; 2 OH N.P. 342(1895, Sep) ("sodomy," man with beast, unspecified).

Melvin v. Weiant, 36 OH St. 184; 38 Am. Rep. 572 (1880, Jan) (slander, charging "sodomy," unspecified).

Mootry et al. v. State, 41 P. 1027; 109 CA 275 (1896, Jan 15) (murder; cites *Medis v. State,* in which accused "were jointly tried for sodomy," unspecified here).

Paterson v. State, 50 N.J.L. 421; 14 A. 125 (1888, Mar 1) (cites NJ law referring to "treason, murder, manslaughter, sodomy [unspecified], rape, arson, burglary, robbery, forgery, or larceny," etc.).

Peak v. State, 53 S.W. 853 (1899, Nov 29) ("sodomy," unspecified).

People v. Boyle, 48 P 800; 116 CA 658 (1897, May 6) ("crime against nature," man in mouth of "boy," age unspecified).

People v. Frey, 112 MI 251; 70 N.W. 548 (1897, Mar 29) (extortion; threat to accuse "sodomy," "bestiality").

People v. Graney, 91 MI 646; 52 N.W. 66 (1892, May 13) ("crime against nature," man with man).

People v. Gleason, 99 CA 359; 33 P. 1111 (1893, Aug 23) (incest; refers to "solicitation to commit incest, adultery, or sodomy").

People v. Hickey, 41 P. 1027; 109 CA 275 (1895, Sep 30)("sodomy," man with person, unspecified; sodomy may also involve a beast, unspecified).

People v. Hodgkin, 94 MI 27 (1892, Dec 3) (sodomy," "buggery," unspecified).

People v. Miller, 66 CA 468; 6 P. 99 (1885, Feb 27) ("crime against nature," man with "boy," 13).

People v. Moore, 103 Cal. 508; 37 Pac. 510; (1894, Aug 11) ("crime against nature," man with man).

People v. Murat, 45 CA 281 (1873, Jan) (reference to "assault" with intent "to commit murder, rape, the infamous crime against nature, mayhem, robbery, or grand larceny").

People v. O'Brien, 26 N.Y.S. 812 (1893, Dec 6) ("crime against nature," man with "boy," 11).

People v. Williams, 59 CA 397 (Ct. App. 1881)(1881, Jul) ("crime against nature," "sodomy," man with man).

People v. Wilson, 51 P. 639, 119 CA 384 (1897, Dec 20) (attempted "crime against nature," man, implicitly with boy, age unspecified).

Prindle v. State, 31 TX Cr. R. 551; 21 S.W. 360; 37 Am. St. Rep. 833(1893, Feb 15) ("sodomy," "crime against nature," man in mouth of "child," age unspecified).

Red v. State, 39 TX Crim. 414; 46 S.W. 408 (1898, Jun 8) (murder; "Appellant proposed to prove . . . that the witness . . . was guilty of incest with his daughter, and was guilty of sodomy [unspecified], and had assaulted the wife of appellant, . . . his granddaughter, with intent to rape her").

Roberson v. Florida, 40 FL 509; 24 So. 474 (1898, Jun ([LEXIS]; Nov 5 ([WESTLAW]) (cites FL law that "persons who have been convicted in any court . . . of murder, perjury, piracy, forgery, larceny, robbery, arson, sodomy or buggery shall not be competent witnesses").

Roesel v. New Jersey, 62 N.J.L. 216; 41 A. 408 (1898 Jul 8 ([LEXIS]; Sep 28 ([WESTLAW]) (murder; cites NJ law referring to persons "committing or attempting to commit sodomy, rape, arson, robbery or burglary, or any unlawful act against the peace of this state, of which the probable consequence may be bloodshed").

Simmons v. State, 41 FL 316, 25 So. 881 (1899, May 2 [WESTLAW]; Jan TERM [case report; LEXIS]) (robbery; cites FL law that "Property obtained by trick or artifice, or by threats of illegal arrest, criminal prosecution, or insinuations against character, except they relate to sodomitical practices, is not taken by 'putting in fear' ").

Singleton v. State, 38 FL 297; 21 So. 21 (1896, Jun ([LEXIS]; Nov 17 [WESTLAW]) (quotes section of FL law "that persons convicted . . . of murder, perjury, piracy, forgery, larceny, robbery, arson, sodomy, or buggery shall not be competent witnesses").

State v. Campbell, 29 TX 44; 94 Am. Dec. 251 (1867) ("crime against nature," "sodomy," man with mare).

State v. Chandonette, 10 MT 280; 25 P. 438 (1890 Dec 1) ("crime against nature," unspecified).

State v. Desforges, 47 LA Ann 1167; 17 S. 811 (1895, Jun 3) (attempting to prevent witness from testifying; court quotes Wharton that solicitations to commit a crime "are indictable . . . when they are . . . offences against public decency, as in the case with solicitations to commit sodomy").

State v. Dolan, 17 WA 499; 50 P. 472 (1897, Sep 7) (murder; citing WA law referring to "assault with intent to commit murder, rape, the infamous crime against nature, mayhem, robbery, or grand larceny").

State v. Frank, 103 MO 120; 15 S.W. 330 (1890, Oct) (attempted "sodomy," man with dog).

State v. Gray, 8 Jones (N.C.) 170 (1860, Dec)(reference to "buggery," unspecified, in case of "carnally knowing and abusing an infant female under the age of ten years").

State v. Grusso, 28 LA Ann. 952 (1876, Dec) ("crime against nature," man with man).

State v. LaForrest, 45 A. 225 (Sup. Ct.); 71 VT 311 (1899, May 6) ("sodomy," unspecified).

State v. Place, 5 Wash. 773 (1893, Feb.18) (attempted "crime against nature," "sodomy," man with man)

State v. Romans, 57 P. 819, 21 WA 284 (1899, Jun 22) (attempted "crime against nature," "buggery," man with man).

State v. Smith, 38 S.W. 717 (MO; 1897, Jan 19) (attempted "sodomy or buggery," man with "boy," age unspecified).

State v. Williams, 34 LA Ann. 87 (Sup. Ct. 1882) (1882, Jan) ("crime against nature," unspecified).

Stewart v. Major, 17 WA 238; 49 P. 503 (1897, Jun 25)(libel; quotes section of WA Code referring to "words falsely spoken of any person charging such person with incest or the infamous crime against nature either with mankind or the brute creation")

Strange v. State, 33 Tex. Crim. 315; 26 S.W. 406 (1894, May 5) (extortion by threat of criminal prosecution for "crime against nature," "sodomy" with beast, unspecified).

Stratham v. State, 53 S.W. 847 (1899, Nov 29) ("sodomy," unspecified).

Territory v. Mahaffey, 3 MT 112 (1878, Jan) ("crime against nature," man with "boy," 14).

Thibault v. Sessions and Phipps, 101 MI 279; 59 N.W. 624 (1894, Jun 26) (libel/slander; teacher accused of "sodomy" with students, sex, age unspecified; "bestiality" referenced).

United States v. Gallagher, 25 F. Cas. 1241 (1832, Mar) (cites PA law re rape, murder, or attempted "crime against nature").

Vieira v. Sowle, 2 HA 346 (1860, Dec 14) ("sodomy"; man with "boy," age unspecified).

Waits v. State, 54 S.W. 1103 (1899, Dec 19) ("sodomy," unspecified).

Wells v. New England Mutual Life Insurance, 191 PA 207; 43 A. 126 (1899, Apr 24) (abortion; Court quotes its earlier decision that abortion "violates the mysteries of nature in that process by which the human race is propagated. It is a crime against nature which obstructs the fountain of life. . . .").

Williams v. Commonwealth, 22 S.E. 859 (VA; 1895, Sep 19) ("buggery," unspecified, by boy, between 10–12).

Willson v. State, 53 S.W. 112 (TX; 1899, Oct 11). ("sodomy," unspecified).

Wood et al. v. State, 47 N.J.L. 180 (1885, Jun 15) (cites NJ law re "murder, manslaughter, sodomy [unspecified], rape, arson, burglary, or robbery").

Woolcott v. Goodrich, 3 Cow. 714 (NY; 1825, Dec) (slander; words charging "He has been with a sow"). (See *Goodrich v. Woolcott*)

Wright v. State, 35 TX Crim. 367; 33 S.W. 973 (1896, Jan 22) ("sodomy," unspecified).

Index